Web 3.0 [Semantic Web]*.

Tim Berners-Lee

Think of Web 1.0 as a library. You can use it as a source of information, but you can't contribute to or change the information in any way. Web 2.0 allows you to still receive information, but you can also contribute to the conversation. Web 3.0 is powered by shared data and linked onotologies (vocabularies)*[Jim Hendler.]

Telementoring in the K–12 Classroom:
Online Communication Technologies for Learning

Deborah A. Scigliano
Duquesne University, USA

INFORMATION SCIENCE REFERENCE

Hershey • New York

Director of Editorial Content:	Kristin Klinger
Director of Book Publications:	Julia Mosemann
Acquisitions Editor:	Lindsay Johnston
Development Editor:	Christine Bufton
Publishing Assistant:	Milan Vracarich Jr.
Typesetter:	Michael Brehm
Production Editor:	Jamie Snavely
Cover Design:	Lisa Tosheff

Published in the United States of America by
Information Science Reference (an imprint of IGI Global)
701 E. Chocolate Avenue
Hershey PA 17033
Tel: 717-533-8845
Fax: 717-533-8661
E-mail: cust@igi-global.com
Web site: http://www.igi-global.com

Copyright © 2011 by IGI Global. All rights reserved. No part of this publication may be reproduced, stored or distributed in any form or by any means, electronic or mechanical, including photocopying, without written permission from the publisher. Product or company names used in this set are for identification purposes only. Inclusion of the names of the products or companies does not indicate a claim of ownership by IGI Global of the trademark or registered trademark.

Library of Congress Cataloging-in-Publication Data

Telementoring in the K-12 classroom : online communication technologies for learning / Deborah A. Scigliano, editor.   p. cm.
  Includes bibliographical references and index. Summary: "This book provides the latest research and the best practices in the field of telementoring, including provide guidance to professionals wanting to implement and improve their telementoring processes"--Provided by publisher. ISBN 978-1-61520-861-6 (hardcover) -- ISBN 978-1-61520-862-3 (ebook) 1. Mentoring in education--Technological innovations. 2. Mentoring--Technological innovations. I. Scigliano, Deborah A., 1951-
  LB1731.4.T457 2010
  372.37'3--dc22

British Cataloguing in Publication Data
A Cataloguing in Publication record for this book is available from the British Library.

All work contributed to this book is new, previously-unpublished material. The views expressed in this book are those of the authors, but not necessarily of the publisher.

Editorial Advisory Board

Laurie Dringus, *NOVA Southeastern University, USA*
Connie Moss, *Duquesne University, USA*
Roderick Sims, *Cappella University, Australia*
Larry Tomei, *Robert Morris University, USA*
Dave Carbonara, *Duquesne University, USA*
Judi Harris, *The College of William and Mary, USA*
Kevin O'Neill, *Simon Fraser University, Canada*

Table of Contents

Foreword xiii

Preface xvi

Acknowledgment xxi

Section 1
Telementoring: Implications for Practice

Chapter 1
Designs for Curriculum-Based Telementoring 1
    Judi Harris, College of William and Mary, USA

Chapter 2
Dimensions of Design in K-12 Telementoring Programs: A Discussion for Designers
and Teachers 15
    Kevin O'Neill, Simon Fraser University, Canada

Chapter 3
Telementoring and Project-Based Learning: An Integrated Model for 21st Century Skills 31
    Joyce Yukawa, St. Catherine University, USA

Chapter 4
You Had to be There: Improving a Telementoring Program through Classroom Observation 57
    Kevin O'Neill, Simon Fraser University, Canada
    Sheryl Guloy, Simon Fraser University, Canada

Chapter 5
The Transformative Capacity of Telementoring on Self-Efficacy Beliefs: A Design-Based
Perspective 72
    Deborah A. Scigliano, Duquesne University, USA

Section 2
Telementoring: Addressing the Needs of Persons with Disabilities

Chapter 6
Fully Including Students, Teachers, and Administrators with Disabilities in Telementoring 89
Sheryl Burgstahler, University of Washington, USA
Terrill Thompson, University of Washington, USA

Chapter 7
Electronic Mentoring in the Classroom: Where Mentors and Students are Persons
with Disabilities 116
Carmit-Noa Shpigelman, University of Haifa, Israel
Patrice L. (Tamar) Weiss, University of Haifa, Israel
Shunit Reiter, University of Haifa, Israel

Chapter 8
Meeting the Needs of Adolescents and Young Adults with Disabilities:
An E-Mentoring Approach 135
Katharine Hill, St. Catherine University, USA & University of St. Thomas, USA
Joe Timmons, University of Minnesota, USA
Christen Opsal, University of Minnesota, USA

Section 3
Telementoring: Professional Development

Chapter 9
Telementoring in Teacher Education 148
Sandy White Watson, University of Tennessee at Chattanooga, USA

Chapter 10
Virtual Mentoring: A Response to the Challenge of Change 173
Thomas T. Peters, South Carolina's Coalition for Mathematics & Science, USA
Terrie R. Dew, Anderson Oconee Pickens Greenville Regional S²MART Center, USA

Chapter 11
Telementoring and Virtual Professional Development: A Theoretical Perspective from
Science on the Roles of Self-Efficacy, Teacher Learning, and Professional Learning
Communities 186
Matthew J. Maurer, Robert Morris University, USA

Section 4
Telementoring: Web 2.0 Technologies

Chapter 12
An Orientation to Web 2.0 Tools for Telementoring.. 206
Robin Hastings, Missouri River Regional Library, USA

Chapter 13
Web 2.0 for Tele-Mentoring... 215
Shari McCurdy Smith, University of Illinois at Springfield, USA
Najmuddin Shaik, University of Illinois Urbana-Champaign, USA
Emily Welch Boles, University of Illinois at Springfield, USA

Compilation of References 254

About the Contributors 284

Index 289

Detailed Table of Contents

Foreword xviii

Preface xxi

Acknowledgment xxvi

Section 1
Telementoring: Implications for Practice

Chapter 1
Designs for Curriculum-Based Telementoring 1
    Judi Harris, College of William and Mary, USA

Telementoring for K-12 students is done primarily outside of school, typically addressing topics that are extrinsic to school curricula. As beneficial as extracurricular telementoring can be, bringing mentors virtually into classrooms to interact with students and teachers over time holds great potential—and considerable challenge—for both. How can telementoring be integrated effectively into content-based curricula taught in face-to-face educational contexts like classrooms? What is key to the success of this type of curriculum-based telementoring? Answers to these questions appear in this chapter, illustrated by examples from an informal taxonomy of curriculum-based telementoring projects that were facilitated by the Electronic Emissary (http://Emissary.wm.edu/), the longest-running formal telementoring program for K-12 students and their teachers.

Chapter 2
Dimensions of Design in K-12 Telementoring Programs: A Discussion for Designers
and Teachers... 15
    Kevin O'Neill, Simon Fraser University, Canada

Teachers and researchers have been designing telementoring programs for more than fifteen years, yet there are many possible program designs that have not yet been attempted, and enormous potential yet to fulfill. An attempt is made to map out the "design space" of K-12 telementoring by discussing the major decisions made in designing a telementoring program, and the relationship of these decisions to one another. Where possible, research findings and examples of specific programs are cited in this discussion. By providing a look "under the hood" of telementoring programs, the chapter aims to help teachers become more equal partners in the effort to refine existing programs and develop new ones. Encouragement is offered to researchers to more fully articulate the rationale behind their designs in their writing, and to carry out more research on the efficacy of particular design choices, so that the field can develop cumulative literature on telementoring design.

Chapter 3
Telementoring and Project-Based Learning: An Integrated Model for 21st Century Skills 31
    Joyce Yukawa, St. Catherine University, USA

While common models of telementoring (ask-an-expert services, tutoring, and academic and career telementoring) can serve a variety of learning objectives, these models are limited with respect to sustained inquiry learning such as project-based learning (PBL). To reach the full potential of PBL with telementoring, this chapter proposes a telementoring model that integrates inquiry learning, information literacy, and digital media literacy and is implemented by a team of experts – subject matter experts as telementors, classroom teachers, school librarians, and instructional technology specialists. The model provides for multifaceted learning experiences for students that involve disciplinary knowledge and habits of mind, critical thinking, collaborative problem solving, and information, media, and technology skills. Brief overviews of inquiry learning approaches, information literacy, and digital media literacy are described in relation to telementoring. Design considerations, the benefits and challenges of the model, and broader implications for educational change are also discussed. Using the integrated telementoring model, the PBL team exemplifies the interdisciplinary collaboration and new literacy skills that students need in today's workplaces and communities.

Chapter 4
You Had to be There: Improving a Telementoring Program through Classroom Observation 57
    Kevin O'Neill, Simon Fraser University, Canada
    Sheryl Guloy, Simon Fraser University, Canada

This chapter makes the case that to fully realize the potential of telementoring for supporting student learning in P-12 schools, teachers and program developers should invest effort in a practice that they traditionally have not – routine observations of how telementoring programs play out in classrooms. Using observational data from a pilot program for secondary social studies called "Compassionate Canada?" the authors illustrate how classroom observations can enable program designers to ask better questions about how a program is working, and why. They also discuss contributions that classroom observations may enable teacher to make to program refinement and professional development.

Chapter 5
The Transformative Capacity of Telementoring on Self-Efficacy Beliefs: A Design-Based
Perspective 72
    Deborah A. Scigliano, Duquesne University, USA

This chapter focuses on the intentional design of telementoring projects to enhance self-efficacy beliefs. The emphasis is on a pragmatic approach to design. Self-efficacy is defined and its importance is detailed. Intentional design which focuses upon addressing the four influences on efficacy of mastery experience, vicarious experience, verbal persuasion, and physiological state is advocated. A design-based drama telementoring research study which employed the best practices of self-efficacy and telementoring research is examined. Capacity, illustrative vignettes, and design implications for each of the four influences on self-efficacy are discussed.

Section 2
Telementoring: Addressing the Needs of Persons with Disabilities

Chapter 6
Fully Including Students, Teachers, and Administrators with Disabilities in Telementoring............... 89
Sheryl Burgstahler, University of Washington, USA
Terrill Thompson, University of Washington, USA

The authors of this chapter discuss challenges that must be addressed to ensure the full inclusion of teachers, administrators, and students with disabilities in telementoring activities in elementary and secondary school environments. Potential barriers to participation relate to the physical environment, the technology used to support a telementoring program, and communication strategies within that environment. Solutions presented to address access challenges employ both universal design and accommodation approaches. The content of this chapter may be useful to administrators, teachers, and technology specialists as they integrate telementoring into elementary and secondary classroom practices; to professionals who seek to promote telementoring in formal and informal settings; and to researchers who wish to identify telementoring topics for further study.

Chapter 7
Electronic Mentoring in the Classroom: Where Mentors and Students are Persons
with Disabilities 116
Carmit-Noa Shpigelman, University of Haifa, Israel
Patrice L. (Tamar) Weiss, University of Haifa, Israel
Shunit Reiter, University of Haifa, Israel

In recent years, we have witnessed a process of growing awareness and increased activity among persons with disabilities toward improvements in their living conditions and their full inclusion into society. Still, persons with disabilities experience difficulty in achieving the interpersonal competencies needed to develop adaptive social behaviors, to achieve and maintain close relationships, and to fulfill their potential. Mentoring appears to promote interpersonal development when it is conducted via traditional face-to-face methods or via electronic means. In particular, electronic mentoring programs that nurture relationships between persons with disabilities appear to have considerable potential for their empowerment. This chapter discusses the relevance, feasibility and utility of e-mentoring intervention programs designed especially for young people with disabilities.

Chapter 8
Meeting the Needs of Adolescents and Young Adults with Disabilities:
An E-Mentoring Approach 135
    Katharine Hill, St. Catherine University, USA & University of St. Thomas, USA
    Joe Timmons, University of Minnesota, USA
    Christen Opsal, University of Minnesota, USA

Resilience in at-risk youth is anchored by supportive adults who may be relatives, neighbors, teachers, employers, or other members of the community. Telementoring or electronic mentoring (e-mentoring) is a promising practice for improving transition-to-adulthood outcomes for youth with disabilities through connections with caring adults. E-mentoring supports the development of technological and social skills and also increases their understanding of the employment and educational opportunities that await youth upon completion of high school. Connecting to Success (CTS) is an e-mentoring program for transition-age youth with disabilities. In this chapter, CTS is discussed in the context of healthy youth development and transition to adulthood. An overview of the CTS program model is provided, and a discussion of future directions is identified.

Section 3
Telementoring: Professional Development

Chapter 9
Telementoring in Teacher Education 148
    Sandy White Watson, University of Tennessee at Chattanooga, USA

This research study involved the telementoring of pre-service teachers by practicing teachers in the fall semester of 2005 and arose out of a need expressed by education students for more contact with practicing teachers that would not require large time and financial commitments. Twelve pre-service education students at the University of Tennessee at Chattanooga (UTC) and 17 practicing K-12 teachers from four states participated. Pre- and post- reflections completed by student participants, email dialogues between pre- and in-service teacher participants, and pre-service student participant email reflections following each dialogue exchange were analyzed to gather project effectiveness data. Results revealed highly positive experiences that provided student participants a unique and practical glimpse of the daily lives of teachers and what teaching is "really like."

Chapter 10
Virtual Mentoring: A Response to the Challenge of Change 173
    Thomas T. Peters, South Carolina's Coalition for Mathematics & Science, USA
    Terrie R. Dew, Anderson Oconee Pickens Greenville Regional S²MART Center, USA

In this chapter mentoring is defined as a sustained relationship between reflective practitioners. The purpose of this relationship is to build capacity to manage the complex classroom environment in ways that bring about instructional improvements. Where there is a difference in experience between these practitioners, what matters for the mentor's effectiveness is expertise with applying reflective practices.

Reflective practices within a virtual (distance) mentoring setting are identified and explored. Developing trust from a distance and understanding representational preferences are essential virtual mentoring practices. These practices were developed as ways to provide ongoing support to field-based instructional coaches charged with improving mathematics and science instruction in South Carolina middle schools. They are applicable in any P-12 classroom mentoring setting.

Chapter 11
Telementoring and Virtual Professional Development: A Theoretical Perspective from Science on the Roles of Self-Efficacy, Teacher Learning, and Professional Learning Communities 186
Matthew J. Maurer, Robert Morris University, USA

In science, examining how teachers can effectively learn content and inquiry-based pedagogy can often be nothing short of an intellectual, cognitive, and motivational maze. Professional development (PD) programs constructed specifically to aid teacher learning may fall short of their goals due to the high background variability of the participants, especially when mixing novice and master-level teachers. Only through conscious reorganization of instructional approaches can PD programs effectively address specific content and pedagogical needs while concurrently aiding the transition from novice to master-level teachers. It is time for a shift in how PD providers think about how teachers learn. Utilizing a theoretical perspective from Science Education, this chapter will demonstrate the benefits of moving to more of a contextual-based discourse that is accomplished through a virtual telementoring-based professional learning community (PLC) in order to enhance content, pedagogy, leadership skills, and positively impact teaching self-efficacy.

Section 4
Telementoring: Web 2.0 Technologies

Chapter 12
An Orientation to Web 2.0 Tools for Telementoring.. 206
Robin Hastings, Missouri River Regional Library, USA

This chapter gives an overview of Web 2.0 technologies and how they can support telementoring partnerships. Web 2.0 tools offer opportunities for increased networking and social interactivity. Synchronous (chats) and asynchronous (email) communication are possible with these tools. Some of the Web 2.0 capabilities that are introduced in this chapter include cloud computing, Facebook, Ning, and Twitter. FriendFeed and Groupware are also discussed as methods to organize and track a number of Web 2.0 applications for ease of use. Stability, data portability, privacy, and security are issues that are indicated for future research.

Chapter 13
Web 2.0 for Tele-Mentoring.. 215
    Shari McCurdy Smith, University of Illinois at Springfield, USA
    Najmuddin Shaik, University of Illinois Urbana-Champaign, USA
    Emily Welch Boles, University of Illinois at Springfield, USA

Web 2.0 technologies are designed to be open, flexible, and collaborative offering many tools to support traditional or non-traditional tele-mentoring activities. The benefit of effortless sharing and connectivity comes with challenges in how we view such things as ownership, privacy, and duplicity. The Web 2.0 toolkit includes applications for web-based note-taking, shared documents, feedback, reflection, informal discussion, and presentation. The collaborative opportunities provided by mashable, social networking platforms allow users to flex time, geography, and projects. Professional educators continue to inform their practice and explore new ways to meet the needs of students. Web 2.0 technologies can support educational professionals by opening doors and classrooms world-wide. The chapter makes a comparison between online and mentoring instructional practice and highlights models for educational use of and aids in identification of tools for mentors and mentees.

Compilation of References 254

About the Contributors 284

Index.. 289

Foreword

When I was hired by Carol Muller in 1998 to be the first Mentoring Specialist and Research Associate for MentorNet, I knew that I was joining a pioneering group who was breaking new ground. After all, it had only been since 1994 that Netscape had made the World Wide Web more accessible to the general public. With Netscape, the business potential of the Internet was immediately recognized. What was more uncertain was the potential that the Internet held for educational or social purposes. So we experimented by developing MentorNet (originally founded in 1995 as the Dartmouth College Women in Science E-mentoring Program), a telementoring program pairing women college students in science and engineering with professionals outside of academic settings.

We were not the only ones experimenting with telementoring. Other pioneering programs, such as the Electronic Emissary Project, DO-IT (Disabilities, Opportunities, Internetworking, and Technology), Telementoring Young Women in Engineering and Computing Project and what became the International Telementoring Project, were also experimenting with this fairly new medium for educational and social justice purposes. While the foci of the programs were varied, many, if not all, of these programs came to some common conclusions. Mainly, that the telementoring relationships established through programs don't just work on their own, they need support. We found that engaged program facilitators had to make good matches, provide regular coaching or prompts to assist the development of the relationships, and intervene when necessary. Also, some of the programs offered group telementoring opportunities to expand the connections among the participants or to serve as a safety net for when the one-on-one relationships were not working.

So it is with great pleasure that over a decade later, I am writing a Foreword to a book that is celebrating the potential telementoring is realizing for improving K-12 educational systems. Telementoring in the K-12 Classroom: Online Communication Technologies for Learning is a must-read for anyone interested in or involved in telementoring for a K-12 audience. If you are interested in starting a telementoring program, or improving a program you are already conducting, this book can provide insights into the process. If you are a researcher interested in programmatic, design, and research issues, this book is for you. Telementoring in the K-12 Classroom addresses issues regarding designing, implementing, and researching telementoring programs. These chapters reflect the current thinking, most pressing issues, and required features of any program.

As I have read these chapters, I am struck that although telementoring programs have been designed, revised, evaluated, and researched for over a decade, over the half of the chapters address technology and design issues. What this tells us is that telementoring programs are highly flexible. They can provide mentoring opportunities unconstrained by time and space. The protégés can be K-1 students, college students studying to be teachers, school or college students with disabilities, or novice teachers just starting out. The mentors can be professionals with varied expertise who directly mentor students or who mentor the students' teachers. The mentors can also be more advanced education college students, novice teachers, or master teachers and may, or may not, be persons with disabilities. The goals of telementoring can be to provide subject matter expertise, to retain education students by giving them a glimpse of their future profession, or professional development. So while some general principles for developing and implementing telementoring programs can be widely agreed upon, each program requires its own set of technology, design and program decisions.

The first section of this book, "Telementoring: Implications for Practice," addresses issues around the design and programmatic features of telementoring programs. If you are planning to develop a telementoring program or have one underway, these chapters will address important issues such as supporting successful telementoring relationships, along with identifying program goals and matching curricula to meet those goals. These chapters also provide practical ways to leverage the expertise of a team of subject matter experts in order to help school students with assigned projects, where the range and scope of the projects would be beyond the knowledge base of any one teacher. Throughout these chapters, we are reminded that the point of telementoring programs is to enhance the knowledge or self-efficacy of the protégés, whether students or novice teachers, and that we can draw from our vast knowledge-base of effective classroom practices to inform the telementoring practices.

In "Telementoring: Addressing the Needs of Persons with Disabilities," the authors present examples of how telementoring has been effective in providing mentoring opportunities to protégés with disabilities. These authors explain how it is not enough to offer mentoring through electronic means to open up the opportunities for protégés with disabilities. Rather, they provide practical program-based and research-based advice for developing programs in such a way that they not only reduce barriers but also address issues of full-inclusion for students, teachers, and administrators with disabilities. These authors make recommendations for program features that are inclusive not only for persons with disabilities but for all. They focus on ways to make sure that the programs are self-empowering for the protégés with disabilities, and they highlight side benefits of such programs, such as when mentors without disabilities replace inaccurate, stereotypical views with enhanced, more realistic views of the abilities and employability of their protégés with disabilities.

The chapters in "Telementoring: Professional Development" provide examples of successful telementoring programs and demonstrate how relying on concepts, such as reflective practice, or theoretical perspectives from science education can enhance telementoring programs for education students or novice teachers. In these chapters, we learn of a successful program requested by pre-service education students who wanted to learn what teaching was really like, before they began their in-service training. Another chapter provides an insightful look at using reflective practice as a mechanism for building trust and establishing effective mentoring relationships that do not have the benefit, or the burden, of visual cues. The final chapter draws from the lessons of science education to present the potential of developing professional learning communities virtually as part of a telementoring program. These chapters help the readers to think conceptually and practically about using telementoring to provide mentoring for future or novice teachers.

The final section "Telementoring: Web 2.0 Technologies" keeps us up-to-date on the latest technologies that can be leveraged to provide opportunities for telementoring. Web 2.0 technologies refer to the many new web applications that allow for information sharing and social networking, such a blogs and wikis. Telementoring came along in its earlier incarnations because researchers, program developers, and social entrepreneurs were creative at using new technologies to provide mentoring opportunities that otherwise may not exist. These two chapters make us aware of how to leverage the latest technologies to expand and enhance current telementoring opportunities. Moving to leverage these new technologies seems natural for the field of telementoring, which has often been on the cutting edge.

Telementoring in the K-12 Classroom is a great resource for newcomers and veterans to the field of telementoring. The insights are directed toward how to use electronic communications to support students and teachers who are a part of K-12 educational systems. Nonetheless, the depth and breadth of the ideas presented can inform anyone who wants to improve the within classroom experiences for students by bringing in resources available over the Web, to inform pre-service education teachers as they are exploring their future career opportunities, or to support novice teachers as they are putting their newly found knowledge into practice. This book will get you to think about telementoring, its promises and possibilities, in a new way.

Peg Boyle Single
Consultant, USA

Peg Boyle Single, *Ph.D., is the author of Demystifying Dissertation Writing: A Streamlined Process from Choice of Topic to Final Text and she writes the "Demystifying the Dissertation" advice column for Inside Higher Education. Dr. Single is an independent consultant who provides writing workshops at universities and offers individual writing coaching through www.pegboylesingle.com.*

Preface

> **Web 2.0** refers to World Wide Web websites that emphasize user-generated content, usability (ease of use) and interoperability (works well with other products) for end users. A Web 2.0 website may allow users to interact and collaborate in a social media dialogue as creators of user-generated content in a virtual community. Examples of Web 2.0 features include social networking sites and social media (eg Facebook), blogs, wikis, folksonomies (tagging)

This book is intended to have two purposes. One purpose is to encourage and support and the other purpose is to extend an invitation. Encouragement and support is provided for those professionals in the P-12 environment who are engaged in the valuable enterprise of telementoring, the practice of online mentoring. A warm invitation is extended to those professionals who have not yet ventured into telementoring to consider, explore, and begin to make use of this beneficial practice. I encourage and invite these professionals who include classroom educators, technology specialists, administrators, teacher educators, and all who seek to promote the use of telementoring to read further and reflect upon the limitless possibilities and outstanding opportunities that telementoring provides.

It is important to understand the richness of the scope of telementoring partnerships and processes in order to facilitate the continuing growth of those who participate in these exciting virtual mentoring relationships. The latest research and best practices in the field of telementoring are presented in this volume. Theoretical and pragmatic viewpoints will provide guidance to the professionals who will use this book to inform their practice and reaffirm their enthusiasm for telementoring. A solid base of current information and an expansive vision of this practice will combine to promote the understanding and the successful implementation of telementoring.

A BRIEF DESCRIPTION OF TELEMENTORING

Telementoring, the practice of online or virtual mentoring, is based upon the traditional roles of a mentoring relationship. The concept of mentoring dates back to Homer's Odyssey when Odysseus entrusted his son, Telemachus, to the tutelage of his trusted friend Mentor. Many of the benefits of mentoring have been documented with telementoring, especially the social connectivity that telementoring provides. One added benefit is that telementoring transcends temporal and spatial boundaries to engage participants in learning that can occur at their convenience instead of a prescribed time and place.

A number of telementoring models involve the use of subject matter experts who mentor students who are engaged in inquiry-based projects. Content-centered processes along with effective telecommunication processes combine to produce successful telementoring projects.

Adult learners have found telementoring to be an opportune means of furthering their learning as well as a functional collaborative tool. When the constraints of a work schedule inhibit collaboration, telementoring opens the door to expansive new possibilities for learning with colleagues.

Text-based media, such as email, form the communication method in many models. Communication can be synchronous or asynchronous. Asynchronous communication is one of the features that facilitates interaction at a time and place that is convenient for the participants.

[Handwritten note at top: Keyword(s), video sharing (YouTube) hosted services, Web applications (apps), collaborative consumption platforms, and mashup applications]

Although telementoring has been in use for several decades at this point, there is still much to learn about its implementation. Telementoring practices and the related research into this valuable process are ever-emerging. The collected wisdom, research, and inspiration in this book will provide abundant resources and new insights for those professionals already engaged in telementoring and those professionals who are about to foray into this enriching endeavor.

TELEMENTORING TODAY

There are a variety of ways that telementoring is put into practice currently. Telementoring is predominantly used between adult subject matter experts and students in the P-12 setting. The use of telelementoring to further professional development is rapidly emerging as another use. Web 2.0 technologies now are able to bring even more interactivity and social connectedness to the telementoring relationship.

In the P-12 setting, telementoring brings adult experts into partnership with students to promote deep learning. These adult subject matter experts act as guides and models. Within these relationships, the students are given control of their learning.

The inclusive nature of telementoring is receiving increasing attention so that participants of all abilities are able to fully participate. All learners can find a place at the table when focus is given to accessibility issues. When inclusivity is considered in the development of telementoring projects and partnerships, each and every learner can benefit from the virtual mentoring experience.

Telementoring is increasingly being used to promote teacher learning. With the time constraints that are placed upon teachers within the school day, virtual mentoring offers a viable solution to promote professional learning. Pre-service and well as teachers in the field are engaging in telementoring to further their learning and gain knowledge and expertise that reach beyond the constraints of time and space.

Perhaps one of the most essential ingredients to a successful telementoring partnership is relationship. Telementoring does indeed hold the potential to create strong relationships which are conducive to learning. Web 2.0 technologies offer a wide range of interactive tools that facilitate the building and sustaining of telementoring relationships. Awareness and understanding of how to effectively use Web 2.0 tools will empower participants to take their virtual partnerships to a new level and strengthen the social connectivity and interactivity that will enrich the telementoring relationship.

ORGANIZATION OF CHAPTERS

The book is divided into four sections: (a) implications for practice, (b) addressing the needs of persons with disabilities, (c) professional development, and (d) Web 2.0 technologies. The chapters in each section will examine issues of practice and research related to each section topic.

The section on Implications for Practice explores issues of practice. The following chapters address these issues.

Designs for Curriculum-Based Telementoring offers a pragmatic and research-based view of the potential and challenges that telementoring provides. Judi Harris focuses on the use of telementoring in the classroom. She discusses the activity types involved in curriculum-based telementoring so that teachers can make informed decisions for the learning in which their students will engage.

Dimensions of Design in K-12 Telementoring Programs discusses issues of design. Kevin O'Neill analyzes the design of telementoring programs and sets forth the premise that knowing what doesn't work is as important as what does work. Teachers are seen as vital in the process of project design and development. It is through sharing research with the intent to find out what needs to be strengthened that can help to move the field of telementoring forward.

Telementoring and Project-based Learning: An Integrated Model for 21st Century Skills focuses on using project-based telementoring to address the need to keep pace with economic and technological changes and challenges that impact education. Joyce Yukawa notes that the Partnership for 21st Century Skills has identified essential skills such as critical thinking, solving complex open-ended problems, creative and entrepreneurial thinking, collaboration with diverse multi-national teams, and using knowledge for innovation. The chapter makes the case for project-based telementoring to address these skills to equip today's students for tomorrow's world.

You Had to be There: What Telementoring Researchers can Learn from Classroom Observations emphasizes the importance for researchers and teachers to actively interact in order to richly develop effective telementoring programs. Kevin O'Neill and Sheryl Guloy invite researchers to consider stepping into the classroom to observe what is happening during the process of telementoring. They note that researchers often rely on captured interchanges to make decisions on the process. Teachers are encouraged to open their classrooms and practice to researcher and to participate in providing valuable insights to guide the design of successful telementoring programs.

The Transformative Capacity of Telementoring on Self-efficacy Beliefs: A Design-Based Perspective examines the tremendous capacity that telementoring holds to impact self-efficacy beliefs, especially with the implementation of intentional design. Self-efficacy is defined and discussed to build context. A research study that focused on using the four influences on self-efficacy of mastery experience, vicarious experience, verbal persuasion, and physiological state is used as an exemplar to show the design possibilities. The capacity of telementoring to address each influence is then discussed along with illustrative vignettes and design implications.

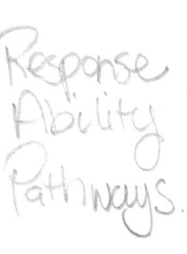

The section on Implications for Addressing the Needs of Persons with Disabilities examines inclusive practices. The following chapters address these issues.

In *Fully Including Students, Teachers, and Administrators with Disabilities in Telementoring* explores the challenges that need to be addressed in the elementary and secondary environments to fully include students, teachers, and administrators with disabilities. Sheryl Burgstahler and Terrill Thompson discuss access issues for telementoring participants with disabilities and present approaches for full inclusion in the telementoring process. Principles of Universal Design are discussed richly and pragmatically in order to guide the successful implementation of telementoring programs that address the needs of all participants.

Electronic Mentoring in the Classroom: Where Mentors and Students are Persons with Disabilities discusses the empowerment that telementoring can provide for individuals with disabilities. E-mentoring intervention programs for young people with disabilities are explored. Carmit-Noa Shpigelman, Patrice L. (Tamar) Weiss, and Shunit Reiter discuss the implementation of two studies that they conducted where protégés with disabilities were partnered with mentors with disabilities. They also describe the four stages of a successful e-mentoring program as well as practical suggestions for implementing a successful e-mentoring program for students with disabilities.

Meeting the Needs of Adolescents and Young Adults with Disabilities: An E-mentoring Approach discusses how telementoring is a promising practice to aid in the transition to adulthood for youth with disabilities. Katharine Hill, Joe Timmons, and Christen Opsal discuss an e-mentoring program, Connecting to Success, which seeks to increase the understanding of educational and employment opportunities for transition-age youth who have disabilities. The ability of e-mentoring to increase resilience in youth with disabilities is explored. Implementation implications are discussed for issues such as safety and confidentiality, mentor training, and mentee/mentor matching.

The section on Professional Development considers the professional development of educators. The following chapters address these issues.

Telementoring in Teacher Education discusses the need that has been voiced by pre-service teachers to know what it is like in the classroom before they reach their student teaching experiences. Virtual mentoring is shown as a way of connecting these pre-service teachers with teachers in the field. Citing the obstacles to face-to-face mentoring between the pre-service and veterans teachers such as time and place constraints, Sandy White Watson notes that telementoring provides a valuable vehicle for the pre-service teachers to be mentored. A study involving a six-week telementoring initiative is discussed. Issues such as classroom management, assessment, and classroom materials were among the real-life teaching experiences that were able to be shared. This virtual glimpse into the practical aspects of life in the classroom gave desired information to the pre-service teachers that otherwise would not have been gained until later in their university experience.

Virtual Mentoring: A Response to the Challenge of Change presents the capacity-building capabilities of virtual mentoring in effecting change. Thomas Peters and Terrie Dew take a pragmatic approach to discussing the improvement of instructional strategies and student achievement. The mentoring relationship is explored in building reflective practitioners who can efficaciously act within ever-increasingly complex school environments. The importance of building trust in a mentoring relationship and how this can be accomplished virtually is a point of emphasis.

Telementoring and Virtual Professional Development: A Theoretical Perspective from Science on the Roles of Self-Efficacy, Teacher Learning, and Professional Learning Communities examines how telementoring can facilitate the involvement in professional learning communities. Matthew Maurer explores one of the goals for this professional learning which is to positively impact teacher self-efficacy. A featured focus of the chapter is the professional development of science teachers. The research-based approach to professional development that professional learning communities provide lends support for inquiry-based learning. Successful examples of telementoring with science-based professional development as well as future recommendations for the use of telementoring in professional development are explored.

The section on Web 2.0 technologies looks at the interactivity that these tools bring to the practice of telementoring. The following chapters address these issues.

An Orientation to Web 2.0 Tools for Telementoring gives an overview of Web 2.0 applications. This guide is designed to familiarize those who are new to the use of Web 2.0 technologies so that they feel more comfortable in implementing them in their telementoring projects. Robin Hastings explores the perfect fit for telementoring relationships that Web 2.0 provides with capabilities that include networking, social sharing, and interactive communication. This chapter focuses on making Web 2.0 tools work to enhance the virtual mentoring relationship.

Web 2.0 for Telementoring explores the collaborative capacity that Web 2.0 tools provide to enhance the telementoring relationship. The constructivist capabilities that Web 2.0 technologies bring to student learning are emphasized. Shari McCurdy Smith, Najmuddin Shaik, and Emily Welch Boles discuss case studies to illustrate successful implementations using Web 2.0 applications to build social presence. An in-depth and extensive discussion of specific applications and their uses is provided.

CONCLUSION

The practice and research of telementoring, although decades old, is a relatively-new and ever-emerging field. The conversations and discussions in each chapter of this book provide new insights, research, and implications that will enhance and broaden the successful use of telementoring and give indications for future research.

For the professionals in the P-12 environment as well as teacher educators, the collected vision provided in this book serves as a research-based and pragmatic guide. Those professionals who are already implementing telementoring projects will find support for their practice as well as new horizon to explore.

The professionals who have not yet engaged in telementoring will find an invitation to engage in this valuable practice. They will find sound and practical advice on how to make the most of telementoring to promote student learning and their own professional learning.

It is my sincere hope that this volume will reaffirm the enthusiasm for those already engaged in telementoring and ignite a spark of willingness to venture into telementoring for those who have not yet tried it. The rich potential of telementoring to impact learning is a call and a challenge to make the best use of this exciting technological relationship. May those who read this book heed that call and take up that challenge.

Deborah A. Scigliano
Duquesne University, USA

Acknowledgment

This book is the result of the collaboration across time and space of a vast network of talented individuals. I am grateful for their dedication, vision, and commitment to bringing the knowledge and experience in this volume to life.

Thank you to all of the contributing authors for sharing their research and experiences to further the field of telementoring. Their practical guidance and visionary perspective of the possibilities that telementoring offers will propel those who engage in this practice into new and richer online mentoring partnerships.

My thanks to the members of my Editorial Advisory Board: Larry Tomei, Roderick Sims, Laurie Dringus, Connie Moss, Dave Carbonara, Judi Harris, and Kevin O'Neill. You have my deepest thanks for your service.

I am deeply grateful to my dedicated reviewers who gave helpful feedback to each author. To Larry Tomei, Dave Carbonara, Joyce Yukawa, Robin Hastings, Laurie Dringus, Roderick Sims, Sheryl Bergstahler, Shellie Hipsky, Sandy Watson, Kevin O'Neill, Connie Moss, David Parker, Sharon McCurdy Smith, Judi Harris, Katharine Hill, Joe Timmons, Carole Duff, Rosemary Mautino, Matt Maurer, Carmit-Noa Shpigelman, and Susie McLaughlin, I extend my deepest thanks for your careful reviews and conscientious attention to detail.

To Peg Boyle Single, I give my heartfelt appreciation for writing the foreword for this book. Peg is a pioneer in the field of telementoring and is deeply supportive of the on-going efforts to enrich the practice which this book offers. Her wisdom, experience, and vision are gratefully welcomed. Her words set the tone so eloquently for this book. Thank you, Peg!

As the final chapters came into being, my second set of proofreading eyes sprang into action. Lindsay McGuirk, our fantastic graduate assistant at Duquesne University, provided the fine-tooth comb look to make sure that all t's were crossed and all i's were dotted. She was able to give attention to these chapters when her schedule was jam-packed. I am deeply appreciative of her timely help and her every-present cheerfulness. Lindsay, thank you!

I had the wonderful opportunity and joy to work with two editorial assistants at IGI Global. Tyler Heath started out on this journey with me. Tyler was always available at the sending of an email or the dialing of a phone. His ready guidance and helpful advice were always appreciated. When he moved on to the journal division of IGI Global, I was placed in the very capable hands of Christine Bufton who has followed this journey to its completion. Christine was ever-helpful with any questions that I had. Her beneficial advice and timely support has been very much appreciated. Whether by email or phone, she has helped to guide this ship into harbor with grace and ease. I am deeply thankful for the support and guidance that Tyler and Christine have provided throughout the completion of this book.

I extend my thanks to our readers who will take this book to heart and use the wisdom contained within to promote the use of telementoring. May the work and words of these individuals inspire you to take telementoring to the next level in your practice.

Deborah A. Scigliano
Duquesne University, USA

Section 1
Telementoring:
Implications for Practice

Chapter 1
Designs for Curriculum-Based Telementoring

Judi Harris
College of William and Mary, USA

ABSTRACT

Telementoring for K-12 students is done primarily outside of school, typically addressing topics that are extrinsic to school curricula. As beneficial as extracurricular telementoring can be, bringing mentors virtually into classrooms to interact with students and teachers over time holds great potential—and considerable challenge—for both. How can telementoring be integrated effectively into content-based curricula taught in face-to-face educational contexts like classrooms? What is key to the success of this type of curriculum-based telementoring? Answers to these questions appear below, illustrated by examples from an informal taxonomy of curriculum-based telementoring projects that were facilitated by the Electronic Emissary (http://Emissary.wm.edu/), the longest-running formal telementoring program for K-12 students and their teachers.

INTRODUCTION

Summarizing the emerging field of social neuroscience, journalist Daniel Goleman (2006, p. 4) asserts that "we are wired to connect." Our brains are designed to be social, and we benefit in measurable ways intellectually, emotionally, and even physically from ongoing, nurturing connections with each other. Given our biological "wiring" and the ever-increasing capabilities and availabilities of social networking tools, is it any wonder that our students are drawn so powerfully to multiple forms of networked communication?

Most of the social networking that so many students enjoy (e.g., texting and cell phone use) is done extracurricularly (Lenhart, Ling, Campbell & Purcell, 2010). Educational technologists are experimenting with "educational networking," seeking to capitalize upon students' attractions to social networking by integrating tool use such as text messaging, microblogging, collaborative document-writing, handheld videoconferencing,

DOI: 10.4018/978-1-60520-861-6.ch001

and wireless phone calls into learning and teaching in K-12 classrooms (Hargadon, 2009). This is challenging work, since more than half of U.S. districts prohibit social networking in school (Deubel, 2009).

Yet one of the oldest and most educationally beneficial forms of social/educational networking — *telementoring* — has been used formally in elementary, middle-level, and secondary classrooms since at least 1992, long before blogs, wikis, wireless networks and even the multimedia Web found their way into most schools. Indeed, informal e-mentoring among adults emerged in the late 1970's and early 1980's, when university-based researchers began communicating using networks that had been reserved previously for U.S. government projects (Single & Single, 2005). Informal online mentoring for K-12 students probably emerged at about the same time, since the first published evidence of email-based educational networking appeared in 1978 (Harris, 2005), and the Free Educational Mail (FrEdMail) network connected schools internationally starting in 1985 ("FrEdWriter and FrEdMail," n.d.).

Telementoring—also called "e-mentoring" and "online mentoring"—is mentoring that happens via educational networking. E-mentoring for K-12 students typically involves sustained exchanges between mentors and protégés, who use electronic mail, discussion forums, texting, and/or video-conferencing to communicate individually or in groups. It differs from using ask-an-expert Web sites (e.g., AllExperts.com) to answer specific questions, because telementoring interactions are much longer and deeper in duration and focus. Curriculum-based telementoring can be an integral part of organized learning for elementary, middle-school, or high school students. It is less common than extracurricular telementoring, however, which typically supports individual students' explorations of career interests, hobbies, and/or personal issues.

When telementoring is designed to function within school-based curricula, rather than extracurricularly, it can help to bring subject matter alive in ways not possible locally, increasing the depth, breadth, and/or authenticity of students' curriculum-based learning. Communicating regularly with content specialists who share active interest, experience, and expertise in curriculum-based topics can increase students' engagement and connection with standards-based learning, due to the interactive, emergent, and personalized nature of telementoring discussions. Integrating regular e-mentoring into students' classroom activities, however, presents pedagogical challenges for teachers who are unfamiliar with planning for and implementing educational networking within classroom-based instruction (Harris, 2010).

Like social networking, much telementoring happens informally and outside of the school day, with an extracurricular focus. Curriculum-based telementoring—the focus of this chapter—is e-mentoring that is a planned part of students' learning that happens in the classroom. Though this type of mentoring has been used episodically for nearly two decades and with considerable success, its potential is still largely untapped. What is curriculum-based telementoring? How is it similar to and different from other types of educational networking? How can it be structured and used to assist and enhance students' curriculum-related learning? Pragmatic answers to these questions begin with teachers' planning for students' learning, the reasons for which can be understood with a metaphor.

BACKGROUND

Eh! Je suis leur chef, il fallait bien les suivre. (Ah well! I am their leader, so I must follow them.)

—Alexandre Auguste Ledru-Rollin
(Aphids Communications, ¶ 33)

Effective, meaningful learning is like enjoying a well-prepared, well-presented, and nutritious meal. A good meal can be eaten at home or away, but when it is partaken at a fine restaurant, it is surely the direct result of careful planning and well-coordinated action, born of both culinary and management expertise. Teachers' work in planning and directing effective, meaningful learning opportunities for their students is much like an experienced chef's work on behalf of the patrons at an award-winning restaurant. To be effective, both instruction and fine dining need to be carefully conceptualized, well-planned, well-executed, competently managed, and evaluated. Both should meet professional standards without sacrificing creative expression or enjoyment.

This metaphor is included here purposefully. Teachers are chefs—not cooks. Though some would say that these two jobs are the same, in reality they require different experience and expertise, warranting different levels of professional respect. This notion is true even across cultures. For example, in Chinese, the word for "chef" translates to "kitchen master," while the word for "cook" translates to "kitchen worker." In French, "chef" means "chief" or "leader," as the quote from Ledru-Rollin above demonstrates. Chefs and teachers are leaders who do much more than prepare nourishment for the body or the mind. They are designers, managers, human relations specialists, artists, and assessors. A successful chef goes beyond following recipes and combining individual dishes into meals. Similarly, teaching that results in students' effective, meaningful, and transferable learning goes far beyond selecting curriculum standards to address, then following directions in teachers' manuals or curriculum guides.

It is true that both chefs and cooks participate in the preparation of food, and cooking without a chef's involvement meets practical needs in many settings outside of popular restaurants. Similarly, many people without professional preparation in education are able informally to help others learn. Yet it is only the professional teacher who has the requisite knowledge, training, experience, and vision to ensure that students' learning meets curriculum-based standards in the most robust, motivating, and appropriately differentiated ways.

Australian author Michael Russell explains the differences between a chef and a cook with the following excerpts from an article posted at a Web site for aspiring chefs. Metaphorically, this also describes the differences between professional and lay teachers.

Being a cook is not synonymous with being a chef. A chef is a cook, but a cook is not necessarily a chef. Yep, it's true that your mom, your Uncle Pete, and your friend can cook. Mom's pancakes are wonderful, Uncle Pete's barbecue makes you drool in anticipation, and your best friend's spaghetti sauce should be patented but alas, they are still merely cooks, not chefs. Chefs must not only be wonderful cooks; they must also develop menus, stay on top of food costs, manage a staff, plus wear the hats of human resource professional, accountant, teacher, sometimes Mom and Dad, and sometimes friend (or enemy), as well.

Creativity plays a major role in a chef's profession. Not only must the food be impeccably prepared; ... its presentation must be artful and designed to appeal to the most discriminating taste buds. Chefs are also expected to create new, never-before-seen dishes, and for this, a mastery of all types of foodstuffs is required: meats, fish, poultry, herbs, spices; even wines. A cook needs nothing more than a desire to work in the kitchen and deftness with a whisk and spatula, while a chef needs years of training and apprenticeship for certification--almost all of it done on his or her feet. ...A true chef MAKES the recipes, THEN follows them. (Russell, 2007)

Similar to Russell's depictions of chefs, professional teachers often manage both resources and assistants (e.g., teachers' aides, student teachers. and parent volunteers), while balancing many different, often conflicting, types of human relationships (e.g., with students, parents, colleagues, and administrators), and the politics inherent in doing so. The most engaging teachers are also often the most creative, yet pragmatic education professionals – the ones who know their students' needs and preferences in ways analogous to how inventive, successful chefs know and serve their clienteles.

For both teachers and chefs, knowledge of new tools, such as educational networking applications, and unfamiliar techniques, such as telementoring, can introduce new possibilities for professional practice. This is especially true for educational technologies and teaching. Yet in the same way that learning to use a food processor or following a recipe to prepare pesto doesn't make someone a chef, mastering the mechanics of using unfamiliar technologies or curriculum-based resources isn't all that is required in integrating those technologies into professional educational practice.

As Russell (2007) asserted, "a true chef makes the recipes, then follows them"—just as a true teacher creates *customized plans for learning* based upon students' needs and preferences, then implements them in the classroom. In doing so, students' learning needs, framed by content-based instructional standards, guide and shape teachers' work. Indeed, as Ledru-Rollin exclaimed in the quotation that began this section, leaders ("chefs") must actually *follow* those whom they serve to lead them effectively. Thus, planning a particular learning experience—such as a curriculum-based telementoring project or exchange—must begin, end, and progress based upon students' learning needs and preferences, rather than an intention to use digital technologies in teaching.

Planning Curriculum-Based Telementoring

During instructional planning, teachers' knowledge is operationalized, in part, through the learning activities that they select, combine, sequence, and redesign (Harris, 2008). Studies of teachers' planning show it to be organized and communicated primarily by learning activities and content goals (John, 2006; Yinger, 1979). Learning activities are "routinized" by teachers over time to simplify the planning and coordinating of classroom activity (Yinger, p. 165), allowing greater flexibility and responsiveness to students in the highly situated and contextualized classroom environment (John, 2006). Unfortunately, comparatively little is known at present about how digital educational technologies are integrated into teachers' planning (Richardson, 2009).

Though planning instruction that is facilitated by use of digital tools and resources can be complex, with each decision influencing aspects of other decisions already made or yet to be determined, planning a particular technologically supported learning event can be described generally as a series of five basic steps:

1. Choosing learning goals.
2. Making practical pedagogical decisions about the nature of the learning experience based upon contextual factors, such as technology access and students' prior experience.
3. Selecting and sequencing appropriate learning activity types that combine to form the learning experience (lesson, project, or unit).
4. Selecting formative and summative assessment strategies that will reveal what and how well students are learning.
5. Selecting tools and resources that will best help students to benefit from the learning experience being planned (Harris & Hofer, 2009, pp. 23-25).

The order in which these steps are completed varies. Some teachers, for example, prefer to choose assessments before selecting other types of learning activities to include in a plan, while others research resources available (such as laptop carts) before considering activity possibilities. New understanding about the interdependent and complex nature of the content, pedagogical, and technological knowledge that teachers use when they integrate educational technologies into curriculum-based learning and teaching—called technological pedagogical content knowledge, or TPACK (Mishra & Koehler, 2006) —has important implications for instructional planning. Recent TPACK work (e.g., Harris & Hofer, 2009, 2011) suggests that no matter what the sequence of the "middle three" steps listed above, it is most effective to choose learning goals or objectives (based upon student learning needs) *first* and the tools that will support their learning *last* during planning. In this way, the curriculum-focused nature of students' learning is ensured, and pedagogies appropriate to content, context, and needs are selected so that technological choices do not drive instructional plans (Harris & Hofer, 2009).

Learning Activity Types

Recent work with the development of teachers' knowledge for technology integration, or TPACK, recommends intentional use of *learning activity types* during instructional planning (Harris, 2008; Harris & Hofer, 2009). Activity types function as conceptual planning tools; they comprise methodological shorthand that educators can use to both build and describe plans for standards-based learning experiences. Each activity type captures what is essential about the structure of a particular kind of learning action as it relates to *what participants do* when engaged in that particular learning-related activity (e.g., "group discussion;" "role play;" "fieldtrip"). Activity types can also serve as efficient communication tools for educators wanting to share their plans for students' learning with each other, as science education lesson study research in Japan has shown (e.g., Linn, Lewis, Tsuchida, & Songer, 2000). Teachers who plan using activities selected from taxonomies of technologically supported learning activity types report that doing so both assists the development of their technology integration knowledge and broadens the range of learning activities that they include in their plans (Harris & Hofer, 2011). (The taxonomies are available online via the Activity Types Wiki: http://activitytypes.wmwikis.net/.)

Previous work with telecollaborative, telecooperative, and teleresearch learning activity types (e.g., Harris, 1998) identified telementoring as just one type of learning activity. However, analysis of the structures of the many telementoring projects facilitated by the Electronic Emissary (http://Emissary.wm.edu)—a pro bono service that has assisted K-12 teachers with planning, implementing, and reflecting upon curriculum-based telementoring projects since 1992—has revealed that there are at least twelve different types of telementoring learning activities.

Based upon emerging results from research and development with other types of technologically supported learning activities (as explained above), it serves to reason that becoming familiar with (and choosing among) the full range of telementoring activity types, especially during instructional planning, should be helpful to teachers who wish to incorporate telementoring into their students' curriculum-based learning. As Shulman (2002) observed,

Distinctions and taxonomies are tools for thought. We make distinctions for the same reasons we carve a turkey or write our books in chapters—to make the world more manageable. And it's only natural that we further order our distinctions and categories into systems, tables, and taxonomies. Categories and distinctions also can call attention to ideas, principles, or values that hitherto have been ignored. (p. 36)

Previous research and development with the TPACK-based learning activity types described above (e.g., Harris, 2008; Harris & Hofer, 2009, 2011) has demonstrated that teachers' planning for technologically enhanced learning and teaching is assisted and eased by reviewing all possible activity types, then selecting the ones that best match content-based goals and pedagogies appropriate to students' learning needs and preferences. (This is step 3 in the planning sequence presented above.) The learning activity types are organized into simple taxonomies to make their review during planning maximally efficient. The twelve *telementoring* learning activity types identified to date are presented in an informal taxonomy below, with accompanying examples of e-mentoring projects supported by the Electronic Emissary illustrating each, to help teachers to understand each and all of the telementoring activity options.

Types of Telementoring Activities

The Electronic Emissary has sponsored and facilitated approximately 800 telementoring projects since its inception in the fall of 1992. While this is by no means the largest number of telementoring efforts assisted by one organization—the International Telementor Program (http://www.telementor.org/) has supported more than 40,000 in three fewer years, for example—the range and variety of different types of telementoring that the Emissary has assisted is broad. Comparing project summaries prepared by participating teachers, mentors, and Emissary staff (project facilitators) reveals different types of telementoring that can be identified according to the *primary communication-based functions and roles that mentors perform,* as demonstrated in Table 1.

How to involve mentors in students' curriculum-based project work is often confusing for teachers and students during early attempts at curriculum-based telementoring. The types of activities listed above address that confusion directly by focusing upon mentors' primary communicative functions. In some telementoring projects, mentors perform only one of the twelve functions listed here. In others, they serve in multiple ways, either simultaneously or in sequence, based upon the specifics of the project work in which students are engaged.

Examples of Telementoring Activity Types

Examples of each of the mentor functions in Table 1 appear below. These are sample project summaries for telementoring efforts sponsored by the Electronic Emissary. They are included here to illustrate the online mentoring functions that distinguish each telementoring learning activity type. They are provided for teachers' review in conjunction with the information in Table 1, to assist with selecting the most appropriate types of telementoring in which teachers will ask their students to engage.

Advise/Coach

"What kinds of berries were eaten by the Indian tribes in Oregon?" Queries such as this and other questions about the livelihoods of the Indians native to Oregon were explored by the fourth grade students in Elise Tickner's class in Parkdale, Oregon. Dr. Ed Liebow, who works with the Battelle Memorial Institute, guided the students through their explorations of village life, dance and religious ceremonies, Indian legends, and other aspects of native Indian culture. Using this information, the students prepared a video demonstrating their knowledge and featuring their completed projects.

Assist

Mellie Lewis' 32 3rd grade students participated in a project focused on saltwater and freshwater living environments. Dr. Carl Berman, from California State University, Monterey Bay, first helped them to learn about coral reefs—in particular the damage to the reefs caused by pollution, and the diversity of life that they support. Ms. Lewis' students originally planned to create a saltwater aquarium in their classroom, but decided instead to create a fresh-water aquarium with local species. Students gathered plant and fish specimens

Table 1. Telementoring activity types

Mentor's Communication	Description
Advise/Coach	Mentors provide suggestions and formative feedback as students progress with their project-related work, focusing upon the former. If the focus is upon providing formative feedback, then the type of telementoring being used is probably Provide Feedback, described below.
Assist	Mentors help students to accomplish a particular task by suggesting techniques, resources, directions, etc. They do not direct, assess, or participate in the project work itself.
Chat	Mentors share personal stories, information about themselves and their families, "behind the scenes" views of their professional work, etc. Typically curriculum- or project-based discussion is not the primary focus for this type of telementoring.
Co-Create	Mentors, teachers, and students work jointly on a particular product or experience.
Discuss/Debate	Mentors dialogue with students and/or teachers, constructively challenging their assertions and views.
Impersonate	Mentors communicate with students in character, typically as an historically accurate or probable person, or as a protagonist in a book that the students are reading.
Problem-Solve	Mentors work alongside students (and often their teachers, too) to solve a complex and longer-term problem jointly. This differs from the Assist activity type in that here, both the mentor and the student(s) are working to solve the problem. In an Assist telementoring activity, the mentor is assisting the students as *they* engage in the learning activity.
Provide Feedback	Mentors send constructive comments and suggestions to students after reviewing successive versions of their work, usually formatively.
Question-and-Answer	Mentors respond to a variety of questions posed by students (individually, in small groups, or as a teacher-led large group). Typically, mentors and students don't share much about themselves or their circumstances in this particular type of telementoring. Some mentors dislike this type of telementoring because their participation can be quite disjointed, time-consuming, and frustrating.
Share Information	Mentors recommend (sometimes gathering and sending) specialized resources to assist the students and/or teachers with their project work.
Supervise	Mentors direct students' project work virtually, functioning as a teacher might direct project work in the classroom.
Tutor	Mentors structure, sequence, and direct individual or small groups of students' learning according to content-related learning goals (typically remedial or advanced).

from a local stream, then monitored their activity in the classroom aquarium.

Dr. Berman provided the class with scientific and technical information to assist all stages of their work with the aquarium. He was also available to answer questions posed by the students and to direct them to both online and offline resources related to their interests. He helped the teacher when she requested assistance, providing additional information on marine topics that were of interest to her. At the end of the project, the students returned all of the specimens from the aquarium to the stream.

Chat

Mentor Susan Gillis Kruman and her high school protégé, Tina, described themselves as "totally engrossed in dancing." Most of their frequent communication consisted of sharing past and present dance experiences, during which they found much in common, despite the difference in their ages. Tina also requested and received help in defining and refining a thesis statement for a senior project on dance. Susan provided both general and specific historical information to help Tina to begin work on the project.

Co-Create

In Dallas, Texas, Marilyn Morgan's 25 sixth grade students enlisted the help of their parents to construct a model built to scale with a heat lamp that simulated the sun's effects upon the Earth. The idea for the model and most of the experiments that the students conducted with it originated with cloud physicist Darrel Baumgardner, who works with the National Center for Atmospheric Research. Dr. Baumgardner guided the students and their teacher through the experiments, helping them with data analysis when necessary. Using Darrel's model, Ms. Morgan's students studied the simulated effects of solar fluctuations, clouds, pollution, and vegetation upon global climate.

Discuss/Debate

The first "Rodney King trial" served as a springboard for discussion and debate among the members of Cindy Hank's senior class in San Angelo, Texas, who worked intensively with anthropologist Steve Maack, who lives and works at a small university in Los Angeles. To help students to understand the charged issues that grew out of this trial and the event that precipitated it, Cindy helped the class to go back in time to learn about and discuss the U.S. Civil Rights Era of the late 1950's and early 1960's. The particular contributions of Martin Luther King, Jr. to the movement were discussed at length, including his philosophy of nonviolence. In response to one student's question, the class discussed and debated whether the dream referenced in Dr. King's speech had been realized in the time that had elapsed. Current ethnic and economic distributions of the San Angelo, Texas population were related to Civil Rights issues. Present-day minority student experiences with police and racism were compared and contrasted with those that were being faced by African Americans in Los Angeles. The second "Rodney King trial" and its aftermath were discussed as the situation was unfolding. Other related current events—notably the deaths of Marian Anderson and Caesar Chavez—were also explored in the context of civil rights history.

Impersonate

Medieval scholar Sharon Michalove, writing in the guise of the "Learned Sage", worked online with a group of sixth-grade "Seekers of Knowledge" from Houston, Texas, on a multidisciplinary project that culminated with a costumed recreation of selected aspects of the Middle Ages given as a presentation to their school. The students videotaped their presentation and sent Dr. Michalove a copy to demonstrate what they had learned with her assistance.

Problem-Solve

Rita Martin and her two classes of eighth graders from Texarkana, Texas explored solutions to the problem of nuclear waste with Dr. Mike Baker, a nuclear engineer at Los Alamos National Laboratory. Their exploration led to many conversations. including presidential candidates' views on nuclear power and weapons, safety precautions for Dr. Baker and others working with nuclear waste, and the effects of nuclear waste on ground water. Thanks to Dr. Baker, Rita and her students also had the opportunity to use antique Geiger counters that Mike donated to the school.

Provide Feedback

The 12 students in Mary McBeth's practical writing class in San Antonio, Texas corresponded with Maria Raymond, an independent historian / writer with a background in journalism living outside Sacramento, California; David Curcio, a lawyer in Houston, Texas; and Rhonda Tuman, an alumni coordinator for a community college in southern Delaware with experience in editing and reporting. These twelve students worked to improve their writing and editing skills. Each professional provided formative feedback to four students' responses to Ms. McBeth's writing activities, while she encouraged the online conversations to delve more deeply into the art and craft of writing.

Question-and-Answer

Brooks Cima's classes of gifted and talented students in grades 1-5 in Katy, Texas. engaged in independent work about "natural extravaganzas" with Dr. Mike Valentine, a professor of geology and environmental science at the University of Puget Sound in Tacoma, Washington. Brooks' students continued the "active questioning" in which they engaged in the classroom with Dr. Valentine online, addressing topics of interest to them such as earthquakes, volcanoes, tsunamis, and undersea events.

Share Information

In McAllen, Texas, Janis Lentz's combined fourth and fifth grade students embarked upon a search for their cultural and historical roots. Dr. Jesus F. de la Teja, an Associate Professor of History at Southwest Texas State University, who specializes in the history of Spanish colonial borderlands, served as their mentor. He guided the students toward an accurate historical depiction of their geographic region by providing a variety of multicultural resources and by engaging in one-to-one email conversations, sometimes in the students' first language, Spanish.

Supervise

Peggy Moates' twenty fifth graders from Talbott Elementary School in Tennessee observed and recorded the behavior of domesticated rats in varying conditions under the virtual supervision of animal ethologist Dr. Beverly Marshall-Goodell. Topics studied included recognizing and rating learned behaviors, recording and reporting data scientifically, and using the scientific method throughout the project. Dr. Marshall-Goodell's questions helped the students to both devise new maze experiments and interpret the authentically "messy data" inevitably collected by novice scientific researchers.

Tutor

Alan Sills, a teacher in North Caldwell, New Jersey, proposed an interesting independent study for two of his students who were very interested in meteorology and weather forecasting. He linked these students with Captain Brian Newton, an Air Force officer assigned to study ways to improve the forecasting of specific atmospheric parameters. With Brian's generous assistance, the students constructed a website that served as a weather forecasting tutorial for other students interested in topics such as how to read weather maps, how severe storms form and are identified, and the weather patterns identified as El Nino.

Note that in many of these project examples, mentors are assuming multiple roles and serving more than one function, as students' interests and learning needs dictate. These shifts are facilitated by active communication with the students' teacher(s), so that the form(s) of the telementoring can evolve as students, teacher(s), and mentor(s) are engaged in project work.

Additional descriptions of Emissary-facilitated, curriculum-based telementoring projects can be found online at http://Emissary.wm.edu/index.php/pastprojects/listall.html.

Participating in Curriculum-Based Telementoring

Despite its long-term (though admittedly sporadic) use and its comparatively low technological threshold, telementoring still proves challenging for many teachers to incorporate into their students' curriculum-based learning. Experience directly facilitating telementoring projects via the Electronic Emissary suggests that there are three primary aspects of in-school telementoring work that explain why it has not been embraced by more K-12 teachers: communication, contexts, and roles. Each is described below.

Communication

Due to students' and teachers' crowded school day schedules, most curriculum-based telementoring at present occurs primarily via electronic mail. Email is asynchronous, primarily text-based, and quick, like many popular social networking applications, but it lacks the full spectrum of visual and audible information that we depend upon in face-to-face exchange. Therefore, telementoring by e-mail requires somewhat specialized interaction strategies to create maximal educational benefit for participating students (Harris, Rotenberg, & O'Bryan, 1997). For example, more frequent and more explicit purpose-setting, progress-reporting, and problem-solving communications are usually necessary online, when compared with face-to-face interchange (Kimball & Eunice, 1999). As Kimball & Eunice explain, "In a face-to-face setting, facilitators watch body language and facial expression and lots of other signals to develop a sense of what's going on. Participants in virtual learning communities convey this same information in different ways." (p. 5)

Contexts

The contexts in which most online mentors work are quite different from K-12 teaching/learning environments. Of particular note are differences in Internet accessibility, and the expectations that such contrasts can create. Most mentors have easy and frequent access to multiple networking tools throughout their workday, and are accustomed to having brief, text-based or videoconferenced conversations with colleagues with quick turnaround times. In most school districts, due to online safety concerns, K-12 students and teachers have much less frequent and much more inconvenient access to educational networking. Whereas a mentor might expect a reply to an e-mail message within 24 hours, many K-12 students are able to respond to e-mail during class only a few times each week. Most mentors working outside the K-12 classroom don't realize how different their working contexts are from what teachers and students experience in their schools. So that potential misunderstandings are minimized, teachers must communicate directly with mentors to help them to adjust their expectations of the amount, frequency, and types of communication that can fit the realities of both working environments (Harris & Figg, 2000).

Roles

When teachers decide to provide curriculum-based telementoring for their students, their role expands to include work as a project facilitator, directing the progress of the project, reading all messages that are exchanged between the mentor and the student, and assessing students' learning as it occurs. Since this can be overwhelming for some teachers, the Electronic Emissary provides facilitation by staff members who are experienced teachers familiar with incorporating telementoring into curriculum-based learning. Unfortunately, not all telementoring services are able to provide facilitation.

Facilitation of telecollaborative work is both emergent and participant-centered. As Kimball & Eunice (1999) explain,

Facilitation is paying attention to what is happening in your group, as distinct from what you wanted or expected would happen...you want to detect where members are now and work with that energy to move in the direction [they] need to go. (p. 5)

What must teachers do to successfully facilitate a telementoring project for their students? Typically, they:

1. Set up, test, and resolve networking technical issues (accounts, filters, etc.).
2. Communicate privately with the mentor, so that the two can be comfortable both personally and professionally while collaborating on the telementoring project.
3. Set realistic project goals and expectations that are in line with curricular standards and sequences.
4. Describe their students and the nature of the learning that they will be doing during the telementoring project to the mentor.
5. Determine and provide answers to procedural questions, both in the classroom and within the online communication that is occurring.
6. Adjust goals and expectations according to project developments over time.
7. Keep communication flowing throughout the project period.
8. Identify, address and resolve miscommunications as promptly as possible.
9. Structure and guide different kinds of online activities, based upon students' learning needs and preferences.
10. Evaluate individual student and group contributions to learning/teaching, ensuring that curriculum standards are met. (Harris & Figg, 2000)

Benefits

Given that these responsibilities are added to the heavy load that teachers already bear, perhaps it is no wonder why more educators haven't chosen to incorporate telementoring – or even educational networking in general – into their professional repertoires. But for those who do, and those who will do so in the future, there is substantial benefit to be gained by students, teachers, and even mentors.

Members of well-functioning telementoring teams engage in in-depth, dynamic exchange. Project evaluation results provided by Electronic Emissary team members have emphasized the importance of the relationships that have developed among the participants. Subject matter can "come alive" for students who interact over time with someone for whom curriculum content is part of everyday life, and a passionate interest. Many participating teachers develop close, apprentice-like relationships with online mentors, requesting and receiving assistance with content-related concepts, resources, and even learning activity design. Mentors typically delight in opportunities to revisit and explore new aspects of their disciplinary specializations as they respond to students' and teachers' questions and requests for assistance. For example, a professor at Yale University who was serving as a mentor with the Electronic Emissary wrote:

Thank you for the opportunity to participate once again in the Electronic Emissary Program. It was a pleasure working with the students, and I found it both helpful and encouraging to communicate with my future students while they were still in their formative years. Some of their questions showed a curiosity and sophistication which unfortunately seems to vanish by the time they make it to college! I regularly showed their questions to my colleagues in different departments here (whose help I often received in formulating a reply, and from whom I steal all the credit <wink>) and they were frequently impressed that their own research interests were mirrored in the students' questions.

The often personal, sometimes challenging, yet in-depth communication co-constructed by people who often have not met face-to-face speaks to the potential power and value of curriculum-based telementoring. As Goleman's (2006) summary of new understandings in neuroscience emphasizes, the importance of deep connections among and between people, especially as children and teens are maturing, cannot be overestimated. Yet paradoxically, at a time when social networking tools seem to provide endless and ever-increasing opportunities for us to connect with each other, the nature of their most popular uses may be minimizing students' opportunities to experience the most beneficial types of connections: those that are longer-term, intellectually stimulating, and compassionate.

FUTURE DIRECTIONS/CONCLUSION

Goleman is among a growing number of writers who see social networking tools as working *against* forming the kinds of interpersonal connections that are crucial to healthy intellectual, emotional, and social development and functioning. He writes, for example:

Then there are the unknowns in the ways humans around the world are connecting—and disconnecting—as technology offers more varieties of nominal communication in actual isolation. These trends all signal the slow vanishing of opportunities for people to connect. This inexorable technocreep is so insidious that no one has yet calculated its social and emotional costs....To the extent that technology absorbs people in a virtual reality, it deadens them to those who are actually nearby. The resulting social autism adds to the ongoing list of unintended human consequences of the continuing invasion of technology into our daily lives. (Goleman, 2006, pp.7-8)

To characterize "technology" in this way is not uncommon, unfortunately. Upon closer examination, however, it becomes clear that it is the predominant *uses* of technology—in this case, social networking tools—that can disrupt and inhibit the kinds of connections that our brains crave and our minds and hearts need. As educators and as citizens, we can choose to use social networking tools in ways that are beneficial and educationally sound. Educational networking can capitalize upon the irresistibly social nature of the tools without sacrificing the potential quality and depth of interpersonal connections. Telementoring is one powerful example of how networked technologies can be used in mutually and maximally beneficial ways.

As other chapters in this book demonstrate, mentoring has long been understood and experienced to be a powerful form of personal and professional learning. Telementoring can be similarly so, though most online mentoring advocates recommend its use only when face-to-face mentoring is impossible or impractical (Single & Single, 2005). Why is curriculum-based telementoring not more commonly used in K-12 classrooms? Though definitive answers to this question have not yet been determined, it is probable that teachers' and students' predominant experiences with the Web as an information portal, and networked communication tools used mostly or exclusively for social purposes, have concealed these tools' powerful educational networking potential. Given models for different types of curriculum-based telementoring, as described in this chapter, along with examples of telementoring efforts and the practical pedagogical advice that appear in this book, it is my hope that more teachers will be inspired and motivated to design and facilitate curriculum-based telementoring for and with their students.

REFERENCES

Aphids Communications. (n.d.). Quotations about politics/government. *The Quotations Archive.* Retrieved August 11, 2010, from http://www.aphids.com/cgi-bin/quotes.pl?act=ShowListingsForSub&Subject=S30

Deubel, P. (2009, September 16). Social networking in schools: Incentives for participation. *Collaboration 2.0 Newsletter.* Retrieved August 10, 2010, from http://thejournal.com/articles/2009/09/16/social-networking-in-schools-incentives-for-participation.aspx

FrEdWriter and FrEdMail. (n.d.). In Global SchoolNet's Global Schoolhouse. Retrieved August 11, 2010, from http://www.globalschoolnet.org/gsnabout/history/fredhistory.cfm

Goleman, D. (2006). *Social intelligence: The revolutionary new science of human relationships.* New York: Bantam Dell.

Hargadon, S. (2009). *Educational networking: The important role Web 2.0 will play in education.* Calgary, Alberta: Elluminate Canada. Retrieved August 10, 2010, from http://www.scribd.com/doc/22279609/Hargadon-Educational-Social-Networking

Harris, J. (1998). *Virtual architecture: Designing and directing curriculum-based telecomputing.* Eugene, OR: International Society for Technology in Education, University of Oregon.

Harris, J. (2005). Curriculum-based telecomputing: What was old could be new again. In Kearsley, G. (Ed.), *Online learning: Personal reflections on the transformation of education* (pp. 128–143). Englewood Cliffs, NJ: Educational Technology Publications.

Harris, J. (2010). Facilitated telementoring for K-12 students and teachers. In Berg, G. A. (Ed.), *Cases on online tutoring, mentoring, and educational services* (pp. 1–11). Hershey, PA: IGI Global. doi:10.4018/978-1-60566-876-5.ch001

Harris, J., & Hofer, M. (2009). "Grounded" technology integration: Planning with curriculum-based learning activity types. *Learning and Leading with Technology, 37*(2), 22–25.

Harris, J., Rotenberg, L., & O'Bryan, E. (1997). *Results from the Electronic Emissary Project: Telementoring lessons and examples.* Denton, TX: University of North Texas, Texas Center for Educational Technology. Retrieved August 9, 2010, from http://www.tcet.unt.edu/pubs/em/em01.pdf

Harris, J. B. (2008). TPACK in inservice education: Assisting experienced teachers' planned improvisations. In AACTE Committee on Innovation & Technology (Eds.). *Handbook of technological pedagogical content knowledge for educators* (pp. 251-271). New York: Routledge.

Harris, J. B., & Figg, C. (2000). Participating from the sidelines, online: Facilitating telementoring projects. *ACM Journal of Computer Documentation, 24*(4), 227-236. Retrieved August 9, 2010, from http://portal.acm.org/citation.cfm?id=353927.353934

Harris, J. B., & Hofer, M. J. (in press). Technological pedagogical content knowledge (TPACK) in action: A descriptive study of secondary teachers' curriculum-based, technology-related instructional planning. *Journal of Research on Technology in Education, 43*(3).

John, P. D. (2006). Lesson planning and the student teacher: Re-thinking the dominant model. *Journal of Curriculum Studies, 38*(4), 483–498. doi:10.1080/00220270500363620

Kimball, L., & Eunice, A. (1999, November). *Zen and the art of facilitating virtual learning communities.* Paper presented at the ThinkQuest Teachers' Summit, Los Angeles, CA.

Lenhart, A., Ling, R., Campbell, S., & Purcell, K. (2010). *Teens and mobile phones* (Research report, April 20, 2010). Washington, DC: Pew Research Center, Pew Internet & American Life Project. Retrieved August 10, 2010, from http://pewinternet.org/Reports/2010/Teens-and-Mobile-Phones.aspx

Linn, M., Lewis, C., Tsuchida, I., & Songer, N. (2000). Beyond fourth-grade science: Why do U.S. and Japanese students diverge? *Educational Researcher, 29*(3), 4–14.

Mishra, P., & Koehler, M. J. (2006). Technological pedagogical content knowledge: A framework for integrating technology in teacher knowledge. *Teachers College Record, 108*(6), 1017–1054. doi:10.1111/j.1467-9620.2006.00684.x

Richardson, K. W. (2009). *Looking at/looking through: Teachers planning for curriculum-based learning with technology* (Doctoral dissertation). Available from ProQuest Dissertations and Theses database. (AAT 3371354)

Russell, M. (2007). The difference between a chef and a cook. Retrieved December 17, 2007, from http://chef-guide.com/a/321859/The+Difference+Between+A+Chef+And+A+Cook.html

Shulman, L. S. (2002). Making differences: A table of learning. *Change, 34*(6), 36–44. doi:10.1080/00091380209605567

Single, P. B., & Single, R. M. (2005). E-mentoring for social equity: Review of research to inform program development. *Mentoring & Tutoring, 13*(2), 301–320. doi:10.1080/13611260500107481

Yinger, R. (1979). Routines in teacher planning. *Theory into Practice, 18*(3), 163–169. doi:10.1080/00405847909542827

Chapter 2
Dimensions of Design in K–12 Telementoring Programs:
A Discussion for Designers and Teachers

Kevin O'Neill
Simon Fraser University, Canada

ABSTRACT

Teachers and researchers have been designing telementoring programs for more than fifteen years, yet there are many possible program designs that have not yet been attempted, and enormous potential yet to fulfill. An attempt is made to map out the "design space" of K-12 telementoring by discussing the major decisions made in designing a telementoring program, and the relationship of these decisions to one another. Where possible, research findings and examples of specific programs are cited in this discussion. By providing a look "under the hood" of telementoring programs, the chapter aims to help teachers become more equal partners in the effort to refine existing programs and develop new ones. Encouragement is offered to researchers to more fully articulate the rationale behind their designs in their writing, and to carry out more research on the efficacy of particular design choices, so that the field can develop cumulative literature on telementoring design.

INTRODUCTION

It is surprising to think that teachers and researchers have been at work on telementoring for as long as we have. The earliest reference in the literature goes back to 1993 (Wighton, 1993), and while I continue to believe that this innovation has tremendous potential for impact on the lives of a broad spectrum of school children and their achievement in school, we have been slower in developing this potential than I had expected when I began my initial forays into this field in the mid-1990s (O'Neill, Wagner, & Gomez, 1996). It seems that like innovators before them, the developers of telementoring programs (some of them at least) assumed that once they demonstrated the potential of this innovation, educators would

DOI: 10.4018/978-1-61520-861-6.ch002

flock to fully realize it (Cuban, 1986). Needless to say this did not happen, and today telementoring maintains a small, though still growing role in K-12 education.

Another surprise is that after all this time, the literature on telementoring continues to be dominated by reports on programs. Furthermore, these are largely reports on successful programs – or at least programs that are *cast* as successes. Cravens' (2003) description of the state of affairs still appears generally accurate:

Most online mentoring programs do not share their own suggested practices publicly or collaborate with other programs; instead, program organizers often promote their specific system of online mentoring as a model for others to follow and, sometimes, as the *only* approach for schools, nonprofit organizations and others who want to bring together volunteers with youth via the Internet. (Cravens 2003, p. 86. Italics in original.)

Cravens offered some explanation for this situation:

[some program coordinators] fear that someone would copy their program materials and methods without involving them or crediting them; other coordinators feared that publicity about their program could shed light on the unresolved problems of their program, or that talking about factors that didn't work in their program could reflect negatively on the agencies involved. (Cravens 2003, p. 89)

This is unfortunate, because there are many unexplored possibilities for the design of telementoring programs, and design does not thrive in an environment in which its practitioners avoid discussing their well-intentioned missteps (O'Donnell, 2004; Vincenti, 1990). Work on telementoring programs to serve the diverse needs of students and teachers would be best supported by an energetic dialogue on design; but to have this we need to openly discuss why *not* to do certain things in our programs, and how challenges or failures demonstrate the limitations of our current knowledge.

Today there is a burgeoning tradition of design-based research in education (Barab & Squire, 2004; Bell, 2004; Collins, Joseph, & Bielaczyc, 2004; Design-Based Research Collective, 2003; Edelson, 2002) that aims to foster a scholarly treatment of the knowledge developed through educational design. In this tradition, teachers and researchers work together to understand how well learning innovations work in particular environments, and why. The designers and implementers of telementoring programs could be important contributors to this literature, and would benefit greatly from thinking about their work in the ways encouraged by a design-based research perspective. This perspective encourages evidence-based reflection on what we learn from each trial of a design, and revision based on what we learn from this reflection.

In this chapter, I will aim to give the designers of telementoring programs and the teachers who use them some of the tools that will be needed to engage in such reflection on design. For designers, I hope to prompt reflection on why we have built our programs the way we have, and whether there might have been better options. For teachers, I hope to provide a view of what unique benefits telementoring programs may offer their students, as well as what their limitations are.

WHAT IS DESIGN?

Since this chapter revolves so much around design, it makes sense to be clear about what this term means. The American Heritage Dictionary defines the verb "to design" as follows:

1a. To conceive or fashion in the mind; invent.
1b. To formulate a plan for; devise.
2. To plan out in systematic, usually graphic form.

3. To create or contrive for a particular purpose or effect.
4. To have as a goal or purpose; intend.
5. To create or execute in an artistic or highly skilled manner. ("Design", 2000)

An important fact about design is that it involves inevitable trade offs (Collins, 1996). The main task of a designer is to *optimize* for desired effects, while *minimizing* undesired ones. Consider, for example, one of the decisions involved in the design of a house. Large windows afford natural light and a (hopefully) pleasant view; but larger window area makes it more difficult to control internal temperature. During the summer, large windows can allow sunlight to overheat the house, and during the winter, windows do not retain heat as well as walls. So, window area is a design choice that is shaped by trade-offs.

As in the design of a house, there are trade-offs at play in the design of telementoring programs. Addressing these trade-offs demands a working understanding of how the various parts of a program design interact and serve to produce the desired outcomes. To do the best job possible for our program participants, we need an explicit understanding of the "design space" (Simon, 1969), or realm of possibilities, in which we work. In this chapter, I will make an attempt to describe our design space, and some of the conundrums we face as we navigate it.

I see this as a fitting contribution for me to make to this volume, because while there are people who run much larger programs than I have, over the past 14 years or so I have had the opportunity to work with a variety of partners in different educational settings to build and closely study a number of small programs. This has enabled me to experiment with a variety of designs in different areas of the school curriculum, and reflect on their advantage relative to one another.

VARIETY IN TELEMENTORING

It is no doubt confusing to those new to telementoring (or e-mentoring) to read about the wide variety of educational programs that call themselves by this name. Programs have been created for for school-aged children generally (Harris, 2003), for particular curricular areas (O'Neill, 2004; Wheeldon & Lehmann, 1999), for special needs students such as the gifted (Siegle, 2003), college students developing careers in particular fields (Kasprisin, Single, Single, & Muller, 2003), and for those in the labor force (Headlam-Wells, Gosland, & Craig, 2006). What is more, telementoring may take place as an extension to an existing face-to-face mentoring program (Shrestha, May, Edirisingha, Burke, & Linsey, 2009), or may take place outside a formal program structure.

This is telementoring: A 34-year-old, white male atmospheric scientist signs up on a university web site during lunch one day, and is later matched with three of thirty-two students working on science fair projects in a teacher's Earth Science class in Illinois. The three girls are average achievers with no particular interest in science, taking a class that is required for high school graduation. They and their mentor work together for 11 weeks, exchanging posts on a class discussion board once or twice per week about their curiosities, the evidence available to address them, and how they can present this evidence at the science fair. After the science fair the students send their mentor a copy of their report, and receive an encouraging reply. The relationship then ends.

This is telementoring: The parents of an elementary school student who has been identified as "gifted" by a school district psychologist submit a request for mentoring to a corporate-sponsored web site. The boy is described as highly intelligent, but unmotivated, or even combative at school. His achievement is below grade level in both math and reading, and he regularly refuses to complete work in class or at home, because he sees little connection between the tasks he has been assigned in school and his interests outside of school. Since he has expressed an interest in computing, he is matched with an executive at the local subsidiary of a multinational computer manufacturer. Over the course of two semesters, she advises him during weekly audio conferences about what she looks for in new employees and how these capabilities relate to schoolwork. Very gradually, his homework completion picks up.

This is telementoring: Over dinner one night, the vice-principal of a middle school in the southwestern US mentions a student of hers to a friend at the police department in a neighbouring city. She is concerned that this promising young woman, always a high achiever, appears to have fallen in with a "rough crowd" lately. Her marks have been suffering, and she has been sent to the office several times for misbehavior. The vice principal is concerned about other 7th grade students becoming engaged in the culture of violence and drug abuse in her community as well. She manages to initiate an e-mail relationship between her friend and the 7th grade class at her school, with the intention of showing the students what danger they can place themselves in by making the "wrong friends." Since the school's computer lab is very busy, the classroom teacher solicits ideas from the class about what they should say to their mentor, and types up the messages on the computer at her desk. When she gets replies, she reads them aloud to the class. Over several weeks the relationship tapers off, but as the school year ends, the vice principal is satisfied that her intervention has been worthwhile.

This variety draws attention the fact that students' educational needs vary, and that peoples' values with regard to education vary from place to place, volunteer to volunteer, and sponsor to sponsor. Even where needs, values and motives are similar, our knowledge of how to do them justice is incomplete enough that quite different approaches appear to have equal chance of success.

Given all this, how do we go about designing a telementoring program to meet particular needs in a particular place and time?

COMMONALITIES AMONG TELEMENTORING PROGRAMS

Our challenge as designers and practitioners interested in telementoring is to use this variety to understand the possibilities we should consider when designing and implementing telementoring programs. There are, in fact, important commonalities among K-12 telementoring programs. We can think of these as the boundaries of our design space. For the purposes of the discussion that follows, I assume that:

- Telementoring is fundamentally a practice that is aimed at developing *relationships* between adults and youth. Telementoring is not a substitute for a face-to-face mentoring relationship, but neither is it less "real" even if the relationships are shorter or more pragmatically driven than spontaneous, face-to-face ones.
- The purpose of telementoring relationships is chiefly to expand students' social mobility – meaning their access to careers, social stations and ways of thinking that they do not necessarily have connections to outside of school (Labaree, 1997). While it serves curriculum goals, telementoring does so in a way that also gives students entrée into communities of discourse and practice they might otherwise not connect with so directly.
- Telementoring is not a "spice" that can be used to make boring curriculum more interesting; but it can be a way to enable teachers to do more challenging and interesting things they otherwise would not feel safe attempting.

Dimensions of Design in K-12 Telementoring Programs

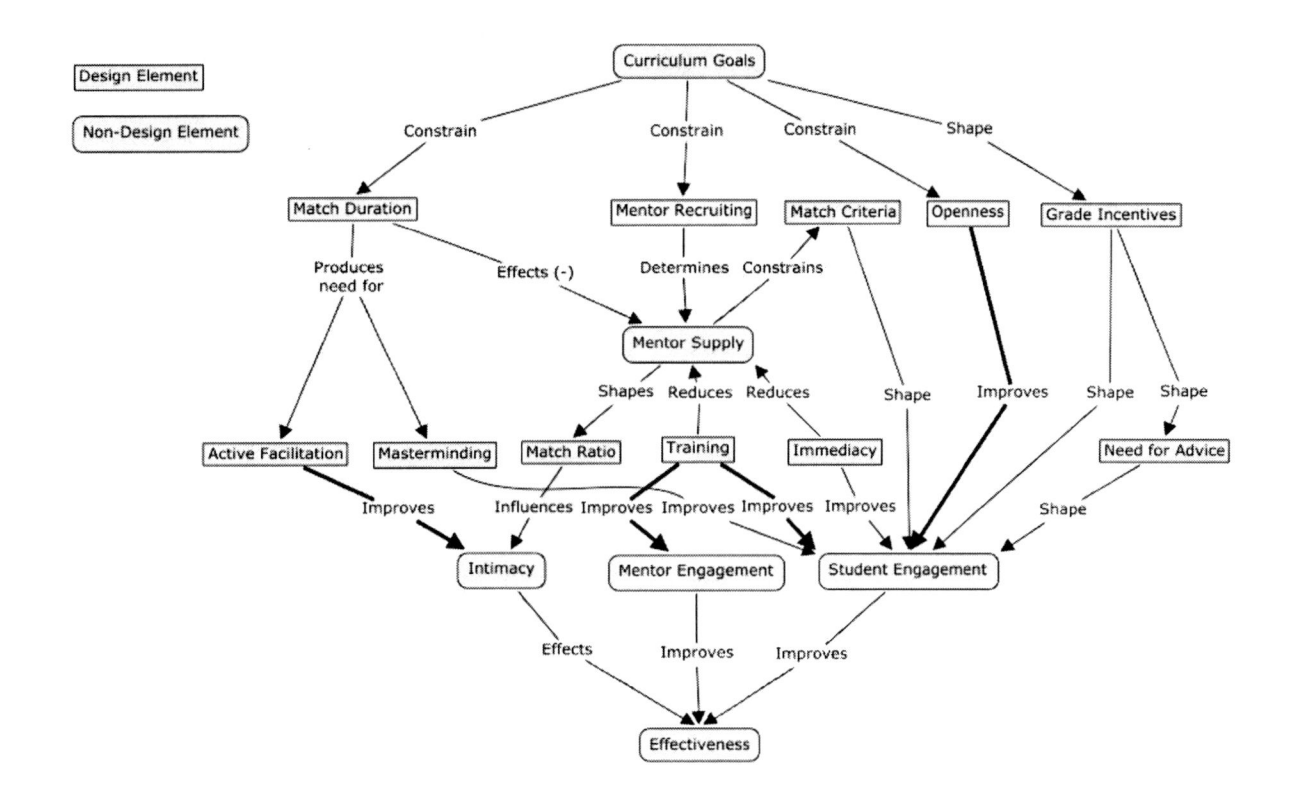

Figure 1. Dimensions of design in K-12 telementoring

Design Dimensions

Having laid out some basic similarities, I now describe some underlying dimensions of telementoring designs in the K-12 arena, using examples from the literature. These dimensions are worth laying out explicitly, since we may sometimes make less optimal design decisions than we could for students if we fail to consider all possibilities, and debate their merits together.

Figure 1 provides an overview of these dimensions and their relationships, as I see them today. The purpose of the diagram is to represent most of the big-picture design choices for those who may be new to the design of telementoring programs; so there are many small, but important choices that are not depicted.

Figure 1 includes two different kinds of objects. The ones with square corners represent design dimensions that I will expand upon below; while the ones with rounded corners represent elements that are not strictly designed, but form part of the design context, or represent outcomes that are somehow affected by our design efforts. For example, mentor supply is *influenced* by many design decisions, but is also dependent on other external variables not represented in the diagram. (It wound up in the centre of the diagram partly because this afforded the least number of crossing arrows and the most clearly readable diagram; but perhaps it is not coincidental that this is a very central concern of the designers of all telementoring programs.)

Below I describe the design dimensions, with some relevant examples from the literature.

Curricular Goals

Wherever we work, everything we do in the K-12 sphere is constrained by the needs of the formal curriculum and the ways in which students' performance is assessed – whether at the classroom level or through large-scale tests. To have a telementoring program that students will invest effort in, we need mentors to make a unique and valued contribution toward curricular goals. After all, why should students and teachers go to the extra effort to work with remote collaborators who can only be contacted by computer? Presumably, it is because the skills and knowledge the mentors bring are uniquely valuable to the work at hand.

As we design a telementoring program, we should be strategic about selecting from among the prescribed learning outcomes those which we believe telementoring is best able to serve. For instance, students in a business class might be willing to cope with the inconvenience of consulting with advertising professionals to refine their campaigns for a big contest. Even if they have to wait a few days for feedback to come, they know that it is feedback they are unlikely to get elsewhere. If, on the other hand, we task mentors with proofreading students' reports (a job that any literate adult could do), the reception is likely to be less positive.

Mentor Recruiting

When people call me up for advice on designing a telementoring program, one of the first questions I ask is "Who would your mentors be?" I have learned to ask this question early on because if there is no ready and sustainable supply of mentors, there is no hope of building a program. One of the questions that every designer of telementoring programs has to ask is, "Where will I find the people with appropriate qualifications to help me achieve my goals with students?" Though the subject of recruiting deserves a whole chapter, here I will explain some of the challenges that I have experienced and other program coordinators have described to me.

As anyone with a Facebook account knows, the Internet can be an extremely efficient and powerful way to assemble groups of people who share a common interest. At times, a group can be assembled to support a cause in a matter of minutes or hours, where it would have taken weeks or months previously. Mentor recruitment can be accelerated online too; however, this usually relies on your prospective mentors having already joined an online group. For instance if you need to find retired doctors and nurses to serve as Biology mentors, you'd better hope that they have already formed their own Facebook group, or that their professional society maintains an e-mail list of retired members. If not, you will be beating the bushes in a more old-fashioned way – perhaps begging a friend for an invitation to the golf club.

In return for the reduced costs and increased speed of recruiting online, we usually sacrifice selectiveness about where our volunteers live. One irony of life on the 'Net is that it can be easier to find someone with matching interests or expertise across the country than in your own neighbourhood. If you find willing volunteers online, you normally don't have to worry about their technical ability to participate in a telementoring program; but you may have to give up on the possibility of them ever meeting their assigned mentees face-to-face. For some program designers and teachers, this is an uncomfortable proposition.

Matching Criteria

The way in which mentors and mentees are matched has long been acknowledged as critical feature of mentoring programs (Noe, 1988; Ragins & Cotton, 1999; Tellez, 1992). After curricular goals, matching criteria may be the most important choice we make in designing a telementoring program. Strangely though, few publications about telementoring programs provide much detail about the matching process followed (Headlam-Wells et al., 2006; Single & Muller, 2000).

Decisions about matching criteria are largely constrained by the program goals we have set out. If the program is designed to help students develop great science fair projects, each mentor ought to know something about the area of science their mentees are working in. If the program is meant to encourage young women to study Computer Science, then your mentors should be computer scientists – and preferably female ones.

We should be careful not to make too many matching decisions intuitively, however, when there is a base of evidence to work from. Gender-based matching makes a good example in this regard. It has been assumed by many designers of formal mentoring programs that same-gender and same-race matches are ideal. The basis of this assumption has been the idea that for a mentoring relationship to succeed, the mentee must identify closely with the mentor (Ragins & Cotton, 1999). However on close examination, researchers have found mixed-gender matches to be equally successful as same-gender matches on most criteria (Bowen, 1985; Burke & McKeen, 1996; Ragins & Cotton, 1999). Large-sample studies have generally found that what a mentor does (the mentoring functions they provide) is more important to successful relationships than her similarity to her mentees.

In discussing this issue, I am conscious that I may be succumbing to the temptation to treat mentor matching in a highly rational way that belies the constraints that most of us work under. It might be *ideal* to collect detailed profile data on every program participant, and match only those mentors and mentees whose profiles have been proven to mesh well in previous research (Turban & Dougherty, 1994); but such an approach is only practical in an environment like a large corporation in which there are thousands of potential matches and you are free to choose among them. In most K-12 programs it will not work. Usually we are lucky to find a sufficient supply of mentors who have the expertise that our students need, or who will serve as appropriate models. When we do not, we usually wind up making sub-optimal matches – asking mentors to "stretch," or boosting the match ratio to ensure that all students are matched. I will say more about match ratio later.

Match Duration

Along with matching criteria, a decision that is constrained, but not *determined* by our program goals is the duration of each mentor "match" (relationship). If our goal for students is social mobility – actually changing their self-concept in such a way that they believe a particular career to be within their reach – a year-long program (or longer) would probably be ideal. It is presumably for this reason that matches in MentorNet and other career-oriented programs are a year in duration (Kasprisin et al., 2003). However even if curriculum time were not an issue (and when is that?), longer matches come with a cost. The longer the time commitment required of mentors, the more difficult it may be to get recruits, and the greater the likelihood that students' participation will lapse. Longer matches generally need more active facilitation to prevent brief lapses from turning into failed relationships, and active facilitation is costly. I will return to this issue later.

To a degree this discussion too is an academic one, since in many circumstances designers are constrained to tie the duration of a match to the duration of a curriculum unit. Units can range in length from a few days to months, but the plausibility of fruitful mentoring relationships is poor on the low end of that scale. Until a few years ago I would have said that the shortest program I would support would be five weeks; but recently my colleagues and I attempted a two-week intensive program with some evidence of student learning based on pre and post assessments (O'Neill & Guloy, 2010).

Match Ratio

From the classical tradition, mentoring has been viewed as a very intimate, personal relationship (Kram, 1985). This has led some program designers to think that matches *must* be one-to-one for the relationships to be "real." For example, to my knowledge the International Telementor Center, which has one of the largest and longest-running K-12 telementoring programs, has always assigned mentors one-to-one (www.telementoring.org). Over the years however, other program designers have (largely for pragmatic reasons) considered larger match ratios (Russell & Perris, 2003). Several years ago I began experimenting with group matches including as many as 10 mentees to a single mentor (O'Neill, 2004), and have continued to do this in a series of projects. Evidence shows that when mated with a high degree of openness, higher ratios can actually improve students' engagement (see the next section). A higher match ratio can also be an adaptive strategy when mentees do not reliably keep mentors as busy as they want to be. (Yes, this happens too.)

Increasing the match ratio must be handled with care, however. As the ratio grows, the relationships may lose intimacy and become more like classroom teaching -- though *without* all the rich contextual supports that teachers have to support their work. It is one thing for a trained teacher to maintain pedagogical relationships with 25 to 30 students at a time when she sees them every weekday and can readily observe their work habits, attitudes, relationships with peers, etc.; it is quite another for a novice telementor to maintain 25 pedagogical relationships based only on occasional e-mails or forum postings. At some point, depending on other factors such as the goals of the program and its duration, the relationships fostered by a high-ratio program would cease to have even a family resemblance to face-to-face mentoring.

Openness

Considering the classical tradition again, there is a conservative view in the field that mentoring relationships must not only be very personal, but very *private*. Of course in K-12 schooling, there must be some oversight of all telementoring relationships for reasons of safety; but some designers seem to assume that without a degree of privacy, mentees will not feel free to express the confusions and concerns in which the learning potential resides (Drayton & Falk, 2003).

Depending on the goals of the program, this might be true. For example, if a program concerns itself with students' career aspirations or is of a remedial nature that carries a stigma, privacy may be essential for telementoring to work. However, in other areas openness may be both possible and beneficial. For example, in most of the programs that I have designed recently, what students are discussing with their mentors are academic matters (history and science projects) that they are generally not shy about discussing in front of other students. Openness can make the program more effective for everyone, since every mentor's advice is available to every participant. Further, in a program with great openness, mentees and mentors have the opportunity to see how well-functioning telementoring relationships work, and are thus able to emulate them (O'Neill, 2004).

Active Facilitation

Even a small telementoring program involves coordinating the actions of quite a few people, some of whom (mentors) are not customarily involved in the work of teaching. The other participants (students and teachers) are not generally used to sharing what they do online. Add all this together and you have quite a lot of potential for confusion. Whose job will it be do manage that?

In some of the earliest telementoring work, Harris and her colleagues recruited facilitators to actively monitor their telementoring matches, and address confusions or lulls in activity as they arose (Harris & Figg, 2000). The special value of active facilitation is reducing the likelihood of relationships trailing off or breaking down, while maintaining a great deal of flexibility in how a program operates. The Electronic Emissary, for instance, has served different grade levels, curriculum areas, and brokered matches of different lengths simultaneously. However this flexibility comes at a rather high cost, since facilitators are normally paid employees with the expertise to help negotiate agreements between the parties involved. Harris generally employs trained teachers with a sophisticated knowledge of computer-mediated communications as her facilitators.

Masterminding

The need for active facilitation can potentially be reduced with additional "masterminding" up front. As I use the term, a masterminded program involves central pre-planning and coordination that go beyond brokering relationships between students and mentors. In addition, the program designers strive to give shape to the mentees' and mentors' work by creating schedules, assignments, grading criteria, etc. that are keyed to curriculum goals. In fact they may create curriculum materials specifically to support the program. In essence, they aim to *create* the needs that the volunteer mentors will then seek to fill.

For example, in a recent project called "Compassionate Canada?" my team worked with three experienced Social Studies teachers to design a telementored unit for 11th grade Social Studies. The design included an overarching question for students to pursue, based on the scope of the curriculum ("Has Canada become a more compassionate country over the last 100 years?"), an activity structure for group work in the classroom, an online archive of materials for students to interpret with their mentors, and classroom activities, such as a live debate that each team's mentor helped them prepare for.

Naturally, masterminding reduces flexibility. It may also reduce scope. The example I gave above focused not only on a single grade level and curriculum area at a time, but a single *unit*. Masterminding places demands on the design team to understand teachers' and students' needs deeply, and have a clear and well-wrought plan that does not need too much tinkering during implementation, since with less active facilitation it is difficult or impossible to re-negotiate criteria, changes in schedule, and so forth while the implementation is in progress. However, the advantage of a masterminded program is that the experience is a more predictable one for all the participants. This can offer advantages for the recruiting of teachers and mentors, and may reduce the stresses placed upon students as well. Student stress comes to be an increasingly large issue as you move up the grade levels into high school.

Immediacy

When I first began studying telementoring around 1995, the general public was just getting used to e-mail, and groupware systems were primitive. Internet bandwidth in many schools and most homes made real-time audio or video links between mentors and mentees out of the question, text chat services such as "MSN Messenger" were not yet popular, and cell phones were too costly for most parents to carry, let alone their children. The situation today is radically different (Gross, 2004; Wallis, 2006). I can expect one student in each class I work with to ask why the volunteer mentors are not available to chat in real time. When a majority of students carry cell phones, you know that their expectation is for virtually instant communication with the people they rely on.

This expectation is a difficult one for telementoring programs to meet. It is hard to find mentors who are willing and able to have their work interrupted in real time; but generally, students are understanding when I inform them that their mentors are at work during the school day or live in a different time zone. They can also appreciate, when told, that their school board does not want them to be in private, real-time communication with adults who are neither parents nor teachers – even if they have been screened as carefully as student teachers are.

From the perspective of program designers, real-time media also have a large downside in that they eliminate the possibility of censoring mentors' (or students') messages on the rare occasions that this becomes necessary. It is also technically more difficult to log real-time interactions for research purposes – particularly when these interactions are mediated by a privately owned server.

Training

One of the better-researched elements of telementoring design is participant training. Early on there were strong assertions in the telementoring literature about the importance of training (Bennett, Hupert, Tsikalas, Meade, & Honey, 1998). Later, quasi-experimental research was conducted to demonstrate the advantages of mandatory training for both mentors and mentees.

In a quasi-experimental study of the MentorNet program involving 400 female undergraduates in science and technology-related programs, mentors and their mentees were randomly assigned either to a condition in which training modules were available but optional, or one in which completion of the training was mandatory. In post-survey measures, mentees reported how frequently they exchanged e-mail messages with their mentors, how satisfied they were with the program, and how much value they felt they derived from the mentoring relationship. Statistical analysis showed that those in the mandatory training group exchanged significantly more messages, though no significant differences were found with respect to satisfaction or value (Kasprisin et al., 2003). A later study of similar design demonstrated that mandatory training for mentees led to greater engagement and satisfaction on the part of mentors (Kasprisin, Single, Single, Ferrier, & Muller, 2008).

These findings refer to college-age women, however. Harris and I have argued that considering the developmental divide that typically separates mentors and mentees at the K-12 level, there are likely to be limitations to what can be achieved through formal training (O'Neill & Harris, 2004). Because of their more limited experience, young mentees are usually not well equipped to anticipate what mentoring functions they will find most helpful or satisfactory. This was illustrated in a study by Asgari and O'Neill (2005), in which high school students were asked prior to a telementoring relationship what they thought a "mentor" should do. After the relationship, they rated their satisfaction with the mentoring they had received and reported the helpfulness of their mentors with respect to the same set of mentoring functions. Strikingly, the functions that correlated with students' satisfaction bore little relation to the functions they had initially anticipated (Asgari & O'Neill, 2005).

So, where does this evidence leave us? While it is clear that training *can* be helpful, there is little discussion in the literature about how that training should be designed in order to achieve the greatest satisfaction among participants, and (more important) the best educational outcomes. Needless to say this area is ripe for research.

Grade Incentives

In the school context, grading weights and criteria are typically how we tell students the ways in which we would like them to channel their effort (D'Amico, 1999; Stiggins, 1992). If we value telementoring exchanges, this tradition would say that we should reward students for making the effort to produce them.

However, grading telementoring exchanges entails a set of problems that is essentially similar to the one we face with grading online discussions in courses. As many have discovered, it can be counter-productive to grade the quantity of students' contributions to online discussions, or mandate a minimum number per week. This can result in the creation of a lot of time-wasting "chaff" as students make trivial posts in order to boost their numbers. The usefulness of the entire forum for learning is then reduced if participants have to read through this chaff to find more substantive posts.

The reason teachers grade on quantity is because grading on quality takes a great deal of effort. One solution to this problem is to have students construct selective portfolios of their best work, using a set of criteria agreed to in advance. To my knowledge this approach has not yet been used in telementoring programs, though it would be very worthwhile to experiment with it.

Grade incentives may be applied to elements of students' work other than their telementoring exchanges as well. In fact, to the extent that we find it necessary to motivate students through grading telementoring exchanges, we ought to question whether we have made other design decisions properly. If students choose not to work with their mentors, it may be that we have not given them an adequate reason to do so. If we believe that working with a mentor will enable students to produce a higher quality of work, then rewarding students for achieving that quality might be all that is necessary.

A SPECULATIVE MODEL OF TELEMENTORING DESIGN

Listing out and describing the design dimensions of K-12 telementoring programs is perhaps a useful beginning; but what would be more useful to designers and evaluators would be to relate these design elements to one another and the outcomes we seek to achieve. In Figure 1, I have made a first attempt to do this based on reflections upon the literature and my own experiences of designing and studying telementoring programs.

It is important to say that the model provided here represents a form of "craft knowledge." There are certainly design dimensions that I have not represented, as well as outcomes and constraining factors (such as funding), which will be important to design decisions at a finer level of granularity. The links I have sketched may also be disputed. In the few instances in which there has been some empirical investigation of the links between design elements (and their outcomes), I have marked these links with bold arrows. Each one of the thinner arrows in the figure should be understood as a product of my reflections on the literature and my experience as a designer, subject to revision as the research base on telementoring continues to expand. I invite (nay, implore) others to dispute the connections I have drawn here based on their own experiences and research, because I believe this is crucial to developing a more useful and defensible scholarship of K-12 telementoring.

Potential Design Trade-Offs

A close examination of my model of telementoring design shows four potential trade-offs. As I stated at the opening of this chapter, my belief is that like design in other fields (Collins, 1996), the design of telementoring programs probably involves some inescapable tradeoffs. Since some readers may choose to study these or dispute them, I should be clear about what I think they are and how I suspect they work.

Match Duration: Long-Term Goals vs. Mentor Supply

While some programs aim for relatively short-term goals, other educational goals may only be achievable with a match duration of months or years. However, as the match length increases, the number of willing volunteers seems likely to decrease. In my experience, volunteer telementors are highly responsible about allocating their time, and are unlikely to volunteer if they believe that other commitments may intrude on their commitments to students.

Training: Quality of Mentor Engagement vs. Mentor Supply

As discussed above, there is good evidence to suggest that the frequency of mentor-mentee communication can be increased with training. This seems to be a good thing, though we should be careful not to confuse frequency of communication with quality. In some of my recent studies, educational outcomes correlated significantly with the mentoring functions students reported receiving, but *not* with frequency of communication (as tracked through server logs) (O'Neill, 2007; O'Neill, Sensoy, & Guloy, 2009). The implication seems to be that as a mentor, *what* you say is more important than how much or how often.

It is also important to consider how mandatory training may affect the supply of willing mentors, since the higher one makes the hurdle to participate, the fewer willing volunteers one is likely to have. It may be argued that if you are going to carry out training, you should also carry out assessment to examine the efficacy of that training. If you are going to carry out assessment, you should be prepared not to "certify" mentors who fail your test. So, implementing a training program inevitably leads to the question of whether you can afford to fail mentors, and how many.

Immediacy: Student Engagement vs. Mentor Supply

Because today's students live in an atmosphere of anytime, anywhere communication, it may feel antiquated for them to post messages and await replies. The longer they must wait, the greater the likelihood that they will disengage from the telementoring relationship. On the other hand, the more program designers seek to intrude on the everyday work routines of people with valuable expertise, the less likely it is that they will volunteer as mentors. Thus, immediacy of communication versus mentor supply likely represents a fundamental trade-off in the design of telementoring programs.

Masterminding: Predictability vs. Flexibility

Above I used "masterminding" as a catch-all term describing the efforts of program designers to plan and shape the engagement of program participants for their maximum benefit. Masterminding generally takes the form of training materials, curriculum, assignments, grading criteria, and routines for actively managing telementoring relationships.

Efforts at masterminding are necessarily based on assumptions about participants' motivations and needs, and these assumptions can sometimes be misguided. Every student and mentor is unique. It could be argued that program designers should make as few assumptions about their participants as possible, and negotiate all the details of the telementoring match from scratch each time. The Electronic Emissary project appears to have taken just this approach, relying on talented facilitators to shepherd these negotiations.

On the other hand, as Barker has said, "settings have plans for their inhabitants' behavior" (Barker, 1963). Schools are settings that place a high value on predictability; so the take-up and engagement with a curriculum-focused program is likely to be greater if it has been carefully tuned to the mandated curriculum. Of course, the more finely tuned a program is to a particular curriculum, the smaller its potential scope is in terms of number of matches.

TAKE-HOMES FOR PROGRAM DESIGNERS AND TEACHERS

In this chapter I have attempted to lay out in a systematic way the major decisions that designers face when structuring a K-12 telementoring program. I have also attempted to describe the relationships of these decisions to one another and the hoped-for outcomes of telementoring in as clear a way as present knowledge allows.

For the program designers and evaluators reading this chapter, my take-home message is that program designs should be discussed explicitly – first among designers and stakeholders, but also in our literature. Sadly, there has not been much detailed discussion in the telementoring literature to date about the rationale behind the design of individual programs. Publications tend to focus instead on the dynamics of the relationships that programs support, on participant satisfaction, or (more rarely) on educational outcome measures – as if all that mattered was that good things happened, not how they came about or whether they could have been better. In this way, we forego the opportunity to develop a cumulative literature to inform the design of telementoring programs, and risk squandering time, effort and money on programs developed "from scratch" without considering all the possibilities.

For the teachers reading this chapter, I have two take-home messages. The first is that telementoring programs are filled with exciting possibilities for their students, and should be entered into as thoughtfully as one makes other instructional decisions, such as the selection of textbooks. Teachers getting involved in telementoring programs should ask themselves: What educational goals are targeted by this program? Does the mentor recruitment, training and matching done by program staff seem likely to support these objectives? Are my students likely to see telementoring as a unique and worthwhile way to learn? Finally, what support will the program, and my students, need from me to make this a success?

My second message for teachers is that they should be partners in the design of telementoring programs. My hope is that this chapter will give teachers a good enough look "under the hood" of telementoring programs that as they become involved with telementoring, they can play an active role in their ongoing refinement.

CONCLUSION

More than 15 years into the development of telementoring as an educational innovation, there remains an enormous amount of unrealized potential in it, and a great deal left to learn. Telementoring could be a tremendous force for educational equity and achievement (Single & Muller, 2000); but in order to make this happen I believe we need to shift our public dialogue toward more systematic discussion and research about design. I hope that this chapter will provide some common vocabulary for designers and teachers to discuss the choices that distinguish one telementoring program from another, and provide a foundation for a stronger cumulative literature on the design of telementoring programs.

REFERENCES

Asgari, M., & O'Neill, D. K. (2005). What do they mean by "success"? Examining mentees' perceptions of success in a curriculum-based telementoring program. In Pascarelli, J., & Kochan, F. (Eds.), *Creating successful telementoring programs* (pp. 225–249). Greenwich, CT: Information Age Publishing.

Barab, S. A., & Squire, K. (2004). Design-based research: Putting a stake in the ground. *Journal of the Learning Sciences*, *13*(1), 1–14. doi:10.1207/s15327809jls1301_1

Barker, R. G. (1963). On the nature of the environment. *The Journal of Social Issues, 19*, 17–38. doi:10.1111/j.1540-4560.1963.tb00456.x

Bell, P. (2004). On the theoretical breadth of design-based research in Education. *Educational Psychologist, 39*(4), 243–253. doi:10.1207/s15326985ep3904_6

Bennett, D., Hupert, N., Tsikalas, K., Meade, T., & Honey, M. (1998). *Critical issues in the design and implementation of telementoring environments* (CCT Technical Report No. 09-1998b). New York: Center for Children and Technology.

Bowen, D. D. (1985). Were men meant to mentor women? *Training and Development Journal*, 30–34.

Burke, R. J., & McKeen, C. A. (1996). Gender effects in mentoring relationships. *Journal of Social Behavior and Personality, 11*(5), 91–104.

Collins, A. (1996). Design issues for learning environments. In Vosniadou, S., De Corte, E., Glaser, R., & Mandl, H. (Eds.), *International perspectives on the psychological foundations of technology-supported learning environments*. Mahwah, NJ: Erlbaum.

Collins, A., Joseph, D., & Bielaczyc, K. (2004). Design research: Theoretical and methodological issues. *Journal of the Learning Sciences, 13*(1), 15–42. doi:10.1207/s15327809jls1301_2

Cuban, L. (1986). *Teachers and machines: The classroom use of technology since 1920*. New York: Teachers College.

D'Amico, L. (1999). *The implications of project-based pedagogy for the classroom assessment infrastructres of science teachers*. Paper presented at the Annual meeting of the American Educational Research Association, Montreal, Quebec, Canada.

(2000). Design. In *American Heritage Dictionary of the English Language* (4th ed.). Boston, MA: Houghton Mifflin Company.

Design-Based Research Collective. (2003). Design-based research: An emerging paradigm for educational inquiry. *Educational Researcher, 32*(1), 5–8. doi:10.3102/0013189X032001005

Drayton, B., & Falk, J. (2003). Discourse analysis of web texts: Initial results from a telementoring project for middle school girls. *Education Communication and Information, 3*(1), 71–104. doi:10.1080/14636310303149

Edelson, D. C. (2002). Design Research: What We Learn When We Engage in Design. *Journal of the Learning Sciences, 11*(1), 105–121. doi:10.1207/S15327809JLS1101_4

Gross, E. F. (2004). Adolescent Internet use: What we expect, what teens report. *Applied Developmental Psychology, 25*, 633–649. doi:10.1016/j.appdev.2004.09.005

Harris, J. B. (2003). Electronic Emissary. In Kovalkchick, A., & Dawson, K. (Eds.), *Education and Technology: An encyclopedia* (*Vol. 1*). Santa Barbara, CA: ABC-CLIO.

Harris, J. B., & Figg, C. (2000). Participating from the sidelines, online: Facilitating telementoring projects. *Journal of Computer Documentation, 24*, 227–236. doi:10.1145/353927.353934

Headlam-Wells, J., Gosland, J., & Craig, J. (2006). Beyond the organization: The design and management of e-mentoring systems. *International Journal of Information Management, 26*, 372–385. doi:10.1016/j.ijinfomgt.2006.04.001

Kasprisin, C. A., Single, P. B., Single, R. M., Ferrier, J. L., & Muller, C. B. (2008). Improved mentor satisfaction: emphasizing protégé training for adult-age mentoring dyads. *Mentoring & Tutoring, 16*(2), 163–174. doi:10.1080/13611260801916424

Kasprisin, C. A., Single, P. B., Single, R. M., & Muller, C. B. (2003). Building a better bridge: Testing e-training to improve e-mentoring programmes in higher education. *Mentoring & Tutoring, 11*(1), 67–78. doi:10.1080/1361126032000054817

Kram, K. E. (1985). *Mentoring at work: Developmental relationships in organizational life*. New York: University Press of America.

Labaree, D. F. (1997). Public goods, private goods: The American struggle over educational goals. *American Educational Research Journal, 34*(1), 39–81.

Noe, R. A. (1988). An investigation of the determinants of successful assigned mentoring relationships. *Personnel Psychology, 41*, 457–479. doi:10.1111/j.1744-6570.1988.tb00638.x

O'Donnell, A. M. (2004). A commentary on design research. *Educational Psychologist, 39*(4), 255–260. doi:10.1207/s15326985ep3904_7

O'Neill, D. K. (2004). Building social capital in a knowledge-building community: Telementoring as a catalyst. *Interactive Learning Environments, 12*(3), 179–208. doi:10.1080/10494820512331383419

O'Neill, D. K. (2007). *Designing a telementoring program to improve secondary students' understanding of history*. Paper presented at the Annual Meeting of the American Educational Research Association, Chicago, IL.

O'Neill, D. K., & Guloy, S. (2010, April, 2010). *The Historical Account Differences survey: Enriching methods for assessing metahistorical understanding in complex school environments*. Paper presented at the Annual Meeting of the American Educational Research Association, Denver, CO.

O'Neill, D. K., & Harris, J. B. (2004). Bridging the perspectives and developmental needs of all participants in curriculum-based telementoring programs. *Journal of Research on Technology in Education, 37*(2), 111–128.

O'Neill, D. K., Sensoy, Ö., & Guloy, S. (2009). *Final research paper, fostering metahistorical knowledge in Canadian history learning project*. Burnaby, BC: Simon Fraser University.

O'Neill, D. K., Wagner, R., & Gomez, L. M. (1996, November). Online mentors: Experimenting in science class. *Educational Leadership, 54*, 39–42.

Ragins, B. R., & Cotton, J. L. (1999). Mentor functions and outcomes: A comparison of men and women in formal and informal mentoring relationships. *The Journal of Applied Psychology, 84*(4), 529–550. doi:10.1037/0021-9010.84.4.529

Russell, A., & Perris, K. (2003). Telementoring in community nursing: A shift from dyadic to communal models of learning and professional development. *Mentoring & Tutoring, 11*(2), 227–237. doi:10.1080/13611260306856

Shrestha, C. H., May, S., Edirisingha, P., Burke, L., & Linsey, T. (2009). From face-to-face to e-mentoring: Does the "e" add any value for mentors? *International Journal of Teaching and Learning in Higher Education, 20*(2), 116–124.

Siegle, D. (2003). Mentors on the net: Extending learning through telementoring. *Gifted Child Today, 26*.

Simon, H. (1969). *The sciences of the artificial*. Cambridge, MA: MIT Press.

Single, P. B., & Muller, C. B. (2000, April 24-28). *Electronic mentoring: Quantifying the programmatic effort*. Paper presented at the Annual meeting of the American Educational Research Association, New Orleans, LA.

Stiggins, R. J. C. Nancy Faires. (1992). *In teachers' hands: Investigating the practices of classroom assessment*. Albany, NY: State University of New York Press.

Tellez, K. (1992). Mentors by choice, not design: Help-seeking by beginning teachers. *Journal of Teacher Education, 43*(3), 214–221. doi:10.1177/0022487192043003008

Turban, D. B., & Dougherty, T. W. (1994). Role of protege personality in receipt of mentoring and career success. *Academy of Management Journal, 37*(3), 688–702. doi:10.2307/256706

Vincenti, W. G. (1990). *What engineers know and how they know it: Analytical studies from aeronautical history*. Baltimore, MD: The Johns Hopkins University Press.

Wallis, C. (2006). The multitasking generation. *Time, 167*(13).

Wheeldon, R. S., & Lehmann. (1999). Establishing a telementoring program that can be used in vocational classes. *Journal for Vocational and Special Needs Education, 21*, 32–37.

Wighton, D. J. (1993). *Telementoring: An examination of the potential for an educational network*. Education Technology Centre of British Columbia.

Chapter 3
Telementoring and Project-Based Learning:
An Integrated Model for 21st Century Skills

Joyce Yukawa
St. Catherine University, USA

ABSTRACT

While common models of telementoring (ask-an-expert services, tutoring, and academic and career telementoring) can serve a variety of learning objectives, these models are limited with respect to sustained inquiry learning such as project-based learning (PBL). To reach the full potential of PBL with telementoring, this chapter proposes a telementoring model that integrates inquiry learning, information literacy, and digital media literacy and is implemented by a team of experts – subject matter experts as telementors, classroom teachers, school librarians, and instructional technology specialists. The model provides for multifaceted learning experiences for students that involve disciplinary knowledge and habits of mind, critical thinking, collaborative problem solving, and information, media, and technology skills. Brief overviews of inquiry learning approaches, information literacy, and digital media literacy are described in relation to telementoring. Design considerations, the benefits and challenges of the model, and broader implications for educational change are also discussed. Using the integrated telementoring model, the PBL team exemplifies the interdisciplinary collaboration and new literacy skills that students need in today's workplaces and communities.

INTRODUCTION

Often associated with apprenticeships in a community of practice, mentoring is the age-old process of wiser, more experienced persons taking younger protégés under their wing. As role models, mentors guide their young initiates into the art, craft, ways of thinking, and values of their community, helping to shape not only knowledge and skills but also the identity and personal and professional maturity of their protégés. Mentoring is rewarding for both the mentee and the mentor. The mentee has a deepening relationship with a special person in his/her life - not a parent, teacher,

DOI: 10.4018/978-1-61520-861-6.ch003

or friend, but a wise guide who listens, cares, encourages, and gives advice. For the mentor, this is a unique opportunity to make a difference in a young person's life and give back to one's profession and community.

Since the rise of the World Wide Web in the 1990s, a variety of online tools has been available to support mentoring beyond the barriers of time and place. Telementoring, also known as online mentoring and e-mentoring, can be defined as:

... using telecommunications technology (including e-mail, conferencing systems, or telephones) to develop and sustain mentoring relationships where face-to-face ones would be impractical. In the field of education, telementoring often involves linking students up with knowledgeable adult volunteers who have an interest in fostering their development. This sort of arrangement allows the participants to take part in intellectual partnerships that would not otherwise take place. (O'Neill, 2000, p. iii)

While communicating online makes telementoring different from traditional face-to-face mentoring, telementoring offers some distinct benefits. Mentors are not limited to the local community and can be drawn from any profession, organization, or geographic location around the world where adults are willing to help a young person develop. And mentors and mentees can communicate at any time, using a wide range of online tools.

Telementoring uses various mentor group configurations to provide different kinds of expert support to students seeking help. MENTOR/National Mentoring Partnership's "Elements of Effective Practice" (http://www.mentoring.org/find_resources/elements_of_effective_practice/) identifies these five types of contemporary group mentoring: (1) traditional mentoring (one adult to one young person); (2) group mentoring (one adult to up to four young people); (3) team mentoring (several adults working with small groups of young people, in which the adult to youth ratio is not greater than 1:4); (4) peer mentoring (caring youth mentoring other youth); and (5) e-mentoring (mentoring via e-mail and the internet).

Expert support online comes in many forms – ask-an-expert services for one-time, discipline-based questions; tutoring for supplementary or remedial study; telementoring for career guidance and academic advice; and telementoring for inquiry learning. Examples of each of these types, as well as their strengths and limitations, will be discussed later in the chapter.

This chapter's main focus is on telementoring for sustained inquiry in the classroom through project-based learning (i.e., project-based telementoring). It is written at a time of extraordinary economic and technological changes and associated challenges to the U.S. educational system. The Partnership for 21st Century Skills, a group of leading education, business, community, and government organizations, has identified essential skills beyond reading, mathematics, and science that students need to "increase their marketability, employability and readiness for citizenship" (Partnership, 2008, p. 10):

- Thinking critically and making judgments about the barrage of information that comes their way every day – on the Web, in the media, in homes, workplaces and everywhere else.
- Solving complex, multidisciplinary, open-ended problems that all workers, in every kind of workplace, encounter routinely.
- Creativity and entrepreneurial thinking – a skill set highly associated with job creation (Pink 2005; Robinson 2006; Sternberg, 1996). Many of the fastest-growing jobs and emerging industries rely on workers' creative capacity – the ability to think unconventionally, question the herd, imagine new scenarios and produce astonishing work.

Telementoring and Project-Based Learning

- Communicating and collaborating with teams of people across cultural, geographic and language boundaries – a necessity in diverse and multinational workplaces and communities.
- Making innovative use of knowledge, information and opportunities to create new services, processes and products. The global marketplace rewards organizations that rapidly and routinely find better ways of doing things. Companies want workers who can contribute in this environment.

Project-based telementoring has the potential to address many of these important skills. Due to the widespread use of the internet and the plethora of free or low-cost technologies for online communication and collaboration, the possibilities for innovative telementoring programs are unprecedented.

Providing the environment and structural support for new types of telementoring is a significant challenge. The New Media Consortium (NMC), a community of hundreds of leading universities, colleges, museums, and research centers, sees the following as the most critical challenges schools will face as they integrate new technologies and reshape the educational experience in the next five years: (1) There is a need for formal instruction in key new skills. (2) Educational practice and materials are changing too slowly to support current student needs. (3) Learning that incorporates real life experiences is not occurring enough and is undervalued when it does take place. (4) New technologies must be adopted and used as an everyday part of classroom activities, but effecting this change is difficult. (5) The fundamental structure of the K-12 education establishment is resistant to any profound change in practice (Johnson, Levine, Smith, & Smythe, 2009, p. 7-8). These trends indicate not only the challenges that schools face, but also the potential of project-based telementoring to contribute to needed changes in structure, teaching practice, and a more relevant educational experience for students.

The next sections of this chapter provide brief overviews of inquiry learning approaches, information literacy (including mastery of information technology), and digital media literacy (particularly with communication and collaboration technologies), as they relate to telementoring. This is followed by an assessment of strengths and weaknesses of common models of telementoring. To reach the full potential of project-based learning, I propose a telementoring model that integrates inquiry learning, information literacy, and digital media literacy and involves a team of specialists – subject matter experts as telementors, classroom teachers, school librarians, and instructional technology specialists. Because of the diverse expertise of this project-based learning (PBL) team, the model provides for multifaceted learning experiences for students that involve disciplinary knowledge and habits of mind, critical thinking, collaborative problem solving, and information, media, and technology skills. Design considerations, the benefits and challenges of the model, and broader implications for educational change are also discussed. Using the integrated telementoring model, the PBL team exemplifies for students the interdisciplinary collaboration and new literacy skills that are increasingly valued in today's workplaces and communities.

INQUIRY LEARNING APPROACHES AND TELEMENTORING

Other chapters in this book explore in depth the use of telementoring in inquiry, problem-based, and project-based learning. The goal of this section is to provide an overview of these approaches as the foundation for a discussion of how well different models of telementoring can meet the learning challenges and address the new media literacy skills needed today.

Scientific inquiry in the classroom is often simplified to a linear process of asking a question, formulating a hypothesis, performing an experiment, collecting data, and drawing conclusions. The University of California Museum of Paleontology's website, *Understanding Science* (http://www.understandingscience.org), aims to accurately communicate "the real process of science" – not only a process of exploration, discovery, and testing ideas, but also of scientific growth based on community analysis and feedback that is shaped by the benefits and outcomes for individuals and society. Science is a process that is dynamic and intensely human:

[S]cientists often begin an investigation by plain old poking around: tinkering, brainstorming, trying to make some new observations, chatting with colleagues about an idea, or doing some reading. Scientific testing is at the heart of the process. In science, all ideas are tested with evidence from the natural world. ... You can't move through the process of science without examining how that evidence reflects on your ideas about how the world works — even if that means giving up a favorite hypothesis. The scientific community helps ensure science's accuracy. Members of the scientific community ... play many roles in the process of science, but are especially important in generating ideas, scrutinizing ideas, and weighing the evidence for and against them. Through the action of this community, science is self-correcting. ... The process of science is intertwined with society. The process of science both influences society ... and is influenced by society. ("A blueprint for scientific investigations," http://undsci.berkeley.edu/article/0_0_0/howscienceworks_03)

Scientific inquiry is clearly a social process as well as a rigorous procedure for testing hypotheses. Identifying a scientific problem and testing one's ideas through communication, collaboration, and peer review are critical aspects of inquiry often missing from the student's classroom experience. Through the partnerships and collaboration enabled through telementoring, a subject matter expert can be one of the most valuable members of the classroom's community of inquiry.

The Telementor's Guidebook (O'Neill, 2000) describes and analyzes a number of telementoring relationships with project groups from a 9th grade class that illustrate the types of guidance subject matter experts can provide. For example, two students doing a research project on earthquakes were matched with a geology graduate student who provided both intellectual and emotional support to help them reach their project goals. Other examples of telementoring by community experts can be found in the project summaries provided on The Electronic Emissary K-12 Telementoring website (http://emissary.wm.edu/project_public.php).

Inquiry learning approaches such as problem-based learning and project-based learning extend the problem beyond a single lesson or two and bring to the classroom some of the complexity, curiosity, creativity, serendipity, and communal effort that more accurately reflect the nature of scientific inquiry. The Illinois Mathematics and Science Academy's PBLNetwork (http://pbln.imsa.edu/model/intro/index.html) provides this definition of problem-based learning:

Problem-based learning (PBL) is focused experiential learning organized around the investigation and resolution of messy, real-world problems. PBL engages students as stakeholders immersed in a messy, ill-structured, problematic situation. PBL organizes curriculum around this holistic problem, enabling student learning in relevant and connected ways. PBL creates a learning environment in which teachers coach student thinking and guide student inquiry, facilitating learning toward deeper levels of understanding while entering the inquiry as a co-investigator.

A challenging issue in problem-based learning is ascertaining problem difficulty in ill-structured problems, with respect to learners' ability to solve such problems. Jonassen (2000; Jonassen & Hung, 2008) identifies a number of factors that contribute to problem difficulty. Factors related to the learner are level of domain knowledge, experience in solving problems, and reasoning skills. Factors inherent in the problem are level of abstraction, stability of problem attributes over time, complexity, and how well- or ill-structured the problem is. Jonassen and Hung (2008, p. 16) recommend that problems should be open ended, moderately ill structured, and with a degree of complexity that is challenging and motivating to students. Appropriate ill-structured problems should "provide opportunities for students to examine the problem from multiple perspectives or disciplines; [be] adapted to students' prior knowledge; [and be] adapted to students' cognitive development and readiness" (p. 16).

An example of a problem statement for elementary students who role play being entomologists shows how problem-based learning can be approached (Goodnough & Hung, 2008, p. 90):

Every summer, Mrs. Bartlett likes to sit in a chair and enjoy her beautiful garden where she has lots of plants and flowers with butterflies flying from one to another. However, before Mrs. Bartlett can enjoy her peaceful summers, she always has to fight with hungry caterpillars who love to eat the leaves of her plants in the spring. ... You and your teammate are entomologists (bug experts) in training. ... What can your team tell Mrs. Bartlett about caterpillars? What can your team do to help Mrs. Bartlett with her problem without destroying her garden? Mrs. Bartlett will choose the best solution to her problem from all the proposals. In order to produce an effective and trustworthy solution proposal, your team should use scientific methods, such as continuous, consistent observation and keep a journal of your research plan, how the plan has been carried out, and whether any revisions to your research plan are needed after a period of doing your research.

Similarly, project-based learning attempts to infuse authenticity, complexity, and community into the learning process. The Buck Institute for Education (BIE, n.d., p. 4) defines project-based learning as "a systematic teaching method that engages students in learning knowledge and skills through an extended inquiry process structured around complex, authentic questions and carefully designed products and tasks." BIE (p. 4-5) criteria for exemplary PBL projects include:

- Recognize students' inherent drive to learn, their capability to do important work, and their need to be taken seriously by putting them at the center of the learning process.
- Engage students in the central concepts and principles of a discipline.
- Highlight provocative issues or questions that lead students to in-depth exploration of authentic and important topics.
- Require the use of essential tools and skills, including technology, for learning, self-management, and project management.
- Specify products that solve problems, explain dilemmas, or present information generated through investigation, research, or reasoning.
- Include multiple products that permit frequent feedback and consistent opportunities for students to learn from experience.
- Use performance-based assessments that communicate high expectations, present rigorous challenges, and require a range of skills and knowledge.
- Encourage collaboration in some form, either through small groups, student-led presentations, or whole-class evaluations of project results.

What does project-based learning look like in the classroom? Planning any educational effort begins with the desired outcomes in mind, known as "backward mapping" (Wiggins & McTighe, 1998). A PBL project begins with developing a project idea, deciding the scope of the project, selecting curriculum standards, working from project design criteria, and creating the optimal learning environment (BIE & Boise State University, 2005). Most projects last several weeks but some can last much longer. Information/data collection that involves library research or active research in the field, such as interviews and community inquiry, can extend the length of the projects. Successful projects usually involve adults, either experts or community representatives, as partners or mentors in a project, necessitating more time. Some projects address broad, open-ended questions with many different solutions, resembling problem-based learning. Complex projects need sufficient time for preparation and student research. Student autonomy is one of the characteristics of PBL, and students can be involved in the project design.

Examples of successful PBL projects at the high school level can be found on the website of High Tech High in San Diego, California (http://www.hightechhigh.org/pbl/index.html). The descriptions of such projects as how drugs affect your body, how human habitation affects the environment, and how math and science affect artistic expression generally include a project overview, standards addressed, a timeline and narrative of activities, lesson plans, assessment rubrics, and teacher and student reflections. Other examples of PBL projects are found in the additional resources listed in Additional Reading.

PBL projects center on driving questions that are "open-ended, go to the heart of a discipline or topic, are challenging, can arise from real world dilemmas that students find interesting, and are consistent with curricular standards and frameworks" (BIE & Boise State University, 2005). While the subject matter specialist may have deeper and more extensive content knowledge than the teacher, the teacher has a unique knowledge base needed for PBL: pedagogical knowledge, knowledge of the students, and pedagogical content knowledge – "the blending of content and pedagogy into an understanding of how particular topics, problems, or issues are organized, represented, and adapted to the diverse interests and abilities of learner, and presented for instruction" (Shulman, 2004, p. 227). PBL projects require teachers to be learning facilitators, drawing on their pedagogical content knowledge. O'Neill (2000, p. 37) provides an example of how the teacher's unique knowledge helps ensure telementoring success:

While teachers may not participate directly in telementoring relationships, they can do a number of other things indirectly, to help them flourish. To begin with, Mr. Wagner [the teacher] set requirements for the students' investigation that gave Dan [the telementor] an appropriate role to play. If the students' assignment had been a more traditional book report, or an investigation of much shorter duration, Dan may have had very little opportunity to become richly involved. Mr. Wagner didn't simply match his students with their mentor and let them go, either: he was there to make decisions about whether or not the students' research proposal was solid enough to go forward, so that Dan was not forced to do this on his own. While Dan had ideas about what the students might be capable of doing, and to what level of perfection, only the teacher had intimate enough knowledge of the students to make a confident decision about this. Finally, during Andy, Cori and Bill's [the students] correspondence with Dan, Mr. Wagner offered the students a substantial amount of behind-the-scenes guidance and support himself. This included helping the students to interpret some of Dan's messages, which they weren't always able to understand easily. Even the very best telementor sometimes talks over mentees' heads unintentionally.

In PBL, teachers are also project managers who structure and guide a project to a successful conclusion while supporting students as they move through an open-ended process of discovery and reflection.

A key consideration is student readiness. Do students have sufficient content knowledge and skills to handle the project successfully? Can they take independent initiative and work collaboratively? Do they have the necessary skills with technology and access to the required tools? Technological resources can be powerful and engaging for students, but they must also be essential tools for learning. Teachers also need fluency with these resources so that the learning can focus on the central content and investigation rather than managing and troubleshooting the technology. While there is no evidence that tools such as virtual learning environments, social software, and other information and communication technologies are being extensively used for project-based learning (Dede, 2007, p. 21), new guides are appearing for how to implement PBL with digital tools, the internet, and Web 2.0 (Boss, Krauss, & Conery, 2008).

Problem-based learning and project-based learning are similar in their emphasis on student autonomy, a shared goal, authentic problems, evidence-based investigations and solutions, collaborative learning, and reflection (Savery, 2006). The primary differences are the goals and the structuring of the activity. Problem-based learning focuses on solving ill-structured problems that require learners to set their own parameters. Project-based learning focuses on an end product. Clear design criteria are essential, with teachers and other adults serving as instructors, coaches, mentors, or project collaborators who provide expert feedback in a timely manner. Ravitz (2009, p. 6) notes that although there are differences among problem-based, project-based, inquiry-based, design-based, and challenge-based learning, "the similarities are more significant, allowing them to be viewed as 'close cousins' with many similar characteristics."

In addition to teachers and subject matter experts, other experts contribute to inquiry learning – helping students think critically and creatively, access and evaluate information, investigate complex problems, and effectively express their ideas. The school librarian and the instructional technology specialist are two of these experts.

INFORMATION LITERACY AND TELEMENTORING

While school librarians are often viewed mainly as the managers of the school library resources, they are much more than that. With credentials and experience in library and information science as well as teaching, school librarians are experts in information literacy and knowing how people seek information. As the complexity of information resources and technologies increases, they are called upon to use their unique skills as learning specialists to help students develop 21st century skills (Zmuda & Harada, 2008). Their roles in PBL are as an instructional partner, a connector with a holistic view of the curriculum who facilitates integration across content areas, and an integrator who links disciplinary concepts with information resources and helps incorporate information literacy skills at various phases of the project (Harada, Kirio, & Yamamoto, 2008b).

The American Association of School Librarians (AASL) has developed new standards that address many of the much-needed skills identified by the Partnership for 21st Century Skills and the New Media Consortium discussed in this chapter's introduction. The *Standards for the 21st-Century Learner* are based on a set of fundamental beliefs (AASL, 2007):

- Reading is a window to the world.
- Inquiry provides a framework for learning.
- Ethical behavior in the use of information must be taught.
- Technology skills are crucial for future employment needs.
- Equitable access is a key component for education.

- The definition of information literacy has become more complex as resources and technologies have changed.
- The continuing expansion of information demands that all individuals acquire the thinking skills that will enable them to learn on their own.
- Learning has a social context.
- School libraries are essential to the development of learning skills.

Within the inquiry learning framework, school librarians aim to assist students with the following skills, dispositions, responsibilities, and self-assessment strategies (AASL, 2007).

Skills:

- Develop and refine a range of questions to frame the search for new understanding.
- Find, evaluate, and select appropriate sources to answer questions.
- Evaluate information on the basis of accuracy, validity, appropriateness for needs, importance, and social and cultural context.
- Make sense of information gathered from diverse sources (e.g., textual, visual, media, digital) by identifying misconceptions, main and supporting ideas, conflicting information, and point of view or bias.
- Apply critical-thinking skills to information and knowledge in order to construct new understandings, draw conclusions, and create new knowledge.
- Use technology tools to access, analyze, and organize information in the pursuit of inquiry.

Dispositions:

- Display initiative and engagement by posing questions and investigating the answers beyond the collection of superficial facts.
- Demonstrate confidence and self-direction by making independent choices in the selection of resources and information.
- Demonstrate creativity by using multiple resources and formats.
- Maintain a critical stance by questioning the validity and accuracy of all information.
- Demonstrate adaptability by changing the inquiry focus, questions, resources, or strategies when necessary to achieve success.
- Display emotional resilience by persisting in information searching despite challenges.
- Use both divergent and convergent thinking to formulate alternative conclusions and test them against the evidence.

Responsibilities:

- Respect copyright/intellectual property rights of creators and producers.
- Seek divergent perspectives during information gathering and assessment.
- Follow ethical and legal guidelines in gathering and using information.
- Use information technology responsibly.
- Connect understanding to the real world.
- Consider diverse and global perspectives in drawing conclusions.
- Use valid information and reasoned conclusions to make ethical decisions.

Self-Assessment Strategies:

- Monitor own information-seeking processes for effectiveness and progress, and adapt as necessary.
- Monitor gathered information, and assess for gaps or weaknesses.
- Seek appropriate help when it is needed.
- Determine how to act on information (accept, reject, modify).

- Reflect on systematic process, and assess for completeness of investigation.
- Recognize new knowledge and understanding.
- Develop directions for future investigations.

Guided by these standards and the imperative to connect learning to student needs, school librarians are taking a larger role in curriculum planning and instructional design. They are partnering with teachers to support inquiry learning (Harada & Yoshina, 2004) and project-based learning (Harada, Kirio, & Yamamoto, 2008a). In the school context, the need for these collaborations is not always self-evident, and the development of partnerships is a challenge under the heavy constraints on time and budget. Two of the bases for successful librarian-teacher partnerships are professional development support and the creation of communities of practice over time (Yukawa, Harada, & Suthers, 2007). When teachers and school librarians participate jointly in sustained, practice-based professional development, significant improvements can occur in the design of inquiry-focused learning and student performance (Yukawa & Harada, 2009).

School and public librarians are increasingly offering chat reference services to students that generally provide factual answers, information resources, and limited research help, much like ask-an-expert services. Among the few studies of librarians as telementors, Yukawa (2005) examined two library and information science graduate students who telementored two high school students doing yearlong senior projects and found that building rapport and relationships were critical for sustaining telementoring.

In published examples and research, it is rare to find PBL projects that are collaboratively designed and implemented with school librarians, despite the fact that the information and technology resources of the library are often essential for background knowledge, research, and the development of final products. For example, High Tech High's San Diego Field Guide project (http://www.hightechhigh.org/pbl/sd-field-guide/) is a 16-week project in which 11th grade students "conduct an environmental assessment of the fauna along the intertidal zone of San Diego Bay. They publish a comprehensive Field Guide including scientific studies, creative writing, photographs, and histories of human development, industry, environmental measures, mapping and other changes to Bay." The interdisciplinary project (biology, humanities, mathematics) is implemented by a subject matter specialist and two high school teachers, but school librarians do not appear to have a role in guiding the information seeking and research processes.

School librarians have a deep understanding of the guidance and instruction that students need to become information literate, a holistic perspective on the school and curriculum, and extensive knowledge of information resources and information technology. In collaboration with other experts on the PBL team, they can provide students with essential project-based learning experiences and resources.

DIGITAL MEDIA LITERACY AND TELEMENTORING

While there is increased use of new technologies for classroom learning (e.g., Moller, Huett, & Harvey, 2008), distance education (e.g., Huett et al., 2008), and library services (e.g., Burger, 2007; Casey & Savastinuk, 2006), there is little evidence that information and communication technologies are being used for project-based learning or telementoring. Email has been the dominant mode of telementoring communication since the 1990s. The selected K-12 telementoring programs listed in Appendix B indicate that most of these programs use email or discussion lists. Newer forms of online communication such as web-based synchronous communication (instant messaging, text messaging, online chat, and videoconferencing) and asynchronous communication (e.g., using wikis and blogs) have the potential to expand telementoring and help reshape learning to meet 21st century educational challenges (Dede, 2007). The instructional technology specialist is the member of the PBL team with the best understanding of how to use and manage these technologies for learning, communication, productivity, and creativity.

As noted in the introduction, The Partnership for 21st Century Skills has implicated information, communication, and collaboration technologies in the innovative, entrepreneurial thinking that students will need for future success. Attaining literacy with these technologies is thus essential. The New Media Consortium defines 21st century literacy as "the set of abilities and skills where aural, visual and digital literacy overlap. These include the ability to understand the power of images and sounds, to recognize and use that power, to manipulate and transform digital media, to distribute them pervasively, and to easily adapt them to new forms" (NMC, 2005, p. 2). Technology is implicated in all of the top trends the NMC has identified as likely to affect teaching, learning, and creativity in the next five years: (1) Technology continues to profoundly affect the way we work, collaborate, communicate, and succeed. (2) Technology is increasingly a means for empowering students, a method for communication and socializing, and a ubiquitous, transparent part of their lives. (3) The web is an increasingly personal experience. (4) Learning environments are increasingly virtual rather than physical spaces. (5) The perceived value of innovation and creativity is increasing (Johnson et al., 2009, p. 6).

Among the technologies likely to have a significant impact on schools within the next five years are collaborative environments, online communication tools, mobile devices, and the personal web (Johnson et al., 2009, p. 6). While research on the learning impact of newer technologies is still emerging, a number of guides for classroom use are available (e.g., Pitler, Hubbell, Kuhn, & Malenoski, 2007; Richardson, 2008; Solomon & Schrum, 2007). These technologies have the potential to be powerful tools for inquiry-, problem-, and project-based learning in the hands of technologically fluent telementors and motivated, tech savvy, creative students.

Collaborative environments are virtual workplaces where students, teachers, telementors, and others can communicate, share information, and work together. Collaborative online spaces come in many forms, from online office suites for document sharing (for examples of these and other tools, see Table 1), online document collaboration, personal publishing, social networking tools to connect people and collect resources, flexible learning management systems, personal web portals, to classrooms in virtual environments. As well as enabling collaboration, the online spaces leave persistent conversations that remain for self reflection and peer critique. These spaces can be used synchronously or asynchronously at a distance, or to support and document collaborative work done in class.

Full-featured wikis such as PBworks (http://pbworks.com) and WetPaint (http://www.wetpaint.com) are powerful tools for telementoring. In addition to supporting the collaborative creation of web pages, these wikis also provide productivity and communication plug-ins such as calendars, spreadsheets, Google gadgets, chat rooms, photo and video integration, and page level discussion threads. Students working on problems or projects can gather resources, post plans, exchange ideas, and write drafts of papers and presentations on wiki pages. Telementors can monitor student progress as it evolves and provide feedback on these wiki pages. Studies have shown that wikis promote collaboration, encourage negotiation, and familiarize students with new technology tools (Elgort, Smith, & Toland, 2008; Hazari, North, & Moreland, 2009). They are also an effective tool for collaborative project planning and documentation (Parker & Chao, 2007), information or data gathering and organization, and or-

Table 1. Technologies for telementoring

	Collaborative Environments	Communication Tools	Mobile Devices	Personal Web	Telementoring Software
Examples	Wikis (PBworks, Wetpaint), blogs (WordPress, Blogger, LiveJournal), office suites (Google Docs, Zoho), flexible learning management systems (Moodle, Sakai), personal web portals (NetVibes, Pageflakes, iGoogle), social networking tools (Flickr, SlideShare, YouTube), virtual environments (Second Life)	Instant messaging (AIM, Meebo, Google Talk), online chat (AIM, Google Talk, Skype), desktop video conferencing (Skype), blogging, micro-blogging (Twitter), voice-over-IP (AIM, Google Talk, Skype), combination voice-video-text messaging (YackPack)	iPhone, BlackBerry	Tagging (Delicious, Diigo), RSS feed aggregators (Bloglines, FeedDemon, Google Reader, Netvibes, Pageflakes), simple, all around personal web tools (Tumblr, Posterous)	Telementoring Orchestrator
Uses	Project planning, document sharing, collaborative writing, personal publishing, social networking, resource collections, portfolios, online classrooms, feedback from teachers, experts, and peers.	One-to-one, one-to-many, and many-to-many communication; archiving messages and conversations; multimedia journals; voice, video, and text communication.	Range of communication options: telephone, email, text messaging, internet faxing, web browsing, multimedia. Third-party applications to support learning and research.	Resource collections, keeping updated on student work, enhanced email communication in a telementoring relationship, portfolios.	Building and describing a mentor pool, matching mentors and mentees, providing opportunities for just-in-time learning, limiting administrative overhead, and preventing mentor overload.

ganizing a personal or team research library (Walsh & Hollister, 2009).

Online communication tools such as instant messaging and online chats via desktop video conferencing are a popular way for students to interact with family and friends online. These familiar tools can also be used to extend learning through telementoring. Desktop videoconferencing, instant messaging services, personal publishing like blogging and micro-blogging, and voice-over-IP enable one-to-one, one-to-many, or many-to-many synchronous communication. As one example, YackPack (http://www.yackpack.com) utilizes voice, video, and text messaging that can also be recorded. This enables one-to-one or one-to-many communication that allows students and telementors to see and hear each other in real time or via archived messages. Students can use blogging tools to set up multimedia journals to share their opinions, ideas, and research. Telementors, teachers, and peers can provide feedback using the comments feature.

Mobiles devices such as the iPhone and the BlackBerry are increasingly being used by young people (Johnson et al., 2009, p. 16). These provide a range of communication options: mobile telephone, email, text messaging, internet faxing, and web browsing. They support multimedia, with a camera and the ability to play music and video. They also incorporate productivity tools such as an address book, calendar, and calculator. Mobile devices have strong potential for educational uses because of the ability to run third-party applications such as GPS and collaborative document software. As of early June 2009, there were approximately 50,000 third-party applications of all types available for the iPhone. It is easy to imagine a wide range of applications being developed for fieldwork, data capture, information organization and analysis, visualization, data sharing, and other research and productivity aids that could support inquiry learning and result in products shared with telementors.

The personal web refers to how we manage the way we view and use the internet, based on "a growing set of free and simple tools and applications that let us create customized, personal web-based environments that explicitly support our social, professional, learning, and other activities" (Johnson et al., 2009, p. 25). The internet has been a major contributor to information overload. Finding, organizing, and evaluating online content are critical for research and learning. Just as researchers and librarians are doing, students can tag and organize web links by subject. Another valuable personal web tool is the feed aggregator, a web application that gathers syndicated web content in one place for easy viewing. News sites, blogs, podcasts, wikis, social networking sites, library websites, and many others provide RSS feeds that automatically appear in personal aggregator content. With the tools of the personal web, teachers, students, and telementors can tag, categorize, annotate, publish, and review work online and build resource collections using web feeds and resources tagged by others. Teachers, students, and mentors can keep track of student work using RSS feeds to import updates of student publishing on the web.

One example of a free, very easy to use personal web tool that can serve a variety of communication and learning functions in telementoring is Posterous (http://www.posterous.com). By simply sending email with attachments to Posterous or grabbing content from the web, one can create a blog with text, video, photos, and music. Posterous provides for privacy, group sites, and email subscriptions to inform each group member of new postings. Posterous could be an effortless way to conduct one-to-one or one-to-many telementoring communication via email, with text enhanced by multimedia in a chronological, open record of the exchanges.

Specialized software may be needed for those who wish to launch their own large-scale telementoring projects and services. One of the best developed is the Telementoring Orchestrator (TMO) from Simon Fraser University's On-line Learning Relationships Lab (http://www.learningrelationslab.org/). TMO streamlines the tasks of building and describing a mentor pool, matching mentors and mentees, and providing opportunities for just-in-time learning, as well as reducing administrative overhead and preventing mentor overload (O'Neill, Weiler, & Sha, 2005, p. 114-115). TMO supports these roles and functions:

Telementoring Orchestrator assumes three roles: (1) mentors, who volunteer by filling out a recruiting form; (2) coordinators, who solicit the assistance of one or more mentors from the volunteer pool, assign them to mentees, and provide oversight for the relationships until they are closed; and (3) an administrator, who configures the TMO software for a particular program or initiative, and creates accounts for coordinators. ... At a minimum, configuring the installation involves: (1) Setting up an e-mail routing account that can be used by mentors and mentees to exchange messages. (2) Specifying a Knowledge Forum 'database' (workspace) in which mentors and their mentees can work together. (3) Defining the varieties of expertise or interests that volunteers might share with their mentees. (O'Neill et al., 2005, p. 115-117)

Freely available, this software currently works only on Mac OS X.

To make effective use of these technologies, schools and classrooms need a reliable technology infrastructure, as well as high-speed internet access. Instructional technology specialists understand how and why technology can be used effectively for learning, communication, and productivity. In collaboration with other experts on the PBL team, they guide students toward achieving better digital media literacy and provide tools for creative expression and the development of innovative, personally meaningful products.

Telementoring and Project-Based Learning

As discussed in this chapter's introduction, schools also face more fundamental and far-reaching challenges as they integrate new information and communication technologies (ICT) and reshape the educational experience. As Dede (2007, p. 35) notes:

At this point in history, the primary barriers to altering curricular, pedagogical, and assessment practices toward the transformative vision of ICT in education ... are not conceptual, technical, or economic, but instead psychological, political, and cultural. We now have all the means necessary to implement alternative models of education that truly prepare all students for a future very different from the immediate past. Whether we have the professional commitment and societal will to actualize such a vision remains to be seen.

TELEMENTORING MODELS

This chapter began with a brief mention of the types of expert advice being provided online – ask-an-expert services for one-time, discipline-based questions; tutoring for supplementary or remedial study; and telementoring for career guidance, academic advice, or sustained inquiry learning in the classroom. With the exception of the last, these types of advice address three learning needs: the need for disciplinary knowledge, the need for academic advice, and the need for career guidance. Our exploration of inquiry learning, information literacy, and digital media literacy provides a backdrop for assessing the strengths and limitations of these types of online expert advice.

Disciplinary Knowledge

Ask-an-expert services provide answers to one-time, discipline-based questions such as "What are simple, complex, and compound fractions?" or "What is the Pythagorean theorem?" Examples of these services are Drexel University's Ask Dr. Math (http://mathforum.org/dr.math/), U.S. Geological Survey's Ask A Geologist (http://walrus.wr.usgs.gov/ask-a-geologist/), and NASA's Ask an Astrophysicist (http://imagine.gsfc.nasa.gov/docs/ask_astro/ask_an_astronomer.html). Students can ask experts questions that they could not ask of others, and receive answers in a timely manner. However, these services can only provide answers to factual questions that are isolated from the learning context. Factual information does not in itself help students develop critical and creative thinking skills. Moreover, the one-time nature of the process does not help them develop disciplinary knowledge over time.

Online tutoring and homework help services provide supplementary or remedial study that supports well-focused learning needs and guides the student in solving well-structured problems. Often these services are a combination of self-paced tutorials and 24/7 help from live tutors, such as the fee-based services, Tutor.com (http://www.tutor.com/) and Homeworkhelp.com (http://www.homeworkhelp.com/). Free homework help sites are also available, many of them developed or sponsored by school and public libraries. The Internet Public Library's Homework Help page (http://www.ipl.org/kidspace/browse/ref8000) lists a number of free sites. The disadvantage of online tutoring is that the questions and problems are provided mostly by the service, not driven by student inquiry. Online tutoring does not help students develop critical and creative thinking skills by solving authentic, ill-structured problems relevant to their own lives and interests.

Academic Advice and Career Guidance

Academic advice and career guidance are often combined in programs that are aimed at vulnerable and at-risk students. This type of mentoring resembles the traditional mentor model of wise counselor to a young protégé. For example, icouldbe.org (http://www.icouldbe.org/standard/

public/lm_index.asp) targets at-risk students from low-income communities. Connecting to Success (http://ici.umn.edu/ementoring/default.html) aims "to promote successful transition of youth with disabilities to adult life." In these types of telementoring programs, mentors encourage students to stay in school and work toward career goals and further education. They provide care and concern, helping with homework and study skills, plans for college, and how to seek and keep jobs. They also help youth improve their communication skills, raise their self-esteem, and change negative and damaging behaviors.

Other telementoring programs are aimed at closing the gender gap in science, technology, engineering, and mathematics (STEM) professions. Programs such as Zoey's Room (http://www.zoeysroom.com/), an online community for middle school girls that fosters interest in STEM subjects, feature chat rooms where girls can interact with professional women with careers in STEM fields.

These programs provide valuable mentoring to specially targeted sectors of students but are not focused on inquiry learning for the development of critical and creative thinking skills. (For those interested in selected programs of these types, Appendix B provides further information).

Integrated Telementoring Model for Project-Based Learning

While ask-an-expert services and academic and career telementoring address important student needs such as the need for factual knowledge, general study skills, career information, and guidance for at-risk students, they are each limited with respect to sustained inquiry learning focused on authentic problems. To reach the full potential of project-based learning, I propose an integrated telementoring model that involves a team of specialists – teachers, subject matter experts, school librarians, and instructional technology specialists.

- *Classroom teachers* manage PBL projects and facilitate learning on many levels – the process of project-based learning, the team process, community building, individual learning, and the achievement of the learning outcomes.
- *Subject matter experts as telementors* encourage, guide, instruct, and model disciplinary practices and ways of thinking.
- *School librarians* guide students to become information literate and help them navigate the increasingly complex terrain of information resources.
- *Instructional technology specialists* help students achieve better digital media literacy and provide opportunities for creative expression using a wide array of technological tools.

Table 2 summarizes the complementary sets of skills and expertise the team brings to PBL. The model provides a framework for rich learning experiences for students and supports scaffolding of disciplinary knowledge and ways of thinking, project-based learning, information literacy, and digital media literacy. This model is further discussed in the next section.

DESIGN CONSIDERATIONS FOR AN INTEGRATED TELEMENTORING MODEL

For the development of 21st century skills, I have proposed that an integrated model of telementoring implemented by a PBL team has the potential to be more effective than current forms of telementoring. This section discusses how the model could be implemented, based on findings from previous studies of telementoring and/or problem-based learning. The main studies referred to are: (1) an examination of the Portals project, funded by the National Science Foundation to support telementoring relationships in project-

Table 2. Integrated telementoring model for project-based learning (PBL)

PBL Team	Teacher	Telementor	School Librarian	Instructional Technology Specialist
Primary Role	**Pedagogy, Project Management** • Pedagogical content knowledge • Knowledge of learners • PBL coordination & facilitation • Project design • Project planning • Project management • Fostering community building	**Disciplinary Inquiry** • Exploration & discovery • Testing ideas – Gathering data • Testing ideas – Interpreting data • Community analysis & feedback • Broader perspectives on the benefits of inquiry to society	**Information Literacy** • Accessing information • Evaluating information • Critical thinking to analyze, organize & use information for decision making • Information ethics • Reflecting on the information seeking process	**Digital Media Literacy** • Technology tools • Uses of tools for learning • Uses of tools for communication • Uses of tools for productivity • Uses of tools for creative expression

based computational sciences classes, involving 40 high school students, five teachers, and 12 mentors (Tsikalas, McMillan-Culp, Friedman, & Honey, 2000); (2) Abbott's (2005) study of eight teachers whose students participated in online learning projects hosted by five established online PBL programs (The Electronic Emissary, iEARN, KidLink, ThinkQuest, and ThinkQuest Jr.); (3) a study by Hmelo-Silver and Barrows (2006) that analyzed the facilitation of a student-centered problem-based learning group in higher education; and (4) Project INSITE, a four-year professional development program to prepare teachers to use problem-centered, inquiry-based science (Lehman, George, Buchanan, & Rush, 2006).

As discussed previously, several components of this model – project-based learning, teacher-librarian collaboration, and the use of information and communications technologies for learning – are in themselves challenging to implement. As an integration of these components, this model is even more challenging, as it involves collaboration among all of the PBL team members and the potential use of a variety of online tools. The model requires careful planning, coordination, ongoing collaboration, and negotiation of roles and responsibilities among members of the PBL team.

The planning is done by the school-based members of the team. During the implementation of the project, the teacher's role is both project manager and learning facilitator. Important factors to consider when designing a project using the integrated telementoring model are commitment to the project, learning goals, roles and functions of participants, the online learning environment, and participant readiness for project-based learning.

Commitment

Project-based learning takes much time to plan and sustained effort to complete (Abbott, 2005). The first and most important factor to consider is the desire and willingness of the school-based team members to tackle project-based learning using this model. Another important factor is the school climate and readiness – whether school administrators and peers welcome innovative uses of technology or not. Access to and funding for new technology may also be key considerations.

Learning Goals

These are some of the typical goals teachers set for project-based learning with telementoring (Abbott, 2005; BIE, n.d.; Hmelo-Silver & Barrows, 2006; Lehman et al., 2006; Tsikalas et al., 2000):

- Students engage in the central concepts and principles of a discipline and develop reasoning skills appropriate to the discipline.
- Students do in-depth exploration of authentic and important topics.
- Students solve complex, multidisciplinary, open-ended problems.
- Students create products that solve problems, explain dilemmas, or present information generated through investigation, research, or reasoning.
- Students engage in self-directed learning.
- Students acquire, evaluate, and use information effectively.
- Students use essential tools and skills, including technology, for learning, self-management, and project management.
- Students effectively communicate and collaborate with each other in teams, and online with adult experts.
- Students reflect on their own work and provide effective feedback to peers.

During planning, the school-based team members align learning goals with various content standards, technology standards, and life skills standards (e.g., McCREL, 2009), as well as information literacy standards (AASL, 2007). These learning goals are also associated with the 21st century student outcomes outlined by Partnership for 21st Century Skills (2008), namely, knowledge in core subjects; learning and innovation skills; information, media and technology skills; and life and career skills.

Roles and Functions

The complex, interdisciplinary, and open-ended nature of project-based learning requires a clear view of general functions and roles, as these maybe taken on flexibly by different members of the team over time. Functions generally fall into four areas: (1) structure, (2) process, (3) facilitation, and (4) community building (Tsikalas et al., 2000). Strategies and functions related to each of these areas may be assumed by any member of the PBL team or by the students themselves, depending on their readiness for PBL.

Structural strategies and functions refer to how activities, communication, and the process of project development are structured. What tasks and activities will be done, when, and by whom? Who will communicate with whom, about what, and when? In their study of the Portals project, Tsikalas et al. (2000) found that structural strategies and functions are generally set by the teachers and mentors. Teachers specify student roles and also set the activity structure in which the telementoring occurs, tied to a set of project deliverables. Mentors often structure the process of project development, advising students on what steps need to be taken to complete the deliverables by the deadline. In the integrated telementoring model, school-based PBL team members would collaborate on these activities and make decisions about how to integrate information literacy and digital media literacy skills in a timely manner.

Process strategies and functions refer to expectations related to the learning conversations over time. Tsikalas et al. (2000) found that these are often set by students, who decide on what role the mentor will take, set expectations, ask good questions, build personal relationships with the mentor, and manage the communication (such as selecting the type of media to use to communicate about certain topics). Mentors also perform process functions – assessing and anticipating student needs, providing information, stimulating students through questioning, directing action, extending students' vision of their projects, and exercising quality control.

Facilitation strategies and functions refer to the means of guiding, supervising, and supporting the learning and communication processes. Facilitation strategies can be considered a form of modeling done by the PBL team. Such strategies include pushing for explanations; restatement; summarizing; encouraging students to generate hypotheses; mediating content by reviewing, digesting, and re-teaching; and redirecting communication from impasses (Hmelo-Silver & Barrows, 2006; Tsikalas et al., 2000). Teachers are critical facilitators in the mentoring groups (Lehman et al., 2006; Tsikalas et al., 2000). They create structures to facilitate mentoring, mediate students' interactions with others, and build community. Some help students rehearse important conversations and provide opportunities for students to teach or mentor. When teachers are involved, student communication with mentors is often richer with ideas, opinions, and emotions (Harris & Jones, 1999). In some cases, teachers take on the role of co-mentor (Tsikalas & McMillan-Culp, 2000).

Community building strategies and functions refer to sharing materials, activities, or messages to promote a shared sense of purpose and benefit from participation in the online community. Tsikalas et al. (2000) found that these are undertaken by students, teachers, and mentors alike. For students, this means primarily collaboration within their team. Teachers help build community by fostering a climate of collaboration in their classrooms. Mentors support community building by helping students to socialize into particular cultures; treating students as colleagues; providing acceptance and encouragement; and referring students to other people for assistance.

The work of teachers as facilitators and project managers is often unknown to mentors. Making this work visible to telementors can provide them with valuable insights into students' knowledge, skills, learning styles, and communication styles. When relevant PBL team communication and collaborative work are conducted or documented in the online spaces, these four types of strategies and functions can be better coordinated and duplication of efforts avoided.

Online Learning Environment

The use of online tools should be carefully planned to meet learning goals, ensure ease of use, and accommodate potentially differing levels of technological fluency among the participants. Factors to consider in structuring the online learning environment include whether online communication will be synchronous, asynchronous, or a combination of both (and which tools to use); whether communication between participants will be private or open to other project teams and mentors; and how to organize resources and individual and group spaces.

Choices about modes of communication and technology tools should be integrated into the regular project planning process – determination of the learning goals, how the learning will be assessed, the skills and understandings expected as outcomes, and the activities that will enable students to achieve those outcomes. For example, if a learning goal is that students understand the structure of a subject, students can organize information in databases (Jonassen, Carr, & Yueh, 1998) or online repositories in wikis and tag each item. Students can then discuss and develop their understanding of conceptual relationships among the tags using a concept map and receive feedback from the PBL team.

In general, the use of separate online tools can be confusing for new users of technology, so the use of a single comprehensive tool (e.g., a full-featured wiki or flexible learning management system) as the main communication center is advisable. The advantage of a wiki over a learning management system is that it can be edited and new pages can be added by any member of a private wiki. At the start of a project, it is important to post goals, project criteria, selected resources, and templates that are accessible to all members of the PBL team, students, and telementors. During the project, wikis are an effective tool for collaborative project planning and documentation (Parker & Chao, 2007). They are also effective for information or data gathering and organization, as well as organizing a personal or team research library that tracks the research process and showcases final products (Walsh & Hollister, 2009). Here, the school librarian plays the major role.

Wiki pages are designed primarily for collaborative writing. Asynchronous discussion and feedback about wiki pages can be done through the page comments or page discussion features available on most wikis. Synchronous discussions may be preferable for brainstorming and other activities that require immediate response. For these, chat plug-ins are available on most wikis. The recorded communication can be used for further collaborative writing, self-assessment, and critique by peers and the PBL team. At the completion of the project, wiki pages and other online spaces can be used for presentations and portfolios.

Telementor-student communication can be done privately and asynchronously via email or synchronously via instant messaging. For group mentoring, O'Neill (2004, p. 182) argues for the importance of "mentoring in the open," where telementoring conversations are visible to other groups and experiences are shared. This provides an opportunity for students to see exemplary telementoring relationships at work and learn from such vicarious, peripheral participation (Lave & Wenger, 1991). Public mentoring discussions can take place asynchronously via discussion forums and synchronously via chat plug-ins in the wiki. These open conversations allow telementors to use the experiences of other groups to guide and scaffold learning, as well as to initiate peer support. When members of the school-based team also participate online or post summaries of face-to-face work in the online spaces, collaboration is strengthened.

Issues and challenges related to mentoring in an online environment are: (1) miscommunication, due in part to the lack of nonverbal cues; (2) slower development of relationships online than face-to-face; (3) the need for competency in written communication and technical skills; (4) a reliable technology infrastructure; and (5) protection of privacy (McLoughlin, Brady, Lee, & Russell, 2007, p. 4).

Participant Readiness

The importance of student readiness cannot be overemphasized. Do students have sufficient content knowledge and skills to handle the project successfully? Do they have the necessary skills with technology and access to the required technology both within school and without? Can they take independent initiative and work collaboratively? Tsikalas et al. (2000) found that students who could communicate and collaborate well with each other tended to do this more effectively with telementors. They also found that mentoring relationships were more successful when students were aware of their needs and proactive about seeking specific assistance. The PBL team can prepare students for the telementoring experience by: (1) encouraging them to be open and honest with their mentors about what they do not understand; (2) providing opportunities to practice describing what they do and do not understand; (3) providing peer and teacher feedback about their communication; and (4) educating them about the various roles and functions mentors may take (Tsikalas et al., 2000, p. 10).

The school-based members of the PBL team need a common understanding of the philosophy, principles, and practice of PBL and preferably some experience either as facilitators or learners. Because implementing PBL online adds complexity, experience with implementing it first face-to-face is beneficial (Savin-Baden, 2007, p. 39). Collaboration requires significant time and effort but also brings rewards in personal learning, professional development, and student achievement. In a study of a yearlong professional development course involving teacher-librarian partners who collaborated on curriculum, Yukawa and Harada (2009, p. 13-14) found that:

Participants characterized the relationship as a partnership of equals, with teachers providing subject expertise and intimate knowledge of their students and librarians providing information literacy expertise, knowledge of resources, technology expertise, and guidance to students through the conceptual and emotional challenges of the research process. Participants appreciated using each other as sounding boards in deepening conversations about unit and lesson planning, standards, essential questions, assessment tools, and information literacy instruction. A key change in roles was the degree to which librarians were integral to the entire process of planning, implementation, and assessment, with joint responsibility and accountability. A valuable theme was the way the partnerships extended to other faculty at the school.

Telementors who join the PBL team from private and public sector organizations outside of the education sector often find it a challenge to understand how telementoring works in the school culture, which may be quite different from their organizational cultures (O'Neill et al., 2005, p. 111). The role of the telementors can be diverse and encompassing. They encourage, offer advice, coach, help students clarify their values or goals, provide information, act as role models, help students socialize into particular cultures, and stimulate students to acquire new knowledge (Tsikalas et al., 2000, p. 10-11). The most likely mentor group configuration for PBL is one telementor to a small group of students, although a telementor may work with a single student or an entire class. At the start of a project, telementors may need an orientation to inquiry learning, project goals and expectations, student learning needs, their role as consultants, the roles of the other members of the team, the school context, technology and software to be used, and tips on how to communicate with the students online (Bennett, Heinze, Hupert, & Meade, n.d.). Advice to telementors should continue as needed throughout the telementoring relationship.

Using the integrated telementoring model, the PBL team serves as a model for students of the interdisciplinary teamwork that is increasingly valued in today's workplaces and communities. As the PBL team members plan, implement, manage, and facilitate project-based learning for students, they model the skills in collaborative problem solving, information literacy, technological fluency, innovation, and leadership that they expect students to demonstrate as a result of their PBL experiences.

BENEFITS AND CHALLENGES OF PROJECT-BASED TELEMENTORING

Although PBL with telementoring is time consuming, many teachers feel it is worthwhile because of the benefits to their students. Student benefits include: (1) increased student engagement and motivation, (2) improved writing and speaking skills, (3) improved information gathering skills, (4), improved reasoning and problem-solving skills, (5) learning science and scientific processes, (6) learning about technology, (7) the transfer of learning into student performance, (8) self-directed learning skills, (9) improved collaboration and cooperative learning skills, (10) opportunities to teach their peers, and (11), self-evaluation techniques (Abbott, 2005; Lehman et al., 2006; Ravitz, 2009).

Interviews with volunteer telementors indicate the self-perceived benefits of telementoring: (1) doing outreach for their employers, (2) cultivating interest in their field, (3) increasing the representation of women and minorities in their field, (4) engaging in the pursuit of challenging inquiry, (5) learning more about teaching and about themselves, (6) giving back, and (7) realizing the potential of the internet (O'Neill, 2000, p. 11-15).

PBL with telementoring also brings benefits to teachers, who value: (1) learning new teaching methods and strategies to increase student motivation, (2) learning more about a discipline, (3) learning new technologies and gaining increased technological competence, (4) becoming less directive and more facilitative to promote student-centered learning, (5) seeing students' success, (6) collaboration with others, (7) increased satisfaction from teaching, and (8) improved personal confidence (Abbott, 2005; Friedman, Zibit, & Coote, 2005; Lehman et al., 2006).

The disadvantages of PBL with telementoring include: (1) heavy demands of time and effort, (2) problems with technology and access to technology, (3) disparity in student technology access or skills, (4) classroom management problems, (5) lack of sufficient materials and supplies, (6) difficulties with group dynamics, (7) problems covering content when PBL interferes with the regular curriculum, and (8) poor collaboration and lack of support from team members (Garcia & Rose, 2007; Lehman et al., 2006).

Another significant challenge is effective facilitation. Although facilitation is generally seen as one of the most important dimensions of PBL, Savin-Baden (2007) points out that "there has still been relatively little discussion about what is being facilitated – whether it is students' understanding and enactment of problem-based learning, the team process, the process of learning, individual learning, or the achievement of the learning outcomes, and to what extent the tutor's ability to facilitate affects all these" (p. 41).

While the process of planning, implementation, and assessment of a telementoring project is an important type of professional development in itself, more structured educational opportunities for learning about PBL may also be necessary. One of the best ways to understand PBL and telementoring is for educators to experience these processes for themselves (Gareis & Nussbaum-Beach, 2007; Hitchcock & Mylona, 2000; Weizman et al. 2008). Experience with telementoring, project-based and problem-based learning, and technology integration should begin with pre-service teacher education (Garcia & Rose, 2007; McLoughlin et al., 2007; Price & Chen, 2003) and be extended with in-service professional development (Dede, 2006; Yukawa & Harada, 2009; Weizman et al., 2008).

CONCLUSION

The purpose of this chapter has been two-fold: (1) to explore the rich potential of telementoring for project-based learning in the context of the urgent need to help students develop new skills and literacies, and (2) to provide the framework for an integrated telementoring model to be tested by new telementoring projects. Using this model, an interdisciplinary PBL team of experts – the subject matter expert serving as telementor, the classroom teacher, the school librarian, and the instructional technology specialist – can provide students with new opportunities for holistic, authentic, personally meaningful learning using emerging technology.

Subject matter experts as telementors encourage, guide, instruct, and model disciplinary practices and ways of thinking. Teachers manage PBL projects and facilitate learning on many levels – the process of project-based learning, the team process, community building, individual learning, and the achievement of the learning outcomes. School librarians guide students to become information literate and help them navigate the increasingly complex terrain of information resources. Instructional technology specialists help students achieve better digital media literacy and provide opportunities for creative expression using a wide array of technological tools. As a team, these experts model the skills in collaborative problem solving, information literacy, technological fluency, innovation, and leadership that are needed in the workplaces and communities of today and tomorrow.

This model requires careful planning, coordination, ongoing collaboration, and a clear view of general roles and functions with flexibility in assuming them. Important factors to consider when designing a project using the integrated telementoring model are commitment to the project, learning goals, roles and functions of participants, the online learning environment, and participant readiness for project-based learning. While collaboration requires significant time and effort, the rewards in personal learning, professional development, and student achievement can be great.

Implementation of the model cannot be divorced from broader educational issues and challenges – the need for formal instruction in new literacy skills for students and educators, professional development on learner-centered approaches like PBL, developing and sustaining school-wide and community-based communities of practice, learning environments that incorporate new technologies, and fundamental changes in the structure of the educational environment. These challenges are also opportunities for project-based telementoring to contribute to needed changes in educational structure, transformations of teaching practice, and more relevant learning experiences for students.

REFERENCES

Abbott, L. (2005). The nature of authentic professional development during curriculum-based telecomputing. *Journal of Research on Technology in Education, 37*(4), 379–398.

American Association for the Advancement of Science (AAAS). 2009. *Science NetLinks*. Retrieved April 2, 2009, from http://www.sciencenetlinks.com/index.cfm.

American Association of School Librarians (AASL). (2007). *Standards for the 21st-century learner*. Chicago: American Library Association. Retrieved August 20, 2009, from http://www.ala.org/ala/mgrps/divs/aasl/guidelinesandstandards/learningstandards/standards.cfm.

American Association of School Librarians (AASL). [n.d.]. *Best web sites for teaching and learning*. Retrieved August 20, 2009, from http://www.ala.org/ala/mgrps/divs/aasl/guidelinesandstandards/bestlist/bestwebsitestop25.cfm.

Bennett, D., Heinze, C., Hupert, N., & Meade, T. (n.d.). *IBM MentorPlace: Starter kit*. New York. *EDC Center for Children and Technology.*

Boss, S., Krauss, J., & Conery, L. (2008). *Reinventing project-based learning: Your field guide to real-world projects in the digital age*. Eugene, OR: International Society for Technology in Education.

Boud, D., & Prosser, M. (2002). Appraising new technologies for learning: A framework for development. *Educational Media International, 39*(2/4), 237–245. doi:10.1080/09523980210166026

Buck Institute for Education (BIE). (n.d.). *Project based learning handbook*. Novato, CA. *Buck Institute for Education.*

Buck Institute for Education (BIE), & Boise State University, Department of Educational Technology. (2005). *PBL Online: Designing your project*. Retrieved April 8, 2009, from http://www.pbl-online.org/pathway2.html.

Burger, L. (2007). Transforming reference. *American Libraries, 38*(3), 5–6.

Casey, M., & Savastinuk, L. C. (2006, September). Library 2.0. *Library Journal, 131*(14), 40–42.

Dede, C. (Ed.). (2006). *Online professional development for teachers: Emerging models and methods*. Cambridge, MA: Harvard Education Press.

Dede, C. (2007). Reinventing the role of information and communications technologies in Education. *Yearbook of the National Society for the Study of Education, 106*(2), 11–38. doi:10.1111/j.1744-7984.2007.00113.x

Elgort, I., Smith, A. G., & Toland, J. (2008). Is wiki an effective platform for group course work? *Australasian Journal of Educational Technology, 24*(2), 195–210.

Friedman, A. A., Zibit, M., & Coote, M. (2004). Telementoring as a collaborative agent for change. *Journal of Technology, Learning, and Assessment, 3*(1). Retrieved March 10, 2009, from http://www.jtla.org.

Garcia, P., & Rose, S. (2007). The influence of technocentric collaboration on preservice teachers' attitudes about technology's role in powerful learning and teaching. *Journal of Technology and Teacher Education, 15*(2), 247–266.

Gareis, C. R., & Nussbaum-Beach, C. (2007). Electronically mentoring to develop accomplished professional teachers. *Journal of Personnel Evaluation in Education, 27*, 227–246. doi:10.1007/s11092-008-9060-0

Goodnough, K. C., & Hung, W. (2008) Engaging teachers' pedagogical content knowledge: Adopting a nine-step problem-based learning model. *Interdisciplinary Journal of Problem-based Learning, 2*(2), 61-90. Retrieved April 2, 2009, from http://docs.lib.purdue.edu/ijpbl/vol2/iss2/6.

Guy, T. (2002). Telementoring: Shaping relationships for the 21st century. In Hansman, C. A. (Ed.), *Critical perspectives on mentoring: Trends and issues, Information series: 388* (pp. 27–37). Columbus, OH: ERIC Clearinghouse on Adult, Career, and Vocational Education, Center on Education and Training for Employment, College of Education, The Ohio State University.

Harada, V. H., Kirio, C. H., & Yamamoto, S. H. (2008b). Project-based learning: Rigor and relevance in high schools. *Library Media Connection, 26*(6), 14–16, 18, 20.

Harada, V. H., & Yoshina, J. M. (2004. *Inquiry learning through librarian-teacher partnerships*. Worthington, OH: Linworth. Harada, V. H., Kirio, C. H., & Yamamoto, S. H. (2008a). *Collaborating for project-based learning in grades 9-12*. Columbus, OH: Linworth.

Harris, J., & Figg, C. (2000). Participating from the sidelines, online: facilitating telementoring projects. *ACM Journal of Computer Documentation, 24*(4), 227–236. doi:10.1145/353927.353934

Harris, J., & Jones, G. (1999). A descriptive study of telementoring among students, subject matter experts, and teachers: Message flow and function patterns. *Journal of Research on Computing in Education, 42*(1), 36–53.

Hazari, S., North, A., & Moreland, D. (2009). Investigating pedagogical value of wiki technology. *Journal of Information Systems Education, 20*(2), 187–198.

Hitchcock, M. A., & Mylona, Z. E. (2000). Teaching faculty to conduct problem-based learning. *Teaching and Learning in Medicine, 12*(1), 52–57. doi:10.1207/S15328015TLM1201_8

Hmelo-Silver, C. E., & Barrows, H. S. (2006). Goals and strategies of a problem-based learning facilitator. *The Interdisciplinary Journal of Problem-based Learning, 1*(1), 21–39.

Huett, J., Moller, L., Foshay, W., & Coleman, C. (2008). The evolution of distance education: Implications for instructional design on the potential of the web. *TechTrends, 52*(5), 63–67. doi:10.1007/s11528-008-0199-9

Illinois Mathematics and Science Academy (IMSA). (2009). *Introduction to problem based learning*. Retrieved April 9, 2009, from http://pbln.imsa.edu/model/intro/index.html.

Johnson, L., Levine, A., Smith, R., & Smythe, T. (2009). *The 2009 horizon report: K-12 edition*. Austin, Texas: The New Media Consortium. Retrieved April 8, 2009, from http://www.nmc.org/pdf/2009-Horizon-Report-K12.pdf.

Jonassen, D. H. (2000). Toward a design theory of problem solving. *Educational Technology Research and Development, 48*(4), 63–85. doi:10.1007/BF02300500

Jonassen, D. H., Carr, C., & Yueh, H. P. (1998). Computers as MindTools for engaging learners in critical thinking. *TechTrends, 43*(2), 24–32. doi:10.1007/BF02818172

Jonassen, D. H., & Hung, W. (2008). All problems are not equal: Implications for problem-based learning. *The Interdisciplinary Journal of Problem-based Learning, 2*(2), Article 4. Retrieved August 20, 2009, from http://docs.lib.purdue.edu/ijpbl/vol2/iss2/4.

Lave, J., & Wenger, E. (1991). *Situated learning: Legitimate peripheral participation.* Cambridge: Cambridge University Press.

Lehman, J. D., George, M., Buchanan, P., & Rush, M. (2006). Preparing teachers to use problem-centered, inquiry-based science: Lessons from a four-year professional development project. *The Interdisciplinary Journal of Problem-based Learning, 1*(1), 9–19.

McLoughlin, C., Brady, J., Lee, M. J. W., & Russell, R. (2007, November). Peer-to-peer: An e-mentoring approach to developing community, mutual engagement and professional identity for pre-service teachers. Paper presented at the Australian Association for Research in Education (AARE) Conference Fremantle, Western Australia. Retrieved April 4, 2009, from http://www.aare.edu.au/07pap/mcl07393.pdf.

Mid-continent Research for Education and Learning (McREL). (2009). *Content knowledge* (4th ed.) Retrieved April 8, 2009, from http://www.mcrel.org/standards-benchmarks/.

Moller, L., Huett, J. B., & Harvey, D. M. (2008). *Learning and instructional technologies for the 21st century: Visions of the future.* New York: Springer.

New Media Consortium (NMC). (2005). *A global imperative: The report of the 21st Century Literacy Summit.* Austin, TX: The New Media Consortium. Retrieved April 8, 2009, from http://archive.nmc.org/pdf/Global_Imperative.pdf.

O'Neill, D. K. (2000). *The telementor's guidebook.* Toronto: Ontario Institute for Studies in Education, University of Toronto.

O'Neill, D. K. (2004). Building social capital in a knowledge-building community: Telementoring as a catalyst. *Interactive Learning Environments, 12*(3), 179–208. doi:10.1080/10494820512331383419

O'Neill, D. K., Weiler, M., & Sha, L. (2005). Software support for online mentoring programs: a research-inspired design. *Mentoring & Tutoring, 13*(1), 109–131. doi:10.1080/13611260500040617

Parker, K. R., & Chao, J. T. (2007). Wikis as a teaching tool. *Interdisciplinary Journal of Knowledge and Learning Objects, 3,* 57–72.

Partnership for 21st Century Skills. (2008). *21st century skills, education & competitiveness: A resource and policy guide.* Retrieved April 8, 2009, from http://www.21stcenturyskills.org/documents/21st_century_skills_education_and_competitiveness_guide.pdf.

Pink, D. H. (2005). *A whole new mind: Why right-brainers will rule the future.* New York: Riverhead.

Pitler, H., Hubbell, E. R., Kuhn, M., & Malenoski, K. (2007). *Using technology with classroom instruction that works.* Alexandria, VA: Association for Supervision and Curriculum Development.

Price, M. A., & Chen, H. H. (2003). Promises and challenges: Exploring a collaborative telementoring programme in a preservice teacher education programme. *Mentoring & Tutoring, 11*(1), 105–117. doi:10.1080/1361126032000054844

Ravitz, J. (2009). Introduction: Summarizing findings and looking ahead to a new generation of PBL research. *Interdisciplinary Journal of Problem-based Learning, 3*(1). Retrieved April 8, 2009, from http://docs.lib.purdue.edu/ijpbl/vol3/iss1/2.

Richardson, W. (2008). *Blogs, wikis, podcasts, and other powerful web tools for classrooms* (2nd ed.). Thousand Oaks, CA: Corwin.

Robinson, K. (2006, February). Do schools kill creativity? Presentation at TED2006 conference, Monterey, CA. Video retrieved from http://www.ted.com/talks/ken_robinson_says_schools_kill_creativity.html.

Savery, J. R. (2006). Overview of problem-based learning: Definitions and distinctions. *Interdisciplinary Journal of Problem-based Learning, 1*(1). Retrieved April 2, 2009, from http://docs.lib.purdue.edu/ijpbl/vol1/iss1/3.

Savin-Baden, M. (2007). *A practical guide to problem-based learning online*. London: Routledge.

Shulman, L. S. (2004). Knowledge and teaching: Foundations of the new reform. In Wilson, S. M. (Ed.), *The wisdom of practice: Essays on teaching, learning, and learning to teach* (pp. 217–248). San Francisco: Jossey-Bass.

Solomon, G., & Schrum, L. (2007). *Web 2.0: New tools, new schools*. Eugene, OR: International Society for Technology in Education.

Sternberg, R. J. (1996). *Successful intelligence.* New York: Simon & Schuster.

Tsikalas, K., & McMillan-Culp, K. (2000). Silent negotiations: A case study of roles and functions utilized by students, teachers, and mentors in project-based, telementoring relationships. In B. Fishman & S. O'Connor-Divelbiss (Eds.), *Fourth International Conference of the Learning Sciences* (pp. 350-357). Mahwah, NJ: Erlbaum. Retrieved April 2, 2009, from http://www.umich.edu/~icls/proceedings/pdf/Tsikalas.pdf.

Tsikalas, K., McMillan-Culp, K., Friedman, W., & Honey, M. (2000, April). *Portals: A window into telementoring relationships in project-based computational science classes.* Paper presented at the Annual Meeting of the American Educational Research Association, New Orleans, LA.

University of California Museum of Paleontology. (2009). A blueprint for scientific investigations. *Understanding science.* Retrieved April 2, 2009, from http://undsci.berkeley.edu/article/0_0_0/howscienceworks_03

University of California Museum of Paleontology. (2009). The real process of science. *Understanding science.* Retrieved April 2, 2009, from http://undsci.berkeley.edu/article/0_0_0/howscienceworks_02.

University of California Museum of Paleontology. *Understanding science.* (2009). Retrieved April 2, 2009, from http://www.understandingscience.org.

Walsh, T. R., & Hollister, C. V. (2009). Creating a digital archive for students' research in a credit library course. *Reference and User Services Quarterly, 48*(4), 391–400.

Weizman, A., Covitt, B. A., Koehler, M. J., Lundenberg, M. A., Oslund, J. A., & Low, M. R. (2008). Measuring teachers' learning from a problem-based learning approach to professional development in science education. *The Interdisciplinary Journal of Problem-based Learning, 2*(2), 29–60.

Wiggins, G., & McTighe, J. (1998). *Understanding by design.* Alexandria, VA: Association for Supervision and Curriculum Development.

Yukawa, J. (2005). *Hearts and minds through hands online: A narrative analysis of learning through co-reflection in an online action research course.* Unpublished doctoral dissertation, University of Hawaii at Manoa, 2005.

Yukawa, J., & Harada, V. H. (2009). Librarian-teacher partnerships for inquiry learning: Measures of effectiveness for a practice-based model of professional development. *Evidence Based Library and Information Practice, 4*(2). Retrieved August 20, 2009, from http://ejournals.library.ualberta.ca/index.php/EBLIP/article/view/4633.

Yukawa, J., Harada, V. H., & Suthers, D. D. (2007). Professional development in communities of practice. In Hughes-Hassell, S., & Harada, V. H. (Eds.), *The School Library Media Specialist and Education Reform* (pp. 179–192). Westport, CT: Libraries Unlimited.

Zmuda, A., & Harada, V. H. (2008). *Librarians as learning specialists: Meeting the learning imperative for the 21st century*. Westport, CT: Libraries Unlimited.

ADDITIONAL READING

American Association for the Advancement of Science (AAAS). (n.d.) *Science NetLinks*. Retrieved April 8, 2009, from http://www.sciencenetlinks.com/index.cfm.

Chard, S. (n.d.) *Project Approach*. Retrieved April 8, 2009, from http://www.projectapproach.org/.

Grant, M. M. (2002). *Getting a grip on project-based learning: Theory, cases, and recommendations*. Retrieved May 22, 2009, from http://www.ncsu.edu/meridian/win2002/514/.

High Tech High. [n.d.]. *Project-based learning: Seven successful PBL projects*. Retrieved August 22, 2009, from http://www.hightechhigh.org/pbl/index.html.

International Society for Technology in Education (ISTE). (n.d.) *Project-based learning resource links*. Retrieved April 8, 2009, from http://www.iste.org/Content/NavigationMenu/EducatorResources/YourLearningJourney/ProjectBasedLearning/Project-Based_Learning_Resource_Links.htm.

Johnson, L., & Lamb, A. (2007). *Project, problem, and inquiry-based learning*. Retrieved June 10, 2009, from http://eduscapes.com/tap/topic43.htm.

McGrath, D. (2008). *Project-based learning with technology*. Retrieved April 8, 2009, from http://coe.ksu.edu/pbl/index.htm.

The Virtual Schoolhouse. (n.d.). Retrieved June 3, 2009, from http://virtualschoolhouse.visionlink.org/index.htm.

Thomas, J. W. (2000). *A review of research on project-based learning*. San Rafael, CA: Autodesk Foundation. Retrieved April 8, 2009, from http://www.bie.org/files/researchreviewPBL_1.pdf.

APPENDIX: SELECTED K-12 TELEMENTORING PROGRAMS (PROGRAMS ARE FREE UNLESS OTHERWISE INDICATED)

Learning Goal	Program	Target Groups	Duration	Mode of communication	Facilitation	Mentor Training
Project based learning One mentor per class	The Electronic Emissary http://emissary.wm.edu/	K-12 students	6 weeks to school year	Email, forum, chat, teleconferencing	Yes	Yes
Project based learning One-to-one mentoring	International Telementor Program http://www.telementor.org/index.cfm	K-12 students	Flexible	Secure, online messaging system	Yes	
Academic & career mentoring One-to-one mentoring	IBM's MentorPlace http://ibm.mentorplace.epals.org/WhatIs.htm	Grades 3-12	School year	Face-to-face at beginning and end of school year; online messaging	Yes	Yes
Academic & career mentoring (fee-based) Many-to-many	Zoey's Room http://www.zoeysroom.com/	Girls age 10-14; math, science, technology	Indefinite	Online only via discussion list	Yes	
Career mentoring One-to-one mentoring	Connecting to Success (Minnesota) http://ici.umn.edu/ementoring/default.html	High school students at-risk & with disabilities	School year	Only email and school-sponsored activities	Yes	Yes
Career mentoring 3 mentors for each student	icouldbe http://www.icouldbe.org/standard/public/lm_index.asp	Middle & high school students at-risk, inner city	School year	Email, discussion board (anonymous)	Yes	Yes
Online tutoring (fee-based) One-to-one tutoring	Tutor.com http://www.tutor.com/	Grades 4-12 homework help	24/7 live homework help	Instant messaging		
Online tutoring (fee-based) One-to-one tutoring	Homeworkhelp.com http://www.homeworkhelp.com/	Grades 4-12 homework help	Tutorials, live homework help	Audio dialogue, text messaging		
Ask an expert Career advice in science, engineering, technology	GEM-SET http://www.uic.edu/orgs/gem-set/index.htm	Girls aged 13-18	Short term	Discussion list (students known by first name only)	Yes	
Ask an expert Astrophysics	NASA Ask an Astrophysicist http://imagine.gsfc.nasa.gov/docs/ask_astro/ask_an_astronomer.html	General	One-time question-and-answer	Email		
Ask an expert Math	Drexel University, Math Forum, Ask Dr. Math http://mathforum.org/dr.math/	K-12 students	One-time question-and-answer	Email		

Chapter 4
You Had to be There:
Improving a Telementoring Program through Classroom Observation

Kevin O'Neill
Simon Fraser University, Canada

Sheryl Guloy
Simon Fraser University, Canada

ABSTRACT

This chapter makes the case that to fully realize the potential of telementoring for supporting student learning in P-12 schools, teachers and program developers should invest effort in a practice that they traditionally have not – routine observations of how telementoring programs play out in classrooms. Using observational data from a pilot program for secondary social studies called "Compassionate Canada?" we illustrate how classroom observations can enable program designers to ask better questions about how a program is working, and why. We also discuss contributions that classroom observations may enable teacher to make to program refinement and professional development.

INTRODUCTION

As other chapters in this volume make clear, telementoring holds enormous potential for supporting student learning in P-12 schools. Fully realizing this potential through any given program relies on several elements, including dedicated and qualified mentors, technology infrastructure, well-designed programs, and the right kind of professional development to help teachers play their part. This chapter makes the case that in order to ensure that the last two of these elements are in place (quality program design and professional development), teachers and program developers should invest effort in a practice that they traditionally have not – routine observations of how telementoring programs play out in classrooms.

One of the benefits that telementoring provides is the opportunity to directly observe how mentoring relationships develop between students and mentors. Prior to the advent of telementoring, program evaluators had to rely almost exclusively on self-report from mentors and mentees to learn what had happened in each relationship. The automatic transcript that text-based telementoring dialogues provide has great potential both for

DOI: 10.4018/978-1-61520-861-6.ch004

program developers' understanding of mentoring relationships and teachers' assessment of student learning. However, despite the richness that telementoring discourse can have, it does not reveal all the contextual factors and offline decisions that contribute to the successful implementation of a telementoring program "on the ground."

In the past, designers (including ourselves) have based their published reports on the analysis of captured correspondence alone (e.g. Brescia, 2005; Harris & Jones, 1999; O'Neill, 2001). (Brescia, 2005; Harris & Jones, 1999; O'Neill, 2001) Martin (2005) pointed out that despite more than a decade of work on telementoring, the research literature did not provide evidence-based guidance to teachers about what they can and should do to effectively support a telementoring program in the classroom (Martin, 2005). To date, program designers have not made it their business to study closely how teachers' work supports what they aim to do with their program designs. We have behaved virtually as if the teacher's only important jobs are to bring students to the program and ensure that they stick with it.

Below, we will illustrate the valuable lessons that program researchers can learn by routinely conducting classroom observations, particularly in the early stages of a program's design and implementation. Using findings from a recently-completed pilot of a program for 11th-grade social studies students called "Compassionate Canada?" we attempt to show how classroom observations can enable program designers to ask and answer better questions about how and why a program is working, and what teachers and designers can do to make it work better.

For teachers, we hope this chapter will make clear why they should invite observations of their classroom practice during the implementation of a telementoring program, and what they may be able to teach program designers and evaluators about how to design better programs. For program designers, we hope this chapter will generate a richer understanding of what makes a P-12 telementoring program work effectively, and how classroom observations can inform better program designs and professional development for teachers.

CONTEXT: THE "COMPASSIONATE CANADA?" UNIT

Under funding from the Canadian Council on Learning (www.ccl-cca.ca), our team recently developed and piloted a telementored curriculum unit designed to develop 11th grade students' conceptions about the nature of historical knowledge. It is necessary to explain some details of the program content and design here, as background to our classroom observations and the lessons they taught us about revisions that were needed in our design.

The goal of the program was to help teachers cover mandated curriculum, while at the same time developing what Lee (2004) referred to as "metahistorical" conceptions – students' ideas about the nature of historical knowledge. What motivated this goal was the belief, shared by many history educators, that today's students need a mature understanding of why conflicting accounts of the past exist (Lee, 2004; Seixas, 2004; Shemilt, 2000; Wineburg, 2001). As society becomes more diverse, we encounter conflicting accounts of the past more often among fellow students, neighbours, and friends. Students need the capacity to understand why this variety of accounts exist, and what to do with them. The assumption that citizenship will thrive if new immigrants assimilate to the majority culture simply will not work anymore (Banks, 2008; Zinn, 2003).

What sorts of ideas should students be equipped with? Working with adolescents in the United Kingdom, Shemilt (1987) (Shemilt, 1987) conducted many hours of interviews to examine how students thought about why historical accounts might differ. The result was a developmental theory of how students move from an early, naïve understanding that there is one self-evidently

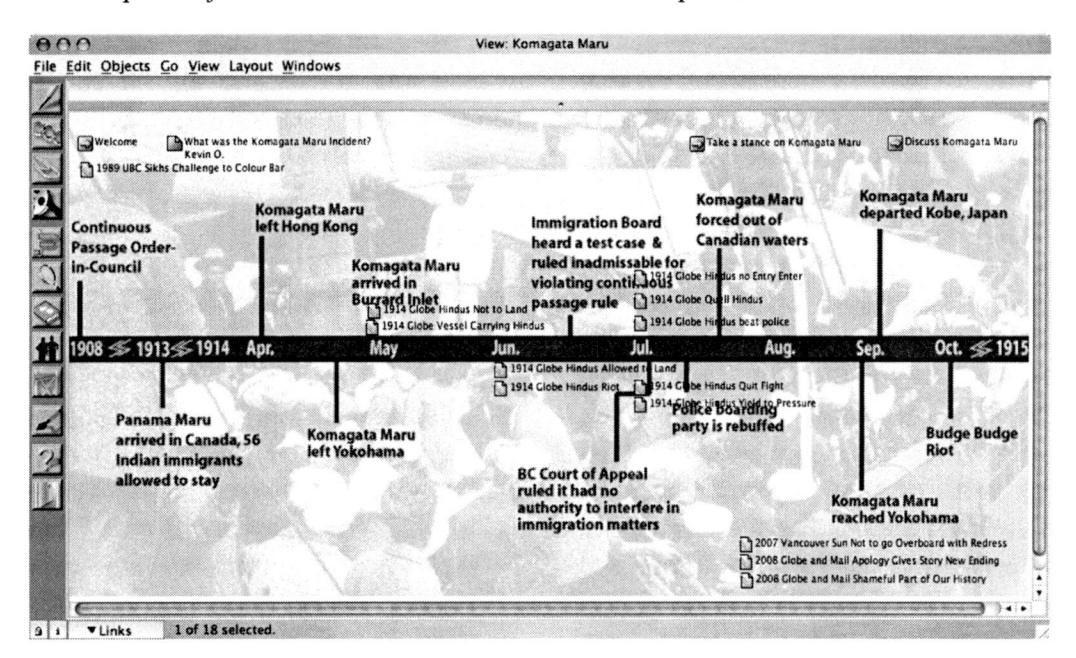

Figure 1. A snapshot of a timeline in the students' online workspace, with source documents attached

true story about any past event, to a more complex understanding that historical accounts are constructed from evidence that is nearly always incomplete. In this more mature conception, historical scholarship involves a certain amount of educated guesswork, directed by questions that change over time.

Because students enter the classroom with a variety of notions about history, reaching the mature ideas Shemilt described requires a process of conceptual change (diSessa, 2002; Vosniadou, 2007). One strategy that psychologists have recommended for creating conceptual change is cognitive conflict (Limon, 2001) – confronting students with the limitations of their existing ideas. We set out to lead students toward more sophisticated ideas about historical knowledge by deliberately orchestrating constructive conflict within students' own minds, and between groups of students (Johnson & Johnson, 2009).

In the "Compassionate Canada?" unit, students spent two weeks working with assigned telementors to pursue a thorny historical question: "Has Canada become a more compassionate country over the last 100 years?" This question, developed by a design team including ourselves and three experienced social studies teachers, was chosen for two main reasons. First, it dealt with the entire scope of the 11th-grade social studies curriculum that we were planning to serve; and second, it required students to think about changes in society over time. In this sense it was a genuinely historical question – not merely about what happened in the past, but *what was going on.*

Our team assembled an online archive of primary source documents covering seven historical cases, some of which illustrate the compassion of Canada's government or its people toward those in need (e.g. Canada's response to Tamil refugees in the 1980s), while others demonstrate unsympathetic, or even abusive actions (e.g. the internment of Japanese Canadians during World War II). Groups of students in each participating class were assigned to pursue the major question of the unit using evidence about a different historical case, under the guidance of a history telementor. A timeline for one case, with attached documents, is shown in Figure 1. A "backgrounder" about the case, prepared for participating students, is included in Appendix.

We expected that the experience of working with telementors to interpret the source evidence would, in itself, contradict some of students' naïve ideas about history. Further, the different cases students were exposed to would lead them to different stances on the overarching question of the unit, arousing some intellectual conflict among them. At the conclusion of the unit, we orchestrated a "horseshoe debate" in which each student team presented its stance on the question of the unit based on its assigned case, then stood on a large horseshoe shape, taped on the school library's floor, where one end represented Yes (Canada has become more compassionate) and the other represented No. After each group presentation, students were invited to move closer to or further away from each end of the horseshoe to represent their views on all the evidence they had heard[1].

We expected our history telementors not only to help students understand the evidence they were working with, but the conflicting perspectives they encountered on the question of the unit as well. Seven volunteer telementors, four men and three women, were recruited from across Canada to serve as telementors. Two had completed PhDs in history, three were PhD candidates, and the remaining two were completing MAs in history. They ranged in age from 25 to 36 years. These telementors shared the students' online environment[2] and could review all the evidence they had been given, as well as post advice and guidance on the various ways the evidence could be interpreted.

Students prepared for the horseshoe debate by posting their speaking notes on a similar-looking online horseshoe days prior to the event, where their telementors could offer encouragement, appreciation, and challenges to the students' interpretations. Figure 2 shows one of these "take a stance" screens, with notes from students and mentors.

After the horseshoe debate, students wrote an in-class essay on the main question of the unit, which was graded and formed part of their preparation for the provincial examination for the course. Students' work with their telementors was not directly assessed.

PILOTING "COMPASSIONATE CANADA?"

A pilot implementation of "Compassionate Canada?" was conducted with almost ninety students in the Vancouver area. All were students of Mr. George, a veteran with over fifteen years of experience teaching history and social studies. His school, Hanover Secondary, is a public school within walking distance of some of the wealthiest and the poorest neighbourhoods in the Vancouver area. The school serves 500 students whose families speak many different heritage languages.

Three sections of Mr. George's Social Studies 11 class participated in the unit, occupying a class period of 1.5 hours approximately every two days. Eighty-seven students were approached for research consent, of whom 41 provided both required approval forms (parent and student). Of those providing consent, 43% were female. Thirty-three percent of the students' mothers and 56% of their fathers were reported to have at least a bachelor's degree. Sixty-six percent planned to pursue post-secondary education. On average, students reported spending 1.8 hours each day on homework, and 8.4 hours per week working at a part-time job.

What We Saw Online

If we had only followed the activity in the online forum, we would have known a few things about what was happening with Mr. George's students and their mentors. We would have noticed that many students were not posting notes (see Figure 3), but that a few — especially in the lead-up

Figure 2. A "take a stance" view with student notes and mentor responses (usernames are obscured for participant anonymity)

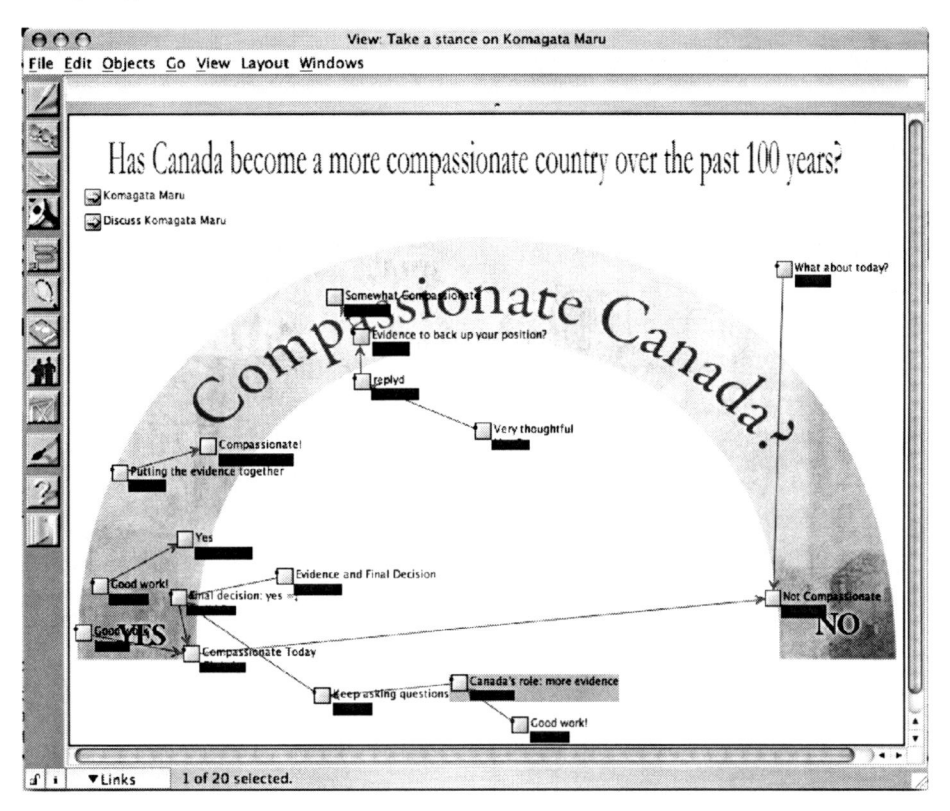

to the horseshoe debate — were engaging in fairly substantive exchanges with their mentors to refine their stances on the "big question." We also would have known that there was very little "lurking" in the forum – that is, that big readers tended also to be big writers, and that students who were not making posts were most often not reading posts, either.

An example of telementoring dialogue from the project will provide a sense of what the online data can and cannot reveal. Linda was the mentor assigned to work with students on the the Komagata Maru case (see Appendix). The Komagata Maru was a Japanese steam liner that arrived in Vancouver in 1914 carrying 376 passengers, primarily Sikhs from Punjab. Although they carried British passports, immigration officials refused to allow them to land, using a legal technicality called the "continuous passage rule." Eventually most of the passengers were forced to leave Canada and land in India.

Linda wrote the following autobiography for her mentees:

My name is Linda, and I am a PhD candidate. I am new to the west coast, having grown up on the prairies. Political history is not my only interest (but I really do love it!). I am really looking forward to being a mentor, not only because I love Canadian history, but because I believe that education works the best, and is the most exciting, when it is a collaborative project. For me what is most exciting about studying history is when I make that connection between historical events and my own life or in the lives of people I know (and this often happens when I least expect it).

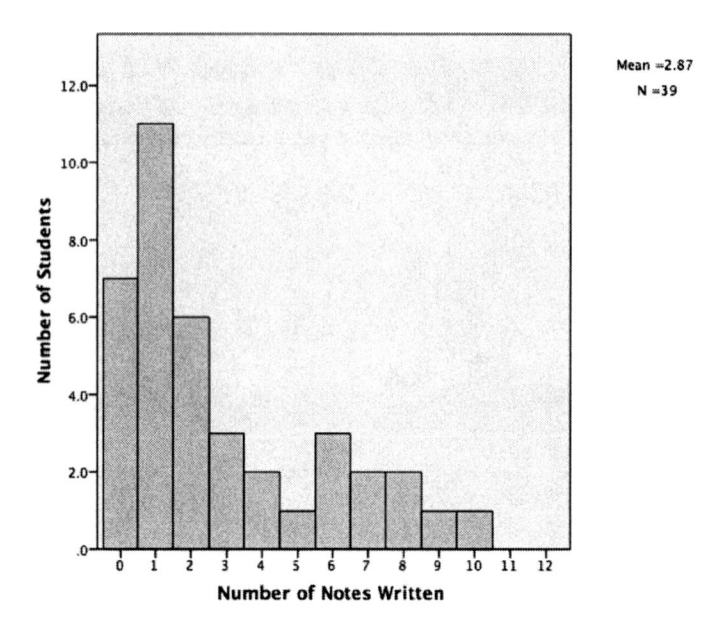

Figure 3. Numbers of notes written by students throughout the unit

[Histogram: Number of Students vs Number of Notes Written. Mean = 2.87, N = 39. Bars approximately: 0→7, 1→11, 2→6, 3→3, 4→2, 5→1, 6→3, 7→2, 8→2, 9→1, 10→1]

Majunder, who was working on the Komagata Maru case with three classmates, was assigned by his group as the liaison to Linda. Shortly before the horseshoe debate, he posted this note:

Majunder: After going over the articles, my group and I have come to a collective agreement, that Canada has become more compassionate over the years. The incidents of the Komagata Maru were not compassionate, but we've reached a conclusion that Canada has followed a better path to make sure that incidents such as the Komagata Maru case don't happen again...Today, Canada has become a more compassionate country, because after all this country is composed of people who have immigrated here. These immigrants have contributed to the building of such a great nation, and they have been recognized for all the hard work they've done in the past.

In response to this note, Linda did just what we would have wanted her to do – push students on questions of evidence:

Linda: Good work. Can you flesh out your argument with some more evidence? What has Canada done to ensure an incident like the K.M. doesn't happen again? Does the presence of immigrants in the country alone make Canada more compassionate? Or do we need to think about how these immigrants are treated? How do we recognize the work they have done?

Majunder responded:

Canada has given equal rights to every Canadian citizen no matter what race they belong to. In my opinion there's much more planning ahead of time for any laws that are being passed. Officials look at all aspects of the laws, who it benefits and who is disadvantaged, and they try to find just the right law. Canada's going through a great learning process, the presence of immigrants is not the only thing which makes Canada compassionate... there's much more today. Canada acts as a peacekeeping nation all around the world. We help out other nations when a natural disaster happens... Canada is compassionate today because we look after nations in need, we care for other countries and try to help our race, the 'human race'.

If data like these represented the limit of what we knew about the implementation prior to our closing interviews, we would likely have framed our follow-up data collection around questions like these:

- How did interest in the unit vary across the classes?
- Why did some of the students not write more?
- Did students get enough time in the computer lab to participate fully?
- How well did students understand what they are supposed to do?

Classroom observations certainly helped us to address some of these questions; but we feel they were equally useful in enabling us to *ask* different questions. We will illustrate what we mean by this in the next two sections.

AN OVERVIEW OF MR. GEORGE'S IMPLEMENTATION

During the pilot implementation, the research team had at least two observers in the classroom at all times. One participated in the class, offering support to the teacher and students when needed. The other took fieldnotes, which were transcribed after each day of observation. At this time, missing details were filled in from memory. All told, 104 single-spaced pages of notes were transcribed, including diagrams of classroom layout and students' seating arrangements.

On day 1, Mr. George and a member of the design team (O'Neill) introduced Compassionate Canada together. This session began with a whole-class discussion of what the term "compassion" meant, and how it was relevant to the curriculum. Students generated criteria for compassion, for example that it included both empathizing with someone in need *and* acting in a helpful way. After this, students were shown the online environment they would be using on a large screen. A five-minute video (produced by the design team) was then shown, which explained what a telementoring relationship is like, and how students should take part in one. The video included sample correspondence between mentors and mentees, taken from a previous history telementoring project implemented by the researchers[3]. A question-and-answer period followed this video, after which Mr. George explained how students' performance on the unit would be evaluated (ie. horseshoe debate and in-class essay). At the end of the session, students were asked to complete a pre-survey for the research team, which provided demographic data and information on students' metahistorical conceptions.

On day 2, the class moved to the school's computer lab. The space was arranged in a fairly typical configuration of rows, and was cramped. Once the class was assembled, Mr. George assigned students to groups of four that he had determined earlier, based on his knowledge of students' existing skills and attendance habits. He was clearly concerned with ensuring that each team's daily work would not be disturbed by the absence of more than one student. Each team was assigned a case to work on, then students were registered to use the online forum. Learning to read and post notes in the forum took the majority of the class session. Before the end of the class, students were directed to read the biographies posted by the mentors for their assigned cases, and introduce themselves either individually or in a group post.

Over the next three days, students continued work in the computer lab, primarily focusing on the historical documents for each case. Mr. George and the team had expected there to be some confusion among students about the source evidence, due to the fact that they had not worked with such source documents so far in the school year.

The documents for each case consisted largely of newspaper articles, some dating back to the early 1900s. These articles not only used arcane English, but discussed events that had not yet been covered in the curriculum. For this reason, the design team wrote a "backgrounder" on each case in modern English. An example is included in the Appendix.

As students began working with the documents in their groups, Mr. George and the designers circulated continuously and listened in, offering students advice and giving direction as requested, or as seemed necessary. During this time, the observer noted the varying ways that teams chose to seat themselves in the lab. Several of the 4-person teams seated themselves along a row of the computer lab, where they could talk as conveniently as the space allowed. Other teams divided up their work and seated themselves far away from one another, speaking rarely. Around this time it became known to the researchers that Mr. George's classes had not previously done group work this school year.

Groups divided the overall work of the unit in different ways. Some divided the evidence, assigning each student to review a portion of the documents for the assigned case and report back. Other groups divided tasks, such as reviewing the evidence, representing the group in the debate, and writing questions to the assigned telementor. While not what we expected, some students felt strongly about the good sense of the latter division of labour. During a class session, one student said to the first author, "Why would I bother asking [my mentor] the same question that everyone else is asking? That's just a waste of the mentor's time."

We also observed some inequitable division of labor among the groups. While some students were working extraordinarily hard interpreting the archival materials and discussing them with their teammates, the lab often seemed too quiet. It became apparent over time that a few students had well-practiced techniques for *appearing* busy. A typical ruse was to fill the computer screen with a pdf document from the online archive and stare at it (usually with one iPod earbud in) until approached. As a teacher or researcher approached, the student would begin to click the mouse rapidly.

Mr. George attempted (with some success) to get students back on task by assigning the whole class worksheets that gave them "accountability" (his word) for how they spent their lab time. His two-column worksheet simplified the task of reviewing the documents into accumulating evidence for and against the claim that Canada acted compassionately in each case. This paper-and-pencil task did help to focus more students' attention, though it also took time away from making contributions to the online discussion or seeking telementors' advice.

On day 6, the final day before the "horseshoe" debate, Mr. George brought the class back to his classroom. He reviewed the plan for the horseshoe debate, explaining that each team should appoint a spokesperson to present their position on the question, "Has Canada become more compassionate?" He then handed out a worksheet, on which he told students to summarize the evidence supporting their case.

Distribution of this worksheet led to a flurry of student activity. Several teams now felt they were short on evidence, so Mr. George allowed a single delegate from each team to go to the computer lab for a few minutes to bring back necessary material for the group's case. At the end of the period, each team was required to turn in the worksheet to ensure that it would be available to the team for the horseshoe debate regardless of who might be absent the next day.

On the final day of the implementation, the "horseshoe debate" took place. This day had a shortened schedule due to an unforeseen change in the school calendar; so the usual 90-minute period was cut to 45 minutes. Students met Mr. George in the school library, which provided more space for students to spread out than was available in the classroom. After setting the scene for his students and handing each team's notes back to them, Mr. George called students up to present in their teams. Most teams had appointed a single spokesperson, who stood on the horseshoe somewhere between the "Yes" (Canada has become more compassionate) and "No" (it has not) ends to indicate its stance on the question based on the case they had studied.

In each of the three periods, the overwhelming majority of the teams stood close to the "Yes" end of the horseshoe, even if they had reviewed a case that clearly demonstrated intolerance on the part of Canadians or their governments. The few teams that stood for the No evoked a strong response from the remainder of the students. The members of most teams stood together to show consensus, though there were some exceptions. Mr. George dismissed most teams with a simple "good job," though in a few instances he probed students for additional justification, or re-voiced their stance to clarify it for himself and the rest of the class. Students asked very few questions of their peers, except when a group stood close to the "No" end of the horseshoe.

In the final days of the implementation, students completed two activities. First, they completed a post-unit survey that re-assessed their metahistorical conceptions, and requested their evaluations of the helpfulness of their telementors. On the following class day, they wrote the in-class essay based on the main question of the unit.

ANSWERS FROM THE CLASSROOM

In this section we will share instances from the classroom observations that address the questions we framed earlier around the online data. In the next section, we develop a series of design-related questions out of these instances, which we believe we would not have asked if we had not carried out our observations.

How Did Interest in the Unit Vary?

On the first day of the implementation, after O'Neill and George introduced the unit, O'Neill asked how the students felt about the project. In response one student, Tommy, exclaimed "I'm excited" and "Let's go!" His body language and tone were not as excited as the statements would seem to indicate, but his tone was not facetious either. At the end of the class, a student is heard to say "That was very interesting." Others are talking about the pre-survey questions as they file out of the classroom.

In another class, there were early signs of resistance to the novelty and challenge of the telementoring project. After the introduction, one student asked, "Is this for grades?" Mr. George explained that the topics for the telementoring project were part of the core curriculum, and that it that would be marked, based on an in-class essay. A student exclaims, "Are you serious?" Students look around at one another. A girl who had arrived late to class asks, "Can we decide not to do this?" Mr. George responds, "I don't recall giving you an option, Jessica." Another student laments, "Oh, man." There is chatter in the class.

Why Did Some of the Students Not Write More?

Classroom observation data suggested a variety of reasons why students did not participate online as much as might have been possible under the circumstances. One clear reason was that students often formulated their posted notes as a group, without explicitly noting this in their text. Group postings had been encouraged as a way to ensure that teams discussed their ongoing work and developed their interpretations of the historical documents together.

Some groups worked together to come up with questions and responses for their mentors; others appeared to work individually, and spoke with one another only occasionally about what they wanted to do. Other groups displayed even less interaction, sitting apart from one another in the computer lab.

A group in the third block provides a useful illustration. The group consisted of Michelle, as team leader; Ken; Adel; and Tania. They seated themselves between two rows of computers. While many students sat four in a row, making it difficult for the whole group to talk, this group sat in two different rows and turned their chairs around so that they were able to face one another.

Michelle says, "What do you guys want to say? We're all athletic. We can say we're great high school students." Ken says, "We can mention we're doing a project." A few minutes later, Michelle is found to be flipping through a book. Ken and Adel are playing with Knowledge Forum, testing out different features.

Later, Michelle and Tania are observed flipping through a book unrelated to the class. Adel is looking over the timelines. After another few minutes, Tania asks, "What are we writing?"

Michelle replies, "No idea. What do you guys want to write?"

Ken says, "Do you have a [piece of] paper?"

Michelle tears a sheet of paper from her binder and hands it to Ken.

Ken asks, "From all of us?"

Michelle says, "Yes."

Ken sets himself to writing out the group response on paper. Adel continues clicking through the case documents on Knowledge Forum. Later, the group is observed watching Michelle as she begins typing out Ken's introduction to the telementor.

Students often divided labour in surprising ways like this, partly due to the physical arrangement of space in the computer lab environment, which was not very conducive to group work. Students were required to take initiative (by moving furniture) or negotiate difficult social situations (asking classmates to move from where they were comfortably seated) in order to work together well. A number of students in each class were evidently not enthusiastic enough about the project to take this kind of initiative. These students fell into off-task behaviour to keep themselves occupied when there was no clear way to contribute to group work.

How Well Did Students Understand What They Were Supposed to Do?

Despite our best efforts to clarify expectations for students, they appeared to face confusion on a number of fronts. These included the nature of the work they were intended to do with primary source documents, and the overarching question of the unit. Because these elements were novel to students, Mr. George and the design team had expected some confusion; and we had hoped that the telementors would play an important role in addressing this confusion. However, at times the level of confusion seemed too great for students to meet it in such a head-on fashion as posting a note to their mentors.

For example, one day in the third block, Darlene (a student) was heard to ask John (her teammate) "Did you read any articles?" John replies: "Yeah, but I don't know what I'm looking for." She then asks, "Do you think Canada is more compassionate or not?" He replies, "I don't think so."

Later in the same class period, Darlene asks O'Neill for help. She and her group are working on the Komagata Maru case. O'Neill says, "Mr. George wants a little more evidence to argue the case." Martin asks, "So, do we have to start with article 1?" O'Neill says, "You don't have to go through each. Let's go back to see what [the case backgrounder] says." Darlene says, "It shows how difficult it was." O'Neill agrees, offering his own interpretation of the story. Then he asks "Do you think an apology [from the government] is enough?" Darlene does not respond.

Martin changes the subject, asking, "How long do our notes for Mr. George have to be?" O'Neill: "Two to three paragraphs; five minutes. You need to explain [the case] to people who haven't read the documents you have, and give them ideas." Martin and Darlene say they are more on track now. O'Neill says, "You asked a good question. Basically, you'll need to be able to explain the case from scratch. What happened? Was it a bad thing? What happened at the end? Has there been any change? You might want to refer to a document at the beginning of the timeline and one at the end of the timeline."

While in this case students consulted a member of the design team and had their attention re-focused on finding evidence of change over time within the case documents, other students understood the question of the unit quite differently. Even at the end of the unit, some students thought that the point of the question, "has Canada become more compassionate" was to compare each historical case to life in the present day. In this light, the preponderance of students advocating for "yes" makes sense. Students correctly interpreted many of the cases as showing that in the past, government policies and actions were prejudicial or abusive to minority groups. Some students then reasoned that if they did not know of similarly prejudicial or abusive actions today, they had to assume that some improvement had taken place. For these students, the notion of working like historians to assess evidence of change in the historical record got lost.

QUESTIONS FROM THE CLASSROOM

The observational data we have discussed here is just a part of what was collected during our pilot of the unit. As mentioned above, our team also collected pre and post assessments of students' metahistorical conceptions, which showed that students made significant progress with regard to the learning objectives we initially set out (O'Neill & Guloy, 2010). Students' appreciation for the methodical work that historians do increased significantly during the two-week unit, and their allegiance to naïve ideas about the existence of "one true story" about any past event reduced in response to their mentors' advice. However, it is possible to do better; and without classroom observation data it would be difficult to know how improvements might be made.

Our classroom observations gave us, as designers, a clearer view of the elements that need to be in place for our program to work more effectively. The instances above, together with others, raised two important design questions.

1. How can we help teachers make students' group work more effective?

As discussed above, much of the teamwork during the unit appeared less effective than it might have been. As designers, we had left both the assignment of the teams and the arrangement of tasks within each team in Mr. George's hands. As it turned out, his class had not done any small-group work earlier in the school year, and had no established routines to guide this. The group work was challenging in itself for the students, but this challenge was compounded by the computer lab setting. Mr. George was a frequent user of technology in his classroom, but he was not a frequent user of the school computer labs. Thus, neither he nor the design team anticipated the challenges students faced working in this cramped environment, where teammates could not easily sit together to negotiate how they would pursue their work.

In a post-unit debriefing, Mr. George suggested that for future implementations, using a lab with one computer per student might not be necessary. Instead, it might be more productive for each team of students to have one or two wireless laptops that they could use in the classroom. In this setting, students could bring their desks together and talk more easily, while still having access to the online archives and their telementors.

Another set of important lessons for us stemmed from the worksheets that Mr. George created to support his students' work. These had significant impact on how students directed their effort, but we might never have known this if we had not been in the classroom ourselves. In future implementations, we will consider using versions of Mr. George's prompts in the online environment. In this way, students would be able to benefit from them while also providing their telementors with more online work to respond to.

2. How might we prevent the main question of the unit from being misinterpreted in the future?

As noted above, we learned that the driving question of the unit was understood by some students in ways that the design team had not expected. Such differing interpretations are important, because students' understanding of the question drove both their exploration of the case evidence and their work with their telementors.

Considering our experiences with the students, the problem may not lie not in the wording of the question itself, but in the way the case materials are organized. We meant for students and their mentors to assess evidence for change within the documents provided for each case, and later (during the debate) between cases. For some students, however, it seemed natural to assume that if they were given documentation about an event in the distant past, a question about change implied comparison with the present. For our next implementation of the unit, we are trying to address this issue by constructing matched pairs of cases – one from the more distant past, and one more recent. In this way we aim to make it clear that the question asks students to examine evidence of change in the documentary record, not to compare the past with the present. This change should help students stay more focused on the evidence, which in turn should make for deeper engagement with telementors and greater improvement in metahistorical conceptions.

CONCLUSION

Part of the reason we committed the resources to observe every class session for Compassionate Canada was that this was a brand-new telementored unit. Despite having carried out several telementoring projects before, there were many unknowns about how students would respond to the overarching question of the new unit and the materials we had prepared. Due to previous experience, we knew that students sometimes have surprising interpretations of tools and practices that seem basic to adults (O'Neill & Weiler, 2006); thus, we felt it was essential to understand the variety of ways in which the unit would be interpreted by the teacher and students "on the ground." As happens in nearly every legitimate process of invention, however, what we learned was different from what we set out to discover (Vincenti, 1990).

Our main purpose in this chapter was to illustrate how classroom observations can benefit the designers of telementoring programs, and the students and teachers they serve. The possible benefits include lessons about specific refinements that may be necessary in program design, insights about infrastructure that might be necessary or helpful for a successful implementation, and most of all, insights about the professional development that participating teachers might find useful. This last point is particularly important, since as Martin (2005) suggested, the literature contains very little in the way of evidence-based advice for teachers pursuing telementoring.

Through our observations we learned at least three lessons that have implications for the professional development we can offer teachers in the future. First, we learned that students sometimes misunderstand the central question of our unit to imply a comparison between each of the historical cases and the present day. So, teachers need to check students' understanding of the question, and guard against this possibility. Second, we learned that paper worksheets can be somewhat effective in guiding students' work with the case evidence, though they also take time away from students' work with their telementors. In the future, if teachers have particular prompts that they feel would work for their students, it may be better for the design team to integrate them into the online environment. Finally, we learned that while having one computer per student might seem ideal for a telementoring project, a more ideal infrastructure may be a smaller number of wireless laptops that could be used flexibly in the classroom, offering fewer impediments to small group work.

Overall, our experience suggests that in the case of a curriculum-focused program like Compassionate Canada, generic training about the nature of telementoring or computer-mediated communications is not likely to be sufficient. Similarly, training that emphasizes administrative practices like checking up on students and keeping them in touch with their mentors will be of limited use. When a program demands intellectually challenging work of students, it is inevitable that teachers will need to provide classroom support, just as Mr. George did. The key question that professional development should help teachers to answer is how to provide this support in ways that are coherent with the goals of the program. With the help of practicing teachers, each program must be able to provide its own answers to this question.

ACKNOWLEDGMENT

We would like to thank the Canadian Council on Learning for its generous support of this research under the Structured Learning program. Several of our teacher colleagues offered invaluable support with regard to the design of the Compassionate Canada unit, its implementation, and/or its evaluation. We would like to thank Daryl Anderson, Jocelyn Beaton, Tom Morton, and Damian Wilmann for all of their guidance and support. Several other members of our research team contributed to the work reported here, including Özlem Sensoy, Fiona MacKellar, Nisha Parhar, Emma Staples and Yi Ran Dong. Finally, we also thank three anonymous peer reviewers for their feedback on an earlier version of this chapter.

REFERENCES

Banks, J. A. (2008). Diversity, group identity and citizenship education in a global age. *Educational Researcher*, *37*(3), 129–139. doi:10.3102/0013189X08317501

Brescia, W. (2005). Developing a telementoring taxonomy to improve online discussions. In Kochan, F., & Pascarelli, J. (Eds.), *Creating successful telementoring programs* (pp. 75–103). Greenwich, CT: Information Age Publishing.

diSessa, A. (2002). A history of conceptual change research. In Sawyer, R. (Ed.), *Cambridge handbook of the learning sciences* (pp. 265–281). West Nyack, NY: Cambridge University Press.

Harris, J. B., & Jones, G. (1999). A descriptive study of telementoring among students, subject matter experts, and teachers: Message flow and function patterns. *Journal of Research on Computing in Education*, *32*(1), 36–53.

Johnson, D. W., & Johnson, R. T. (2009). Energizing learning: The instructional power of conflict. *Educational Researcher*, *38*(1), 37–51. doi:10.3102/0013189X08330540

Lee, P. (2004). Understanding history. In Seixas, P. (Ed.), *Theorizing Historical Consciousness*. Toronto: University of Toronto Press.

Limon, M. (2001). On the cognitive conflict as an instructional strategy for conceptual change: A critical appraisal. *Learning and Instruction*, *11*, 357–380. doi:10.1016/S0959-4752(00)00037-2

Martin, A. (2005). *Shared responsibilities of teachers and mentors in a curriculum-based telementoring project in the humanities.* Unpublished Master's thesis, Simon Fraser University, Burnaby, British Columbia.

O'Neill, D. K. (2001). Knowing when you've brought them in: Scientific genre knowledge and communities of practice. *Journal of the Learning Sciences, 10*(3), 223–264. doi:10.1207/S15327809JLS1003_1

O'Neill, D. K., & Guloy, S. (2010, April, 2010). *The Historical Account Differences survey: Enriching methods for assessing metahistorical understanding in complex school environments.* Paper presented at the Annual Meeting of the American Educational Research Association, Denver, CO.

O'Neill, D. K., & Weiler, M. J. (2006). Cognitive tools for understanding history: What more do we need? *Journal of Educational Computing Research, 35*(2), 179–195. doi:10.2190/H22P-7718-81G5-0723

Seixas, P. (Ed.). (2004). *Theorizing Historical Consciousness.* Toronto: University of Toronto Press.

Shemilt, D. (1987). Adolescent ideas about evidence and methodology in History. In Portal, C. (Ed.), *The History curriculum for teachers.* London, England: The Falmer Press.

Shemilt, D. (2000). The caliph's coin: The currency of narrative frameworks in History teaching. In Stearns, P. N., Seixas, P., & Wineburg, S. (Eds.), *Knowing, teaching and learning History: National and international perspectives* (pp. 83–101). New York: New York University Press.

Vincenti, W. G. (1990). *What engineers know and how they know it: Analytical studies from aeronautical history.* Baltimore, MD: The Johns Hopkins University Press.

Vosniadou, S. (2007). Conceptual change and education. *Human Development, 50*(1), 47–54. doi:10.1159/000097684

Wineburg, S. (2001). *Historical thinking and other unnatural acts: Charting the future of teaching the past.* Philadelphia: Temple University Press.

Zinn, H. (2003). *A people's history of the United States, 1492-present.* New York: HarperCollins.

ENDNOTES

[1] We are indebted to Dr. Roland Case for the concept of the horseshoe debate.
[2] We used Knowledge Forum as our online workspace. See www.knowledgeforum.com for details.
[3] The video is available at http://www.sfu.ca/compassionatecanada/resource.html

APPENDIX: STUDENT BACKGROUNDER FOR THE KOMAGATA MARU CASE

On May 23, 1914 the Japanese steam liner The Komagata Maru dropped anchor in Burrard inlet [along the shoreline of Vancouver] after having picked up passengers as she had sailed from Hong Kong, to Shanghai and then on to Japan before arriving in Canadian waters. The ship had been carrying 376 passengers—the majority of whom were Sikhs originally from Punjab. Aside from 22 individuals who were returning to Canada, authorities refused to allow the remaining passengers to land as it was claimed that they had violated an Order-in-Council requiring immigrants from Asia to come via direct passage to Canada.

While a heated legal battle took place on land between immigration officials and lawyers for the passengers (who had had been arranged by members of the Indian community then living in British Columbia), the passengers—all of whom had British passports—were forced to remain on the ship. For many weeks, officials refused to allow basic provisions such as food and water to be taken on board.

By the end of June, the Immigration Board agreed to hear the case of Mushi Singh, a young Sikh farmer, as a test case. It was subsequently found that Mr. Singh had violated the continuous passage regulation and further that he was not in possession of the monies required for entry--$200 to be paid to the government of Canada and an additional $300 owed to the province.

After a failed attempt was made by officials to board and take control of the ship, the Komagata Maru was forced to leave Canadian waters on July 23. After heading back to East Asia, the ship eventually made its way to India. Destined for Calcutta, Indian officials forced the remaining passengers to disembark. In the events that ensued, a number of the passengers were shot and killed, and over two hundred were jailed.

Chapter 5
The Transformative Capacity of Telementoring on Self-Efficacy Beliefs:
A Design-Based Perspective

Deborah A. Scigliano
Duquesne University, USA

ABSTRACT

This chapter focuses on the intentional design of telementoring projects to enhance self-efficacy beliefs. The emphasis is on a pragmatic approach to design. Self-efficacy is defined and its importance is detailed. Intentional design which focuses upon addressing the four influences on efficacy of mastery experience, vicarious experience, verbal persuasion, and physiological state is advocated. A design-based drama telementoring research study which employed the best practices of self-efficacy and telementoring research is examined. Capacity, illustrative vignettes, and design implications for each of the four influences on self-efficacy are discussed.

INTRODUCTION

This chapter will look at the central influence that self-efficacy has on human action and how telementoring has the capacity to enhance students' self-efficacy beliefs. Three sections form the discussion.

The first section of this chapter will examine self-efficacy. Research has shown that there is a direct link between self-efficacy and achievement. The importance of finding ways to build self-efficacy in students will be discussed.

The second section will take a look at a design-based research study that examined the effects of a drama telementoring model on students' self-efficacy beliefs. Through this model, the importance of design will be seen in action. The self-efficacy research and the telementoring research that informed the drama telementoring model and the results of the model on the students' self-efficacy beliefs will be examined.

The third section of the chapter will look at capacity and design issues to promote the enhancement of self-efficacy beliefs through telementoring. The capacity that telementoring holds to address the four influences on self-efficacy will be

DOI: 10.4018/978-1-61520-861-6.ch005

discussed. The implications of intentional design to address each of the influences to maximize the effect of telementoring to enhance self-efficacy beliefs will be explored.

THE IMPORTANCE OF SELF-EFFICACY

The important role that self-efficacy beliefs play in human agency must be known and understood. The following poem reveals the pivotal influence that self-efficacy has in determining one's course of action.

State of Mind
If you think you are beaten, you are.
If you think that you dare not, you don't.
If you'd like to win, but think you can't,
It's almost certain that you won't.
If you think that you'll lose, you've lost.
For out in the world you'll find,
Success begins with a fellow's will,
It's all in the state of mind.
If you think you are outclassed, you are.
You've got to think high to rise.
You've got to be sure of yourself before
You can ever win a prize.
Life's battles don't always go
To the stronger or faster man,
But sooner or later, the man who wins
Is the man who thinks he can.

—*Jesse Owens*

The person in this poem who has the attitude that he can win is most likely a person with high self-efficacy beliefs. But, what does self-efficacy mean? What is so important about self-efficacy beliefs? Why does telementoring hold the powerful capacity to transform one's self-efficacy beliefs? These are the questions that will be explored, examined, and discussed in this chapter.

Self-Efficacy Defined

According to Bandura (1997), self-efficacy is the belief "...in one's capabilities to organize and execute the courses of action required to produce given attainments" (p. 3). Bandura (1997, 2004) stated that of all the factors in human action, none is more pervasive or more central than personal self-efficacy beliefs. Our beliefs of whether we think that we can or cannot accomplish a certain action will determine our engagement in that endeavor.

Studies have shown that people with high self-efficacy beliefs will be more motivated, will establish higher goals for themselves, will persist in pursuing those goals even in the face of obstacles or set-backs, and will ultimately achieve more than a person with low self-efficacy beliefs (Bandura, 1997, 2004; Pajares, 1996). Bandura (1997) found that high self-efficacy beliefs will increase student achievement.

All of these indicators point to the power that self-efficacy holds in each person's life. How, then, are self-efficacy beliefs formed?

Four Influences

There are four influences on self-efficacy: (a) mastery experience, (b) vicarious experience, (c) verbal persuasion, and (d) physiological state. From these four sources, one selects, interprets, integrates, and recalls information to form judgments concerning self-efficacy (Bandura, 1997, 2004; Pajares, 1997; Pintrich & Schunk, 2002).

Mastery experience is the strongest source of self-efficacy information (Bandura, 1997, 2004; Hackett & Betz, 1981; Pajares, 1993; Schunk, 1996; Usher & Pajares, 2008). This influence is based on the successful performance of prior behaviors and actions. Successful performance is the strongest way to build self-efficacy beliefs. This influence is the most powerful because it provides authentic information about one's capabilities. As one experiences an improvement in skills, an increase in self-efficacy is usually experienced (Usher & Pajares, 2008).

Vicarious experience has a weaker influence on efficacy beliefs than mastery experience (Pajares, 1997). Watching someone who is similar in competence to yourself perform something successfully gives you information to believe that you can also accomplish that (Usher & Pajares, 2008). This influence involves modeling which is an effective way to promote self-efficacy. A significant model can help to instill influential self-efficacy beliefs (Bandura, 2004; Pajares, 1997; Pintrich & Schunk, 2002; Usher, 2009; Woolfolk Hoy, 2003/2004).

Verbal persuasion involves feedback from others that they believe that you can accomplish something. This influence is weaker than mastery experience and vicarious experience (Pajares, 1997). High quality feedback can promote the self-efficacy beliefs of students (Wang & Wu, 2008). Efficacy is built when persuasion is from a trusted source (Pintrich & Schunk, 2002). Bandura (2004) noted that effective persuasion to build efficacy involves structuring successful tasks and avoiding placing people in situations that could lead to pre-mature failure. Pajares (1997) noted that "Persuaders must cultivate people's beliefs in their capabilities while at the same time ensuring that the envisioned success is attainable" (p. 4).

Physiological state refers to information such as heart rate, sweating, and mood that gives indications that will guide efficacy judgments (Bandura, 1997, 2004; Pintrich & Schunk, 2002; Schunk, 1996; Usher & Pajares, 2008). If a person has sweaty palms before giving a speech, he may interpret that as a sign that he is lacking the necessary skills to perform the action successfully which would indicate a low sense of self-efficacy for speaking. Conversely, if that same person experiences sweaty palms and attributes them to the fact that the room is hot, this same physical information will not lower his self-efficacy beliefs for speaking. A positive mood can enhance self-efficacy while a depressed mood can decrease efficacy (Bandura, 2004).

Subskill Structure

Successful accomplishment of complex tasks is mastered if they are broken into subskills. These subskills should be arranged in a hierarchical fashion from simple to complex (Bandura, 1997). A subskill structure should aid in the development of perceived self-efficacy beliefs. Pintrich and Schunk (2002) noted that "Progress toward difficult goals raises efficacy because it conveys that students are improving" (p. 165).

This holds important information for building self-efficacy beliefs in those who are involved in telementoring projects. The telementoring project should be designed to begin with simpler tasks that will be easily mastered. This will build self-efficacy beliefs. As each performance is mastered, increasingly more difficult tasks can be added. The information from the successfully-completed tasks will build the self-efficacy to engage in the more difficult tasks.

Specificity

Although a general sense of self-efficacy does exist within each person, self-efficacy beliefs are more predictive of achievement when examined in reference to a specific performance (Pajares, 1996; Pintrich & Schunk, 2002). One might have high self-efficacy in writing and low self-efficacy in mathematics.

Therefore, efforts to increase self-efficacy are best served by focusing on achievements in specific domains (Wang & Wu, 2008). Increasing efficacy beliefs in arts, content areas, social interaction, technology, specific sports, or other specific areas are indicated in the design of telementoring projects.

Implications of Self-Efficacy for Schools

Self-efficacy beliefs are influential in the choices that people make and the courses of action that they decide to pursue. Raising self-efficacy increases motivation and achievement. Self-efficacy research has demonstrated the importance of a high sense of self-efficacy to engage, sustain effort and, ultimately, achieve, in chosen activities. One needs a strong sense of efficacy to overcome constant rejections in their endeavors.

The effects of personal self-efficacy on the large society point to the imperative to find education practices that will raise student self-efficacy beliefs. Inefficacious-feeling people will not make an efficacious group (Bandura, 1982). The power of the effects of personal self-efficacy on society is indicated by Bandura's (1982) statement "Our own collective efficacy will shape, in turn, how future generations will live their lives" (p. 145). This collective efficacy has implications for schools to find practices that will build self-efficacy.

The importance for schools to cultivate efficacy in students was reflected in three statements by Bandura (1997). Bandura (1997) stated:

Peoples' regrets commonly center on educational opportunities forsaken, valued careers not pursued, interpersonal relationships not cultivated, risks not taken, and failures to exercise a stronger hand in shaping one's life course. Turning visions into realities is an arduous process with uncertain outcomes. Societies enjoy the considerable benefits of the eventual accomplishments in the arts, sciences and technologies of its persisters and risk takers. Optimistic self-appraisals of capability raise aspirations and sustain motivation in ways that enable people to get the most out of their talents. (pp. 71-71)

From these statements, the importance of building self-efficacy can be envisioned. Schools have a vital role to play in shaping efficacy beliefs. Telementoring, in particular, holds the capacity to transform the efficacy beliefs of those who are involved in the telementoring experience.

Implications for the Transformative Capacity of Telementoring upon Self-Efficacy Beliefs

The powerful influence of self-efficacy upon the choices that shape lives, both individually and collectively, has been demonstrated in the literature. The need for ways to build efficacy in students is indicated. How, then, can telementoring be used to transform self-efficacy beliefs?

The four influences on efficacy of (a) mastery experience, (b) vicarious experience, (c) verbal persuasion, and (d) physiological state provide the avenues by which to transform self-efficacy beliefs. Hackett & Betz (1981) noted, "These four avenues by which self-efficacy can be strengthened or weakened interact complexly and require comprehensive interventions which address at least several sources of efficacy information" (p. 337). Telementoring offers an optimal venue for addressing each of the influences and transforming self-efficacy beliefs.

The remainder of this chapter will examine the capacity of telementoring to influence self-efficacy beliefs in each of the four influences. Educational practices that seek to build efficacy beliefs need to address the four influences on efficacy judgments (Scigliano, 1999).

The design implications for creating telementoring projects that build students' self-efficacy beliefs will be explicitly discussed.

Telementoring and Self-Efficacy: Design in Action

Drama Telementoring Model

The drama telementoring project in the Scigliano (1999) study consisted of twenty 30-minute class sessions. The project goal was the writing and enactment of a play. The students were mentored online by a practicing artist who was a children's theatre director.

The telementor acted as a guide, coach, and model. Serving in these roles as an expert, the telementor had the capacity to influence self-efficacy beliefs through the influences of mastery experience and verbal persuasion. The feedback that was given by the telementor served to inform the students of their progress.

Prior to beginning the project, the telementor introduced himself to the students via e-mail. The telementor presented a brief biographical portrait so that a personal presence was mediated. The importance of establishing this personal presence was noted by Shamp (1991) who found that in the absence of personal content, the perceptions of the computer-mediated communication partners were similar to computer characteristics.

E-mail correspondence occurred through the classroom teacher. The students composed their correspondences which the teacher transmitted to the telementor. The telementor's responses were sent to the teacher who then printed out individual copies for each student.

Frequent e-mail exchanges were encouraged between the students and the telementor. Twice a week was the goal with a quick turn-around time from the telementor.

The playwriting tasks were designed to progress from simpler to more difficult tasks. The initial sessions were devoted to writing dialogues. These dialogues were written by students in groups of two and three. The dialogues of other students and adult playwrights were read and analyzed during this time period.

The remaining sessions were devoted to writing scenes. Prior dialogues were discussed to decide if they could be used to enlarge into scenes or if new scenes needed to be created. The finalized scenes became the final pieces that were enacted in a school performance.

Students read aloud their works-in-progress. They critiqued each other's work. The students shared their work with the telementor and received feedback, encouragement, and guidance.

Individual reflection on the writing process was an integral part of the sessions. The shared reflection that occurred in person and on-line added to the individual reflection.

The culminating sessions were devoted to the rehearsal and performance of each group's scenes. The performance was enacted for the students of the school.

Design

This research-based model was informed and designed using the best practices of telementoring research and self-efficacy research. The intentional design of this model was to promote self-efficacy beliefs. Following are the best practices that informed the design of this telementoring project. First, the telementoring best practices will be addressed; then, the information to inform the influences of self-efficacy will be discussed.

The telementoring literature revealed the importance of clearly communicating a telementoring project's goals (Harris & Jones, 1999; Tsikalas, 1997; Wighton, 1993). Prior to the commencement of the project, a clear explanation of the project's goals was communicated by the researcher to the telementor and the classroom teacher. This was done in order to have input into the design of the project from the telementor and the teacher. The development and planning of the project was a combined effort of the teacher, the telementor, and the researcher.

Sharing information, such as teaching strategies, with the telementor was noted to be essential to a successful telementoring project (Harris, O'Bryan, & Rotenberg, 1996; McGee, 1997). Lenert and Harris (1994) expressed that teachers should "...be willing to share information about their curriculum instructional strategies, and students when necessary...." (p. 15). This sharing of information was demonstrated in the Sanchez and Harris (1996) study when the teacher gave the telementor tips on tailoring his presentation for their learning. The telementor was able to experience greater success with his mentored students because of the teacher's guidance.

The self-efficacy literature revealed essential elements to inform the design of the telementoring project to promote the development of self-efficacy beliefs in the areas of writing efficacy and social efficacy. The first design element was the sub-skill structure.

According to Bandura (1992, 1997) complex tasks are mastered if they are broken into sub-skills and arranged in a hierarchical fashion. This structure also addressed Harris et al.'s (1996) advice for telementoring projects to contain "...a strong subtask structure...." (p. 55). To employ this subskill structure, the playwriting tasks were designed to provide a progression from simpler to more difficult tasks. Writing dialogues comprised the first sessions of the project. The students progressed to writing scenes. Finally, the students enacted their scenes in front of others.

The drama telementoring project was designed to incorporate all four influences on self-efficacy. The influence of mastery experience was informed through the writing and enacting of dialogues and scenes. The influence of verbal persuasion was seen in the feedback from the telementor, teacher, and classmates. The influence of vicarious experience was addressed by watching and listening to classmates' performances and writing as well as through the modeling and coaching of the telementor. Physiological state information was gained through the students' performance of their work and their reflections on their physical reactions.

Results

Qualitative data revealed in the students' journals and interviews showed increases in writing efficacy. The influences on self-efficacy were reported by the students to affect their writing self-efficacy beliefs. Additionally, the subskill structure was found to aid the development of the students' perceived self-efficacy beliefs.

The subskill structure was reported by the participants to be beneficial in building their writing self-efficacy. All of the participants responded that the structure of the project, progressing from writing dialogues to writing scenes and finally performing their work, helped to inform their efficacy for writing. One participant noted, "Because once I saw that I could write the dialogue, it made it easier for me to think that I could write a play and eventually progress to performing."

Mastery experience was found to be the most frequently reported influence on the students' writing self-efficacy judgments. A total of 50 statements were presented that noted mastery experience as the source for efficacy judgments. The authentic mastery experiences of writing scenes and dialogue provided by the design of the drama telementoring model may have been responsible for this predominance of mastery experience statements. Additionally, it was documented that there was more frequent communication to the telementor than correspondence from the telementor. The frequency of writing to the telementor, another mastery experience, may have contributed to the increases reported in writing efficacy. Some of the participant statements included "I believe that I effectively expressed how our characters felt", "My partner and I made sense with our writing", and "I'm getting better at explaining myself".

Verbal persuasion was the second most frequently noted source of efficacy judgments. Ten statements were reported that indicated verbal persuasion as an efficacy source. The design of this project provided a number of avenues for verbal persuasion to occur. These avenues included teacher to student, student to student, and telementor to student interaction. The wording of the interview question for verbal persuasion referred to the telementor as the only source for this influence. There is a possibility that if the question had been broadened to include classroom teacher and classmate feedback, this may have been a more strongly reported influence. Participant responses for this influence included

"Because...having the telementor really helped me" and "After we performed, a lot of the people that we asked how they felt about our play, they said it was really good and it was interesting and it was strong...".

Vicarious experience was the third most frequently reported influence. There were a total of 6 statements citing this influence on efficacy judgment. Self-efficacy research has shown that this influence is stronger than verbal persuasion. Although this study did not support this finding, vicarious experience was definitely present as described by the participants. The design of the project may have contributed to this lowered reporting of this influence. The project was designed to use feedback from the telementor and other project participants thus allowing more opportunities for verbal persuasion to operate as an influence. Integrating more opportunities to view other students' work into the design may have increased the influence of vicarious experience to operate. "We listened to other people's plays today. I think ours compares pretty well with everyone else's...." and "Today my group finished our story....Also we heard other people's plays. Our story was pretty good compared to others."

The least reported influence was physiological state. Four statements referred to physiological state as an influence on efficacy judgments. Affective information from physiological state has been shown to be the weakest of the four influences of self-efficacy beliefs. The presence of this information was noted especially during the performance phase of the project. One participant responded, "I was really nervous because I practiced it so much so I knew I could do it."

Hackett and Betz (1981) discussed the importance of interventions that address the influences on self-efficacy beliefs. "These four avenues by which self-efficacy can be strengthened or weakened interact complexly and require comprehensive interventions which address at least several sources of efficacy information" (Hackett & Betz, 1981, p. 337).

Telementoring has demonstrated the capacity to transform student self-efficacy beliefs. It is through the intentional design of telementoring projects to address the four influences on self-efficacy beliefs and promote a subskill structure that this transformative capacity will have the greatest opportunity to operate.

The influences on self-efficacy will now be discussed in four sections. Each section will examine telementoring's capacity to address the information received through each influence, provide an illustrative vignette from the research to show telementoring in action that addresses each influence, and the design implications to bring about changes in efficacy beliefs through each influence.

Mastery Experience

Capacity

The most powerful influence on self-efficacy beliefs is mastery experience, also known as performance accomplishment (Bandura, 1997, 2004; Gresham, Evans, & Elliott, 1988; Hackett & Betz, 1981; Pajares, 1997; Schunk, 1996). According to Gresham et al. (1988), "Performance accomplishments represent the strongest basis of personal efficacy because individuals have the personal experience of successfully performing certain behaviors in the past" (p. 238).

Telementoring works best when used in connection with a specific project or task (Cobb, 1997; Donker, 1993; Doyle, 1995; Harris et al., 1996; Lenert & Harris, 1994; Harris & Jones, 1999; McGee, 1997; O'Neill, 1996; O'Neill & Harris, 2004/2005; Sanchez & Harris, 1996; Wighton, 1993). The use of actual performances addresses the capacity of telementoring to influence mastery experience, the strongest of the influences on self-efficacy beliefs.

Science has been one of the most widely-implemented uses of telementoring (Amill, 2002; Dimock, 1996; Far West Lab., 1995; O'Neill,

2001, 2004; O'Neill & Harris, 2004/2005; O'Neill, Wagner, & Gomez, 1996; Weir, 1992). The arts and humanities have also been used successfully to create telementoring projects (Sanchez & Harris, 1996; Scigliano, 1999).

The engagement in specific projects or tasks which increase competence has the capacity to increase self-efficacy beliefs in that particular domain. Self-efficacy is most predictive of achievement when specificity is involved. Pajares (1996) noted that assessments of students' self-efficacy beliefs are more predictive when they are asked to show their confidence in math or writing rather than omnibus measurements of efficacy.

Illustrative Vignette

The capacity for the development of self-efficacy in critical thinking skills through the influence of mastery experience can be seen in the following telementoring vignette. O'Neill and Harris (2004/2005) detailed the profound effect that engagement in a 10th Grade Social Studies project had upon the students who were involved in it. This telementoring project was titled "Tracking Canada's Past". Students from a number of cities participated in this project each year for 10 weeks.

One mentee developed a keen interest in a controversial Canadian figure whose fate of arrest and hanging for treason is still debated by historians. The telementor asked guiding questions without giving clear-cut answers. Through this process, the mentee was given the opportunity to crucially read the historical accounts and then synthesize and evaluate them for herself.

This synthesis and evaluation can be seen in an excerpt from this mentee's final paper. The first sentence reflects the majority viewpoint of Canadian historians; the remainder shows the thoughts and questions of the mentee's reflections as she challenges the majority perspective that the effect that the building of the Canadian Pacific Railway had on the native peoples of Canada:

The Canadian Pacific Railway linked the hearts of all Canadians....However, is this the real picture of what the CPR brought to ALL Canadians? What about the First Nations?...Did the CPR link their hearts also?...Their hearts were torn into pieces as Donald Smith drove the last spike of the CPR. (O'Neill & Harris, 2004/2005, p. 115)

Through this process, the mentee was able to create a successful mastery experience. The guiding questions of the telementor helped her to analyze and synthesize her own view of the historical events, even to the point of being able to challenge the majority viewpoint of these events.

Design Implications

The design of a telementoring project that will promote success is a crucial first step in promoting efficacy beliefs through the influence of mastery experience. The nature of the project should be active and student-driven as noted in the telementoring literature (Lenert & Harris, 1994; McGee, 1997). Telementoring communications should be student-centered with active, inquiry-based interaction (Harris et al., 1996). The project should be designed to yield benefits to inform students through the successful attainment of specific achievement.

Although success builds a "robust efficacy" (Bandura, 2004, p. 79), easy success is not a goal for which to aim. Bandura (2004) noted that easy success can lead to discouragement when faced with failure. Instead, a sense of resilient efficacy is developed through overcoming obstacles and learning how to manage failure (Bandura, 2004). Telementors can inform their mentees how to cope with setbacks and failures while persevering in their development of skills and knowledge.

An important design principle consider in order to accomplish this goal is the use of a subskill structure. Unfold your desired outcome for the mentee's achievement and examine the necessary skills that will be needed to attain that outcome. Arrange the skills in a hierarchy from simple to complex. Provide suitable opportunities to engage in the performance of these skills at each level in order to promote success.

Vicarious Experience

Capacity

Watching similar others perform successfully increases our self-efficacy beliefs that we can also accomplish those tasks (Bandura, 1992, 2004). Schunk (1996) found that peer observation will raise efficacy beliefs. Also, a significant model can help to influence self-beliefs (Bandura, 1997, 2004; Gresham et al., 1988; Pajares, 1997; Usher, 2009; Woolfolk Hoy, 2003/2004).

Bandura (1997) noted that the situation of modeling can be seen to develop knowledge and skills with the help of proficient models. The comparison to one's current skill level with an eye to improved skill development through the aid of the proficient model helps to promote a positive self-appraisal.

Telementors provide this proficient modeling role. There are several models of telementoring including (a) one-to-one, (b) small group to one telementor, (c) whole class to one telementor, and (d) mentoring in the open. Each of these involves the observation of others either as similar others or as an expert model. This observational learning demonstrates the capacity of telementoring to influence self-efficacy beliefs through the influence of vicarious experience.

Illustrative Vignette

O'Neill (2004) illustrated the capacity of telementoring for addressing vicarious experience. This study examined groups of telementors and mentees who used a software application which allowed the groups to view each other's work. This model was referred to as telementoring in the open.

Exemplary work was shared in this open online environment. This permitted students to see models and to vicariously learn from these experiences. The following response by a mentee illustrated this vicarious learning. "But if something was really helpful, [our mentor] would highlight it. She would tell us, 'OK, go into Andrea's [note] and see.' She would say, 'Alright, she did this, and this is what you were supposed to do'..." (O'Neill, 2004, pp. 199-200).

Those students who watched the mentoring relationships of others in this online environment became more selective in what they expected of the telementoring experience. The students were able to self-regulate their performance by watching their peers. They began to model the best practices that they observed in their peers and their peers' telementors (O'Neill, 2004).

Design Implications

There are two factors to keep in mind when designing a telementoring experience that will use the influence of vicarious experience. One is to provide opportunities to watch similar others perform. Another is to provide opportunities for modeling to occur.

Building opportunities to share works in progress will help students to increase their efficacy judgments. "Observing the success of peers can enhance both achievement and self-efficacy if the peers are perceived as similar in competence" (Bandura, 1992, p. 333).

Bandura (1997) noted that dissimilar others can also be vicarious builders of efficacy. "Progressive mastery of modeled skills and strategies through observational learning increases perceived similarity to initially dissimilar proficient models" (Bandura, 1997, p. 101). This speaks directly to the capacity that telementors can provide in modeling skills and behaviors for their mentees. Mentees can learn vicariously from the skilled telementor through observational learning.

As students correspond with their telementors, they can share their progress during the duration of the project. Designing regular opportunities to share work during the telementoring experience will allow the influence of vicarious experience to operate. The culmination of the project provides an additional time to share the completed work and give the students another opportunity to watch their peers.

The telementor and the classroom teacher each can serve as models for students. A significant model in one's life can help to instill influential self-beliefs (Pajares, 1997). Telementors give support and encouragement which are similar to traditional mentor roles (White-Hood, 1993).

Communicating with the telementor prior to the commencement of the telementoring experience will enhance the likelihood of modeling taking place. Informing the telementor of role-appropriate behavior will also increase the success of the telementor (Sanchez & Harris, 1996).

Proficient models help to develop a person's knowledge and skills (Bandura, 1997). Telementors are proficient models and play an important role in developing the mentee's skills and knowledge through modeling. One point to keep in mind in effectively modeling skills is to explicitly discuss strategies and thought processes that are needed for problem-solving endeavors (Bandura, 1997). This thinking-made-visible will help to develop needed cognitive skills.

Verbal Persuasion

Capacity

Feedback from others can influence self-efficacy beliefs. Schunk (1996) noted the importance of giving progress feedback to students in order to build self-efficacy. Proximal, short-term, goals would lead to increased self-efficacy.

High quality feedback serves to promote students' efficacy beliefs (Wang & Wu, 2008). The messages that students receive concerning their academic competence from significant adults in their lives may linger with them for the rest of their lives (Usher, 2009).

Bandura (2004) noted that persuaders do more than give positive feedback.

In order to build efficacy, one must structure experiences that will bring success and avoid premature failure. "Pep talks without enabling guidance achieve little" (Bandura, 2004, p. 7).

The influence of verbal persuasion may indeed prove to be even more important for students with low self-efficacy beliefs. Usher (2009) found that students with high self-efficacy reported persuasive messages that were beneficial to them and encouraged them to reach their goals and surpass others' achievements. However, students with low self-efficacy reported that they received limited or no positive feedback which, in turn, lowered their self-efficacy beliefs.

The capacity for telementoring to increase students' self-efficacy beliefs through the influence of verbal persuasion is considerable. Telementors provide feedback (Friedman, Zibit, & Coote, 2004, Kerka, 1998, Wolf & Witte, 2005). With the appropriate understanding of the nature of effective feedback for enhancing self-efficacy beliefs, telementors are in a key position to help to promote students' self- efficacy.

Influence in Action: Telementoring Vignette

The capacity for the feedback from telementors to influence self-efficacy beliefs through verbal persuasion can be seen in this vignette from Sanchez and Harris' 1996 study. A 10-year-old student was working on an extracurricular project with a 74-year-old English professor Emeritus. The student compared her online experience with her classroom learning. The immediacy of the feedback was a feature that she liked. She also noted that she felt that she was understood by the telementor. When the professor complimented her use of vocabulary or her questions, she felt that she was being taken seriously.

This feedback that is provided by telementors shows the powerful capacity that they hold to influence their mentees' self-efficacy beliefs through verbal persuasion. The self-efficacy literature holds guidance on how to make the most of this influence.

Design Implications

The telementor has the ability to influence self-efficacy beliefs through verbal persuasion. Maximize the role of feedback by informing the telementor of the importance of this element and sharing information on the effective use of feedback. Motivation and self-efficacy are increased when students think that they are progressing towards their goals and increasing in competence (Schunk, 1996).

Bandura (2004) addressed the importance of short-term goals as motivational agents for change. Telementors can assist in the process of helping their mentees to set achievable subgoals that result in success. Establishing realistic plans and strategies will impact the realization of goals (Bandura (2004).

The effect of feedback that addressed achievable subgoals can be seen in a 2004 writing telementoring study by Friedman et al. (2004). Friedman et al. (2004) found that all of the telementors had initial difficulties in providing effective feedback. The initial feedback was extensive in scope and provided in language that was not readily understood by their young mentees. This ineffective feedback resulted in second drafts that were not markedly changed from the first drafts.

However, over time the telementors developed effective and focused feedback that gave information to the mentee on what was working and what needed to be developed. The following excerpt from the telementor illustrates this more effective feedback, "I think you have some very good ideas here. I especially like how you have included quotations to support your ideas. I have a suggestion about writing mechanics. Capitalize the first letter of each sentence" (Friedman et al., 2004, p. 22).

The use of proximal goals and specific goals were found to promote self-efficacy more than distant goals and general goals (Pintrich & Schunk, 2002). Pintrich and Schunk (2002) suggested that contracts can be designed that state a series of short-term subgoals that progress to more distant and complex goals.

Schunk and Gunn (1986) found that ability feedback, "You show a strength in this", promoted higher self-efficacy than effort feedback, "You really worked hard on this". Pintrich and Schunk (2002) also noted that ability feedback enhances efficacy beliefs more than effort feedback.

Pajares (1997) noted, "Persuaders must cultivate people's beliefs in their capabilities while at the same time ensuring that the envisioned success is attainable" (p. 4). This is an important understanding for telementors. Cultivate this understanding by designing time into the telementoring experience to inform telementors of this prior to the commencement of the telementoring experience. Provide support, guidance, and feedback to the telementor throughout the process to maintain and enhance the most effect use of feedback.

Putnam (2009) offered specific advice for giving feedback to increase self-efficacy in students. Explicit teaching of strategies to meet goals is needed. Students need constant feedback to support the attainment of their goals. Putnam (2009) used a sandwich approach to feedback. First a strength that the student demonstrated was discussed, then an area for improvement, and finally, another area of strength. Putnam (2009) noted that it is important to note the progress that the student has made and to celebrate achievements of small goals which will lead to greater confidence.

Wang and Wu (2008) found that students who received more elaborated feedback increased their self-efficacy significantly. Dempsey, Driscoll, and

Swindell (as cited in Wang and Wu, 2008) noted that elaborated feedback gives an explanation of why the student's responses are correct or incorrect and gives information that will encourage the students to reason or evaluate correct responses.

Feedback from the teacher and class peers also provide another source of verbal persuasion. As with vicarious experience, opportunities should be provided to interact with class peers and the classroom teacher to receive feedback. Usher (2009) noted that the students in her study relied on modeling from parents, peers, and self to inform their efficacy judgments in math; however, students with high math efficacy referred to peer feedback more than they commented on feedback from adults. This finding suggests the importance of designing telementoring projects that include peer interaction and peer-assessment to help to inform self-efficacy beliefs through the influence of verbal persuasion.

The role of the telementor as a provider of feedback and as a persuader commands the necessity for understanding effective feedback that will build self-efficacy beliefs. In the design of the telementoring project, special attention needs to be paid to promoting the ability of the telementor to provide effective persuasive feedback to enhance the efficacy beliefs of the mentee.

Physiological State

Capacity

Physiological state information gives indications that guide judgments of self-efficacy (Bandura, 1997, 2004; Pintrich & Schunk, 2002; Schunk, 1996; Usher & Pajares, 2008). This information includes such things as heart rate and sweating. If a student experiences anxiety, he may believe that he lacks the necessary skills to perform successfully. Pajares (1997) stated that people often gauge their confidence by the emotions they experience as they think about an action.

This influence of physiological state informs efficacy rather than the other way around. The belief of the reason for the physical manifestations determines the information gained from the reaction. If a person has sweaty palms before performing a task and attributes the reason to feelings of incompetence, the person experiences low self-efficacy judgment for that task. If that person believes that the cause for the sweaty palms is a hot room, than efficacy is not in question (Bandura, 1997).

Usher (2009) found that all of the students in the study reported moments of heightened physiological discomfort in math. The only students who interpreted this information to show that they were not competent in math were students with low math self-efficacy. Those students who experienced the momentary disequilibrium and who had high self-efficacy in math reported feelings of content and belief in their capabilities.

Influence in Action: Telementoring Vignette

Probing questions in the post-study interview conducted by Scigliano (1999) revealed the students' feelings of self-efficacy as influence by their physiological state. The question was "Did the way you feel affect how you thought about your ability to do this?"

The responses that indicated the influence on physiological state totaled four. These were: (a) "…it (the way the participant felt) helped me to think that I could but when we actually started the play, it kind of made me feel the opposite", (b) "I was really nervous because I practiced it so much so I knew I could do it", (c) "We were excited about presenting it to some of the grades in the school so we wanted to make it interesting so that the people in the other classes would like it, like watching it", and (d) "When I was tired, I practically felt like doing nothing, when I was sick, the same thing….".

Design Implications

There are ways to inform efficacy through the influence of physiological state. Bandura (2004) stated that indications for modeling efficacy beliefs concerning physiological state include reducing stress and depression as well as addressing misinterpretations of the information gained from people's physiological states. This holds design implications for telementors to ascertain the physiological information that mentees hold that influence their self-efficacy beliefs.

Reflection is one way to access this information. The opportunity to reflect on one's physical state can help students to gauge their confidence through their emotions as they think about an action.

The implications of Usher's (2009) study indicate the need to pay close attention to the perceptions of students with low self-efficacy concerning the physiological state information that they experience. These students may experience distress, disheartenment, and paralysis (Usher, 2009). Bandura (2004) indicated the need to address the misinterpretations of the physiological perceptions of students with low self-efficacy. Telementors can play a vital role in this process.

Build reflection into the telementoring experience. Ask guiding questions that probe the affective state at times. Provide reflection for feelings of calm, anxiety, excitement, and the judgments of efficacy that these emotions indicate.

CONCLUSION

Telementoring has the capacity to transform self-efficacy beliefs. It has been shown to address the four influences of self-efficacy: (a) mastery experience, (b) vicarious experience, (c) verbal persuasion, and (d) physiological state. However, intentional design is needed in order to reap the most benefits from this transformative capacity.

There are design lessons to be learned as indicated in the literature. One overarching design implication is to incorporate as many influences on self-efficacy into telementoring experiences as possible. Telementoring has the capacity to address all of the four influences of mastery experience, vicarious experience, verbal persuasion, and physiological state.

Another design implication is to inform the telementor of the goals and intent of the project at each stage and invite and encourage the participation in the design of the project from the beginning. The telementor needs to know the importance of self-efficacy beliefs and how this telementoring role of the telementor can address these beliefs. The clear communication of how the telementoring process can transform self-efficacy will build awareness, knowledge, and intentional actions by the telementor to influence the efficacy beliefs of their mentees.

The use of a subskill structure is indicated in the design of telementoring projects. This crafting of tasks that proceed from simple to complex will aid in the development of self-efficacy beliefs.

The specificity of self-efficacy beliefs are to be taken into account when designing projects to build efficacy beliefs. Focus on specific areas of achievement in order to increase self-efficacy.

Telementoring holds great potential to affect the efficacy of those who are engaged in the experience. Intentional design will increase the capacity of any telementoring project to transform self-efficacy beliefs.

REFERENCES

Amill, L. (2002). *Telementoring: A view from the facilitator's screen.* Retrieved November 20, 2006, from http://www.serviceleader.org/old/w/direct/laura.html

Bandura, A. (1982). Self-efficacy mechanism in human agency. *The American Psychologist, 37*, 122–147. doi:10.1037/0003-066X.37.2.122

Bandura, A. (1992). Albert Bandura's social-cognitive theory. In M. E. Gredler, *Learning and instruction: Theory into practice* (pp. 302-345). New York: MacMillan Publishing Co.

Bandura, A. (1997). *Self-efficacy: The exercise of control*. New York: Freeman.

Bandura, A. (2004). Social cognitive theory for personal and social change by enabling media. In Singhal, A., Cody, M. J., Rogers, E. M., & Sabido, M. (Eds.), *Entertainmenteducation and Social Change: History, Research, and Practice* (pp. 75–96). Mahwah, NJ: Lawrence Erlbaum.

Cobb, B. (1997). *HP e-mail mentor program evaluation. September 1996 – May 1997*. Retrieved September 12, 1998 from http://mentor.external.hp.com/eval/eval9697.html

Dimock, K. V. (1996). *Building relationships, engaging students: A naturalistic study of classrooms participating in the electronic emissary project*. Retrieved September 20, 1998, from http://www.tapr.org/emissary/

Donker, H. (1993, November). *Experiences in telementoring during a computer-mediated communication (CMC) process*. Paper presented at the Conference of the New Educational Technologies and the TEMUS Programme – A Contribution to their Dissemination in Bulgaria, Sofia, Bulgaria. Retrieved September 12, 1998 from http://nsn.bbn.com/telementor_wrkshp/tmlink.htm

Doyle, C. S. (1995). Telementoring takes off in California: The telemation project develops integrated curriculum. *Internet Research: Electronic Networking Applications and Policy, 5*, 40–45. doi:10.1108/10662249510084453

Friedman, A. A., Zibit, M., & Coote, M. (2004). Telementoring as a collaborative agent for change. *Journal of Technology, Learning, and Assessment, 3*(1). Retrieved January 29, 2010 from http://www.jtla.org

Gresham, F. M., Evans, S., & Elliott, S. N. (1988). Self-efficacy differences among mildly handicapped, gifted, and nonhandicapped students. *The Journal of Special Education, 22*, 231–241. doi:10.1177/002246698802200208

Hackett, G., & Betz, N. E. (1981). A self-efficacy approach to the career development of women. *Journal of Vocational Behavior, 18*, 326–339. doi:10.1016/0001-8791(81)90019-1

Harris, J., O'Bryan, E., & Rotenberg, L. (1996). It's a simple idea, but it's not easy to do! Practical lessons in telementoring. Learning and leading with technology. *The ISTE Journal of Educational Technology Practice and Policy, 24*, 53–57.

Harris, J. B. & Jones, G. (1999). A descriptive study of telementoring among students, subject matter experts, and teachers: Message flow and function patterns. *Journal of Research on Computing in Education, 32*.

Kerka, S. (1998). *New perspectives on mentoring*. Retrieved October 5, 1998, from http://www.peer.ca/Perspectives.html

Lab, F. W. For Educational Research and Development. (1995). *Telemation project evaluation, Final report* (ERIC Document Reproduction Service No. ED 396 705). Sacramento, CA: California State Department of Education.

Lenert, K. F., & Harris, J. B. (1994). *Redefining expertise and reallocating roles in text-based asynchronous teaching/learning environments*. Retrieved October 8, 1998 from http://www.tapr.org/emissary/

McGee. P. (1997). *Collaboration and unintentional teacher learning in telementoring contexts.* Retrieved October 7, 1998 from http://www.tapr.org/emissary/

O'Neill, D. K. (2001). Knowing when you've brought them in: Scientific genre knowledge and communities of practice. *Journal of the Learning Sciences, 10*(3), 223–264. doi:10.1207/S15327809JLS1003_1

O'Neill, D. K. (2004). Building social capital in a knowledge-building community: Telementoring as a catalyst. *Interactive Learning Environments, 12*(3), 179–208. doi:10.1080/1049482051233183419

O'Neill, D. K., & Harris, J. B. (2004/2005). Bridging the perspectives and developmental needs of all participants in curriculum-based telementoring programs. *Journal of Research on Technology in Education, 37*(2), 111–128.

O'Neill, D. K., Wagner, R., & Gomez, L. M. (1996). Online mentors: Experimenting in science class. *Educational Leadership, 54*(37), 39–42.

O'Neill, K. (1996). Telementoring: One researcher's perspective. *National School Network Testbed Newsletter, 12*, 223–264.

Pajares, F. (1993). *Self-efficacy defined.* Retrieved September 1, 1998 from http://userwww.service.emory.edu/~mpajare/eff.html

Pajares, F. (1996, April). Assessing self-efficacy beliefs and academic outcomes: The case for specificity and correspondence. In B. J. Zimmerman (Chair), *Measuring and mismeasuring self-efficacy: Dimensions, problems, and misconceptions.* Symposium conducted at the annual meeting of the American Educational Research Association, New York, NY.

Pajares, F. (1997). Current directions in self-efficacy research. In Maehr, M., & Pintrich, P. R. (Eds.), *Advances in motivation and achievement* (Vol. 10, pp. 1–49). Greenwich, CT: JAI Press.

Pintrich, P. R., & Schunk, D. H. (2002). *Motivation in Education.* Upper Saddle River, NJ: Pearson Education, Inc.

Putman, M. (2009). Running the race to improve self-efficacy. *Kappa Delta Pi Record, 45*(2), 53–57.

Sanchez, B., & Harris, J. (1996). Online mentoring: A success story. Learning and leading with technology. *The ISTE Journal of Educational Technology Practice and Policy, 23*, 57–60.

Schunk, D. H. (1996, April). *Self-efficacy for learning and performance.* Paper presented at the Annual Conference of the American Education Research Association, New York, NY.

Scigliano, D. (1999). *The effects of a drama telementoring model upon students' self-efficacy beliefs.* Published doctoral dissertation, Duquesne University, Pittsburgh, PA.

Shamp, S. (1991). Mechanomorphism in perception of computer communication partners. *Computers in Human Behavior, 7*, 147–161. doi:10.1016/0747-5632(91)90004-K

Tsikalas, K. (1997). *Telementoring now.* Retrieved September 15, 1998 from http://www.uwnyc.org/7mentor.htm

Usher, E. L. (2009). Sources of middle school students' self-efficacy in mathematics: A qualitative investigation. *American Educational Research Journal, 46*(1), 275–314.. doi:10.3102/0002831208324517

Usher, E. L., & Pajares, F. (2008). Sources of self-efficacy in school: Critical review of the literature and future directions. *Review of Educational Research, 78*(4), 751–797. doi:10.3102/0034654308321456

Wang, S., & Wu, P. (2008). The role of feedback and self-efficacy on web-based learning: The social cognitive perspective. *Computers & Education, 51*(4), 1589–1598.. doi:10.1016/j.compedu.2008.03.004

Weir, S. (1992). *Electronic communities of learners: Fact or fiction*. Cambridge, MA/Washington, D. C.: TERC Communications/Department of Education and National Science Foundation.

Wighton, D. J. (1993). *Telementoring: An examination of the potential for an educational network.* Retrieved September 15, 1998 from http://mentor.creighton.edu/htm/telement.htm

Wolf, S. E., & Witte, M. M. (2005). Technology and mentoring practices within academic settings. In F. K, Kochan & J. T. Pascarelli (Eds.), *Creating Successful Telementoring Programs* (pp. 105-121). Greenwich, CT: Information Age Publishing.

Woolfolk Hoy, A. (2003/2004). Self-efficacy in college teaching. *Essays on Teaching Excellence: Toward the Best in the Academy, 15*(7). Retrieved on July 7, 2008 from http://gozips.uakron.edu/~mcgurk/number7.htm

KEY TERMS AND DEFINITIONS

Mastery Experience: The successful performance of prior behaviors and actions.

Mentee: The protégé in a telementoring relationship.

Physiological State: Physiological information such as heart rate, sweating, and mood.

Self-Efficacy: The belief one's capability to perform a given action.

Telementor: The expert in a telementoring relationship.

Telementoring: Mentoring which occurs electronically.

Verbal Persuasion: Feedback from others that they believe that you can accomplish something.

Vicarious Experience: Watching similar others perform an action successfully.

Section 2
Telementoring:
Addressing the Needs of Persons with Disabilities

Chapter 6
Fully Including Students, Teachers, and Administrators with Disabilities in Telementoring

Sheryl Burgstahler
University of Washington, USA

Terrill Thompson
University of Washington, USA

ABSTRACT

The authors of this chapter discuss challenges that must be addressed to ensure the full inclusion of teachers, administrators, and students with disabilities in telementoring activities in elementary and secondary school environments. Potential barriers to participation relate to the physical environment, the technology used to support a telementoring program, and communication strategies within that environment. Solutions presented to address access challenges employ both universal design and accommodation approaches. The content of this chapter may be useful to administrators, teachers, and technology specialists as they integrate telementoring into elementary and secondary classroom practices; to professionals who seek to promote telementoring in formal and informal settings; and to researchers who wish to identify telementoring topics for further study.

INTRODUCTION

Telementoring, which is also referred to as online mentoring or e-mentoring, has the potential to engage students, teachers, and mentors in meaningful learning activities. However, some of the physical locations, technological tools, and engagement strategies used in telementoring can erect barriers for potential participants with disabilities. For example, a mentor might suggest that students view an online video that demonstrates a topic being discussed. If that video is not captioned, a student who is deaf will not be able to access the content unless special accommodations are made. Similarly, if classroom computer equipment is placed in an inaccessible location, a student with a wheelchair will not have access

DOI: 10.4018/978-1-61520-861-6.ch006

to that resource. Teachers also need to ensure that mentor and protégé relationships are facilitated in such a way that positive, educational interactions take place for everyone, including students with disabilities. If accessibility issues are addressed as programs are being developed, all potential participants can fully benefit from telementoring opportunities.

The objectives of this chapter are to increase the knowledge of elementary and secondary educators, administrators, and technology specialists about issues related to the full inclusion of teachers, administrators, and students with disabilities in telementoring activities. After a summary of background information, the authors present an overview of access issues for students, educators, and administrators with disabilities; approaches for ensuring that telementoring environments are inclusive of people with disabilities; key strategies for developing an effective telementoring community; and suggestions for future research.

BACKGROUND

Telementoring has been defined as an approach that uses "e-mail or computer conferencing systems to support a mentoring relationship when a face-to-face relationship would be impractical" (O'Neill, Wagner, & Gomez, 1996, p. 39). Interactions between students and mentors can augment teacher-student engagement in a classroom. Well-established communication technologies (e.g., email) as well as rapidly-emerging electronic tools (e.g., social networking websites) provide creative teachers with an exciting array of options for engaging students in authentic learning experiences that "reflect how knowledge is built and used in the world" (Electronic Emissary, n.d.a).

Leaders of the Electronic Emissary Project, which has supported hundreds of teams of students, teachers, facilitators, and subject matter experts in telementoring relationships, report that

Today, a teacher no longer needs to be the sole content matter expert in the classroom. It is possible, for example, for students to learn about weather phenomena from meteorologists studying weather as it occurs, or to discuss the paleontological implications of a recent T-Rex skeleton discovery with evolutionary scientists, using simple telecomputing tools such as email and chat. Volunteer subject matter experts, such as the meteorologists and paleontologists mentioned above, can work virtually with students over an extended period of time, developing and sustaining mentor-protégé relationships that contribute to the richness and relevance of curriculum-based learning in elementary, middle-level, and secondary classrooms. (Electronic Emissary, n.d.b)

Members of Electronic Emissary teams have engaged in dynamic exchanges using Internet-based tools such as email, text-based chats, and websites. Project evaluations have revealed high value of these relationships to both mentors and protégés.

Subject matter "came alive" for students who could interact with someone for whom curriculum content is part of everyday life… Subject matter experts often reported delighting in opportunities to revisit and delve deeper into their disciplinary specializations by interacting with interested, but less knowledgeable others. (Harris, 1999)

It is likely that the intention of teachers who implement telementoring practices in their classrooms is to engage all learners in a rich learning environment and to recruit the best mentors. Depending on how it is implemented, however, telementoring can serve to level the playing field for students with disabilities and their nondisabled peers or to further widen the gap in the educational attainment between these two groups. It can also be designed to include all potential mentors, or restrict recruitment to only those who have specific abilities and use certain types of technology.

The goal to ensure that students with disabilities have access to telementoring activities can be motivated by the commitment of teachers and administrators to make learning opportunities available to all students in their classrooms. The goal is to attract the best mentors, who may have disabilities themselves. However, accessible practices are sometimes motivated by legal mandates. For example, almost all educational entities are covered by both Section 504 of the Rehabilitation Act of 1973 and the Americans With Disabilities Act of 1990 (ADA). These laws prohibit discrimination on the basis of disability. Although they do not specifically mention information technology (IT), they are generally interpreted to require that schools plan for, purchase, and use educational technology that is accessible to students and educators with disabilities (Patrick, 1996). In addition, the Individuals with Disabilities Education Act (IDEA) mandates states and public agencies to provide early intervention, special education, and related services to children with disabilities to ensure that all students receive a public education that is free, appropriate to their individual needs, and in the least restrictive environments (U.S. Department of Education, n.d.). A broad range of disabilities are covered by relevant legislation; they include conditions that affect mobility, sight, hearing, speech, learning, attention, cognitive skills, and social interactions.

The next section of this chapter includes a discussion of accessibility issues regarding technologies and other aspects of telementoring environments. This section is then followed by one that shares an approach for addressing these access barriers.

THE PROBLEM: ACCESSIBILITY ISSUES WITH TELEMENTORING

Telementoring program structures can take on several different forms, including one-on-one mentoring, where one student is assigned to one mentor; group mentoring, where communication takes place between a group of protégés and one or more mentors; or ask-an-expert, where students primarily ask questions of mentors with specific expertise often over a short period of time (Burgstahler, 2006a; Guy, 2002; Perez & Dorman, 2001). Multiple aspects of each telementoring approach can impose distinct challenges related to accessibility for teachers, mentors, and protégés with disabilities. In the following paragraphs the authors summarize issues related to the physical environment, computers, asynchronous and synchronous telementoring technologies, and interaction strategies.

Physical Environments

For all current and potential students to be able to participate in telementoring activities, the technologies they will be using (e.g., computers, monitors) must be placed in environments that facilitate learning and that are accessible to people with a broad range of abilities. Students who use wheelchairs, canes, walkers, and those who simply have difficulty walking can face challenges in accessing computers placed in locations that are physically inaccessible to them. Some wheelchair users may not be able to use computers that are placed on work surfaces that cannot be adjusted in height. Also, some work areas have inadequate room for left-handed users. Students with visual impairments can face challenges when computer equipment is placed in cluttered areas, is frequently moved, or is located where lighting cannot be adjusted. Additionally, students with attention deficits may find it difficult to work in noisy environments or in settings with other distractions, such as activities taking place outside a window.

Computer Technology

People with disabilities were the original pioneers in alternative input and output technologies, as they have long been users of custom colors, font sizes, and other individualized settings, as well as specialized hardware and software called "assistive technology." Dozens of alternatives to the standard keyboard and mouse make it possible for individuals with mobility impairments to fully operate computers with head motion, eye gaze, speech, and other controls (Closing the Gap, n.d.). People who are blind can use "screen readers", a software feature that reads the content and controls of websites and software applications in a synthesized voice. Some people who are blind or deaf-blind can access electronic content using a refreshable Braille output device, which presents content in a row of tactile Braille dots that refreshes as users navigate through the website or application. Individuals with low vision may use screen magnification software or, depending on the severity of their visual impairment, may simply enlarge the font size using the built-in capabilities of their operating systems or browsers (most browsers now support text enlargement via a simple keystroke, such as Ctrl + in Microsoft Windows browsers and Apple + in Macintosh browsers). Some individuals with learning disabilities such as dyslexia also use software that reads the screen in a synthesized voice, often in conjunction with visual highlighting and alternative presentation schemes.

To participate in a telementoring experience, some students with disabilities require access to assistive technology. In most cases, assistive technology can be purchased when a specific student faces an upcoming need (e.g., when they enroll in a class that will require access to a particular product). However, it is a good idea, especially for large schools, to have some assistive technology on hand, particularly inexpensive items such as trackballs, that can benefit students who might not otherwise request them. Educators and lab staff should also be aware of accessibility features that are available in operating systems and software programs. For example, all major desktop operating systems (e.g., Microsoft Windows, Mac OS, Linux) include features that allow users to customize keyboards and pointing devices in ways that make them more usable for people with physical disabilities, and to modify default color and font configurations so that they are more usable by people with visual impairments or learning or cognitive disabilities. Also, all major operating systems include built-in assistive technologies such as screen readers, screen magnification software, and on-screen keyboards. These tools generally provide basic features and functionality and cannot therefore be relied upon as complete accommodations for some students with disabilities. However, they can be helpful for users who need quick access on computers they do not usually use, who wish to try out a particular access approach, or who are waiting for more fully-featured commercial software to be procured and installed.

Many popular software applications, in addition to supporting the custom settings defined with the operating system, also provide their own accessibility features. For example, most word processing software includes a feature by which users can magnify the font on the screen without altering the text size in the printed document. Similarly, most modern web browsers provide functions that allow users to increase the font size with a single keystroke. If teachers, technical support staff, and mentors are aware of these features and how to activate them, sharing this information with protégés with disabilities is a step toward opening doors for their full participation in telementoring and other computer-supported activities.

Telementoring Technologies

Given the diversity in how individuals with and without disabilities access technology, problems arise when software products and websites are designed for an audience with a narrow range of characteristics, rather than for a contemporary audience comprised of individuals using a rich variety of technologies. People access websites and services in a growing variety of ways that include web-enabled wireless mobile devices, televisions, gaming systems, coffee table computers, and an expanding array of browsers and operating systems. One can no longer assume that a person is accessing a computer using the traditional combination of keyboard and mouse for input, and monitor for output. Telementoring involves the use of one or more synchronous and/or asynchronous communication technologies. Asynchronous technologies include email, email-based discussion lists, web-based interactive forums, and social networking tools such as Facebook. Synchronous communication technologies include audio or video conferencing, and online meeting and collaborative environments that include virtual worlds such as Second Life. Unfortunately, as shared in the following paragraphs, many of the technologies used in telementoring are not accessible to everyone.

Asynchronous Technologies

Email-based communication. Email is an "older" technology, but its maturity is a strength. It provides a standard format that is supported across a wide variety of applications and devices. Users have plenty of choices for tools to use in reading and writing email messages, including many products that are fully accessible to people with disabilities. Communication by email traditionally consists of plain text communication, with little or no explicit structure within a message. In contrast, web pages have headings, subheadings, lists, tables, paragraphs, and other features that very clearly communicate structure. Plain text email has none of these features. Structure is important, especially for screen-reader users, as it helps them to clearly see how a message is organized. One potential solution is formatting email using Hypertext Markup Language (HTML), the primary language used in encoding web pages. However, this approach creates new problems for users whose devices or web browsers don't reliably support HTML. Additionally, structure within HTML email messages is not well-supported by screen readers.

Workarounds to the structure limitation include familiar conventions such as prefacing each line of a quotation with the ">" character when replying to an email and indicating emphasis by surrounding words in *asterisks* or _underlines_. These conventions help keep communications organized and understandable, but email can still become unwieldy if a conversation involves multiple messages back and forth between parties and, therefore, includes multiple levels of quotations within quotations. This situation can be especially challenging for screen-reader users to navigate and understand, but can also be challenging for individuals with learning disabilities, attention deficits, or cognitive disabilities. Also, in today's highly active electronic communication climate, if individuals have overflowing inboxes, poor spam filters, or inadequate skills in managing large quantities of communication, email can easily get lost or go unnoticed.

The advantages and disadvantages of email apply to all email-based communications, including discussion lists, where messages are posted to the list and delivered to subscribers' email addresses. Despite the deficiencies described in the preceding two paragraphs, the medium is technically accessible, and may be more familiar to most teachers, mentors, and protégés than other potential telementoring technologies. The DO-IT Center (Disabilities, Opportunities, Internetworking, and Technology) at the University of Washington has used this technology for many years to facilitate communication within dozens of online mentoring communities. DO-IT discussion lists include *doitchat* (for nearly 300 high school students, college students, and professionals with disabilities); and several smaller mentoring communities that focus on specific disabilities, including communities addressing learning disabilities and attention deficits, mobility and health impairments, blindness and low vision, deaf and hard of hearing, mobility impairments, and autism spectrum disorders. Membership on these specialized lists averages around 50 participants, including both mentors and protégés. As the topics suggest, the participants on these lists are individuals with specific disabilities. List activity demonstrates that, despite shortcomings of email, it is accessible to and usable by individuals with all types of disabilities and can be used effectively to support participation in a telementoring program.

Web-based forums. Web pages, in contrast to email, can be highly structured. HTML is ripe with structural markup, including headings, subheadings, lists, tables, and paragraphs. This structural markup provides cues that are especially helpful for screen-reader users, allowing the users to quickly determine, for example, how many items are in a list, how many rows and columns are in a table, and where they are currently positioned within that structure. Also, screen readers support keyboard shortcuts that allow users to jump between HTML headings on a page, which allows them to navigate the page quickly, much like sighted users do. The opportunity for structure is an important benefit of web-based forums, where all communication takes place through a website. Typically, participants can read the communications of others by browsing tables or lists with topics, subjects, and messages, along with useful information about each.

One example of a web-based forum is E-Forum, hosted by MentorNet. MentorNet is a nonprofit initiative whose mission is to "further the progress of women and others underrepresented in scientific and technical fields through the use of a dynamic, technology-supported mentoring network" and "to advance individuals and society, and enhance engineering and related sciences, by promoting a diversified, expanded and talented global workforce" (MentorNet, n.d.a). MentorNet pairs students, faculty, and experienced professionals in email-based mentoring relationships, but also provides E-Forum, a website through which mentors, protégés, and other participants can communicate on dozens of topics, such as career development; disabilities; diversity issues; grants, fellowships, scholarships; and societal benefits of engineering and science (MentorNet, n.d.b). MentorNet's E-Forum is organized using HTML tables. After logging in, the participant is presented with a table of discussion groups where each discussion group occupies a row in the table. Columns in the table include the name and description of the discussion group, the number of topics, the number of messages, and the date and time of the most recent post. When a participant selects a discussion group, they are taken to a new web page and presented with a table of subjects within that discussion group. Each subject is presented within a single row of the table, with metadata about each subject available in columns. If the participant selects a subject, he or she is taken to yet another web page, this one showing all the messages related to that subject. Again, this information is presented in a table, with two columns, author, and message. Each message concludes with the date and time posted, and an extra table row that includes reply and other buttons.

The layout in this example is fairly easy for screen-reader users to understand and navigate. With a table-based layout, questions arise such as whether the rows in the table can be sorted and whether additional HTML markup such as headings or access keys are available that would further help users find and quickly access the content of interest. Also, as interfaces become more complicated, the need for additional accessibility markup becomes increasingly critical. For example, if tables include nested rows or columns, it can be difficult for screen-reader users to understand their position within that structure. If a user's current focal position is a cell within a table, they need to know which row and column headings apply to that cell. Fortunately, HTML provides markup that allows this information to be communicated to screen-reader users, and most screen readers support this markup.

Clearly, web-based forums have the potential to be a highly accessible medium for communication in a telementoring program. Unfortunately, this potential for accessibility is not fully realized when forums are designed without using HTML appropriately to communicate structure and without regard to other accessibility issues.

Social networking websites. Social networking websites, such as Facebook and LinkedIn, offer the same potential advantages as any web-based communication, as well as a variety of additional interactive features. These sites also have the advantage of familiarity, as growing numbers of individuals, including students and professionals, use them regularly. A search for "mentoring" on Facebook returns over 500 groups, including many with hundreds of members. The same search on LinkedIn returns 592 groups, including the Professional and Amateur Mentoring Group, which has over 2,000 members and was created to help mentors and protégés, especially in the field of engineering, connect with each other in mentoring relationships (LinkedIn, n.d.).

Unfortunately, most of the major social networking sites pose significant problems with respect to accessibility. An assessment conducted by AbilityNet (2008) found that MySpace, Facebook, YouTube, Yahoo, and Bebo were all difficult or impossible for people with some types of disabilities to use. As AbilityNet points out, "in many cases a user is not even able to register with the website." Issues common to all five websites identified in the study were that (a) there was no help provided that addressed the unique needs of individuals with disabilities; (b) some content was inaccessible to keyboard-only users (including those who use an alternative keyboard but do not have access to mouse functions); (c) many graphics lacked alternate text for screen-reader users; (d) all sites used a CAPTCHA (Completely Automated Public Turing Test to Tell Computers and Humans Apart) image to prevent automatic user registrations, but did not provide a usable alternative for individuals who couldn't see the CAPTCHA image; and (e) all sites supported uploading videos, but did not support uploading captions or prompt users regarding the importance of captions.

In 2007, a group of frustrated Facebook users created a Facebook group called the Official Petition for a More Accessible Facebook, which soon attracted more than 2,000 members (Facebook, n.d.b). The American Foundation for the Blind also offered to help Facebook improve its accessibility. Since then, Facebook has taken some steps to address accessibility problems (Augusto, 2009), as described in part on its page of frequently asked questions and answers related to accessibility (Facebook, n.d.a). However, Facebook and other social networking sites continue to employ inaccessible features. Therefore, accessibility issues should be carefully considered before choosing to utilize these sites in telementoring programs.

Another popular social networking service is Twitter, which allows users to post short messages (140 characters or less) called "tweets", which are then distributed to people who "follow" that user. Twitter users include experts in a variety of fields who regularly post information related to their current work, thereby providing followers with insights into their activities, knowledge, and experience. Many of these same experts are willing to respond to questions. This creates a climate that is well-suited for telementoring.

As of the time of this writing, the Twitter website is not fully accessible. For example, screen-reader users and keyboard-only users can read others' tweets, but the icons for replying to them, adding them to their favorites, or deleting them are not available to these users because they require the use of a mouse or other pointing device. Also, when writing a tweet, a counter displays the number of characters remaining, starting at 140 and counting down as the user types. This information is not automatically communicated to screen-reader users. To access this information, users would have to leave the form field, navigate to the counter, read the number of remaining characters, and then navigate back to the form field. This is a cumbersome process.

Fortunately, Twitter includes an application program interface (API) that allows developers to create their own websites, widgets, and software programs for accessing Twitter content and features. As a result, there are scores of Twitter clients that run on the web as well as on mobile devices, including an accessible Twitter site (Lembree, 2009), a script for accessing Twitter using Freedom Scientific's popular screen reader JAWS (Randall, 2009), and a Greasemonkey script which adds an accessible layer on top of the existing Twitter website (Lemon, 2009).

A potential benefit of tools like Twitter is flexibility. In fact, Twitter and email share this characteristic. Since both support communication across a wide variety of client software, websites, widgets, and devices, participants in a mentoring relationship have plenty of choices as to which tool they use, and their choice has no impact on the choice of the person with whom they're communicating.

Synchronous Communication Technologies

Audio conferencing. If telementoring activities take place via audio conference, it is important to consider that some potential participants are unable to hear audio and that some cannot speak intelligibly. Nevertheless, individuals in these groups can participate in conferences using standard assistive technologies or services. Therefore, organizers of telementoring activities should be aware of the need to offer and provide these accommodations.

Typically, individuals who are deaf or hard of hearing communicate with remote participants using text rather than voice. This can be done over the Internet, but more traditionally is done using a teletypewriter (TTY), also known as a telecommunications device for the deaf (TDD). A basic TTY consists of a keyboard, display screen, and modem, which operates over standard telephone lines. To participate in an audio teleconference, users of text-based telecommunication systems send and receive communication via text, while hearing participants send and receive audible communication. Communication between parties using each of these two methods requires translation by a third party. Similarly, people with speech impairments may have difficulty being understood on the phone; thus, they too may require translation by a third party. Such third-party translation is known as a relay service. Specifically, the relay service for the deaf and hard of hearing is known as Telecommunication Relay Service (TRS), and the relay service for people with speech disabilities is known as Speech-To-Speech (STS) relay service. STS is staffed by communications assistants who are skilled in language recognition and trained to understand many different speech patterns. Both relay services are mandated by Title IV of the Americans with Disabilities Act of 1990 and are available free of charge (Federal Communication Commission, n.d.). Traditional TRS is expanding to include a growing variety of text streaming options, including specialized audio phones that include a caption display, and real-time relay captioning of phone calls over the Internet.

Video conferencing. Like audio conferences, video conferences require accommodations for participants who are deaf or hard of hearing. The accommodations are fundamentally the same as those provided for audio conferences: If a person is unable to hear the audio, it must be translated into a format he or she can access. Ideally this accommodation is delivered using the same medium in which the video conference itself is delivered. For example, if a video conference is delivered using a web-based application, that application should be capable of supporting an embedded text stream and a relay operator or live captionist who can type what is being spoken so that the person who is deaf or hard of hearing can access the content on the screen in real time. Alternatively, users may prefer Video Relay Service (VRS), which is similar to TRS, but a relay operator provides translation between spoken word and sign language, rather than between spoken word and text. Hearing participants communicate by voice and non-hearing participants communicate by video using sign language. The relay operator serves as a liaison, communicating by voice to the hearing party and by sign language to the non-hearing party. VRS is an important alternative to TRS since, for many individuals who are deaf, sign language is their primary language and they are not as proficient with written language. All of these services are freely available from telecommunications providers in most U.S. states.

Individuals who are blind or have low vision may also face challenges in a video conference, in particular, if content is presented visually and is not otherwise described. This situation is similar to an on-site presentation. If content is presented visually (e.g., slides or demonstrations), the presenter should describe all of this content orally. This is a good practice regardless of whether an individual with a visual impairment is involved in the conference, since participants seated in the back of the room may be unable to see the content, older students experience worsening vision, and some participants prefer to listen while taking notes. All participants may find it helpful when slides or other materials are made available ahead of time and are also available by request in accessible formats such as electronic text, large print, and Braille.

If video conferencing occurs within an interactive web application such as those designed for webinars and online meetings, special attention should be given to accessibility when selecting a product or service. In addition to supporting relay and caption services as described above, the interactive features of these environments can be highly complex, and the accessibility of these features is equally complex and critical. These applications might include presenter slides, live audio or video, interactive panes in which participants can ask questions of the instructor, chat with other participants, send private messages to other participants, and browse lists of participants. Primary accessibility considerations revolve around whether participants can navigate efficiently between and within these features and operate their controls with or without a mouse and with or without eyesight (using a screen reader). Further, screen-reader users and users whose disabilities affect their ability to attend or focus may need to close distracting panels or turn off automatic prompts that often accompany private messaging and chat features.

Virtual worlds. Virtual reality has been gaining popularity for many years, but Second Life (n.d.c), launched in 2003 by Linden Lab, may be the first to be taken seriously by many sectors of society, including education. Users, called "residents" in Second Life, create animated avatars to represent themselves, then explore, interact with other residents, and participate in individual and group activities. Second Life has its own economy; residents buy and sell goods and services, create businesses, hold jobs, and own virtual property. Many colleges and universities own land in Second Life, and are building virtual campuses and meeting there for a wide variety of courses, projects, simulations, and learning experiences (Conklin, 2007; Kelton, 2007).

Not surprisingly, Second Life has its own mentorship program, which trains volunteers to serve as mentors for other residents, teaching them how to explore Second Life and "develop the skills needed to have a positive experience" (Second Life, n.d.b). Also, over twenty science and technology related organizations, including government agencies such as NASA, NOAA, and National Physics Laboratory; museums such as the International Spaceflight Museum and the Tech Museum of Innovation; and several universities, are working collaboratively to provide education, share ideas, and plan future projects in SciLands, a Second Life "mini continent and user community... devoted exclusively to science and technology" (SciLands, n.d.). This is one of many examples of real-world people and organizations having a virtual world presence where they are available to students for online communication.

There are many potential accessibility problems within virtual environments. The most obvious of these is that the environment is highly visual, which can make it difficult or impossible for people without sight to navigate, read virtual print material, and participate in activities. In addition, many objects and features in the virtual world are only accessible to mouse users; a virtual interface may or may not support participant needs for custom colors and fonts; and many events and activities that include streaming audio are not transcribed or captioned. Second Life residents, including research scientists at universities and major corporations, have worked actively to address these issues (e.g., IBM, 2008; TextSL, n.d.; Pascale, Mulatto, & Prattichizzo, 2008) and Second Life provides a forum in which users can share accessibility information (Second Life, n.d.a). Since the Second Life viewer is an open source software application, it is possible for third parties to create custom interfaces that work for specialized populations or a single customizable interface that meets the needs of multiple populations.

Interaction Strategies

Students with certain types of disabilities face specific challenges with respect to online engagement. For example, students with learning disabilities that affect reading skills (e.g., dyslexia) and those with developmental delays may have difficulty reading messages that are long and use vocabulary with which they are unfamiliar; they may also have difficulty composing their thoughts into a text-based message. Students who have conditions such as Asperger's syndrome may have difficulty interpreting social cues embedded within messages from mentors; this is most impactful in one-on-one and group mentoring programs, but less so in ask-an-expert formats that focus primarily on information-sharing.

The lack of social distinctions—e.g., gender, race, ethnicity, physical characteristics, disability—can make some students in telementoring environments more willing to share their views than they are in face-to-face communications. However, race/ethnicity, differences in economic status, and other social distinctions observed within in-person interactions are often reflected in online communication as telementoring participations make assumptions from the content, tone, choice of vocabulary, and grammar in messages (Center for Children & Technology, 1998; Guy, 2002; Halbert, 1999). It has also been found that e-mentoring participants with disabilities are affected by a second marginalized status. For example, in one study female protégés with disabilities communicated more frequently and on a greater variety of themes than their male counterparts (Burgstahler & Doyle, 2005; Burgstahler & Chang, 2007). Further, females with disabilities were more likely to discuss personal and social issues, while males were more likely to both provide and seek information about computers, the Internet, and other technical content (Burgstahler & Doyle, 2005). The results are consistent with other studies that suggest that gender plays a role in mentoring and online communication—e.g., females more often confide in others, whereas males refrain from expressing emotions (Ragins, 1989; Monnier, Stone, Hobfoll, & Johnson, 1998); females turn to peers, whereas men more often seek support from superiors (Greenglass, 1993); females respond more favorably and benefit more from social support than males (Day & Livingstone, 2003; Beehr, Farmer, Glazer, Gudanowski, & Nair, 2003); and male mentors provide more career mentoring to their protégés and female mentors provide more psychosocial mentoring (Allen & Eby, 2004).

Although gender differences may be diminishing, it has been found that boys are still more likely than girls to like computers, are more confident in their use, and use computers more frequently out of school (Colley & Comber, 2003); there is some evidence that older girls hold the most negative attitudes about computer use, possibly due to gender stereotyping (Colley & Comber, 2003). Race, ethnicity, and other social factors likely impact interactions between mentors and protégés as well. One study found that, when considering both race and gender, level of contact and protégé satisfaction with mentors were higher for protégés who perceived themselves to be more similar to their mentors; and race pairing was positively related to protégés' perceptions of the amount of career support and to mentors' liking of protégés (Ensher & Murphy, 1997). Consideration of all diversity issues should be made to ensure that telementoring communities are welcoming, accessible, and productive for all potential protégés and mentors (Hansman, 2002).

THE SOLUTION: UNIVERSAL DESIGN OF TELEMENTORING

Myriad issues must be addressed in any telementoring program. They include access to computers in schools, selection of telementoring technology, management of participant expectations, participant training, mentor recruitment, online facilitation of telementoring relationships, and student safety (Center for Children & Technology, 1998; Garringer, M., Fulop, M., & Rennick, V., 2003; O'Neill & Harris, 2005). To ensure equity, leaders should make decisions in each of these areas that take into consideration the wide range of participant characteristics, including those related to the cultures, native languages, reading levels, technical skills, and disabilities of potential students, teachers, and mentors. This approach—where a broad range of participant characteristics is addressed when creating and selecting products and environments—is called "universal design."

The concept of universal design originated in the field of architecture. The phrase was coined by Ron Mace, a research professor in the architecture department at the College of Design at North Carolina State University. In 1989, he founded the Center for Accessible Housing, which later became the Center for Universal Design (CUD, n.d.a). Mace defined universal design as "the design of products and environments to be usable by all people, to the greatest extent possible, without the need for adaptation or specialized design" (CUD, n.d.b, p. 1). First applied to the physical environment, universal design has expanded and found application in many other contexts as well, including IT communities (Burgstahler, 2008).

Universal Design of Physical Environments

Universal design strategies can be applied to the environment where technology is used, such as a computer lab or classroom. To ensure access to everyone, educators and computer lab staff should make sure that all levels of the facility are connected via wheelchair-accessible routes of travel. Aisles should be kept wide and clear of obstructions for students and teachers with mobility and/or visual impairments. Placing at least one of the workstations students use on an adjustable-height table ensures physical access for potential students who use wheelchairs or are exceptionally tall or short in stature. For students who are easily distracted, it is good to provide options for quiet work areas where noise and other distractions are minimized. Ample high-contrast, large-print directional signs and equipment labels throughout a lab or classroom also benefits many students (Burgstahler, 2006b; Thompson, 2008).

Universal Design of Telementoring Technologies

To make telementoring experiences accessible to everyone, the technology used to support the telementoring environment must address the wide range of abilities of potential users and the assistive technologies they may employ. Some practitioners have been concerned about accessibility issues since the early days of the microcomputer. By 1992, representatives from industry, education, and government, as well as consumers and researchers developed the Guidelines for More Accessible Design (Vanderheiden & Vanderheiden, 1992) that address technology access issues related to sensory, physical, cognitive, and seizure disorders as well as language barriers. Organized by technology function, each guideline presents an objective as well as examples regarding how to design a product to achieve the objective. Some guideline content follows.

1. *Output/displays,* which includes auditory and visual output: Maximize the number of people who can hear auditory output clearly enough, not miss important information if they can't hear, have line of sight to visual output and reach printed output, and see visual output clearly.
2. *Input/controls,* which includes keyboards and all other means of communicating to the product: Maximize the number of people who can reach the controls, find the individual controls/keys if they can't see them, read the labels on the controls/keys, physically operate and understand how to operate controls and other input mechanisms, and connect special alternative input devices.
3. *Manipulations,* which includes all actions that must be directly performed by a person in concert with the product (e.g., inserting a disk, changing an ink cartridge): Maximize the number of people who can physically insert and remove objects as required to operate a device, and understand how to physically handle and/or open the product, remove, replace, or reposition often-used detachable parts.
4. *Documentation,* with a focus on operating instructions: Maximize the number of people who can access the documentation and understand the content.
5. *Safety,* including alarms and other protections from harm: Maximize the number of people who can perceive hazard warnings and use the product without injury. (Vanderheiden & Vanderheiden, 1992, Part III, Sections 1-5)

The World Wide Web originally emerged in the early 1990s and was primarily used in post-secondary education and research settings. Tim Berners-Lee, a computer scientist, is credited with inventing the web when he implemented the first successful communication between a Hypertext Transfer Protocol (HTTP) client and server via the Internet on December 25, 1990. In June 1993, Berners-Lee wrote an informal specification for HTML, the original and primary language used for creating websites. Even in this early specification, Berners-Lee included support for alt attributes on images, which provide text alternatives to users who are unable to see images (Berners-Lee, 1993).

Berners-Lee founded the World Wide Consortium (W3C) in 1994 and continues to serve as its director. The W3C is an independent non-profit organization that develops and maintains protocols to ensure interoperability of the web. According to Berners-Lee, "the power of the Web is in its universality. Access by everyone regardless of disability is an essential aspect" (World Wide Web Consortium, n.d.a., p. 1). Despite Berners-Lee's best intentions, accessibility was not a requirement for web designers, and concerns and interests grew with respect to accessible (e.g., Laux, McNally, Paciello, & Vanderheiden, 1996; Nielson, 1996; Rowland & Smith, 1999) and universal (e.g., Burgstahler, Comden, & Fraser, 1997; Waters, 1997) web design. In 1997, W3C announced its Web Accessibility Initiative (WAI) to develop guidelines for the accessible design of websites. The WAI promotes universal, as well as accessible design, pointing out that:

Web accessibility also **benefits** *people without disabilities. For example, a key principle of Web* *accessibility is designing Websites that are flexible to meet different user needs, preferences, and situations. Such* **flexibility** *benefits people with disabilities, but also those without disabilities, such as people using a slow Internet connection, people with "temporary disabilities" such as a broken arm, and people with changing abilities due to aging. (Web Accessibility Initiative, 2005)*

In 1999, the Web Content Accessibility Guidelines (WCAG 1.0) were published as a W3C recommendation (World Wide Web Consortium). The WCAG 1.0 included fourteen broad guidelines, each of which was further explained by specific checkpoints, most of which pertained to specific web coding practices in HTML. Altogether, there were 65 checkpoints, each assigned a priority level (1-3), where Priority 1 checkpoints were those most critical for ensuring access for one or more groups of users.

In parallel to the work of the W3C, congress worked on legislation that would mandate that IT developed, maintained, procured, or used by the federal government meet accessibility standards (United States Department of Justice, 2005). In 1998 this legislation was enacted as Section 508 of the Rehabilitation Act of 1973, as amended. According to the Department of Justice, accessible IT

can be operated in a variety of ways and does not rely on a single sense or ability of the user. For example, a system that provides output only in visual format may not be accessible to people with visual impairments and a system that provides output only in audio format may not be accessible to people who are deaf or hard of hearing. (2005, p. 18)

Section 508, as amended in 1998, charged the U.S. Access Board (n.d.; 2007) with producing minimum accessibility standards for the IT used by federal agencies. In response, the Board produced the Electronic and Information Technology Accessibility Standards, commonly known as the "Section 508 standards." These standards were organized into six categories of technology: software applications and operating systems; web-based Intranet and Internet information and applications; telecommunications products; video and multimedia products; self contained, closed products; and desktop and portable computers (Office of the Federal Registrar, 2000). In developing the standards for "web-based Intranet and Internet information and applications," the Access Board drew extensively on the work of the W3C, and, as a result, the Section 508 standards roughly parallel the Priority 1 checkpoints of WCAG 1.0. Although the Section 508 standards technically apply only to products used by the federal government, the standards have been voluntarily adopted by some states, educational institutions, and other organizations as one way to meet their obligations under the ADA. Thus, WCAG 1.0 has more broadly promoted the integration of flexible and inclusive features within mainstream IT.

Both the Section 508 standards and the WCAG define specific techniques for developing web pages that are accessible to a wide range of possible users. The web has evolved considerably since these guidelines and standards were published. Static HTML web pages have given way to dynamic, interactive applications. In response, both sets of accessibility standards have undergone and continue to undergo revision. In July 2006, the Access Board assembled the Telecommunications and Electronic and Information Technology Advisory Committee (TEITAC) and charged the committee with recommending updates to the Section 508 standards (WebAIM, n.d.). On April 3, 2008, the TEITAC submitted their formal recommendation for updates to the Access Board (TEITAC, 2008). As of the time of this writing, the Board has not yet acted on this recommendation.

Parallel to this effort, the W3C announced WCAG 2.0 as an official recommendation in December 2008 (World Wide Web Consortium, 2008b). In developing WCAG 2.0, the W3C sought to develop standards that would be enduring as the web continued to evolve. To do so, they identified accessibility issues and corresponding success criteria that were "technology independent," that is, they could be applied across a wide range of technologies. The W3C continues to recommend best practices that expand the reach of the web to everyone. In fact, the W3C mission statement includes the core principle Web for All that the W3C describes as follows:

The social value of the Web is that it enables human communication, commerce, and opportunities to share knowledge. One of W3C's primary goals is to make these benefits available to all people, whatever their hardware, software, network infrastructure, native language, culture, geographical location, or physical or mental ability. (W3C, n.d.b.).

WCAG 2.0 is organized according to four broad principles that define web accessibility:

- *Perceivable*. All content and communication must be perceivable by the user. This principle relates to computer output. Keep in mind that there are many ways that people perceive electronic information. Many do so visually, but even among visual users there is much diversity across screen size and resolution (e.g., older desktops with lower resolution, modern laptops with extremely high resolution, cell phones, and other handheld wireless devices with small screens). There are also visual differences in terms of user's preferred font size and color (e.g., some people are color blind, and some have used their browser or operating system to customize unique color schemes). In addition to the variation among visual users, there are growing numbers of people who perceive electronic information audibly (e.g., blind people using screen reading software, and people using speech-based services to access the web via their cell phones), as well as blind or deaf-blind individuals who perceive information using a refreshable Braille output device.
- *Operable*. The tools used in communicating with mentors must be operable by the user. This principle relates to computer input. In order for participants to use a tool, they must be able to operate its controls, including links, buttons, menus, and other controls. Many software products and web-based applications are built with the erroneous assumption that everyone can use a mouse. Applications often require users to hover over or click on controls in order to trigger some dynamic effect such as the display of a submenu. Many people are physically unable to use a mouse, including individuals with limited fine motor ability, amputees, and individuals who are unable to see the pointer on the screen. These users may be operating the computer with keyboard alone, or using an assistive input device such as a system that tracks head movement or eye gaze. Some people are using technologies that don't include a mouse, such as speech recognition technology, or handheld wireless devices that users control with a stylus or by touch. Regardless of input method, all of these individuals must be able to operate the controls in order to participate in the communication.
- *Understandable*. Tools must be easy to use for their intended purpose. If the purpose is communication between mentor and protégé, tools should facilitate this communication rather than make it more challenging. A simple, consistent design helps to make an application easy to use. However, it is important to consider that users will be approaching the application using different modalities. An application that looks

simple visually must also be presented in an easy-to-understand way to non-visual users who are navigating audibly or using a tactile interface.
- *Robust.* As described earlier in this chapter, the world is rich with web-enabled devices and programs that are designed to render information content. If tools are designed to facilitate communication over the web, they should work equally well across all of these devices and applications. Regardless of which hardware device, operating system, browser, configuration settings, or assistive technologies a user happens to be using, they should be able to participate in the communication.

By following these principles and considering the needs of all users in developing a website or web-based application, a web developer is practicing universal design. The fact that universal design benefits people with and without disabilities is sometimes referred to as "the curb cut effect" because of the wide range of users (e.g., parents with strollers, delivery people with carts, bicyclists) who benefit from curb cuts, a technology originally designed for individuals who use wheelchairs. On the web, alternate text for images benefit people who are blind, but they also benefit people with low bandwidth or minimal screen real estate (e.g., cell phone users), as these users can turn off bandwidth- and space-consuming graphics yet still access content. There are, in fact, many web design techniques that benefit mobile web users in addition to users with disabilities (W3C, 2008a). Similarly, captions on video presentations provide access to the deaf or hard of hearing, but they also benefit people who temporarily have no sound on their computers (e.g., in a quiet computer lab or classroom with no headphones). Additionally, captions make full-text searching of video possible (e.g., DO-IT, n.d.).

Universal Design of Learning

Since the 1980s, the Center for Applied Special Technology (CAST) has been a leader in expanding "learning opportunities for all individuals, especially those with disabilities, through the research and development of innovative, technology-based educational resources and strategies" (CAST, n.d.b). CAST defined "universal design for learning" (UDL) as "a research-based set of principles that together form a practical framework for using technology to maximize learning opportunities for every student" (Rose & Meyer, 2002, p. 5*).* UDL provides "rich supports for learning, and reduces barriers to the curriculum, while maintaining high achievement standards for all" (CAST, n.d.c, p. 1). UDL applies the results of brain research and the capabilities of IT to develop educational software components to teach students with diverse language and preferences, interests, abilities, cultural backgrounds, and other characteristics in the same class. This includes students with attention issues; learning disabilities; physical disabilities; sensory impairments; and those who have difficulty with note taking, reading, handwriting, or spelling. These students may be using a wide variety of assistive technology. Products that employ UDL reach high degrees of flexibility by applying three guiding principles to all aspects of learning activities:

- *Multiple means of representation,* to give learners various ways of acquiring information and knowledge.
- *Multiple means of action and expression,* to provide learners alternatives for demonstrating what they know.
- *Multiple means of engagement,* to tap into learners' interests, offer appropriate challenges, and increase motivation. (CAST, n.d.a, p. 1)

In a UDL environment:

- The learning goals and objectives provide an appropriate challenge for each student.
- The curriculum has a flexible format, supporting transformation between media and multiple representations of content to support each student's learning style.
- Methods are flexible and diverse enough to provide appropriate learning experiences, challenges, and support for all students.
- Assessment is sufficiently flexible to provide accurate, ongoing information that helps teachers adjust instruction and maximize learning. (Hitchcock, Meyer, Rose & Jackson, 2002; Hitchcock & Stahl, 2002; Rose, Meyer, & Hitchcock, 2005)

Most developers do not take a diverse range of abilities and other characteristics into account when they develop IT products. As a result, they erect barriers to potential users (Golden, 2002; National Council on Disability, 2004). In a study undertaken by the National Council on Disability (2004), researchers found that rapid changes in technology often cause decreases in accessibility and that sales associates are often unaware of the accessibility features of technology even when they do exist. They arrived at the following conclusions:

- IT products and services that accommodate a variety of physical and cognitive differences benefit both users and companies.
- Section 508 has had some impact on increasing the accessible and universal design efforts of the IT industry.
- A significant market exists for products and services that are universally designed.
- Universal design principles are not difficult to incorporate into the design practices of IT developers.
- Even when IT products and services are designed to be accessible to people with disabilities, they are often not fully usable because the developers did not understand the needs of users with disabilities, and people with a variety of disabilities were not included in design and testing processes. (National Council on Disability, 2004)

It is unlikely that a developer would intentionally design IT products and services to be inaccessible to specific populations. Instead, inaccessible design is often the result of a lack of awareness by educators, technology developers, and administrators regarding a variety of factors. These factors include the barriers erected by the design of IT, the benefits of universal design for all technology users, their legal obligations for providing accessible content, and the availability of guidelines for designing accessible IT.

Universal Design of Telementoring Interactions

Projects for youth with disabilities, racial/ethnic minorities, and women have identified promising practices for bringing these students into fields where they have been underrepresented, such as science and engineering. Key among these practices is mentoring (American Association for the Advancement of Science, 2001; Benz, Doren, & Yovanoff, 1998; Burgstahler & Cronheim, 2001; Doren & Benz, 1998; National Science Foundation, 2001; Kim-Rupnow & Burgstahler, 2004). Mentors can help young people learn academic content, explore career options, identify resources, strengthen interpersonal skills, and develop a sense of identity (Saito & Blyth, 1992). To best serve all participants, telementoring leaders should incorporate strategies that address disability, gender, race, ethnicity, culture, and other characteristics of protégés and mentors, with special consideration of those with double-minority status. With understanding of such differences, educators and mentors are better equipped to promote skills, confidence, and motivation for all protégés through universal design of mentor selection and assignments, discussion facilitation, and participant training that promotes effective communication with all users, including those with disabilities.

Mentor Recruitment

Since a key to forming effective telementoring relationships is the development of trust between the individuals involved (Guy, 2002), the best mentors are selected for more than their content expertise alone. They are effective in engaging youth with diverse interests, knowledge, and backgrounds; respect the viewpoints of others; are good listeners; are sensitive to the different styles of communication of young people; and are patient. They give students a great deal of control over how discussions progress, but know when to draw them back to a topic; point out various viewpoints and facilitate discussions of alternatives; offer expressions of encouragement; and seek and utilize advice from the classroom teacher. In contrast, less effective mentors do not allow time to develop mutual trust and respect; do not communicate with protégés on a regular basis; demand that youth play an equal role in initiating contact; make judgmental statements about the attitudes of participants; preach their values and opinions on others; or ignore the advice of program staff (Burgstahler, 2006a; Sipe, 1996).

Communication Issues of Diverse Learners

Mentoring is all about communication. For protégés, communication challenges may involve difficulty in reading text that includes words for which they are unfamiliar; the teacher can remind mentors to define terms as they go and help students develop skills (e.g., looking up definitions on the Internet) in dealing with unknown words. For some students, who find reading is difficult, the teacher might arrange to provide speech output and headphones. Communication issues may involve social abilities that might be faced by a student with Asperger's syndrome. In this case, giving very specific instruction, modeling appropriate communication, and monitoring communications and providing feedback may help a student learn to communicate effectively in a telementoring environment. Having the student begin telementoring in an ask-the-expert model that focuses on information sharing may provide a good foundation that could lead to success in more engaging one-on-one and group telementoring.

Telementoring leaders should also attend to other social distinctions of participants. For example, in discussing concepts of self, Gilligan (1982) delineated "separate" versus "connected" knowing, which tend to be preferred by males and females, respectively. Separate knowing includes the more solitary approaches such as logic and deduction, whereas connected knowing relies on context, intuition, and induction; it may be an avenue for engaging girls in telementoring communities. Females might be more comfortable with more conversational patterns of online communication, while males might be more comfortable with factual content (Burgstahler & Doyle, 2005). Practitioners can learn from some telementoring research and practice that has focused on serving women and racial/ethnic minorities (e.g., Center for Children & Technology, 1998; Guy, 2002; MentorNet, n.d.a), but less research and practice has focused on other underrepresented groups, including those defined by disability.

Participant Training

There is evidence that mentor training is effective, but has limitations. Since mentor and protégé perceptions of their roles may differ, facilitators should help them build their understanding of these roles in the context of a specific telementoring program (O'Neill & Harris, 2005). The use of multiple methods to train students and mentors might be most effective, facilitating the development of relationships, presenting models of communication, and allowing for practice and feedback (O'Neill & Harris, 2005). Mentors and protégés can even be engaged in identifying the most effective means by which communication can occur. This in itself can be an excellent experience for students with disabilities, as they can learn to address communication issues related to their disabilities and to identify and self-advocate accommodations as needed. Mentors can benefit from instruction and guidance on general strategies for positive youth development, as well as how to deal with the diverse characteristics of students in the classroom as they promote success for all students. Mentors need to be prepared for the frustrations they may encounter in communicating with some students as well as have realistic expectations regarding their impact. Orientation for students and mentors should cover program goals, technology issues, communication tips, expectations, boundaries, how to understand frame of reference, how to clearly express feelings, and other key content. Program educators and administrators can consult resources that address the training of participants in mentoring communities in general (Center for Children & Technology, 1998; Harris, O'Bryan, & Rotenberg, 1996; Herrera, Sipe, & McClanahan, 2000; Jucovy, 2001) as well as those specifically related to students with disabilities (Burgstahler, 2006a, 2007; Campbell-Whatley, 2001; Sword & Hill, 2002).

Facilitation

Building relationships can be challenging for both protégés and mentors. To ensure the safety of students and of appropriate interactions between mentor and protégé, it is important that discussions in a telementoring community be monitored and guided by the teacher or other facilitator. This same individual should periodically request feedback from mentors and students regarding their satisfaction, collect their suggestions for improvements, assess the impact of telementoring participation in supporting program goals, and make appropriate adjustments. Leaders can model for students and mentors how to engage in appropriate behavior, make clear when a statement is a fact or opinion, and welcome and respect all points of view (O'Neill & Harris, 2005). Facilitators should step in as necessary, and use specific incidents as constructive, teachable moments for everyone.

FUTURE RESEARCH DIRECTIONS

As telementoring increases in popularity and new technologies continue to emerge for its implementation, new accessibility challenges will manifest themselves. Since one cannot assume that telecommunications technologies are accessibly- or universally-designed, when selecting products to support online communication it is important for teachers, administrators, or technical support staff to ask developers for details about how their products support accessibility. They should also seek input from a specialist in the accessibility field or ask individuals with disabilities to give products a test run.

It is important that researchers and practitioners remember that accessibility considerations apply to mentors and teachers as well as student participants and that policy issues need to be addressed with respect to accessibility in a telementoring program. For example, one of the most active mentors in the DO-IT program is a blind researcher who works at the National Oceanic and Atmospheric Administration (NOAA). She uses speech and Braille output devices to access Internet content. If telementoring tools are inaccessible to screen readers, she is unable to participate as a mentor. Keeping this in mind, DO-IT has adopted a policy that any technology used in its e-mentoring community is accessible to all members, including those who use screen readers. Since schedules vary greatly for mentors, administrators, and participants, the communication tool must be asynchronous. Since some participants are under the age of 18, the communication tool selection and use must be acceptable to parents. Since all participants have computers, but not all have cell phones, it has been decided that only computer-based technologies will be used in the large mentoring community of all participants.

At the time this chapter was written, DO-IT continues to use email and email-based discussion lists as the primary e-mentoring tool because it is asynchronous and accessible to all participants and potential participants. In smaller, focused mentoring groups, however, other choices for technology can be explored, as long as they are accessible to all members of the group at the time, and the tool will be changed if someone joins the group and the technology is not accessible to him or her. For example, DO-IT supports a very small e-mentoring community for program participants with Asperger's syndrome. Since at the current time there are no members who use screen readers, the group might choose to use an online tool that is not fully accessible to screen readers; participants understand that if a new member joins the group for which their current technology choice is not accessible, a new tool will be selected. This approach emphasizes the importance of access without creating undue restrictions for a specific group with known participants, as well as having a plan in place for adjusting the choice of telementoring tool when accessibility issues arise.

The content presented in this chapter suggests the following questions for future research:

1. Besides gender, disability, and minority status, what other factors influence the level and content of mentor-protégé interactions (e.g., age, academic interest, specific disability type)?
2. What effect does having opportunities to meet face-to-face have on mentor-protégé relationships primarily sustained online?
3. How does the content of mentor-protégé messages change over time?
4. How do the telementoring experiences of students with disabilities compare with those of students who do not have disabilities?

CONCLUSION

The basic concept of telementoring is quite simple. However, implementing a program that is fully inclusive of all participants is a challenge. If a technology-enhanced learning or mentoring environment is carefully built following principles of universal design, the environment will be flexible in meeting the needs of diverse groups of students. However, if inclusive design is not considered, a specific student or mentor may be unable to fully participate. In this chapter, authors shared access barriers that must be addressed in order for everyone to fully participate in telementoring—including challenges related to technology used to support telementoring environments, interaction approaches, and the physical environment. They proposed solutions to access challenges that employ both universal design and accommodation approaches. The content may be useful to administrators, teachers, and technology specialists as they integrate telementoring into classroom practices; to professionals who seek to promote telementoring in formal and informal settings; and to researchers who wish to identify telementoring topics for further study.

Much work remains to be done to ensure that the physical environment, interaction methods, and technology are fully accessible to all potential teachers, mentors, and students in telementoring communities. Listed below are some guidelines for making telementoring activities welcoming and accessible to students, teachers, and administrators with disabilities (and everyone else!).

1. *Consider accessibility early.* Conduct a formal assessment of the current state of accessibility of a mentoring program and environment. Identify whether technology tools and methods are accessible, and to what extent staff and mentors are aware of diversity and accessibility issues. Use this information to identify areas needing improvement, and document a specific strategy,

with timelines and responsible parties, for creating a program that better embraces the spirit of universal design.
2. *Use accessible tools and methods.* When deciding what technology tools to use and how communication will take place, consider accessibility of those tools and methods. Ask vendors about the accessibility of their products, but don't assume their answers are always correct. Investigate. Seek help from accessibility-focused organizations. Seek out previous users for accessibility-related product-specific feedback.
3. *Provide diversity-related training to mentors.* Be sure that mentors are aware of individual differences related to culture, gender, ethnicity, and disability, and are equipped to work creatively and effectively with these differences in their communication strategies. Work to raise mentors' awareness of accessibility issues with communication technologies. Mentors do not need to be technology experts, but they should be able to identify possible barriers and know where to turn for solutions.
4. *Provide support.* Ensure that individuals who are charged with supporting the mentoring program on its technology needs are aware of technology accessibility issues. Seek out training opportunities for these individuals, and develop a list of resources that can provide additional assistance with accessibility as needed.
5. *Be flexible.* Provide a number of options for communication in a telementoring environment. Blended, flexible solutions increase the likelihood that all parties' needs and preferences will be met, and that more effective mentoring relationships will be established.
6. *Expect challenges.* Recognize that we live in a world that has great technological diversity. What works for some participants might not work for others. If tools have been selected that are flexible and customizable, participants can use a variety of operating systems and telementoring tools.
7. *Share successes.* If a mentoring program is successful in including individuals with disabilities as mentors or protégés, promote this as a promising practice. Become a mentor to other programs, encouraging them to pursue similarly inclusive programs.

ACKNOWLEDGMENT

This chapter is based on work supported by the National Science Foundation under grant #HRD-0833504 in Research in Disabilities Education [RDE]) and #CNS-0540615 and #CNS-0837508 in Computer and Information Science and Engineering [CISE]. Any opinions, findings, and conclusions or recommendations expressed in this material are those of the authors and do not necessarily reflect the views of the National Science Foundation.

REFERENCES

W3C. (1999). *Web content accessibility guidelines 1.0: W3C recommendation 5-May-1999*. Retrieved February 1, 2010, from http://www.w3.org/TR/WAI-WEBCONTENT/

W3C. (2007). *W3C Mission*. Retrieved May 13, 2009, from http://www.w3.org/Consortium/mission

W3C. (2008a). *Relationship between Mobile Web Best Practices (MWBP) and Web Content Accessibility Guidelines (WCAG)*. Retrieved February 1, 2010, from http://www.w3.org/TR/mwbp-wcag/

W3C. (2008b). *Web content accessibility guidelines (WCAG) 2.0*. Retrieved February 1, 2010, from http://www.w3.org/TR/WCAG20/

W3C. (n.d.b.). *W3C Mission.* Retrieved March 1, 2010, from http://www.w3.org/ Consortium/mission

AbilityNet. (2008, January 18). *State of the eNation Reports: Social networking sites lock out disabled users.* Retrieved May 13, 2009, from http://www.abilitynet.org.uk/enation85

Allen, T. D., & Eby, L. T. (2004). Factors related to mentor reports of mentoring functions provided: Gender and relational characteristics. *Sex Roles, 50*(1-2).

American Association for the Advancement of Science. (2001). *In pursuit of a diverse science, technology, engineering, and mathematics workforce.* Washington, DC: Author.

Americans With Disabilities Act of 1990. 42 U.S.C.A. § 12101 et seq.

Augusto, C. (2009, April 6). *Making Facebook accessible for everyone.* Retrieved February 1, 2010, from http://blog.facebook.com/blog.php?post=71852922130

Beehr, T. A., Farmer, S. J., Glazer, S., Gudanowski, D. M., & Nair, V. (2003). The enigma of social support and occupational stress: Source congruence and gender role effects. *Journal of Occupational Health Psychology, 8*(3), 220–231. doi:10.1037/1076-8998.8.3.220

Benz, M., Doren, B., & Yovanoff, P. (1998). Crossing the great divide: Predicting productive engagement for young women with disabilities. *Career Development for Exceptional Individuals, 21*(1), 3–16. doi:10.1177/088572889802100102

Berners-Lee, T. (1993, June). Hypertext Markup Language (HTML). Retrieved February 1, 2010, from http://www.w3.org/MarkUp/draft-ietf-iiir-html-01.txt

Burgstahler, S. (2006a). *Creating an e-mentoring community: How DO-IT does it and how you can do it too.* Seattle: University of Washington. Retrieved February 1, 2010, from http://www.washington.edu/doit/Mentor/

Burgstahler, S. (2006b) *Equal access: Universal design of computer labs.* Seattle: University of Washington. Retrieved February 1, 2010, from http://www.washington.edu/doit/Brochures/Technology/comp.access.html

Burgstahler, S. (2007). Accessibility training for distance learning personnel. *Access Technologists Higher Education Network (ATHEN) E-Journal, 2.* Retrieved February 1, 2010, from http://athenpro.org/node/56

Burgstahler, S. (2008). Universal design of technological environments: From principles to practice . In Burgstahler, S. E., & Cory, R. C. (Eds.), *Universal design in higher education: From principles to practice* (pp. 213–224). Cambridge, MA: Harvard Education Press.

Burgstahler, S., & Chang, C. (2007). Gender differences in perceived value of components of a program to promote academic and career success for students with disabilities. *Journal of Science Education for Students with Disabilities, 12*(1).

Burgstahler, S., Comden, D., & Fraser, B. (1997). Universal access: Designing and evaluating Websites for accessibility. *CHOICE: Current Reviews for Academic Libraries, 34*(Suppl.), 19–22.

Burgstahler, S., & Cronheim, D. (2001). Supporting peer-peer and mentor-protégé relationships on the internet. *Journal of Research on Technology in Education, 34*(1), 59–74.

Burgstahler, S., & Doyle, A. (2005). Gender differences in computer-mediated communication among adolescents with disabilities: A case study. *Disability Studies Quarterly, 25*(2).

Campbell-Whatley, G. (2001). Mentoring students with mild disabilities: The "nuts and bolts" of program development. *Intervention in School and Clinic, 36,* 211–216. doi:10.1177/105345120103600403

CAST. (n.d.b). *R & D projects.* Retrieved May 13, 2009, from http://www.cast.org/research/projects/index.html

CAST. (n.d.c). *What is universal design for learning?* Retrieved February 1, 2010, from http://www.cast.org/research/udl/

Center for Applied Special Technology [CAST]. (n.d.a). *CAST Transforming education through universal design for learning.* Retrieved February 1, 2010, from http://www.cast.org

Center for Children & Technology. (1998, September). *Critical issues in the design & implementation of telementoring environments.* Retrieved March 1, 2010, from http://cct.edc.org/admin/publications/report/09_1998.pdf

Center for Universal Design [CUD] (n.d.a) *About the Center: Ronald L. Mace.* Retrieved February 1, 2010, from http://www.design.ncsu.edu/cud/about_us/usronmace.htm

Closing the Gap. (n.d.). *Closing the Gap solutions: Producers.* Retrieved February 1, 2010, from http://www.closingthegap.com/solutions/producers/

Colley, A., & Comber, C. (2003). Age and gender differences in computer use and attitudes among secondary school students: What has changed? *Educational Research, 45*(2), 155–165. http://www.informaworld.com/smpp/content~content=a713766213~db=all~order=page Retrieved February 1, 2010. doi:10.1080/0013188032000103235

Conklin, M. (2007, February 25). *101 uses for Second Life in the college classroom.* Retrieved March 3, 2010, from http://citeseerx.ist.psu.edu/viewdoc/download?doi=10.1.1.133.9588&rep=rep1&type=pdf

CUD. (n.d.b). *About UD.* Raleigh: CUD. Retrieved May 13, 2009, from http://www.design.ncsu.edu/cud/about_ud/about_ud.htm

Day, A. L., & Livingstone, H. A. (2003). Gender differences in perceptions of stressors and utilization of social support among university students. *Canadian Journal of Behavioural Science, 35,* 73–83. doi:10.1037/h0087190

DO-IT. (n.d.). *DO-IT video search.* Retrieved February 1, 2010, from http://www.washington.edu/doit/Video/Search/

Doren, B., & Benz, M. R. (1998). Employment inequity revisited: Predictors of better employment outcomes of young women with disabilities in transition. *The Journal of Special Education, 31*(4), 425–442. doi:10.1177/002246699803100402

Electronic Emissary. (n.d.a). *What is the Electronic Emissary?* Retrieved February 1, 2010, from http://emissary.wm.edu/index.php?content=what.html

Electronic Emissary. (n.d.b). *Project overview.* Retrieved February 1, 2010, from http://emissary.wm.edu/index.php?content=project_overview.html

Ensher, E. A., & Murphy, S. E. (1997). Effects of race, gender, perceived similarity, and contact on mentor relationships. *Journal of Vocational Behavior, 50,* 460–481. doi:10.1006/jvbe.1996.1547

Facebook (n.d.a). *Accessibility and assistive technology.* Retrieved February 1, 2010, from http://www.facebook.com/help.php?page=440

Facebook (n.d.b). *The official petition for a more accessible Facebook.* Retrieved February 1, 2010, from http://www.facebook.com/home.php#/group.php?gid=2384051749

Federal Communications Commission. (n.d.). *What you need to know about TRS*. Retrieved February 1, 2010, from http://www.fcc.gov/cgb/dro/trs.html

Garringer, M., Fulop, M., & Rennick, V. (2003). *Foundations of successful youth mentoring: A guidebook for program development*. Portland, OR: National Mentoring Center. Retrieved February 1, 2010, from http://gwired.gwu.edu/hamfish/merlin-cgi/p/downloadFile/d/20699/n/off/other/1/name/foundationspdf/

Gilligan, C. (1982). *In a different voice: Psychological theory and women's development*. Cambridge, MA: Harvard University Press.

Golden, D. C. (2002). Instructional software accessibility: A status report. *Journal of Special Education Technology, 17*(1), 57–60.

Greenglass, E. R. (1993). Structural and social-psychological factors associated with job functioning by women managers. *Psychological Reports, 73*(3), 979–987.

Guy, T. (2002). Telementoring: Shaping mentoring relationships for the 21st Century. In C. A. Hansman (Ed.), *Critical Perspectives on Mentoring: Trends and Issues* (pp. 27-38). Columbus, OH: Center on Education and Training for Employment. Retrieved May 13, 2009, from www.calpro-online.org/eric/docs/mott/mentoring1.pdf

Hansman, C. A. (2002). Facing forward: Implications for practice and suggestions for future research. In C. A. Hansman (Ed.), *Critical Perspectives on Mentoring: Trends and Issues* (pp.49-52). Columbus, OH: Center on Education and Training for Employment. Retrieved May 13, 2009, from http://www.calpro-online.org/eric/docs/mott/mentoring7.pdf

Harris, J. (1999). *About the Electronic Emissary Project*. Retrieved February 1, 2010 from http://emissary.wm.edu/index.php?content=about.html

Harris, J., O'Bryan, E., & Rotenberg, L. (1996). It's a simple idea, but it's not easy to do! Practical lessons in telementoring. *Learning and Leading with Technology, 24*(2), 53–57.

Herrera, C., Sipe, C., & McClanahan, W. S. (2000). *Mentoring school-age children: Relationship development in community-based and school-based programs*. Philadelphia, PA: Private/Public Ventures.

Hitchcock, C., Meyer, A., Rose, D., & Jackson, R. (2002). Providing new access to the general curriculum: Universal design for learning. *Teaching Exceptional Children, 35*(2), 8–17.

Hitchcock, C., & Stahl, S. (2002). Assistive technology, universal design, universal design for learning: Improved learning opportunities. *Journal of Special Education Technology, 18*(4).

IBM. (2008). *What is Virtual Worlds User Interface for the Blind?* Retrieved February 1, 2010, from http://services.alphaworks.ibm.com/virtualworlds/

Jucovy, L. (2001). *Training new mentors*. Philadelphia, PA: Public/Private Ventures.

Kelton, A. J. (2007). *Second Life: Reaching into the virtual world for real-world learning*. EDUCAUSE Center for Applied Research (ECAR) Research Bulletin, 2007 (17). Retrieved February 1, 2010, from http://www.educause.edu/ECAR/SecondLifeReachingintotheVirtu/161863

Kim-Rupnow, W. S., & Burgstahler, S. (2004). Perceptions of students with disabilities regarding the value of technology-based support activities on postsecondary education and employment. *Journal of Special Education Technology, 19*(2), 43–56.

Laux, L. F., McNally, P. R., Paciello, M. G., & Vanderheiden, G. C. (1996). Designing the World Wide Web for people with disabilities: A user centered design approach. In *Proceedings of the Second Annual ACM Conference on Assistive Technologies*. Association for Computing Machinery, Special Interest Group on Accessible Computing, Vancouver, B. C., 94-101.

Lembree, D. (2009). *Accessible Twitter*. Retrieved February 1, 2010, from http://www.accessibletwitter.com

Lemon, G. (2009). *Twitter focus*. Retrieved February 1, 2010, from http://juicystudio.com/article/twitter-focus.php

LinkedIn. (n.d.). *Professional and Amateur Mentoring Group*. Retrieved February 1, 2010, from http://www.linkedin.com/groups?gid=36602

MentorNet. (n.d.a). *About MentorNet*. Retrieved February 1, 2010, from http://www.mentornet.net/documents/about/

MentorNet. (n.d.b). *MentorNet E-Forum*. Retrieved May 13, 2009, from http://www.mentornet.net/community/eforum/

Monnier, J., Stone, B. K., Hobfoll, S. E., & Johnson, R. J. (1998). How antisocial and prosocial coping influence the support process among men and women in the U.S. Postal Service. *Sex Roles*, *39*(1-2), 1–20. doi:10.1023/A:1018821631246

National Council on Disability. (2004). *Design for inclusion: Creating a new marketplace*. Washington, DC: Author. Retrieved February 1, 2010, from http://www.ncd.gov/newsroom/publications/2004/online_newmarketplace.htm#afbad

National Science Foundation. (2001). *Programs for persons with disabilities: Regional Alliances for Persons with Disabilities in Science, Mathematics, Engineering and Technology Education* (NSF 01-67). Retrieved February 1, 2010, from http://www.nsf.gov/pubs/2001/nsf0167/nsf0167.htm

Nielsen, J. (1996, October). Accessible design for users with disabilities. *Albertox: Current Issues in Web Usability*. Retrieved February 1, 2010, from http://www.useit.com/alertbox/9610.html

O'Neill, D. K., & Harris, J. B. (2005). Bridging the perspectives and developmental needs of all participants in curriculum-based telementoring programs. *Journal of Research on Technology in Education, 37*(2), 111-128. Retrieved May 13, 2009, from http://www.eric.ed.gov:80/ERICDocs/data/ericdocs2sql/content_storage_01/0000019b/80/2a/0d/16.pdf

O'Neill, D. K., Wagner, R., & Gomez, L. M. (1996). Online mentors: Experimenting in science class. *Educational Leadership*, *55*(3), 39–42.

Office of the Federal Register, National Archives and Records Service, General Services Administration. (2000, December 21). Electronic and information technology accessibility standards. *Federal Register*, *65*(246), 80499–80528.

Pascale, M., Mulatto, S., & Prattichizzo, D. (2008). Bringing haptics to Second Life. In *Proceedings of the 2008 Ambi-Sys workshop on Haptic user interfaces in ambient media systems* (pp.1-6). Quebec City, Canada: Haptic in Ambient Systems.

Patrick, D. L. (correspondence to Senator Tom Harkin, September 9, 1996). Retrieved February 1, 2010, from http://www.usdoj.gov/crt/foia/cltr204.txt

Perez, S., & Dorman, S. M. (2001). Enhancing youth achievement through telementoring. *The Journal of School Health*, *71*(3), 122–123. doi:10.1111/j.1746-1561.2001.tb07307.x

Ragins, B. R. (1989). Barriers to mentoring: The female manager's dilemma. *Human Relations, 42*, 1–22. doi:10.1177/001872678904200101

Randall, S. (2009). Jawter: Twitter from Jaws with no software in the middle. *Randy Laptop*. Retrieved May 13, 2009, from http://randylaptop.com/software/jawter-2/

Rehabilitation Act of 1973. 29 U.S.C. § 79 et seq.

Rose, D. H., & Meyer, A. (2002). *Teaching every student in the digital age: Universal design for learning*. Alexandria, VA: Association for Supervision and Curriculum Development.

Rose, D. H., Meyer, A., & Hitchcock, C. (Eds.). (2005). *The universally designed classroom: Accessible curriculum and digital technologies*. Cambridge, MA: Harvard Education Press.

Rowland, C., & Smith, T. (1999). Web site accessibility. *The Power of Independence* (Summer Edition), 1–2. Logan: Center for Persons with Disabilities, Utah State University.

Saito, R. N., & Blyth, D. A. (1992). *Understanding mentoring relationships*. Minneapolis, MN: Search Institute.

SciLands. (n.d.). SciLands Virtual Continent. Retrieved February 1, 2010, from http://www.scilands.org/

Second Life (n.d.a). *Accessibility—Second Life Wiki*. Retrieved February 1, 2010, from http://wiki.secondlife.com/wiki/Accessibility

Second Life (n.d.b) *Volunteer Portal*. Retrieved March 02, 2010, from http://wiki.secondlife.com/wiki/Volunteer_Portal

Second Life (n.d.c). *Second Life*. Retrieved May 13, 2009, from http://secondlife.com

Section 504 of the Rehabilitation Act of 1973. 29 U.S.C. § 794.

Section 508 of the Rehabilitation Act of 1973. (1998, amended). 29 U.S.C. 794(d). Retrieved February 1, 2010, from http://www.access-board.gov/sec508/guide/act.htm

Sipe, C. L. (1996). *Mentoring: A synthesis of P/PV's research: 1988-1995*. Philadelphia, PA: Public/Private Ventures.

Sword, C., & Hill, K. (2002). Creating mentoring opportunities for youth with disabilities: Issues and suggested strategies. *Issue Brief: Examining Current Challenges in Secondary Education and Transition, 1*(4). Retrieved February 1, 2010, from http://www.ncset.org/publications/viewdesc.asp?id=704

Telecommunications and Electronic and Information Technology Advisory Committee [TEITAC]. (2008). *Report to the Access Board: Refreshed accessibility standards and guidelines in telecommunications and electronic and information technology*. Retrieved February 1, 2010, from http://www.access-board.gov/sec508/refresh/report/

Text, S. L. (n.d.). *TextSL a Second Life client for visually impaired and blind users*. Retrieved February 1, 2010, from http://textsl.org/

Thompson, T. (2008). Universal design of computing labs . In Burgstahler, S. E., & Cory, R. C. (Eds.), *Universal design in higher education: From principles to practice* (pp. 235–244). Cambridge, MA: Harvard Education Press.

United States Access Board. (n.d.). *Section 508 home page: Electronic and information technology*. Retrieved February 1, 2010, from http://www.access-board.gov/508.htm

U.S. Access Board. (2007). *Update of the 508 Standards and the Telecommunications Act Guidelines*. Retrieved February 1, 2010, from http://www.access-board.gov/sec508/update-index.htm

U.S. Department of Education. (n.d.). *Building the legacy: IDEA 2004*. Retrieved February 1, 2010, from http://idea.ed.gov/explore/home

U.S. Department of Justice Civil Rights Division. (2005, September). *A guide to disability rights laws*. Retrieved February 1, 2010, from http://www.ada.gov/cguide.htm

Vanderheiden, G. C., & Vanderheiden, K. R. (1992). Guidelines for the design of consumer products to increase their accessibility to people with disabilities or who are aging (Working Draft 1.7). Madison, WI: Trace Research and Development Center. Retrieved February 1, 2010, from http://trace.wisc.edu/docs/consumer_product_guidelnies/toc.htm

WAI. (2005). *Introduction to Web accessibility*. Cambridge, MA: World Wide Web Consortium. Retrieved February 1, 2010, from http://www.w3.org/WAI/intro/accessibility.php

Waters, C. (1997). *Universal Web design*. Indianapolis, IN: New Riders.

WebAIM. (n.d.). TEITAC Archives. Retrieved February 1, 2010 from http://www.webaim.org/teitac/

World Wide Web Consortium [W3C]. (n.d.a.). *Web Accessibility Initiative (WAI)*. Retrieved February 1, 2010, from http://www.w3.org/WAI/

ADDITIONAL READING

Burgstahler, S. (2006). *Creating an e-mentoring community: How DO-IT does it and how you can do it too*. Seattle: University of Washington. Retrieved February 1, 2010, from http://www.washington.edu/doit/Mentor/

Burgstahler, S. (2007). Accessibility training for distance learning personnel. *Access Technologists Higher Education Network (ATHEN) E-Journal*, 2. Retrieved February 1, 2010, from http://athenpro.org/node/56

Burgstahler, S. (2008). Universal design of technological environments: From principles to practice. In *Universal design in higher education: From principles to practice* (pp. 213–224). Cambridge, MA: Harvard Education Press.

Center for Applied Special Technology. (n.d.). Retrieved February 1, 2010, from http://www.cast.org/

Center for Universal Design. (n.d.). Retrieved February 1, 2010, from http://www.design.ncsu.edu/cud/

Jucovy, L. (2001). *Training new mentors*. Philadelphia, PA: Public/Private Ventures.

Kelton, A. J. (2007). *Second Life: Reaching into the virtual world for real-world learning*. EDUCAUSE Center for Applied Research (ECAR) Research Bulletin, 2007 (17). Retrieved February 1, 2010, from http://www.educause.edu/ECAR/SecondLifeReachingintotheVirtu/161863

O'Neill, D. K., & Harris, J. B. (2005). Bridging the perspectives and developmental needs of all participants in curriculum-based telementoring programs. *Journal of Research on Technology in Education, 37*(2), 111-128. Retrieved February 1, 2010, from http://www.eric.ed.gov:80/ERICDocs/data/ericdocs2sql/content_storage_01/0000019b/80/2a/0d/16.pdf

Slatin, J., & Rush, S. (2003). *Maximum accessibility: Making your web site more usable for everyone*. Boston: Addison-Wesley.

Sword, C., & Hill, K. (2002). Creating mentoring opportunities for youth with disabilities: Issues and suggested strategies. *Issue Brief: Examining Current Challenges in Secondary Education and Transition, 1*(4). Retrieved February 1, 2010, from http://www.ncset.org/publications/viewdesc.asp?id=704

The Center for Universal Design in Education. (n.d.) Retrieved February 1, 2010, from http://www.washington.edu/doit/CUDE

WebAIM. (n.d.). *Introduction to Web accessibility.* Retrieved February 1, 2010, from http://www.webaim.org/intro/

Chapter 7
Electronic Mentoring in the Classroom:
Where Mentors and Students are Persons with Disabilities

Carmit-Noa Shpigelman
University of Haifa, Israel

Patrice L. (Tamar) Weiss
University of Haifa, Israel

Shunit Reiter
University of Haifa, Israel

ABSTRACT

In recent years, we have witnessed a process of growing awareness and increased activity among persons with disabilities toward improvements in their living conditions and their full inclusion into society. Still, persons with disabilities experience difficulty in achieving the interpersonal competencies needed to develop adaptive social behaviors, to achieve and maintain close relationships, and to fulfill their potential. Mentoring appears to promote interpersonal development when it is conducted via traditional face-to-face methods or via electronic means. In particular, electronic mentoring programs that nurture relationships between persons with disabilities appear to have considerable potential for their empowerment. In this chapter we discuss the relevance, feasibility and utility of e-mentoring intervention programs designed especially for young people with disabilities.

INTRODUCTION

Historically, persons with disabilities were a marginalized group, a fact that reflected broad societal judgments of pity, at best, fear and, in some cases, loathing at worst. Since the 1970s, society's views of persons with disabilities have become more enlightened. Towards the end of the 20th century, the concept of a person with a disability has changed from the traditional medical model to the newer humanistic and social model. According to the medical model of disability, persons with disabilities are viewed as defective and in need of being "fixed," rather than being included as

DOI: 10.4018/978-1-61520-861-6.ch007

individuals with a range of capabilities. In contrast, the humanistic and social model emphasizes the personality and the competences of the person; it is the relationship between the impairment and society's structure and treatment of people with disabilities that is likely to determine the degree to which the disability is limiting. Individuals who use a wheelchair will find an inaccessible physical environment to be "disabling" whereas a barrier-free environment is not (Reiter, 2008).

During the past two decades, following the legislation of new laws around the world, we have witnessed a process initiated in response to the needs of persons with disabilities, in which public buildings and cultural centers have been made more accessible by, for example, removing physical barriers, installing ramps and lifts, and providing vocal signals at pedestrian crossings (Preiser & Ostroff, 2001). In the educational system, with the aid of new legislation in the field, the movement towards integration has been greatly accelerated. We also witness increased proactivism among persons with disabilities, as they demand improvements in their living conditions and their complete inclusion in the larger community (Poetz, 2003).

Despite a slow paradigm shift from strict adherence to the medical model to consideration of the social model of disability, loneliness and alienation are prevalent among young people with disabilities (Albert, 2006; Smith & Erevelles, 2004, Fish, Rabidoux, Ober, & Graff, 2006; Abbott & Mcconkey, 2006; Chadsey & Beyer, 2001; Allen & Sigafoos, 2000). Regardless of enlightened laws, integration does not always result in a child's meaningful inclusion in school and in the community (Dinerstein, 2004; McConkey, 2005). Based on extensive work in England, South Africa and developing countries in Asia and Africa, Albert (2006) suggests that the persistence of traditional medical and welfare approaches to disability still prevail even among 'well-meaning' organizations. He states that "although many aid organizations have adopted the human-rights language and slogans of the disability movement, with few exceptions, their attitudes and actions remain rooted in a medical understanding of disability and its concomitant top-down, charity-like, 'professional-know-the-best' approach to disabled people themselves" (pp.1-2).

Despite technological progress and some signs of a growing awareness, in most countries around the world persons with disabilities are still regarded as 'sick' and 'imperfect' who not able to be 'like everyone else'. It appears that the major obstacle that persons with disabilities will face in the third millennium will remain that of social inaccessibility. Social inaccessibility leads to loneliness. Persons with disabilities are here with us but don't really belong. They are not an integral part of the general community (Longmore, 2003; Michalko, 2002). According to the social model of disability, an effort should be made to promote the participation of persons with disabilities in political and legislative decisions concerning their lives and they should be encouraged to take part in research and projects that address these issues (Albert, 2006). Indeed, inclusion should be regarded as a bilateral process. Through education we can assist persons with disabilities to be able to take an active part in changing their social status (Reiter, 2008).

However, in order to promote full inclusion of persons with disabilities into society, we have to construct educational programs which allow social involvement, respect, meaning, and self-fulfillment of these persons. Mentoring programs that are integrated into the lives of persons with disabilities at an early stage of childhood or adolescence can promote their positive development. It is critical that mentoring programs address the interest of these youth through approaches that are strength-based, and accord control to them, work toward their goal attainment and engage also mentors with disabilities (McDonald, Balcazar, Keys, 2005).

E-MENTORING AS ALTERNATIVE COMMUNICATIVE TOOL

The Internet has opened up a range of new communication opportunities, especially for persons with disabilities, through increased avenues for communication, improved educational outcomes and greater employment opportunities (Hasselbring & Williams Glaser, 2000). Computer-Mediated Communication (CMC) may contribute to their social and emotional well-being (Rhodes, 2003). A related development, which has a considerable potential for persons with disabilities, is the ever increasing number of mentoring programs conducted via the Internet (Walther & Boyd, 2002). E-mentoring, also referred to as *Telementoring*, *Online Mentoring* or *Virtual Mentoring*, refers to a dyadic relationship in which a mentor, a person senior in age or experience, provides guidance and support to a less experienced or younger person, the protégé, via CMC (DuBois & Karcher, 2005).

The term *Telementoring* is routinely used when the mentoring relationships are conducted via telephone or media that electronically transmits voice communication while the term *E-mentoring* often refers to text-based electronic communication (Single & Single, 2005). CMC was originally defined as a form of asynchronous electronic written communication (e.g., email). As computer technologies have progressed, e-mentoring programs have expanded to include synchronous communication (e.g., chat rooms, instant messaging) with the aid of audio and video tools such as microphone and webcam (Barak, Hen, Boniel-Nissim, & Shapira, 2008b; Barnes, 2003; Leh, 2001).

The growing number of e-mentoring websites (e.g., http://www.mentornet.net; http://www.imentor.org; http://www.mentorplace.org) provide mostly vocational and career support. These websites offer advice, provide feedback and coaching, and may link to influential organizations (Ensher, Heun & Blanchard, 2003). In addition, American national policy directed at the needs of at-risk youth has encouraged the establishment of mentoring programs designed especially for persons with disabilities and included electronic communication. For example, Disabilities, Opportunities, Internetworking & Technology (DO-IT) is an e-mentoring program that matches between mentors and protégés with similar disabilities in order to encourage individuals with disabilities to participate in postsecondary academic programs and careers through outreach programs to students with disabilities, disability awareness training, and information dissemination. (http://www.washington.edu/doit). The protégés are DO-IT scholars, college-bound high school students with disabilities (hearing, mobility, vision, and health impairments as well as learning disabilities) who are interested in science, engineering, mathematics, and technology. They use computers, assistive technology, and the Internet to communicate with each other and with the mentors who are DO-IT staff and adult volunteers who also have disabilities and are enrolled in postsecondary institutions or are employed. Mentors are encouraged to contact protégés-scholars with interests via email and occasionally meet with them face-to-face (Burgstahler & Cronheim, 2001)

MENTOR, the American national mentoring partnership, also established an e-mentoring program designed to promote successful transition of youth with disabilities to adult life (http://www.mentoring.org; http://ici.umn.edu/ementoring). This program facilitates interactions between a student with a disability and an employer through CMC and focuses on building a career path. Another e-mentoring program which matches youth and adults with disabilities is conducted under the auspices of the Partners for Youth Disabilities (PYD) in the United States (Seeger, 2007).

The effectiveness of these online support interventions has been questioned due to the lack of social context cues, absence of immediate clarification and time delays which characterized computer-mediated environments (Mallen, Vogel, Rochlen, & Day, 2005; Rochlen, Zack, &

Speyer, 2004). With regard to the issue of social context cues, attainment of a feeling of social presence may be a compensation for the lack of shared physical space in a computer-mediated environment. *Social presence*, which refers to the feeling of being together, of social interaction with a virtual or remotely located communication partner, may be obtained through adding emoticons (i.e., symbols designed to supplement a text message with emotional content), visual or audio files (Barnes, 2003; Leh, 2001; Lombard & Ditton, 1997). Achieving a greater sense of "presence" in a computer-mediated environment may lead to disinhibition which encourages the removal of social stigmas, possibly facilitating self-disclosure and self-reflection (King et al., 2006; Suler, 2004). Moreover, writing about one's concerns or conflicts may contribute to a feeling of well-being and relief (Pennebaker, 1997; Mallen et al., 2005; Rochlen et al., 2004).

THE UTILITY OF E-MENTORING FOR PERSONS WITH DISABILITIES

Studies that have explored the effectiveness of e-mentoring programs suggest that individuals who are isolated, stigmatized, or lack real-world social support may be especially motivated to participate in and gain from these online support interventions (Andersson et al., 2005; Barak & Dolev-Cohen, 2006; Lewis, Coursol, & Herting, 2004; Miller & Griffith, 2005; Rhodes, Spencer, Saito, & Sipe, 2006b). Burgstahler and Cronheim (2001) compared peer-peer and mentor-protégé relationships of youth with disabilities conducted via the Internet. The participants communicated via email using the DO-IT program. The results supported CMC as a favorable environment in which to provide peer and mentor psychological, academic, and career support for youth with disabilities. In particular, peer-peer relationships were shown to be more personal (i.e., the information exchanged was about personal lives, family, feelings, friendships and hobbies) than mentor-protégé relationships. Most of the messages exchanged between mentors and protégés are related to academics, careers, disabilities and technical issues.

Cohen and Light (2000) also conducted an e-mentoring program for adolescents and young adults with cerebral palsy who use augmentative and alternative communication (AAC). Four mentor-protégé dyads were instructed to communicate weekly via e-mail on topics of interest to them over a period of at least six months. Most of the participants reported satisfaction with the e-mentoring program. The results indicated that e-mentoring by successful users of AAC (i.e., the mentors) may be effective in easing the transition of younger users of AAC. The training of mentors, the careful matching of protégés and mentors, the provision of guidelines and expectations of frequency of message exchanges, reliable Internet service, and opportunities for additional methods of contact (face-to-face interactions) appeared to be important steps in developing an effective e-mentoring program.

Van Uden-Krann et al. (2008) interviewed 32 persons with somatic diseases (breast cancer, fibromyalgia, or arthritis) who participated in online support groups, in order to explore if, and in which ways, they felt empowered by their participation. The findings revealed that online support groups can make a valuable contribution to the emergence of empowered persons with disabilities. The participants were being better informed, felt confident in the relationship with their physicians, their treatment, and their social environment. They also achieved greater acceptance of the disease, and increased their optimism, control, self-esteem and social well-being. The study of Bowker and Tuffin (2007) also emphasized that online experiences afford people with disabilities an opportunity to enjoy greater social acceptability and self-esteem, independent of their identity as a person with a disability. The researchers investigated the psychology of the online process for people with physical and sensory disabilities. Results indicated that the physical and attitudinal barriers that impinge upon the ability of people with disabilities to demonstrate their competencies are reduced during the online experience.

The above studies highlight the unique communication features of e-mentoring interventions. These include freedom from the restrictions of location and time, greater access to diverse sources of information, anonymity which appears to encourage frankness and intimacy and may lead to greater self-disclosure due to a lessening of the apprehension of stigma related to illness and disability (Barak, 2003; Barak et al., 2008b; Wright & Bell, 2003). In addition, negative feelings related to one's physical appearance (e.g., overweight, disability) and vocal characteristics (e.g., stutter) as well as inept social skills are lessened in computer-mediated environments (Rhodes, 2003; Rice & Katz, 2001; White & Dorman, 2001; Wright, 2000). These unique features imply that online support interventions such as e-mentoring may become a useful alternative for persons with disabilities (Braithwaite, Waldron, & Finn, 1999).

THE FEASIBILITY OF E-MENTORING FOR STUDENTS WITH DISABILITIES

We conducted companion studies which explored the feasibility and utility of social and emotional support through an e-mentoring intervention program between protégés and mentors who both had disabilities (Shpigelman, Reiter, & Weiss, 2008; 2009a; Shpigelman, Weiss, & Reiter, 2009b). The protégés were teen-aged students (12 to 20 years old) from Israeli special education schools with a wide range of impairments (physical, emotional, behavioral or intellectual impairments). The mentors were university students (22 to 28 years old) with sensory or physical impairments. The first study was a three-month pilot e-mentoring intervention, which provided mutual self-disclosure and socio-emotional support for five mentor-protégé pairs with disabilities. The second study was conducted over a one academic year (i.e., an eight-month period) and included 13 mentor-protégé pairs.

The selected protégés were recommended by a professional school staff based on their need for socio-emotional support. They had a basic ability to communicate via the Internet, and were interested in participating in the e-mentoring intervention program. Student mentors were recruited from a national mentoring program run on all university campuses known as "PERACH" (http://www.perach.org.il/English). This program provides educational, social and emotional one-on-one support to school children from disadvantaged families or from the special education system. The support is provided by university students who receive a reduction in tuition for serving as mentors or tutors for the school children. The mentors were selected by the coordinator after a personal interview which demonstrated that they were adept at using a computer and the Internet, had an available Internet connection, and had a strong willingness to volunteer and contribute via an e-mentoring program. After selection, the coordinator made appropriate matches of mentor-protégé pairs while taking into consideration factors such as gender, shared interests and hobbies (Ensher et al., 2003).

The program coordinator was trained and supported by professional PERACH staff in consultation with the researchers (Shpigelman et al., 2008; 2009b). Prior to and during the e-mentoring intervention program, the coordinator conducted four, two-hour training workshops for the mentors. These focused on issues related to mentoring adolescents with special needs and to electronic social and emotional support and coping techniques via CMC, e.g., the ability to handle acting-out behavior and intensity of emotion as expressed in the protégés' messages, and encouraging the protégés to communicate and express themselves (Ensher et al., 2003).

Each mentor was matched separately with two protégés. Both mentors and protégés were requested to send at least two messages per week via email. The e-mentoring intervention program was conducted under the auspices of the school computer science teacher who helped the protégés develop their computer and Internet usage skills. During the intervention each mentor-protégé pair was requested to meet face-to-face three times. Between these meetings, the mentors and the protégés continued to communicate via email and some of them also used synchronous communication, such as instant messaging or phone.

Qualitative content analysis of the electronic correspondence provided support for the relevance and feasibility of e-mentoring for persons with disabilities and indicated that the protégés learned to use a computer and the Internet to develop interpersonal communication skills, and to gain a friend. Communication with young adults, the mentors, who also had disabilities, gave the protégés an opportunity to experience an accepting relationship with less prejudice. The teachers reported that the protégés started to develop more meaningful relationships with their classmates, developed sensitivity and consideration toward persons with disabilities, and the intervention appeared to lead to an increase of their self-image and self-esteem. The intervention contributed also to the mentors themselves. The mentors felt they had an opportunity to give and to assist others, and for the first time they felt as if they were not disabled. In general, e-mentoring relationships appeared to be valuable for personal empowerment of persons with disabilities by the learning of communication skills, exposure to various coping strategies related to living with a disability, and the opportunity to assist others (Shpigelman et al., 2008; 2009b).

The content analysis of the electronic correspondences indicated that the development of the e-mentoring relationship paralleled the process typically found for face-to-face mentoring, as shown in Table 1. The process commenced with the phase of personal acquaintance (self-presentation such as age, family, studies, hobbies), and then continued at the mentors' initiative to exploring mutual interests. The mentors endeavored to establish realistic expectations for the e-mentoring process and to prepare a foundation for a more personal, intimate, informal and longer-term relationship.

The next phase consisted of a deepening of the relationship. Content analysis revealed three central themes: perceptions of the relationship, definition of the mentor's roles, and developing and maintaining of the relationship. The e-mentoring relationship was perceived by the participants on a continuum ranging from a superficial relationship (having fun and meeting a new person) to a "deeper" relationship (mutual assistance and being friends). The mentor's roles, achieved primarily by utterances as guided by the program coordinator, were categorized into two major themes: "Being a friend" and "Being an adviser". Being a friend meant that the mentor and the protégé corresponded informally and shared personal information. This was perceived by the protégés to be one of the mentors' major roles whereas the mentors perceived it to be minor, mainly as a means to achieve the role of being an adviser. Being an adviser was perceived as being a supportive role model for the protégé through listening, advising, giving constructive feedback and encouraging (i.e., providing emotional, instructional and educational support).

Developing and maintaining the relationship was driven primarily by the mentors and occurred at two levels. The first level was superficial and referred to the efforts made to ensure the protégés' diligence and compliance with the targeted sequence of electronic correspondence. The second level referred to the efforts made by the mentors to promote a relationship based on social and emotional openness, trust, reflection, mutual consideration and regard and the sharing of personal information including the disability issue. The majority of the mentors chose to raise

Table 1. Development of an e-mentoring relationship

Core themes	Sub-themes	Description	Examples
Establishment of the relationship	Self-presentation	Basic information: personal name, age, living area, studies, hobbies, etc.	Protégé: "My name is X and I study in the eighth grade at Y school. I live with my mother in Z. I very much like computer science lessons and I like mostly to surf the Internet, and I have a computer at home."
	Exploring mutual interests	Mentors wrote about their interests and asked the protégé to do the same.	Mentor: "Both of us like the sea." Mentor: "I haven't read this book; will you tell me a little bit more about it?"
	Coordination of expectations	Mentors defined their expectations and asked the protégé to do the same.	Mentor: "We will get to know each other step by step, and you may feel free to ask whatever you want. I will always be there, on the other side of the Internet, to respond."
Deepening of the relationship	Perceptions of the relationship	Having fun	Mentor: "It's a lot of fun to open the electronic mailbox and find there is a letter waiting for me."
		Acquaintance of a new person	Protégé: "Have you already taught children in a classroom?" Mentor: "I would like to hear more about you - what do you like to study, what are your hobbies or even your favorite TV shows and the singers that you admire."
		Mutual assistance	Mentor: "I also ate so much during that holiday. I have been thinking that maybe we'll search the Internet together to find diet recipes - tasty and not fattening ones. So what do you say?"
		Being friends	Protégé: "I was very sorry that we didn't meet at your home; my mother and I had an argument and she punished me by canceling our meeting." Mentor: "Thank you for taking a picture with me and especially thank you for your trust in me and that you shared a private thought with me."
	Definition of the mentor's roles	Being a friend	Mentor: "Feel free to write anything you think and want to share with me. I would like to be a mentor and a good friend for you."
		Being an advisor	Mentor: "If you think about it, when we restrain from something, the restraint itself makes us become stronger, and then when we finally do the anticipated thing we enjoy it a lot more."
	Developing and maintaining of the relationship	Superficial level - writing about hobbies, family, studies, etc.	Mentor: "I remember that you study fashion design so I have collected some fashion catalogs and they will be waiting for you at our next meeting."
		Deeper level - writing about personal issues, such as weight, diet, and disability.	Protégé: "Sorry about this question, I have heard that you have a problem with your eyes." Mentor: "I'm glad that you have raised this issue. I will be glad to talk about it if you have more questions."
Determination of the relationship	Meeting face-to-face and sending a good-bye email message.	Most of the pairs closed the process only though a face-to-face meeting.	Mentor: "I would like to wish you good luck in your Math matriculation exam. I understand that your exam will be tomorrow... I cross my fingers for you and count on you that you'll succeed."

the disability issue in the very first message. In contrast, the protégés usually did not refer to their disability although they referred to their mentor's disability by asking questions or making statements which indicated care and consideration. For example, a 12-year-old protégé, who had intellectual impairment, wrote to his mentor: *"How can you see if you don't see in one eye; do you have special glasses?"*

Overall, most of the mentors and the protégés referred to their disabilities minimally and only at the start of the intervention. As the intervention progressed, however, they chose to focus on daily experiences and concerns via the electronic correspondence, such as hobbies, relationships with family members, friends and teachers, and future plans such as continued education and career options (Shpigelman et al., 2009b). Previous studies (Shaw, Hawkins, McTavish, Pingree, & Gustafson, 2006) have indicated that online support interventions, such as e-mentoring, which are not limited to specific topics, may not encourage participants to focus on a "shared situation", (e.g., the disability issue). Interactions that are too general may also remain impersonal (Shpigelman et al., 2009b). However, they appeared to be valuable for the enjoyment, development and empowerment of persons with disabilities, as shown also in other studies (Adelman, Parks, & Albrecht, 1987; Amichai-Hamburrger, MaKenna, & Tal, 2008; Barak & Sadovsky, 2008; Pitts, 2004).

During the phase of a deepening of the e-mentoring relationship, the mentors, and especially the protégés, expressed a strong need for more tangible feedback such as visual and vocal interactions. The last phase of the e-mentoring process was termination of the relationship. The mentors had been instructed to end the relationship at a face-to-face meeting and to then send a goodbye email message.

In accordance with a debate related to the effectiveness of online support interventions (Barak et al., 2008b; Mallen et al., 2005; Rochlen et al., 2004), the findings of our studies (Shpigelman et al., 2008; 2009b) revealed different viewpoints held by the mentors and the protégés. On the one hand, the e-mentoring process, which has been characterized by anonymity, asynchronicity, and lack of non-verbal communication cues, was considered to be a protective environment for the disclosure of personal information and the development of personal relationships by youth with disabilities (Barak, 2007; Bowker & Tuffin, 2007; Coulson, 2005; Joinson, 2001; Suler, 1996-2005; Tidwell & Walther, 2002; Wehmeyer, Smith, Palmer, & Davis, 2004). For example, a 16-year-old female protégé with an emotional impairment remarked: *"Regarding the e-mentoring relationship - it is easier to write the words than say it face-to-face. I would like to go on participating in this program because it is fun, there is someone you can tell anything to, and you can count on him. I feel comfortable with it."* The use of informal language, such as slang phrases (e.g., "What's up man?" or "Sweetie, how are you?"), by the mentors and the protégés, indicated a progression towards greater intimacy as the intervention progressed (Shpigelman et al., 2008).

On the other hand, most of the mentors, and especially the protégés, considered the e-mentoring process to be a barrier to development of a personal relationship, as indicated by an 18-year-old female protégé with an emotional impairment: *"The process was just correspondence. I still feel distant from my mentor"*. While the mentors attributed failure to achieve a more intimate relationship to a lack of mutual commitment, the protégés viewed it to be more related to a lack synchronous communication, such as on-site communication and more frequent face-to-face meetings. The results also indicated that youth with disabilities, similar to their peers who do not have disabilities, consider face-to-face relationships to be stronger than electronic relationships due to the frequency and quality of communication which they consider necessary to promote a building of trust and to encourage self-disclosure (Mesch & Talmud, 2006; Paine, Joinson, Buchanan, & Reips, 2006).

The results of our studies supported previous studies (Bowker & Tuffin, 2007; Burgstahler & Cronheim, 2001) and demonstrated that a rapport developed between the mentor-protégé pairs, becoming a positive and supportive relationship. Communicating via email appeared to reduce the

Table 2. Four stages for conducting a successful e-mentoring program

Main Stages	Description
1. Personal acquaintance	Introduction and searching for topics of mutual interest.
2. Moderated communication	Focusing directly or indirectly on issues that concern adolescents, such as social life, relationships in the family, studies, career, travel, and other issues that can be raised by the protégé. During this stage it is recommended to set an individual face-to-face meeting in order to deepen the bond between the mentor-protégé pairs.
3. Online activities	Playing web games, planning a trip via the retrieval of information from websites, chatting online and sharing information. During this stage it is recommended to set another face-to-face meeting.
4. Saying "Goodbye"	Preparing the mentors and the protégés for the end of the program including planning a common souvenir, such as creating a web album or presentation. It is recommended to set a last individual face-to-face meeting in order to achieve closure to the program.

visibility of the participants' disability, which enabled them to speak about life experiences (e.g., family, friends, hobbies, studies) and to help them feel that they share some characteristics with typical youth (Andersson et al., 2005; Barak et al., 2008b; Bowker & Tuffin, 2007; Cohen & Light, 2000). According to the development process of e-mentoring relationships (see Table 1), a successful e-mentoring program should be conducted following four major stages, as shown in Table 2.

To summarize, the literature review demonstrates the considerable potential of an e-mentoring relationship for positive development of persons with disabilities, especially in adolescence. Youth with disabilities can be empowered by communication via the Internet since they can be viewed as people without disabilities, and also by the exposure to other ways of coping with a disability. They, like their peers without disabilities, can also enjoy using the Internet for leisure and social activities and benefit by such pursuits (Barak, Boniel-Nissim, & Suler, 2008a; Gross, Juvonen, & Gable, 2002; Weiss, Bialik, & Kizony, 2003).

Furthermore, pairing mentors and protégés who have disabilities in a computer-mediated environment has a considerable potential to nurture a relationship to empower the protégés. A young person with a disability can be positively influenced especially by a successful adult with a disability (McDonald et al., 2005; Sword & Hill, 2003). Mentors with disabilities can identify with the difficulties experienced by protégés with disabilities, and can support their personal growth through exploring career options, setting academic and career goals, examining different lifestyles, developing social and professional contacts, strengthening interpersonal competencies, achieving higher levels of autonomy, and developing a vigorous sense of identity (Burgstahler & Cronheim, 2001).

However, our studies revealed some difficulties that the protégés encountered during the e-mentoring intervention including language limitations (e.g., lack of reading comprehension, expressive written communication and typing skills), technical problems due to inappropriate and cognitively difficult Internet-access software, a need for more visual and vocal cues when using CMC and emotional difficulty when trying to write about their disability and to accept the mentor's disability, (Shpigelman et al., 2008; 2009b). These difficulties highlighted that even a mentoring program designed especially for students with disabilities may not be able to meet the needs of all persons, as shown also in a study conducted by Todis, Powers, Irvin and Singer (1996).

In addition, in order to conduct successful e-mentoring programs, a conceptual framework aimed to guide the establishment and implementation of such interventions, is needed. Based on the literature and the results of our studies

(Amichai-Hamburrger et al., 2008; Burgstahler & Cronheim, 2001; Cohen & Light, 2000; McDonald et al., 2005; Shpigelman et al., 2008; 2009b), we will present, in the next section, a conceptual framework that we have developed and used to guide an electronic social and emotional support (ESES) process for persons with disabilities.

PRACTICAL SUGGESTIONS: HOW TO IMPLEMENT AN E-MENTORING PROGRAM FOR STUDENTS WITH DISABILITIES?

The growing literature on mentoring has included models related mainly to traditional face-to-face mentoring and at-risk populations (Ensher et al., 2003; Hamilton & Scandura, 2003; Miller & Griffiths, 2005). Unfortunately, to date, only few e-mentoring programs have made an active attempt to include persons with disabilities, in part, due to the difficulties in making the program settings, activities or transportation accessible for this population (Rousso, 2001). When policy makers, caregivers and/or educators plan and conduct a mentoring intervention which is based on electronic communication and aimed to support populations with disabilities, they have to cope with the obstacles described above. In order to fulfill the considerable potential of the electronic medium for students with disabilities, it is recommended to follow the proposed conceptual framework. First we will review theories and models related to mentoring, support, CMC and disabilities. Then, we will present the ESES conceptual framework.

Cutrona and Suhr (1992) developed a framework of Social Support Behavior Code (SSBC) which emphasizes the influence of help-intended communicative behaviors on coping with stressful life events. According to Cutrona and Suhr (1992), social support consists of five types of support:

a. Informational support - providing information about a stressful event or how to deal with it.
b. Tangible assistance - providing or offering to provide goods or services needed in a stressful event.
c. Esteem – expressing confidence in abilities and intrinsic value.
d. Emotional support - communicating caring, concern, empathy and sympathy.
e. Social support - communicating belonging to a group of persons with similar interests and concerns.

In their view, although communicative behaviors ranging from quiet listening to active problem solving can be helpful, they will have less impact, or even a negative impact, if provided in the wrong context. Contextual factors that influence the degree to which help-intended communications will be helpful include the nature of the relationship between the helper and the recipient, whether help was provided spontaneously or upon request, the timing of the help-intended communication, the personality of the recipient, and the nature of the stressful event. Although Cutrona and Suhr's (1992) framework was originally developed for supportive behaviors occurring during face-to-face interactions, it appears to provide a basis for identifying which supportive behaviors will have an impact during CMC.

The Online Social Support (OSS) Theory of Perreault LaCoursiere (2001) expanded the focus of the social support process to computer-mediated environments. The OSS theory encompasses the factors effecting online social support, based initially on a nursing perspective but also integrating research findings from an open system, multidisciplinary perspective (e.g., anthropology, sociology, psychology, communication science, computer science and management). The OSS theory presents a dynamic process which occurs through three filters: perceptional filter – the feeling or emotional state of a person seeking social support; cognitive filter – the intellectual processing of information; and transactional filter – an evaluation of all information received through electronic support interchanges. Then, three processes -- support mediation, information processing and evaluation -- lead to a synthesis of an individual's experiences and result in changes of behaviors, thought, feelings and actions (Perreault LaCoursiere, 2001).

O'Neill, Weile and Sha (2003) add five instructions that educators should take into consideration when they plan and implement an e-mentoring program:

- Building and describing an available and up-to-date "pool" of volunteer mentors.
- Matching mentors and protégés in ways appropriate to the needs being served.
- Providing opportunities for just-in-time learning which means that the participants learn about mentoring relationships while experiencing them.
- Preventing mentor overload since CMC is fast and there might be a temptation to match metros large numbers of protégés. It is important especially when the mentors and the protégés are persons with disabilities.

Based on the above theories, models and previous studies (Shpigelman et al., 2008; 2009b), we have developed a conceptual framework, which delineates the optimal electronic socio-emotional support (ESES) process for students with disabilities (Shpigelman et al., 2009b). As illustrated in Figure 1, the drive for commencing the ESES process may emanate from intrinsic and/or extrinsic sources. An individual with disabilities may seek electronic support on his own if he is sufficiently motivated and aware of its possibilities. Due to physical or psychological difficulties, some students with disabilities may have difficulty in making use of electronic support. To rectify such problems, caregivers, referred to as extrinsic sources, are encouraged to expose these students to the new opportunities offered by CMC. In accordance with Bierema and Merriam (2002) and the humanistic model (Childress, 2000; Reiter, 2008), mentoring relationships can be nurtured but not forced. Caregivers must allow these individuals a free choice of participation in e-mentoring interventions. The relative contribution of the internal and external factors is dynamic, depending on the individual's personality and supports in his environment (Suler, 2001).

The next components are preconditions which are needed to enable and facilitate the process. Preconditions consist of adapted hardware and software that make computer access possible for students with disabilities, the availability of technical support and being computer literate, i.e., being adept at computer and Internet usage, having sufficient communication skills to interact via the Internet such as reading comprehension, expressive written communication, and the ability to find, evaluate and use information technology (Hoffman & Blake, 2003). Consistent with our studies (Shpigelman et al., 2008; 2009b) and Bowe's study (2002), the precondition, referred to as requiring computer literacy skills, is considered to be an important factor in order to engage an individual with a disability in sufficiently frequent communication including reciprocal self-disclosure. Appropriate training and the type and the quality of CMC (sufficiently frequent, two-way and task-based) are also crucial for this process. Indeed, the provision of such CMC elements to enhance the sense of "social presence", such as visual and auditory graphic icons (emoticons and earcons) designed to supplement a text message with emotional content, is essential (Barak, 2003; 2007; Barnes, 2003; Leh, 2001).

Pre-training is also an important component that must be provided for all participants in an e-mentoring program, including the mentors, the protégés and the coordinators. Pre-training may enhance individuals' confidence in their ability to participate in such programs. It may also lead

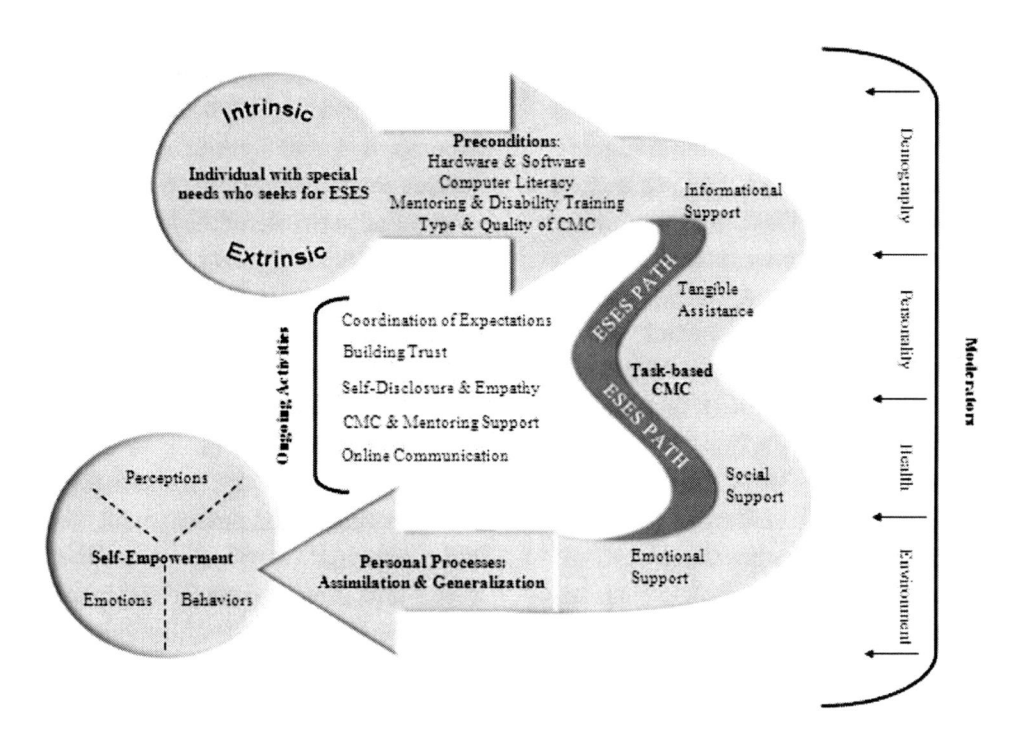

Figure 1. Electronic socio-emotional support (ESES) process

to a feeling of self-efficacy and, in return, to facilitate desired positive outcomes during the e-mentoring process. With regard to the protégés, our previous work (Shpigelman et al., 2008; 2009b) highlighted the need to deal also with the issue of self-acceptance, specifically awareness of one's own disability, and acceptance of one's self as a person with unique competencies. That is, it is recommended to conduct disability-centered pre-training in order to benefit from relationships with mentors who also have disabilities (Burgstahler & Cronheim, 2001). In addition, the pre-training should focus on support and coping techniques via CMC, such as the ability to handle acting-out behavior and intensity of emotion as expressed in the email messages, and encouraging participants to communicate and express themselves.

Furthermore, an e-mentoring program should focus on a defined task or area of learning which will make electronic communication more authentic and attractive (Miller & Griffiths, 2005).

According to Rhodes' (2002; 2005) Model of Youth Mentoring, the socio-emotional developmental process and the cognitive developmental process are interrelated and can be furthered via mentoring relationships. By engaging in cognitive tasks conducted via interactions with mentors, protégés may acquire and refine new thinking skills, becoming more receptive to adult values, advice, and perspectives (Rhodes & DuBois, 2008). Herrera, Sipe and McClanahan (2000) also indicated that mentors who reported engaging in a larger number of social and academic activities with protégés tended to rate their relationships as significantly closer. That is, the addition of a task-based CMC to the ESES path is an essential part of conducting an e-mentoring program (Rhodes et al., 2006a). Task-based CMC, which is considered to be more concrete for youth with disabilities, will probably enhance their engagement in the e-mentoring process.

When sufficient preconditions are in place, the ESES path commences. Based on Cutrona and Suhr's (1992) framework, the ESES path should include informational support, tangible assistance, social support and emotional support. Throughout the ESES process, there is a need for ongoing support, i.e., CMC and mentoring support. These should be coordinated in terms of expectations, building trust, self-disclosure and empathy, and it should also include online communication, as indicated also by Asgari and O'Neill (2005). In accordance with face-to-face mentoring models (Parra, DuBois, Neville, & Pugh-Lilly, 2002; Keller, 2005; Rhodes, 2002; 2005), building trust was found to be correlated with self-disclosure and empathy. Ongoing CMC and mentoring support and guidance may assist building and maintaining an e-mentoring relationship (Rhodes, Spencer, Keller, Liang, & Noam, 2006a). Studies (Shpigelman et al., 2008; 2009b) have emphasized the need for visual and vocal cues when using CMC by youth with disabilities. These may be obtained through online communication, such as synchronous text, audio and video electronic communication (Weiss, Whiteley, Treviranus, & Fels, 2001), and also face-to-face meetings as conducted in the current e-mentoring interventions.

However, the process is influenced by moderators which have to be taken into consideration when conducting an e-mentoring program, especially for individuals with varying disabilities (DuBois, Holloway, Valentine, & Cooper, 2002; Perreault LaCoursiere, 2001; Rhodes, 2002; 2005; Shpigelman et al., 2009b). The moderators encompass four categories: (1) Demographic factors – traditional descriptors such as age, gender, race, marital status, and socioeconomic status; (2) Personality factors – psychological dimensions of the personality such as stressfulness, shyness, coping ability, social isolation, self-awareness, and self-disclosure. The personality factors are affected also by internal (personal events) and external circumstances (national or cultural events); (3) Health factors – the complexity of the disability including the quantity (one or more impairments), the type (physical, mental or intellectual impairments), the degree of disability stability (stable / chronic or changeable / temporary), and functional status (dependent or interdependent areas); (4) Environmental factors - the social networks of the individual such as family members, caregivers, friends, acquaintances, neighbors, school staff persons, classmates, which provide multi-dimensional support (psychological, social, instructional, economic, medical, etc.).

Finally, the ESES path leads to two intertwined personal processes -- assimilation and generalization -- which are valuable beyond the computer-mediated environment. The transition from electronic communication to face-to-face communication is an essential step toward preparing individuals with disabilities for independence and self-fulfillment (Reiter, 2008). At this stage, protégés are encouraged to synthesize information, thoughts and feelings experienced via electronic support, to make their own meaning of the support experience and to integrate this within the context of their life goals. The ESES process may ultimately result in self-empowerment of an individual with disabilities (Amichai-Hamburrger et al., 2008). It thus aims to facilitate changes in the protégé's emotional, perceptual and behavioral states. The goal is for the protégé to become more self-aware and confident of his abilities. In addition, the protégé will become more adept at communicating with others within and beyond the Internet (including face-to-face communication).

To summarize, e-mentoring programs appear to be feasible and effective for young people with disabilities. Previous work (Huston, Cooper, & Ford, 2002; Shpigelman et al., 2008; 2009b; Weiss et al., 2001) suggests that an e-mentoring program should include:

- Synchronous text, audio and/or video on-line communication
- Face-to-face meetings
- Frequent and task-based CMC

- Training and ongoing support for the protégés, provided by a coordinator who will assist them to process the e-mentoring experience
- Coordination of expectations between the mentors and the protégés.

Furthermore, it is recommended to explore the optimal duration of the e-mentoring process for students who have different disabilities and personalities. These refinements may enable the protégés to obtain greater personal benefit from the e-mentoring process through internalization of thoughts and feelings experienced via the electronic process, deriving their own meaning from the support experience, and integrating all of these within the context of their life goals.

REFERENCES

Abbott, S., & Mcconkey, R. (2006). The barriers to social inclusion as perceived by people with intellectual disabilities. *Journal of Intellectual Disabilities*, *10*, 275–287. doi:10.1177/1744629506067618

Adelman, M. B., Parks, M. R., & Albrecht, T. L. (1987). Beyond close relationships: Support in weak ties. In Albrecht, T. L., & Adelman, M. B. (Eds.), *Communicating Social Support* (pp. 127–147). Newbury Park, CA: Sage.

Albert, B. (Ed.). (2006). *In or out of the mainstream? Lesson from research on disability and development cooperation*. Leeds: The Disability Press.

Albert, M., Becker, T., Mccrone, P., & Thornicroft, G. (1998). Social networks and mental health service utilisation – A literature review. *The International Journal of Social Psychiatry*, *44*, 248–266. doi:10.1177/002076409804400402

Allen, L. J., & Sigafoos, J. (2000). Friendship and loneliness among Australian children with special education needs. *The Journal of International Special Needs Education*, *3*, 12–20.

Amichai-Hamburrger, Y., MaKenna, K.Y.A., & Tal, S.A. (2008). E-empowerment: Empowerment by the Internet. *Computers in Human Behavior*, *24*(5), 1776–1789. doi:10.1016/j.chb.2008.02.002

Andersson, G., Bergström, J., Holländare, F., Carlbring, P., Kaldo, V., & Ekselius, L. (2005). Internet-based self-help for depression: randomized controlled trial. *The British Journal of Psychiatry*, *187*, 456–461. doi:10.1192/bjp.187.5.456

Asgari, M., & O'Neill, D. K. (2005). What do they mean by "success"? Examining mentees' perceptions of success in a curriculum-based telementoring program. In Pascarelli, J., & Kochan, F. (Eds.), *Creating Successful Telementoring Programs*. Greenwich, CT: Information Age Publishing.

Barak, A. (2003, December). *Psychological determinates of emotional experiences on the Internet*. Paper presented at the workshop of Rationality and Emotion, Haifa, Israel.

Barak, A. (2007). Phantom emotions: Psychological determinants of emotional experiences on the Internet. In Joinson, A., McKenna, K. Y. A., Postmes, T., & Reips, U. D. (Eds.), *Oxford handbook of Internet psychology* (pp. 303–329). Oxford, UK: Oxford University Press.

Barak, A., Boniel-Nissim, M., & Suler, J. (2008a). Fostering empowerment in online support groups. *Computers in Human Behavior*, *24*, 1867–1883. doi:10.1016/j.chb.2008.02.004

Barak, A., & Dolev-Cohen, M. (2006). Does activity level in online support groups for distressed adolescents determine emotional relief? *Counselling & Psychotherapy Research*, *6*(3), 186–190. doi:10.1080/14733140600848203

Barak, A., Hen, L., Boniel-Nissim, M., & Shapira, N. (2008b). A comprehensive review and a meta-analysis of the effectiveness of Internet-based psychotherapeutic interventions. *Journal of Technology in Human Services, 26*, 109–160. doi:10.1080/15228830802094429

Barak, A., & Sadovsky, Y. (2008). Internet use and personal empowerment of hearing-impaired adolescents. *Computers in Human Behavior, 24*, 1802–1815. doi:10.1016/j.chb.2008.02.007

Barnes, S. B. (2003). *Computer-mediated communication: Human-to-human communication across the Internet*. Boston, USA: Allyn and Bacon.

Bierema, L. L., & Meriam, S. B. (2002). E-mentoring: Using computer mediated communication to enhance the mentoring process. *Innovative Higher Education, 26*(3), 211–227. doi:10.1023/A:1017921023103

Bowe, F. G. (2002). Deaf and hard of hearing Americans' instant messaging and e-mail use: A national survey. *American Annals of the Deaf, 147*(4), 6–10.

Bowker, N. I., & Tuffin, K. (2007). Understanding positive subjectives made possible online for disabled people. *New Zealand Journal of Psychology, 36*(2), 63–71.

Braithwaite, D. O., Waldron, V. R., & Finn, J. (1999). Communication of social support in computer-mediated groups for people with disabilities. *Health Communication, 11*(2), 123–151. doi:10.1207/s15327027hc1102_2

Burgstahler, S., & Cronheim, D. (2001). Supporting peer-peer and mentor-protégé relationships on the Internet. *Journal of Research on Technology in Education, 34*(1), 59–74.

Chadsey, J., & Beyer, S. (2001). Social relationships in the workplace. *Mental Retardation and Developmental Disabilities Research Reviews, 7*, 128–133. doi:10.1002/mrdd.1018

Childress, C. A. (2000). Ethical issues in providing online psychotherapeutic interventions [online]. *Journal of Medical Internet Research, 2*(1). http://www.jmir.org/2000/1/e5/ Retrieved July, 2007. doi:10.2196/jmir.2.1.e5

Cohen, K. J., & Light, J. C. (2000). Use of electronic communication to develop mentor-protégé relationships between adolescent and adult AAC users: Pilot study. *Augmentative and Alternative Communication, 16*, 227–238. doi:10.1080/07434610012331279084

Coulson, N. S. (2005). Receiving Social Support Online: An Analysis of a Computer-Mediated Support Group for Individuals Living with Irritable Bowel Syndrome. *Cyberpsychology & Behavior, 8*(6), 580–584. doi:10.1089/cpb.2005.8.580

Cutrona, C. A., & Shur, J. A. (1992). Controllability of stressful events and satisfaction with spouse support behaviors. *Communication Research, 19*(2), 154–174. doi:10.1177/009365092019002002

Dinerstein, R. D. (2004, January). *Disability and the Law*. Paper presented at the inaugural conference of MISHAL – The Israeli University Center on Disabilities – Education, Empowerment & Research. Haifa, Israel: University of Haifa.

DuBois, D. L., Holloway, B. E., Valentine, J. C., & Cooper, H. (2002). Effectiveness of mentoring programs for youth: A meta-analytic review. *American Journal of Community Psychology, 30*(2), 157–197. doi:10.1023/A:1014628810714

DuBois, D. L., & Karcher, M. J. (2005). Youth mentoring. In DuBois, D. L., & Karcher, M. J. (Eds.), *Handbook of youth mentoring* (pp. 2–11). Thousand Oaks, CA: Sage.

Ensher, E. A., Heun, C., & Blanchard, A. (2003). Online mentoring and computer-mediated communication: New directions in research. *Journal of Vocational Behavior, 63*, 264–288. doi:10.1016/S0001-8791(03)00044-7

Fish, T. R., Rabidoux, P., Ober, J., & Graff, V. L. W. (2006). Community literacy and friendship model for people with intellectual disabilities. *Mental Retardation*, *44*, 443–446. doi:10.1352/0047-6765(2006)44[443:CLAFMF]2.0.CO;2

Gross, E. F., Juvonen, J., & Gable, S. L. (2002). Internet use and well being in adolescence. *The Journal of Social Issues*, *58*, 75–90. doi:10.1111/1540-4560.00249

Hamilton, B. A., & Scandura, T. A. (2003). E-mentoring: Implications for organizational learning and development in a wired world. *Organizational Dynamics*, *31*, 388–402. doi:10.1016/S0090-2616(02)00128-6

Hasselbring, T. S., & Williams Glaser, C. H. (2000). Use of computer technology to help students with special needs. *The future of children – Children and computer technology, 10*(2), 102-122.

Herrera, C., Sipe, C. L., & McClanahan, W. S. (2000). *Mentoring school-age children: Relationship development in community-based and school-based programs*. Philadelphia: Public/Private Ventures. (Published in collaboration with MENTOR/National Mentoring Partnership, Alexandria, VA.

Hoffman, M., & Blake, J. (2003). Computer literacy: Today and tomorrow. *Journal of Computing Sciences in Colleges*, *18*(5), 221–233.

Houston, T. K., Cooper, L. A., & Ford, D. E. (2002). Internet support groups for depression: A 1-year prospective cohort study. *The American Journal of Psychiatry*, *159*(12), 2062–2068. doi:10.1176/appi.ajp.159.12.2062

Joinson, A. N. (2001). Self-disclosure in computer-mediated communication: The role of self-awareness and visual anonymity. *European Journal of Social Psychology*, *31*, 177–192. doi:10.1002/ejsp.36

Keller, T. E. (2005). The stage and development of mentoring relationships. In DuBois, D. L., & Karcher, M. J. (Eds.), *Handbook for youth mentoring* (pp. 82–99). Thousand Oaks, CA: Sage.

King, R., Bambling, M., Lloyd, C., Gomurra, R., Smith, S., Reid, W., & Wegner, K. (2006). Online counseling: The motives and experiences of young people who choose the Internet instead of face to face or telephone counseling. *Counselling & Psychotherapy Research*, *6*, 169–174. doi:10.1080/14733140600848179

Leh, A. S. C. (2001). Computer-Mediated Communication and Social Presence in a Distance Learning Environment. *International Journal of Educational Telecommunications*, *7*(2), 109–128.

Lewis, J., Coursol, D., & Herting, W. (2004). Researching the cybercounseling process: A study of the client and counselor experience. In Bloom, J. W., & Walz, G. R. (Eds.), *Cybercounseling & cyberlearning: An encore* (pp. 307–325). Alexandria, VA: American Counseling Association.

Lombard, M., & Ditton, T. (1997). At the heart of it all: The concept of presence. *Journal of Computer Mediated Communication, 3*(2). Retrieved November, 2007, from http://jcmc.indiana.edu/vol3/issue2/lombard.html

Longmore, P. (2003). *Why I burned my book and other essays on disability*. Philadelphia, PA: Temple University Press.

Mallen, M. J., Vogel, D. L., Rochlen, A. B., & Day, S. X. (2005). Online Counseling: Reviewing the Literature from a Counseling Psychology Framework. *The Counseling Psychologist*, *33*(6), 819–871. doi:10.1177/0011000005278624

McConkey, R. (2005*). Inclusion in society: Delivering on the promise.* Paper presented at the International Special Education Conference on Inclusion: Celebrating diversity? 1st – 4th August, Galsgow, Scotland.

McDonald, K. E., Balcazar, F. E., & Keys, C. B. (2005). Youth with disabilities. In DuBois, D. L., & Karcher, M. J. (Eds.), *Handbook of youth mentoring* (pp. 493–507). Thousand Oaks, CA: Sage.

Mesch, G. S., & Talmud, I. (2006). Online friendship formation, communication channels, and social closeness. *International Journal of Internet Science, 1*(1), 29–44.

Michalko, R. (2002). *The difference that disability makes*. Philadelphia, PA: Temple University Press.

Miller, H., & Griffiths, M. (2005). E-Mentoring. In DuBois, D. L., & Karcher, M. J. (Eds.), *Handbook of youth mentoring* (pp. 300–313). Thousand Oaks, London, New Delhi: Sage.

O'Neill, D. K., Weiler, M., & Sha, L. (2003). *The telementoring orchestrator: Research, design and implementation*. Paper presented at the annual meeting of the American Educational Research Association, Chicago, IL.

Paine, C., Joinson, A. N., Buchanan, T., & Reips, U. D. (2006, April 22-27). Privacy and self-disclosure online. *Conference on Human Factors in Computing Systems* (pp. 1187-1192). Montréal, Québec, Canada.

Parra, G. R., DuBois, D. L., Neville, H. A., & Pugh-Lilly, A. O. (2002). Mentoring relationships for youth: Investigation of a process-oriented model. *Journal of Community Psychology, 30*(4), 367–388. doi:10.1002/jcop.10016

Pennebaker, J. W. (1997). Writing about emotional experiences as a therapeutic process. *American Psychological Society, 8*, 162–166.

Perreault LaCoursiere, S. (2001). A theory of online social support. *ANS (Nijmegen), 24*(1), 60–77.

Pitts, V. (2004). Illness and Internet empowerment: Writing and reading breast cancer in cyberspace. *Health, 8*(1), 33–59.

Poetz, C. L. (2003). Reflections on 30 years of involvement in self-advocacy. *Journal of Intellectual & Developmental Disability, 28*, 84–87. doi:10.1080/1366825031000086920

Preiser, W. F. E., & Ostroff, E. (Eds.). (2001). *Universal Design Handbook* (pp. 3.3–3.14). New York: McGraw-Hill.

Reiter, S. (2008). *Disability from a humanistic perspective: Towards a better quality of life*. New York: Nova Science Publishers.

Rhodes, J. E. (2002). *Stand by me: The risks and rewards of mentoring today's youth*. Cambridge, MA: Harvard University Press.

Rhodes, J. E. (2003). Online mentoring: The promise and pitfalls of an emerging approach. *National Mentoring Partnership*. Retrieved August, 2004, from http://www.mentoring.org/research_corner/11_03_online.adp

Rhodes, J. E. (2005). A model of youth mentoring. In DuBois, D. L., & Karcher, M. J. (Eds.), *Handbook of youth mentoring* (pp. 30–43). Thousand Oaks, London, New Delhi: Sage.

Rhodes, J. E., & DuBois, D. L. (2008). Mentoring relationships and programs for youth. *Current Directions in Psychological Science, 17*(4), 254–258. doi:10.1111/j.1467-8721.2008.00585.x

Rhodes, J. E., Spencer, R., Keller, T. E., Liang, B., & Noam, G. (2006a). A model for the influence of mentoring relationships on youth development. *Journal of Community Psychology, 34*(6), 691–707. doi:10.1002/jcop.20124

Rhodes, J. E., Spencer, R., Saito, R. N., & Sipe, C. L. (2006b). Online mentoring: The promise and challenges of an emerging approach to youth development. *The Journal of Primary Prevention, 27*(5), 497–513. doi:10.1007/s10935-006-0051-y

Rice, R. E., & Katz, J. E. (Eds.). (2001). *The Internet and health communication: Experiences and expectations*. Thousand Oaks, CA: Sage.

Rochlen, A. B., Zack, J. S., & Speyer, C. (2004). Online therapy: review of relevant definitions, debates, and current empirical support. *Journal of Clinical Psychology, 60*(3), 269–283. doi:10.1002/jclp.10263

Rousso, H. (2001). What do Frida Kahlo, Wilma Mankiller, and Harriet Tubman have in common? Providing role models for girls with (and without) disabilities. In Rousso, H., & Wehmeyer, M. (Eds.), *Double jeopardy: Addressing gender equity in special education* (pp. 337–360). Albany: State University of New York Press.

Seeger, K. L. (2007). *Mentoring youth with disabilities: The mentor's lived experiences*. Unpublished master's thesis, The School of Human Resource Education and Workforce Development, Louisiana State University, U.S.A.

Shaw, B. R., Hawkins, R., McTavish, F., Pingree, S., & Gustafson, D. H. (2006). Effects of insightful disclosure within computer mediated support groups on women with breast cancer. *Health Communication, 19*(2), 133–142. doi:10.1207/s15327027hc1902_5

Shpigelman, C. N., Reiter, S., & Weiss, P. L. (2008). E-mentoring for youth with special needs: Preliminary results. *Cyberpsychology & Behavior, 11*(2), 196–200. doi:10.1089/cpb.2007.0052

Shpigelman, C. N., Reiter, S., & Weiss, P. L. (2009a). A conceptual framework for electronic socio-emotional social support for people with special needs. *International Journal of Rehabilitation Research. Internationale Zeitschrift fur Rehabilitationsforschung. Revue Internationale de Recherches de Readaptation, 32*(4), 301–308. doi:10.1097/MRR.0b013e32831e4519

Shpigelman, C. N., Weiss, P. L., & Reiter, S. (2009b). E-mentoring for all. *Computers in Human Behavior, 25*(4), 919–928. doi:10.1016/j.chb.2009.03.007

Single, P. B., & Single, R. M. (2005). E-mentoring for social equity: Review of research to inform program development. *Mentoring & Tutoring, 13*(2), 301–320. doi:10.1080/13611260500107481

Smith, R. M., & Erevelles, N. (2004). Towards and enabling education: The difference that disability makes. Book Reviews. *Educational Researcher*, (November): 31–36. doi:10.3102/0013189X033008031

Suler, J. (2001). Assessing a person's suitability for online therapy: The ISMHO clinical case study group. *Cyberpsychology & Behavior, 4*(6), 675–679. doi:10.1089/109493101753376614

Suler, J. (2004). The online disinhibition effect. *Cyberpsychology & Behavior, 7*(3), 321–326. doi:10.1089/1094931041291295

Suler, J. (1996-2005). *The psychology of cyberspace* [online]. Retrieved 13 July 2008 from http://www-usr.rider.edu/~suler/psycyber/psycyber.html

Sword, C., & Hill, K. (2003). Creating mentoring opportunities for youth with disabilities: Issues and suggested strategies. *American Rehabilitation, 27*(1), 14–17.

Tidwell, L. C., & Walther, L. B. (2002). Computer-mediated communication effects on disclosure, impression and interpersonal evaluations: Getting to know one another a bit at a time. *Human Communication Research, 28*, 317–348. doi:10.1111/j.1468-2958.2002.tb00811.x

Todis, B., Powers, L., Irvin, L., & Singer, G. (1996). A qualtitive study of a mentor intervention with children who have multiple disabilities. In Powers, L., Singer, G., & Sowers, J. (Eds.), *On the road to autonomy: Promoting self-competence for children and youth with disabilities* (pp. 237–254). Baltimore: Paul H. Brookes.

Van Uden-Kraan, C. F., Drossaret, C. H. C., Taal, E., Lebrun, C. E. I., Drossares-Bakker, K. W., & Smit, W. M. (2008). Coping with somatic illnesses in online support groups: Do the feared disadvantages actually occur? *Computers in Human Behavior, 24,* 309–324. doi:10.1016/j.chb.2007.01.014

Walther, J. B., & Boyd, S. (2002). Attraction to computer-mediated social support. In Lin, C. A., & Atkin, D. (Eds.), *Communication technology and society: Audience adoption and uses* (pp. 153–188). Cresskill, NJ: Hampton Press.

Wehmeyer, M. L., Smith, S. J., Palmer, S. B., & Davis, D. K. (2004). Technology use by students with intellectual disabilities: An overview. *Journal of Special Education Technology, 19*(4), 1–33.

Weiss, P. L., Bialik, P., & Kizony, K. (2003). Virtual reality provides leisure time opportunities for young adults with physical and intellectual disabilities. *Cyberpsychology & Behavior, 6,* 335–342. doi:10.1089/109493103322011650

Weiss, P. L., Whiteley, C. P., Treviranus, J., & Fels, D. I. (2001). PEBBLES: A personal technology for meeting educational, social and emotional needs of hospitalized children. *Personal and Ubiquitous Computing, 5,* 157–168. doi:10.1007/s007790170006

White, M., & Dorman, S. M. (2001). Receiving social support online: Implications for health education. *Health Education Research, 16*(6), 693–707. doi:10.1093/her/16.6.693

Wright, K. B. (2000). Perceptions of on-line support providers: An examination of perceived homophily, source credibility, communication and social support within on-line support groups. *Communication Quarterly, 48,* 44–59.

Wright, K. B., & Bell, S. B. (2003). Health-related support groups on the Internet: Linking empirical findings to social support and computer-mediated communication theory. *Journal of Health Psychology, 8*(1), 39–57. doi:10.1177/1359105303008001429

Chapter 8
Meeting the Needs of Adolescents and Young Adults with Disabilities:
An E-Mentoring Approach

Katharine Hill
St. Catherine University, USA & University of St. Thomas, USA

Joe Timmons
University of Minnesota, USA

Christen Opsal
University of Minnesota, USA

ABSTRACT

Resilience in at-risk youth is anchored by supportive adults who may be relatives, neighbors, teachers, employers, or other members of the community. Telementoring or electronic mentoring (e-mentoring) is a promising practice for improving transition-to-adulthood outcomes for youth with disabilities through connections with caring adults. E-mentoring supports the development of technological and social skills and also increases their understanding of the employment and educational opportunities that await youth upon completion of high school. Connecting to Success (CTS) is an e-mentoring program for transition-age youth with disabilities. In this chapter, CTS is discussed in the context of healthy youth development and transition to adulthood. An overview of the CTS program model is provided, and a discussion of future directions is identified.

INTRODUCTION

Healthy youth development is an issue of considerable national importance, as evidenced by the many federal and state policies and programs which fund such opportunities for adolescents and young adults (including the Federal Youth Coordination Act, AmeriCorps and other service learning opportunities, and federal and state support for 4-H, after school programs, mentoring programs, and workforce development). We know that preparing young people for academic, vocational, and social success takes the proverbial village, yet we also know that many, many youth reach adulthood without the tools, resources, and supports they need to live independently and safely.

There are many "markers" that can predict if youth are increasingly likely to struggle in the transition to adulthood; these include poverty, chronic illness, chemical dependency, teen parenthood, language and cultural issues, and disability. Disability is widespread in the United States — more than eighteen percent of Americans have a diagnosed or undiagnosed disability (U.S. Census Bureau, 2005). This chapter will detail some of the issues related to youth with disabilities, discuss a framework for meeting their needs, and provide an overview of an e-mentoring program for youth with disabilities which has been successfully used in schools across the country.

BACKGROUND

Youth with Disabilities and Transition

In public schools, students may receive special education services and supports under the Individuals with Disabilities Education Improvement Act of 2004 if they have an impairment involving one of thirteen conditions—mental retardation, hearing impairments (including deafness), speech or language impairments, visual impairments (including blindness), serious emotional disturbance, orthopedic impairments, autism, traumatic brain injury, other health impairments, or specific learning disabilities—and can show that they need "special education and related services" as a result (P.L. 108-446). A disability may be diagnosed and interventions put into place (through written plans such as an Individualized Education Program) or, in a large number of cases, a disability may be undiagnosed (or not acknowledged) with no interventions in place.

From ages 14-21, special education students are considered to be in "transition", a period of planning and preparation for life after secondary education. Transition planning was formalized in part because data show that youth with disabilities are at particularly high risk during their transition to adulthood. They are less likely to graduate from high school, find employment, and participate in postsecondary education than their same-age peers (Johnson et al., 2002). More than one in four youth with disabilities leave school without receiving a diploma, and youth with certain disabilities drop out of school at much higher rates (Wagner, Newman, Cameto, Garzo, & Levine, 2005). For example, 44% of youth with emotional disturbances drop out (Wagner et al., 2005). Only about 30% of youth with disabilities attend either 2- or 4-year colleges; this is less than half the rate of postsecondary attendance for their same-age peers (Wagner et al., 2005). Estimates of the prevalence of youth with all types of disabilities in juvenile corrections range from 32% to 50% of the total juvenile corrections population (Quinn, Rutherford, & Leone, 2001).

As a consequence, employment rates for young adults with disabilities are much lower than those of young people without disabilities. According to the Bureau of Labor Statistics (2009), "the employment-population ratio for persons with a disability was 19.9 percent, compared with 64.9 percent for persons with no disability," which means that many more individuals with disabilities have left the labor market and are not actively looking for work. Timmons, Mack, Sims, Wills, and Hare (2006) contend that "many youth with disabilities have not had the same opportunities as their peers without disabilities to be exposed to necessary career preparation options" (p. 2), such as part-time employment, internships, or mentoring, which also contributes to the disparity in outcomes between youth without disabilities and youth with disabilities.

Mentoring: A Successful Approach for Promoting Healthy Youth Development

Resilience in at-risk youth, or the "capacity to rise above adversity and forge lasting strengths in the struggle" (Wollin & Wollin, 1993, p. ii), is anchored by supportive adults who may be relatives, neighbors, teachers, employers, or other members of the community. In fact, research on factors which promote resilience in at-risk youth has shown that the consistent presence of just one caring adult can have a significant positive impact on a young person's growth and development (Beir, Rosenfeld, Spitalny, Zanksy, & Bontempo, 2000).

Benson and Pittman (1991) define healthy youth development as the:

ongoing growth process in which all youth are engaged in attempting to meet their basic personal and social needs to be safe, feel cared for, be valued, be useful, and be spiritually grounded, and to build skills and competencies that allow them to function and contribute in their daily lives. (p. 94)

Benson, Scales, Hawkins, Oesterle, and Hill (2004) identify eight dimensions of successful adult functioning: physical health, psychological or emotional well-being, life skills, ethical behavior, healthy family and social relationships, educational attainment, constructive engagement, and civic engagement. At-risk youth with limited resources are likely to struggle with these indicators and may, after leaving school, never have opportunities to catch up. The National Collaborative on Workforce and Disability for Youth (NCWD/Y) recommendations for healthy youth development for young with disabilities specifically advocate mentoring activities in both formal and informal settings with mentors both with and without disabilities (2003). The National Alliance for Secondary Education and Transition (NASET) established national standards and quality indicators that describe the transition supports and services that all youth need. These research-based benchmarks cite mentoring programs as a key component in career preparation and youth development (NASET, 2004). For example, youth participating in mentoring programs may be able to:

- participate in career awareness, exploration, and preparatory activities in school- and community-based settings, such as work experience, on-the-job training, internships, community services, service-learning, or volunteer work;
- use a career planning process (e.g., assessments, career portfolio, etc.) incorporating their career goals, interests, and abilities;
- develop interpersonal skills, including communication, decision-making, assertiveness, and peer refusal skills, and have the ability to create healthy relationships; and
- engage in experiential learning and have opportunities for genuine leadership, taking primary responsibility for developing plans, carrying out decisions, and solving problems

Mentors can stimulate mentees' academic performance and clarify mentees' future occupational goals (Rhodes, Grossman, & Resch, 2000). Campbell-Whatley (2001) found that mentoring may positively impact transition goals such as developing career awareness, succeeding academically, overcoming barriers, and developing social skills. Youth with disabilities who participate in mentoring programs are exposed to new and different careers, leading to a richer understanding of potential areas of employment. Youth with disabilities often need extra opportunities for these career activities because they don't have as much access to afterschool employment, summer jobs, or internships that youth without disabilities have.

Finally, youth with disabilities' participation in mentoring programs helps to build understanding of disability and disability issues in the community. Hernandez (2000) reported that employers express numerous concerns about employing individuals with disabilities, with individuals with psychiatric disabilities, epilepsy, and learning disabilities generally eliciting especially negative attitudes from employers. In focus groups of rehabilitation providers and employers, Fabian, Edelman, and Leedy (1993) found that both groups cited negative attitudes and prejudice as the most significant barriers to job placement. Mentoring offers the potential for mentors to learn more about the skills and abilities of youth with disabilities, while minimizing some of the myths about the occupational potential of this population.

ELECTRONIC MENTORING FOR TRANSITION-AGE YOUTH WITH DISABILITIES

Mentoring initiatives hold promise in assisting youth with disabilities to achieve more meaningful and positive post-school outcomes. There is solid evidence that effective mentoring programs can change the direction of a youth's life, reduce substance abuse, and improve academic performance (Grossman, 1999). We have seen in our own work that mentoring activities support learning and skill development integral to successful transition, including career awareness, career planning, work experience, interpersonal skills, decision-making, assertiveness, leadership, and problem solving. Mentoring activities also have helped our students develop critical skills to access and utilize technology, understand workplace expectations and norms, communicate with others, and become strong self-advocates, skills useful for postsecondary education and employment. E-mentoring provides these benefits in a safe environment and also builds career awareness among youth with disabilities and promotes disability awareness among mentors.

New opportunities exist for using technology to expand mentoring opportunities; for example, electronic mentoring (e-mentoring) utilizes a combination of e-mail and face-to-face meetings to facilitate mentoring relationships between youth and adults. As web-based technologies continue to expand and change, it is likely that other electronic forums for mentoring relationships will be identified. E-mentoring provides high-quality community and work-based learning in a forum that is easy and efficient for mentors, teachers, and students. It is a strategy that uses technology to make mentoring accessible and effective for both working adults and busy young people.

Connecting to Success

In 1999, the National Center on Secondary Education and Transition (NCSET) at the University of Minnesota received initial start-up funds from the Presidential Task Force on Employment of Adults with Disabilities to develop and pilot test Connecting to Success (CTS), an electronic mentoring program for transition-age youth with disabilities. The goals of CTS include: (a) connecting youth with disabilities to positive role models in the world of work, (b) improving technology skills, (c) building students' motivation to increase academic achievement, (d) enhancing self-esteem, (e) improving students' skills in writing, and (f) assisting students in their career development. Another major goal of CTS is to integrate e-mentoring with the students' transition/Individualized Education Program (IEP) goals.

Aspects of the CTS were based on the earlier work of Youth Trust, a Minneapolis nonprofit organization. Youth Trust developed an adopt-a-classroom e-mentoring model that was being used successfully by Minneapolis Public Schools in partnership with General Mills and other Minnesota-based corporations. Evaluations of the project found that students and teachers felt that students improved their writing skills and career readiness by corresponding via e-mail with mentors (Moen, 2000). The project generated excitement in the Minneapolis area because it linked students with mentors in a convenient way that enhanced academic performance. NCSET staff quickly realized that e-mentoring was compatible with an inclusive philosophy, providing an innovative format for classroom career-readiness activities that involve all youth, including youth with disabilities.

CTS emphasizes specific learning goals for students, including the development of effective writing and communication skills, occupational awareness and career development, and social skills, with the added intent of improving student motivation for learning. The program model calls for weekly e-mail exchanges between the mentor and the student, as well as a minimum of two face-to-face visits over the course of the academic year. Teachers are strongly encouraged to adapt the model, within guidelines, to best serve the needs of their students and their classroom goals.

Each CTS implementation site may vary in the specifics of the program, adapting to best fit the needs of the students and teachers, and the expertise of the employers. Key elements at each site include the presence of an intermediary liaison between the school and the employer, the inclusion of specific learning goals for the students, and a focus on career development and occupational awareness. The intermediary acts as the point person for both the classroom teacher and the employer, in order to minimize the time demands of participating in CTS, to protect the privacy of participants, and to ensure the program is implemented smoothly. The liaison's responsibilities include recruiting classrooms and employers, and providing training and information on CTS, disability, and mentoring to all participants, as needed. The liaison may also assist in additional, supporting activities, such as coordinating face-to-face social activities between students and mentors, or visits to job sites or college campuses.

Because CTS is oriented to address career development and occupational awareness, the focus of e-mail exchanges should remain in these areas. This does not mean that personal relationships don't develop, or that other topics are not discussed. However, the focus of the mentoring relationship remains on the development of career awareness and skills for the young person. This focus is facilitated by the learning goals for each student that are developed by their classroom teacher. Often, these goals will align with the young person's IEP goals, as well as with classroom activities or curricula.

In some CTS settings, all of the mentors for a given classroom are employed at a single business. In other settings, mentors are recruited from multiple local businesses. In either case, the mentor recruitment, screening, and training are conducted by the liaison. Mentors are asked to complete a brief application, which includes basic demographic information, information about their job responsibilities, educational background, and if they have ever worked with or known a young person with a disability. CTS sites have relied on the employer's human resources screening policies, rather than conducting their own background checks. Additionally, mentors are forbidden to share personal contact information with students (including their e-mail address) or to meet with them face-to-face outside of structured CTS activities.

CTS participants and mentors are matched by the student's classroom teacher, a representative of the business and the CTS liaison. Every effort is made to make matches based on similar interests; for example, shared hobbies, or a specific educational or employment goal. Once the match is made, the mentor writes an introductory e-mail to their student match which is then sent to the classroom teacher and forwarded on to the student.

Each CTS participant (student) e-mail their mentors once a week on a variety of topics linked to the students' learning goals. In some settings, the topics are pre-determined by the teacher to match specific course or transition goals; in other settings, the e-mail "conversation" is less structured. However, the focus of the mentoring relationship is always employment and the development of employment skills. Topics may include general career advice, assistance with developing resumes or filling out job applications, development of specific tools or products, such as brochures, spreadsheets, or other written work, or sharing wisdom and experience gained by the mentor. All e-mails pass through their teacher's e-mail address (in other words, the students send their e-mail to their teacher, who after reviewing it, forward it on to the mentor) in order to protect mentor's privacy and to monitor the content of the e-mails. Students also participate in several face-to-face meetings with their mentors over the course of the academic year, often visiting mentors at their job sites or hosting them in their classroom.

Qualitative evaluations were conducted at four of the CTS pilot sites during the first years of the program's implementation. Each of the pilots took place with high school students, ranging in age from 14 to 21. The settings included alternative high schools, continuing transition programs (for youth between the ages of 18 and 21), and traditional special education classrooms. Participants had a variety of disability diagnoses, including emotional/behavioral disorders, learning disabilities, and developmental disabilities. Mentors were drawn from a number of settings. At two of the sites, all of the mentors for a given classroom came from the same, large employer. In the two others, they were drawn from many small, local businesses, including realtors, government offices, banks, manufacturers, and restaurants. The evaluations were conducted by internal evaluators and gathered data through interviews with classroom teachers, mentors, and student participants.

Evaluation findings included:

- For youth: greater career awareness and development of career goals, greater motivation for academic success, improved grades, improved self-advocacy skills, improved attendance, and greater sense of competence to overcome obstacles. Students found that participation increased their academic motivation; some reported an improvement in their reading and writing skills; they reported greater knowledge of careers and workforce readiness; and they enjoyed the friendship of a caring adult.
- For teachers: an increase in the support of adults and the community for the educational process, an improvement in students' grades and attendance, greater collaboration with employers and service agencies, and an increased understanding of the needs of business and industry.
- For mentors: greatly increased awareness of the employability and potential contributions of youth with disabilities to communities.

Obstacles in implementing CTS included challenges with technology, recruiting mentors who matched with student interests, and maintaining the mentoring connection over the course of the school year, including over breaks and vacation periods.

Safety and Confidentiality

In order to ensure the safety of the youth participating in CTS, mentors are screened using several different methods before they are allowed to contact a student. The first and most important screening occurs at the time that the individual is hired by the company that employs them. The company's hiring process is the first, and certainly most extensive, vetting process. Once prospective mentors are recruited, they must fill out an application form which is then shared with the Employer Liaison, the teacher, and the Program Coordinator. The application asks about prospective mentors' interests and hobbies, previous employment and volunteer experiences, previous experience with youth with disabilities, and interest in participating in the program. There are several key safeguards incorporated into CTS to ensure the safety and privacy of all participants. First, all e-mails are sent and received from school or business computers—participants are strictly prohibited from communicating from their home or private e-mail addresses and are not given each other's home information. In addition, both mentors and students receive training prior to program implementation regarding appropriate boundaries to the relationship (i.e., no contact with your mentor or the student outside of school, no unsupervised contacts), confidentiality issues, on the monitoring that takes place as an inherent part of CTS, and on the necessity of reporting any indications of child abuse, child neglect, or threat of harm to the appropriate authority. Finally, a teacher or teacher's assistant reads all e-mails to assure that content is appropriate within the scope of CTS before they are sent on to either recipient. If an e-mail indicates that either a mentor or mentee are violating the boundaries of the program, the issue would be immediately addressed by the teacher. Teachers are considered mandated reporters—they are required to assess whether information is reportable and to report it to the proper authorities if appropriate.

Mentor Training

After mentors are accepted for participation in Connecting to Success, they are required to participate in an initial orientation and training, as well as ongoing trainings throughout the academic year. Much of this work can be done electronically, through e-mail or on a website. The training is often conducted by an intermediary (a trained staff person from a local community organization), participating teachers, and students who have been e-mentored in the past, if possible. At minimum, the face-to-face mentor training should include:

- Program overview
- Specific classroom and learning objectives and how mentors help accomplish them. This may include discussion of IEPs and transition goals in general, an overview of the curricula used in the classroom, and a discussion of the teacher's hopes for CTS in supporting their work with students.
- Policies, procedures, and guidelines
- Expectations of mentors, including frequency of communication, methods of communication, topics to be discussed, and protecting all participants' privacy
- Orientation to the school and students
- Tips on mentoring youth
- Specific curriculum or technical training that mentors need to help their students complete assignments. For example if the students are learning to develop brochures, they may be sending practice ones to their mentor for feedback and critiques.

Mentor/Mentee Matching

The mentor/student matching process can be adapted to fit the needs and expectations of each setting. However, the process must meaningfully involve the classroom teacher and representatives from the employer. The employer liaison and the teacher work collaboratively, using professional judgment, the mentors' application forms, the student's application forms, and their personal knowledge of the students and employees to match participating students with mentors. Consideration is given to gender of the participants, the disability-related needs of the students and the skills of the mentors, as well as interests and hobbies.

An advantage of this approach to matching is that the mentors and students have ongoing contact with the people who made the match and are able to provide constant feedback on the suitability of the match. If, for any reason, the match is thought to not be beneficial, all of the people involved in potentially making a change are easily accessible and aware of the issue. Every effort is made to match students with mentors who will best help them reach their learning goals.

CTS: Implementation Examples

One CTS implementation site matched mentors from local businesses with students in an alternative education setting in Minneapolis, Minnesota. The students, who were all in their late teens, had emotional or behavioral disorders and were close to dropping out of school; several also had learning disabilities. In an effort to increase engagement with school and to support individual career development, students were matched with volunteers from a large manufacturer of food products that also had positions in marketing, advertising, information technology, accounting, and human resources. In this program site, grant funds supported a liaison at a nonprofit mentoring organization who served as the "go-between" and organizer for the program. This liaison, working with the classroom teacher, recruited and trained mentors, matched the students with their mentors, and provided trouble-shooting and logistical support over the course of the year-long mentoring relationship. Based on student interest, matches were made in several different company divisions and relationships were built with general career goals in mind. Face-to-face visits at the company's world headquarters were highlights of the school year and had profound effects on most students' willingness to write weekly e-mails, participate in career exploration activities, and to attend school more regularly.

Another e-mentoring project that does not use grant funds but exists solely with volunteer support is set at the SUMIT (Skills Uniquely Marketable in Technology) Program, in St. Paul (Minnesota) Public Schools. SUMIT joins with community and business partners to train students with disabilities who are interested in utilizing technology for employment. SUMIT, which is open to students aged 16-21, provides intensive work-based computer application training, career exploration in technology fields, and the development of internships in business settings. Students learn graphic design, database management, animation, and spreadsheet accounting and, depending on the available work, may do production jobs for the district or community partners.

Since 2003, SUMIT has also included an e-mentoring component where students are matched with staff from the University of Minnesota, who pass on expertise and resources related to postsecondary educational opportunities, career development, and overall youth development. Students have the opportunity to "practice" the skills they are learning in school through projects with their mentors—for example, designing notepads or note cards for their mentors to use at work. Face-to-face meetings are held at the SUMIT program site and on campus. While on campus, students take a tour of the university, look and learn about myriad job opportunities as well as have more informal time with their mentors, usually over a meal.

FUTURE DIRECTIONS

The research on mentoring programs for youth with disabilities (for example, Campbell-Whatley, 2001) as well as the wider mentoring literature indicate that mentoring is an effective intervention to build career awareness, relationships with caring adults, and positive youth development. Although research has demonstrated that youth with disabilities are at increased risk for poor transition outcomes compared with their same-aged peers (Wagner et al., 2005), and that mentoring in any form can help all youth succeed, there have been too few e-mentoring programs which are specifically designed to accommodate the needs of youth with disabilities in transition. This is changing as more schools and organizations learn about the benefits and the importance of mentoring, especially for at-risk youth.

With a national focus on mentoring, we hope that more research will take place that explores more fully the short and long-term benefits and impacts that these activities have on youth with disabilities. We also look for more examples of promising practices to be highlighted in journal articles or Websites.

As the CTS experience indicates, it is not more complicated to implement a mentoring program inclusive of youth with disabilities as it is to implement one that is not. Providing training to mentors and employers on disability issues and building on the supports and accommodations that are provided as part of special education can reduce or remove the barriers to including youth with disabilities. Beside the CTS materials developed by the University of Minnesota, http://ici.umn.edu/ementoring/default.html, these other sources can be accessed for those interested in e-mentoring youth with disabilities:

- The National Collaborative on Workforce and Disability for Youth: Mentoring http://www.ncwd-youth.info/topic/mentoring
- Minnesota High School/High Tech E-Connect http://ici.umn.edu/mnhighschoolhightech/econnect.html
- NCSET: E-mentoring http://ncset.org/topics/mentoring/default.asp?topic=32

CONCLUSION

E-mentoring is a promising practice for improving transition outcomes for youth with disabilities. It provides youth participants with important technological and social skills and also increases their understanding of the employment and educational opportunities that await them upon their completion of high school. Additionally, participation in e-mentoring with youth with disabilities carries benefits for the mentors, including increasing their understanding of disability and disability issues, and building stronger connections between local businesses and schools.

The Connecting to Success e-mentoring program provides a safe, research-based approach to e-mentoring for youth with disabilities. CTS has proven itself to be flexible to the needs of different communities while providing a consistent base on which to build a successful e-mentoring program. However, regardless of the model selected, it is imperative that e-mentoring opportunities be inclusive of transition-age youth with disabilities, so that all youth can benefit from mentoring programs.

REFERENCES

American Youth Policy Forum. (1997). *SOME things DO make a difference for youth*. Washington, DC: Author. Retrieved December 4, 2009 from http://www.aypf.org/publications/compendium/comp01.pdf

Beier, S. R., Rosenfeld, W. D., Spitalny, K. C., Zansky, S. M., & Bontempo, A. N. (2000). The potential role of an adult mentor in influencing high-risk behaviors in adolescents. *Archives of Pediatrics & Adolescent Medicine, 154*, 327–331.

Benson, P. L., & Pittman, K. J. (2001). *Trends in youth development: Visions, realities, and challenges*. Boston: Kluwer Academic Publishers.

Benson, P. L., Scales, P. C., Hawkins, J. D., Oesterle, S., & Hill, K. G. (2004). *Successful young adult development. A report submitted to The Bill & Melinda Gates Foundation*. Retrieved December 4, 2009 from http://depts.washington.edu/sdrg/SuccessfulDevelopment.pdf

Bureau of Labor Statistics. (2009). New monthly data series on the employment status of people with a disability. Retrieved December 4, 2009 from http://www.bls.gov/cps/cpsdisability.htm

Campbell-Whatley, G. (2001). Mentoring students with mild disabilities: The "nuts and bolts" of program development. *Intervention in School and Clinic, 36*, 211–216. doi:10.1177/105345120103600403

Fabian, E. S., Edelman, A., & Leedy, M. (1993). Linking workers with severe disabilities to social supports in the workplace: Strategies for addressing barriers. *Journal of Rehabilitation, 57*, 118–124.

Grossman, J. B. (1999). The practice, quality and cost of mentoring. In J. B. Grossman (Ed.), *Contemporary issues in mentoring* (pp. 5-9). Philadelphia: Public/Private Ventures. Retrieved December 4, 2009 from http://www.ppv.org/ppv/publications/assets/37_publication.pdf

Hernandez, B., Keys, C., & Balcazar, F. (2000). Employer attitudes toward workers with disabilities and their ADA employment rights: A literature review. *Journal of Rehabilitation, 66*, 4–16.

Individuals with Disabilities Education Improvement Act of 2004. (P.L. 108-446). Retrieved December 4, 2009 from http://idea.ed.gov/download/statute.html

Johnson, D., Stodden, R., Emmanuel, E., Luecking, R., & Mack, M. (2002). Current challenges facing secondary education and transition services: what research tells us. *Exceptional Children, 68*(4), 519–531.

Kaye, S. (2000). Disability and the digital divide. *Disability Statistics Abstract, 22*. Retrieved December 4, 2009 from http://dsc.ucsf.edu/publication.php?pub_id=6

Kessler, M. (2004). *The transition years: Serving current and former foster youth ages eighteen to twenty-one.* Tulsa: University of Oklahoma, National Resource Center for Youth Services.

Moen, D. (2000). *Cargill/Olson e-mentoring program evaluation report 1999-2000: Linking youth with employees through the use of computer technology.* Unpublished manuscript.

National Alliance for Secondary Education and Transition. (2004). *NASET overview.* Retrieved December 4, 2009 from http://www.nasetalliance.org/about/index.htm

National Collaborative on Workforce and Disability for Youth. (2003). *The guideposts for success.* Washington, DC: Author. Retrieved December 4, 2009 from http://www.ncwd-youth.info/resources_&_Publications/guideposts/

National Organization on Disability and Harris Survey. (2004). *Landmark disability survey finds pervasive disadvantages.* Retrieved December 4, 2009 from http://www.nod.org/index.cfm?fuseaction=feature.showFeature&FeatureID=1422&C:\CFusion8\verity\Data\dummy.txt

Osgood, D., Foster, E., Flanagan, C., & Ruth, G. (2004). *Why focus on transition to adulthood for vulnerable populations?* (Research Network Working Paper No. 2). Network on Transitions to Adulthood. Retrieved December 4, 2009 from http://www.transad.pop.upenn.edu/downloads/vulnerable.pdf

Presidential Task Force on Employment of Adults with Disabilities. (1999). *Report from the subcommittee on expanding employment opportunities for young people with disabilities to the Presidential Task Force on Employment of Adults with disabilities.* Washington, DC: Author.

Quinn, M., Rutherford, R., & Leone, P. (2001). *Students with disabilities in correctional facilities.* Arlington, VA: ERIC Clearinghouse on Disabilities and Gifted Education, Council for Exceptional Children. (ERIC Document Reproduction Service No. ED461958). Retrieved December 4, 2009 from http://www.ericdigests.org/2002-4/correctional.html

Rhodes, J. E., Grossman, J. B., & Resch, N. L. (2000). Agents of change: Pathways through which mentoring relationships influence adolescents' academic adjustment. *Child Development, 71*, 1662–1671. doi:10.1111/1467-8624.00256

Timmons, J., Mack, M., Sims, A., Hare, R., & Wills, J. (2006). *Paving the way to work: A guide to career-focused mentoring for youth with disabilities.* Washington, DC: Institute for Educational Leadership, National Collaborative on Workforce and Disability for Youth. Retrieved December 4, 2009 from http://www.ncwd-youth.info/paving-the-way-to-work

U.S. Census Bureau. (2005). *Americans with disabilities: 2005.* Retrieved December 4, 2009 from http://www.census.gov/hhes/www/disability/sipp/disable05.html

Wagner, M., Newman, L., Cameto, R., Garza, N., & Levine, P. (2005). *After high school: A first look at the postschool experiences of youth with disabilities. A report from the National Longitudinal Transition Study-2 (NLTS2). (Executive Study).* Menlo Park, CA: SRI International. Retrieved December 4, 2009 from http://www.nlts2.org/reports/2005_04/index.html

Wolin, S., & Wolin, S. (1993). *The resilient self: How survivors of troubled families rise above adversity.* New York: Villard Books.

Youth Connections. (n.d.). Improving transition outcomes: An innovative state alignment grant for improving transition outcomes for youth with disabilities through the use of intermediaries. Youth Connections: E-Mentoring and Vocational Exploration for Students with Disabilities. Retrieved December 4, 2009 from http://publications.iowa.gov/5618/2/ementoring_RepTemp.txt

ADDITIONAL READING

Campbell-Whatley, G. (2001). Mentoring students with mild disabilities: The "nuts and bolts" of program development. *Intervention in School and Clinic, 36*, 211–216. doi:10.1177/105345120103600403

Connecticut, L. E. A. R. N. S. (2000). *Workplace mentoring guide f*or education, business and industry partners of Connecticut's school-to-career initiative: Connecticut LEARNS. Middletown, CT: Author. Retrieved December 4, 2009 from http://www.sde.ct.gov/sde/lib/sde/PDF/DEPS/Career/WB/mentoring.pdf

Ferber, T., Pittman, K., & Marshall, T. (2002). *Helping all youth to grow up fully prepared and fully engaged.* Takoma Park, MD: The Forum for Youth Investment.

Garringer, M., & McRae, P. (Eds.). (2007). The ABCs of school-based mentoring: effective strategies for providing quality youth mentoring in schools and communities. *Foundations of successful youth mentoring: A guidebook for program development.* Portland, OR: National Mentoring Center. Retrieved June 4, 2009 from http://gwired.gwu.edu/hamfish/merlin-cgi/p/downloadFile/d/20696/n/off/other/1/name/abcspdf/

Jekielek, S., Moore, K. A., & Hair, E. C. (2002). *Mentoring programs and youth development: A synthesis.* Washington, DC: Edna McConnell Clark Foundation. Retrieved December 4, 2009 from http://www.childtrends.org/what_works/clarkwww/mentor/mentorrpt.pdf

National Collaborative on Workforce and Disability for Youth. (2004). *Youth development and leadership.* Washington, DC: Author. Retrieved December 4, 2009 from http://www.ncwd-youth.info/topic/youth-development

Peer Resources. (2002). *A guide to the mentor program listings*. Retrieved December 4, 2009 from http://www.mentors.ca/mentorprograms.html

Sword, C., & Hill, K. (2002, December). *Creating mentoring opportunities for youth with disabilities: Issues and suggested strategies*. Minneapolis, MN: University of Minnesota, Institute on Community Integration, National Center on Secondary Education and Transition. Retrieved December 4, 2009 from http://www.ncset.org/publications/viewdesc.asp?id=704

Timmons, J., Podmostko, M., Bremer, C., Lavin, D., & Wills, J. (2004). *Career planning begins with assessment*. Washington, DC: National Collaborative on Workforce and Disability for Youth. Retrieved December 4, 2009 from http://www.ncwd-youth.info/career-planning-begins-with-assessment

Section 3
Telementoring:
Professional Development

Chapter 9
Telementoring in Teacher Education

Sandy White Watson
University of Tennessee at Chattanooga, USA

ABSTRACT

This research study involved the telementoring of pre-service teachers by practicing teachers in the fall semester of 2005 and arose out of a need expressed by education students for more contact with practicing teachers that would not require large time and financial commitments. Twelve pre-service education students at the University of Tennessee at Chattanooga (UTC) and 17 practicing K-12 teachers from four states participated. Pre- and post- reflections completed by student participants, email dialogues between pre- and in-service teacher participants, and pre-service student participant email reflections following each dialogue exchange were analyzed to gather project effectiveness data. Results revealed highly positive experiences that provided student participants a unique and practical glimpse of the daily lives of teachers and what teaching is "really like."

INTRODUCTION

Education students at the University of Tennessee at Chattanooga (UTC) have many times voiced the need for more current and practical information about teachers and teaching, citing that many of their education professors have not taught in a K-12 setting in several years, if at all, and often have outdated perceptions of what today's teachers face as a part of their daily teaching routines. Often it is not until students near the end of their programs of study that they have the immersive student teaching experience in which they are exposed to and participate in the routines and procedures of schooling unless they have the opportunity to participate in a Professional Development School prior to student teaching. The education students who are nearing the student teaching phase of their programs and who have had only sporadic field and observational experiences in the K-12 setting often demonstrate anxiety about student teaching and question their teaching preparedness.

DOI: 10.4018/978-1-61520-861-6.ch009

In an effort to give such students much needed contact with practicing teachers in their subject/grade level areas, who could possibly provide more current information about today's teaching culture, student populations, and teaching responsibilities, but not cause a time or financial hardship, a telementoring project was developed with practicing teachers serving as mentors to pre-service teachers (mentees) via an email format.

In this chapter, as background information, the author will explore mentoring in general (beginning with its classical origins), face-to-face mentoring and the beginning teacher, disadvantages of traditional face-to-face mentoring, mentoring and the pre-service teacher, telementoring, examples of initiatives involving telementoring, telementoring and the pre-service teacher, and telementoring studies involving pre-service teachers. Next, the author will introduce her research study involving the telementoring of pre-service teachers at the University of Tennessee at Chattanooga by practicing mentor teachers in four states. The need for the study will be addressed as well as the specifics of the study: the participants, procedure, data analysis (including an examination and discussion of emergent themes), and conclusion, including research questions and implications.

BACKGROUND

Mentoring's Classical Origins

Mentoring's classical origins rest in Homer's epic poem *The Odyssey* in which we find the character named Mentor, who is given the responsibility of overseeing both the son (Telemachus) and home of Odysseus while Odysseus is away fighting in the Trojan War. While Telemachus is under Mentor's care, Mentor helps him find his father and also guides Telemachus toward a new self-understanding. Because of the relationship between Mentor and Telemachus in *The Odyssey*, "mentor" later became a word commonly utilized to describe an experienced individual who offers wisdom, support and guidance to an inexperienced individual. Anderson and Shannon (1988) studied the relationship between Telemachus and Mentor and deemed it a positive example of mentoring.

Colky and Young (2006) describe mentoring as a "process that brings together the inexperienced and the experienced in the hope that the former gains knowledge, skills, self-confidence, and other benefits" (p. 437). According to Zelditch (1990):

Mentors are advisors, people with career experience willing to share their knowledge; supporters, people who give emotional and moral encouragement; tutors, people who give specific feedback on one's performance; masters, in the sense of employers to whom one is apprenticed; sponsors, sources of information about and aid in obtaining opportunities; models, of identity, of the kind of person one should be to be an academic. (p.11)

Kram (1983) lists four distinct phases of mentoring: (1) initiation; (2) cultivation; (3) separation; and (4) redefinition. Each phase contains significant roles of both the mentor and the mentee that must be fulfilled for mentoring success.

In Kram's (1983) initiation phase, the mentor and mentee introduce themselves to one another and discuss the goals of the relationship. The mentor and mentee then evaluate the current progress of the mentee, and together fashion a means by which the progress is furthered so that the mentee eventually reaches an objective, identified by both parties in the initiation phase. In a traditional face-to-face mentoring setting, the initiation phase could last between six and twelve months (Colky & Young, 2006).

The cultivation phase is a long-term phase in which trust develops between the mentor and mentee. A sense of accomplishment and mutual respect is also often realized in this phase. The mentor and mentee become fully committed to the relationship in this phase, which can last from two to five years in the traditional face-to-face mentor setting (Kram, 1983).

The third phase, separation, involves the beginning of a departure between the mentor and mentee as the mentee becomes increasingly independent and autonomous. The mentor sometimes must offer additional encouragement at this phase as the mentee might experience separation anxiety (Kram, 1983).

The final phase, redefinition, is the complete separation phase. The mentee is no longer dependent on the mentor and establishes his or her own identity and often physically leaves the presence of the mentor to pursue work that is separate from that of the mentor (Kram, 1993).

Nykodym, Freedman, Simonetti, Nielson, and Battles (as cited in Peyton, Morton, Perkins, and Dougherty, 2001) identify several types of mentors who are often found in the corporate setting: peer mentors; information mentors; competitor mentors; retiree mentors; and grandparent mentors. In the educational setting, information mentors are most often utilized. The informational mentor provides information to the mentee and acts as a teacher to the mentee. The informational mentor is selected to be a mentor because that person has expertise in the needed area, is a good communicator, and is willing to share his or her information, resources, and support with the mentee (Kram, 1983). In the school setting, new teachers are often assigned mentor teachers who are veteran teachers willing to share with the new teacher the hidden curricula of the school (how things are done at that particular school, the culture of the school, the routines and procedures of the school), classroom management strategies, teaching strategies,

lesson plans, teaching resources, and overall support and encouragement. The mentor teacher acts as a coach to the new teacher and ideally, the new teacher feels he or she can fully trust the mentor teacher.

Face-to-Face Mentoring and the Beginning Teacher

The first year teacher faces a myriad of obstacles that often become insurmountable and ultimately result in his or her abandonment of the profession within the first five years (Ingersoll, 2002; Schlichte, Yssel, & Merbler, 2005). In fact, in the United States, fully half of all beginning teachers exit the profession within their first five years (Gareis & Nussbaum-Beach, 2008; Ingersoll, 2002). Reasons that have been reported by beginning teachers for leaving the teaching profession have included feelings of isolation, lack of professional and personal support, overwhelming workloads, lack of a collaborative school environment, excessive paperwork, the principal's mode of administration, and the realization that the teaching profession was not what it was expected to be (Abbott, 2003; Billingsley & Cross, 1992: Gersten, Keating, Yovanoff, & Harniss, 2001). Not cited as direct reasons for leaving the profession, but listed as contributing factors are feelings of isolation, worries of acceptance by veteran teachers, concerns of their own effectiveness as teachers, classroom management issues, administrator evaluation worries, and concerns about meeting the individual needs of students (Achilles & Gaines, 1991; Chubbuck, Clift, Allard, & Quinlan, 2001; Martin & McGrevin, 1990; Moran, 1990; Smith & Scott, 1990). The first year for a beginning teacher can often be traumatic and is well described by Ganser (1997): "Being a beginning teacher is like being in water over your head. You are floating on a tiny piece of foam that crumbles away every day just a little bit" (p. 106).

Clearly, the attrition of teachers is a significantly critical issue in education. Much research has focused on addressing the unique problems of beginning teachers in the hopes of improving teacher retention rates. Several initiatives seem to be positively influencing the retention of new teachers; one effective strategy has been the assignment of mentors (veteran teachers) to new teachers during the critical first year of teaching.

The positive significance of mentoring to the retention of beginning teachers has been well documented in the literature (Alvarado, 2006; Chubbock, Clift, Allard, & Quinlan, 2001; Gareis & Nussbaum-Beach, 2008; Heider, 2005; Ingersoll & Kralik, 2004). Many of the earlier causal factors for beginning teacher attrition are effectively eliminated when a new teacher is assigned a veteran teacher as a mentor and an effective, long-term mentor/mentee relationship develops. Kilgore and Griffin (1998) maintain that teacher socialization within the school setting is crucial for the well-being of beginning teachers. Having an experienced teacher mentor who offers advice, professional and emotional support, and friendship is critical to the success of the beginning teacher. Mentoring has also been shown to increase the effectiveness of new teachers (Gareis & Nussbaum-Beach, 2008). In addition, mentored beginning teachers demonstrate a greater commitment to professional development, are more content with their chosen profession, are twice as likely to continue in the teaching profession, and are more effective teachers than their non-mentored counterparts (Deshler, Ellis, & Lentz, 1996; Seabrooks, Kenney, & LaMontagne, 2000; Spuhler & Zetler, 1994). The mentoring of beginning teachers has also been associated with long-term positive change in teacher practice (Gentry, Denton, & Kurz, 2008). The overwhelmingly positive implications of a mentoring program for new teachers now means that over fifty percent of states in the United States have implemented and require participation in such programs (Feiman-Nemser, 1998).

Disadvantages of Traditional Face-to-Face Mentoring

Ideally, face-to-face mentor and mentee are in close proximity to one another, usually housed in the same building or in buildings within walking distance of one another. If a mentor and mentee are separated geographically, the relationship becomes much more problematic, and often creates a financial commitment, usually on the part of the mentee, who must bear the cost of traveling to the location of the mentor.

Mentees separated from their mentors by significant distance end up devoting more time to the relationship, as traveling time must be considered. Obviously, the greater the distance, the greater the time sacrifice involved to maintain the relationship and the more likely it is that the relationship will be aborted prematurely (Noe, 1988).

Mentees seeking traditional face-to-face mentors are very limited according to geographic location, so have a very finite number of mentees from which to choose. Factoring in the need to secure a mentee within one's specific career area further decreases the available mentor population for the mentee when geographic location is a factor.

Face-to-face mentoring usually occurs within a prescribed time frame. If one hour is allotted for the mentoring relationship per week (as an example), then all exchanges must occur within that hour. If mentee and mentor have not carefully planned how that hour will be spent, only surface-level topics may be addressed, time could be lost in introductory conversation, significant issues may not be considered because they were forgotten or thoughtful responses from mentors may not be supplied due to time constraints. Face-to-face mentoring is also subject to interruption if care has not been taken to carefully plan where and when the meetings are to take place.

Mentoring and the Pre-Service Teacher

Pre-service teachers, if paired with committed cooperating teachers during their student teaching experience, should receive mentoring from these veteran teachers. If education students have the opportunity to participate in a Professional Development School (PDS), they may also receive mentoring from the teachers with whom they are placed. But the student teaching experience does not usually occur until the students' senior year of college/university and many institutions of higher education have not implemented Professional Development School programs. So where does that leave the pre-service teacher in the beginning to middle portion of his or her teacher educational program who has not participated in a Professional Development School program? How much contact do these pre-service teachers actually have with veteran teachers? Likely, contact between these pre-service teachers and practicing teachers is sporadic (taking place as limited field experience components of certain education courses) prior to the student teaching experience.

What about the education professors teaching education courses? Weren't they all (at one time) practicing teachers in the K-12 setting? Surprisingly, that is not always the case, and many education students complain that education professors are out of touch with what is currently taking place in the K-12 school setting as many education professors have been out of the K-12 classroom for many years. Education students in the early stages of their programs of study often indicate the need for more contact with practicing teachers who can share practical information, such as what a typical teaching day is like, how to prepare for the daunting first year of teaching, how to manage a classroom, and how to effectively manage time as a new teacher (Clowes, 1997; Watson, 2006).

Because the literature clearly shows the value of mentoring to beginning teachers, we can surmise that a similar relationship between a pre-service teacher and a veteran teacher would be similarly beneficial to pre-service teachers. The need for the establishment of a connection between pre-service teachers in the beginning to middle stages of their education programs with practicing teachers in their projected subject areas or grade levels is therefore evident. However, a mentoring program between pre-service teachers and practicing teachers outside of student teaching, the Professional Development School and random field experiences is difficult to initiate. Practicing teachers are busy people. Face-to-face mentoring of a pre-service teacher requires an additional time commitment that most practicing teachers cannot spare and a financial commitment for pre-service teachers that most can ill afford. One possible solution is to initiate a telementoring program between pre-service teachers and veteran in-service teachers.

What is Telementoring?

Telementoring is also known as virtual mentoring, electronic mentoring, computer-mediated conversation, e-mentoring, cyber-mentoring and online mentoring (Gareis & Nussbaum-Beach, 2008). Colky and Young (2006) describe virtual or telementoring as mentoring relationships that take place electronically between individuals who "are not geographically co-located" (p. 433).

Early informal types of electronic mentoring likely began with the creation of email and expanded to more formal and larger scaled mentoring programs with the advent of America On-line (AOL) and Netscape (an easy to use email program widely marketed in the United States) (Single & Single, 2005). The need for telementoring arose for several reasons, some identical to those that resulted in face-to-face mentoring; other reasons were directly related to what a telementoring program could provide that a face-to-face mentoring program could not. Telementoring has the potential to "level the playing field" for individuals who, for a variety of reasons, may not otherwise be able to participate in a face-to-face mentoring program. For example, many early telementoring projects "focused on creating educational and professional opportunities for underprivileged or underrepresented populations (such as women in engineering or underprivileged students), or focused on areas of national need (such as school-aged students' access to science and scientists)" (Single & Single, 2005, pp. 202-203).

If we revisit Kram's (1983) four phases of mentoring, we can see how telementoring influences those phases. The telementoring initiation phase takes place quickly and therefore *swift trust* must take place immediately between mentee and mentor. According to Myerson, Weick and Kramer (1996), "there is less emphasis on feeling, commitment, and exchange and more on action, and heavy absorption in the task" (p. 191) in the telementoring initiation phase. In the second phase, cultivation, the telementoring relationship fast forwards and requires the mentor and mentee "delve into the relationship, and the goals of the relationship, very quickly and intensively" (Colky & Young, 2006, p. 440). Trust is still an important component in this phase and must be quickly established. In the telementoring separation phase, the mentor must coach the mentee on self-reliance, as in the virtual relationship, the life-cycle is limited and mentees must be ready to become independent from mentors much sooner than those who are in a face-to-face mentoring relationship (Kram, 1983). Because telementoring is usually a much more short-term project, the mentee must not become attached to his or her mentor, and must be ready to quickly separate from the mentee at the culmination of the relationship in the final phase of redefinition. Thus, telementoring greatly decreases the time commitment of a mentoring relationship, which addresses one of the most often mentioned reasons for face-to-face mentoring relationship failure: time constraints (Noe, 1988).

Additional benefits of telementoring are many and varied: it is cost efficient, is more accessible to mentees than face-to-face mentoring, and is space, and place independent (Colky & Young, 2006). There are virtually no monetary costs associated with telementoring as no one is out travel costs to meet and large blocks of time are not required that take from the responsibilities of the mentors' and mentees' daily work loads. Participants usually choose to communicate via email (rather than in an online chat forum), which is asynchronous, allowing them greater flexibility as to when they choose to post responses. Telementoring is space and place independent. Telementoring could thus occur anywhere the mentors and mentees have access to a computer and the Internet, and would not require the use of a particular meeting area. Another advantage to telementoring according to Single and Muller (1999) is that "communicating using email allows for the construction of thoughtfully written messages without the pressure of immediately responding, such as in communicating orally" (p. 237). In some instances, individuals are assigned mentors to improve their performance in specific career skills areas, and in those cases electronic mentoring can allow for a remediation process that can be kept relatively secret to alleviate possible embarrassment on the part of mentees at having to be mentored (National Mentoring Center, 2002).

Clearly, telementoring has some advantages over face-to-face mentoring, but many experts caution that this form of mentoring should only occur when face-to-face mentoring is not possible, practical, feasible, or appropriate (Muller, 1997; National Mentoring Center, 2002; O'Neill, Wagner & Gomez, 1996). There are many disadvantages to telementoring. Experts in telementoring (Harris, O'Bryan & Rotenberg, 1996; O'Neill, Wagner & Gomez, 1996; and Single & Muller; 2001) have reported the need for programmatic support for sustained telementoring as a distinct disadvantage. The technology and infrastructure required to support a telementoring program can be quite costly and complicated (Dickey, 1997; Noe, 1988). In addition, Sproull & Kiesler (1992) indicate that telementoring is lacking in reinforcement cues necessary for the sustainment of an electronic mentoring relationship. It is much easier for an individual to sign up for a telementoring program and then discontinue it or to ignore emails from mentors or coordinators because the likelihood of personally facing those individuals is greatly reduced in a telementoring format.

Examples of Initiatives in Telementoring

Telementoring is a rapidly developing phenomenon that has been in place for well over a decade (Gareis & Nussbaum-Beach, 2008) and many promising studies of such initiatives involving university students have been reported in the literature (Freedman, 1992; Kasprisin, Single, Single & Muller, 2003; Muller, 1997; Single & Muller, 2001). One such program, MentorNet, pairs women pursing science and engineering careers at 36 United States colleges and universities with "individuals who are industry professionals in the students' desired technical or scientific career areas" (Watson, 2006, p. 169). Participants in MentorNet have reported increased knowledge in their chosen career fields and a greater awareness of career opportunities (Single & Muller, 2001). The College of William and Mary, in partnership with the Center for Teacher Quality, has also developed an online mentoring initiative between beginning and veteran teachers known as ENDAPT—Electronically Networking to Develop Accomplished Professional Teachers (Gareis & Nussbaum-Beach, 2008). Waycross College in Georgia, electronically pairs matriculating minority students with faculty for mentoring purposes (Single & Muller, 2001). High school students indicating an interest in a particular career field are paired with adults working in those career fields in an organization called icouldbe.org (Colky & Young, 2006). Bonnett, Wildemuth & Sonnenwald (2006) describe a mentoring program between "pairs of corporate research scientists and university biology students" (p. 21). In yet another example, Arizona State University's graduate music education students are linked electronically with music professionals around the world for discussions concerning the music profession, which in turn become topics for discussion in their music education course (Bush, 1998). Writing students from Nanyang Technological University and Singapore Polytechnic (Cavallaro and Tan, 2006), were linked electronically in a peer-to-peer mentoring project (Nanyang students were university-aged students while the students from Singapore Polytechnic were all 17-18 years old). Nanyang students served as writing mentors for the Singapore students. Results showed that not only did the younger, less experienced Singapore students improve their writing skills as a result of the mentoring program, but the Nanyang students also indicated benefitting from the relationship as they reported an increased desire to perform well for their mentees.

Additional accounts of electronic mentoring, benefiting groups other than university students have also been documented in the literature. The Committee of the Advancement of Women Chemists (COACh) provides electronic forums to address the unique concerns of academic female chemists (Sylwester, 2005). The University of Tasmania in Australia has implemented a highly successful electronic relationship between beginning and senior level faculty to develop and support the research skills and attempts of beginning faculty. Senior mentors provide feedback to junior faculty on research proposals and often edit and correct their writing (Mihkelson, 1997). Many telementoring programs have resulted in the pairing of K-12 students with professionals in many career areas: the Electronic Emissary Project (Harris, Rotenberg, & O'Bryan, 1997); the Telementoring Young Women Project (Bennett, Tsikalas, Hupert, Meade, & Honey, 1998); and the Hewlett Packard Email Mentoring Project (Bennett, Harris, Klemmer & Neils, 1997). And finally, a unique mentoring initiative was developed for children with disabilities who are interested in pursuing higher education. Called DO-IT (Disabilities, Opportunities, Internetworking, and Technology), this project pairs students as young as 13 with college students and professionals who have similar disabilities, have been successful in postsecondary education and professions and live independently (Cory & Burgstahler (2007). This program has been critical in helping participant mentees connect with individuals like themselves who serve as role models and examples of what they might also one day be able to accomplish, despite their disabilities.

Telementoring and the Pre-Service Teacher

Because there is ample evidence in the literature for the positive benefits of mentoring for the beginning teacher, we could surmise that the same would hold true for the pre-service teacher. Face-to-face mentoring is usually employed for the beginning teacher (from a veteran teacher on site) at the direction of the school's administration and as was previously indicated, is now required in approximately half of all U.S. schools. Face-to-face mentoring for the pre-service teacher is much more difficult to establish for a plethora of reasons. Practicing teachers and pre-service teachers are separated by place; the practicing teacher spends his/her days in the K-12 school setting while the pre-service teacher is in the university setting, and these two locations could be miles apart. It would be a financial burden on pre-service teachers (who are often already struggling financially) to bear the cost of traveling to a school for mentoring. Traveling to a K-12 setting would be particularly problematic for the pre-service teacher who might not have access to a car or public transportation. Practicing teachers are already overloaded with teaching responsibilities: lesson planning, parent conferences, before and after school faculty and parent meetings, special education meetings, extracurricular activities they sponsor, tutoring, bus duty before and after school, etc. Setting aside an additional block of time to mentor a pre-service teacher, is often not possible, even though the desire to do so may exist. Locating a teacher mentor who meets the specific subject and grade level requirements of the pre-service teacher may also be limited within a geographical area. There are just so many music education teachers in one small school district, for example. All of these obstacles to face-to-face mentoring for the pre-service teacher could be eliminated via the utilization of telementoring.

Telementoring would eliminate the need for the pre-service teacher to physically travel to the school where the practicing teacher is located, eliminating possible transportation and cost dilemmas, which can be particularly problematic for the pre-service teacher who resides in a rural setting. Also a problem for pre-service teachers in rural areas seeking a face-to-face mentor is the lack of access to a large pool of practicing teachers (Harrington, 1999). Practicing teachers might be more likely to agree to mentor pre-service teachers if they could do so electronically, in an asynchronous format. With no obligation to meet at a certain time and place for a prescribed amount of time, the veteran teacher may not view mentoring the pre-service teacher as yet another time consuming responsibility. Instead, the veteran teacher (and the pre-service teacher) could converse whenever they had the time to do so (in the evenings after supper, when the children are in bed, on a Sunday afternoon). In addition, because the conversation occurs asynchronously via email (although it can occur synchronously in a chat format), the quality of the conversation could improve, becoming more reflective and thoughtful (Muller, 1999).

Telementoring Studies Involving Pre-Service Teachers

There are few examples of studies in which pre-service teachers are electronically mentored by practicing teachers in the literature, although several studies are cited that involved face-to-face mentoring between practicing and pre-service teachers. Seabrooks, Kenney and LaMontagne (2000) conducted an electronic mentoring program involving pre-service and practicing special education teachers.

In Seabrooks, Kenney and LaMontagne's (2000) study, special education pre-service teachers were paired electronically with practicing in-service special educators for mentoring purposes, which ultimately resulted in the pre-service teachers' reporting an increased confidence in themselves as developing teachers. Their research provides evidence of the critical role a mentor practicing teacher plays in the pre-service teacher's introduction to education. According to Seabrooks, et al (2000):

During these relationships practicing teachers support pre-service teachers in exploring, sharing, reflecting, and refining their knowledge and skills about teaching....Mentor teachers can be instrumental in facilitating a pre-service teacher's reflection related to daily classroom changes. Through their guidance and support, mentors share critical information related to the practical application of instructional management. (p. 222)

The other study found in the literature regarding the telementoring of pre-service teachers by in-service teachers is Watson's research at the University of Tennessee at Chattanooga (2006), which is the foundational study for this chapter.

ELECTRONIC MENTORING OF PRE-SERVICE TEACHERS AT THE UNIVERSITY OF TN AT CHATTANOOGA

Need for Study

Watson's study took place in the fall semester of 2005 at the University of Tennessee at Chattanooga (UTC) (Watson, 2006). The study was initiated as a response to a recurring voiced concern from pre-service teachers that their teacher education professors were out of touch with practical issues in K-12 education because the professors had not been K-12 teachers in many years or did not have any current contact with teachers in K-12 settings or both. Pre-service teachers indicated a dire need for practical information about teaching (what a typical day in the life of a teacher is like, how currently practicing teachers handle classroom management issues, how much time current teachers devote to planning, how specific subject area teachers address certain content area issues, etc.) from currently practicing teachers in the K-12 educational arena (Watson, 2006).

Specifics of Study: Participants

Twelve teacher education students (all seniors in their programs of study) enrolled in EDUC 433, a secondary curriculum course, were electronically paired with seventeen (some pre-service participants had more than one mentor) practicing K-12 teachers across the country in ten different school systems across Tennessee, Georgia, Kentucky, and Florida. Pre-service teachers selected their mentors from a list of practicing teachers in Education World's database of U.S. schools, from a selection of practicing teachers known by the instructor, or they could elect to enter into a mentoring relationship with practicing teachers they already knew who were willing to serve as mentors. To be selected for the study, mentor teachers had to be teaching and licensed in the same subject area and/or grade level as the pre-service teacher was seeking, and have at least two years of teaching experience. The mentor teachers participating in the projected had varying levels of education: four had bachelor's degrees in education, ten had master's degrees in education, and three held educational specialist degrees. Teaching experience of mentor teachers in the project ranged from two to thirty years. Average years of mentor teaching experience was fourteen (Watson, 2006).

Specifics of Study: Procedure

Watson's (2006) telementoring project took place over a span of six weeks, during which mentors and mentees were expected to engage in pertinent conversations two times per week.

Watson (2006) listed four primary goals for the telementoring project initiated at UTC:

(1) The pairing of a pre-service teacher with an experienced, practicing teacher in his/her desired subject/grade level.
(2) The provision of a support source (mentor) for the pre-service teacher (mentee).
(3) The provision of opportunities for pre-service teachers to engage in conversation about pedagogical issues in his/her content area with a practicing teacher in that same content area.
(4) To aid in the development of reflective practice on the part of pre-service teachers. (p. 170)

These goals were identified for the student participants at the beginning of their course in the fall semester of 2005, along with a description of and expectations for the project. Student participants were also asked to present their perceptions of the project previous to its implementation via a pre-reflection survey. This survey asked the participants to relate their feelings about the project (trepidation, excitement, dread, etc.), what they hoped to learn as a result of the project, and their predictions of possible problems that could arise during the project (Watson, 2006).

Next, the student participants were given a thorough description of how the project would proceed, beginning with the explanation of several components/documents pertinent to the project. Students were given a model letter of introduction that would serve as the initial contact between themselves and their potential mentees. This initial contact required mentees to introduce themselves, identify their programs of study, share the goals of the telementoring initiative, obtain biographical information of mentors to be certain mentors met the previously mentioned criteria for the project, and ask the veteran teachers if they would serve as mentors for the project (Watson, 2006).

Students were then supplied a list of possible educational conversational topics that could be initiated with mentor teachers in an interview format. The list was only intended to be used as a conversational guide and could be deviated from, insuring that the interviews were semi-formal in nature. Topics in the list provided included socialization issues (informal relationships with other teachers, student/faculty relationships, relationships with administrators, etc.), classroom management and discipline concerns (paperwork items, behavioral contracts, handling student violence, etc.), curricula and resource issues (how to write grants to obtain additional funding, what resources media centers provide teachers, time management, professional conference attendance, report cards, etc.), assessment and reporting concerns (standardized testing, parent conferences, etc.), time management, pedagogical strategies, teacher certification, legal issues, and concerns about teaching special needs students. Students were advised to add any additional items they wanted to include to the list of topics and then prioritize the list according to importance, due to the limited length of the project (there would not be enough time to address every issue) (Watson, 2006).

Next, the electronic process to follow during the project was clarified. Students were asked to keep a running commentary of their conversations with mentors by clicking "reply" each time a new conversation began rather than starting a new document. This running commentary allowed mentees to easily scroll back in time to revisit previous comments or questions for further clarification and expansion. Student participants were also advised to copy each conversational exchange to the instructor immediately after it took place so the instructor could monitor all conversations for appropriateness and value. Hard copies of each email exchange were also created and stored in a notebook (telementoring journal) by student participants to be turned in at the culmination of the project (Watson, 2006).

Following each twice weekly conversational exchange (Watson, 2006), student mentees completed a reflective journal entry with responses to the following four questions:

(1) Did the mentor adequately respond to your questions? Why or why not?
(2) What surprised you, if anything, about his/her responses?
(3) What information, suggestions, ideas, etc. did your mentor provide that were particularly helpful to you?
(4) Based on your questions and your mentor's responses in this particular exchange, where would you like to see the discussion go in the next interaction? What follow-up questions do you intend to pose? (p. 171)

These reflective pieces were inserted into their telementoring journals following each conversational exchange. At the culmination of the six-week project, student participants completed a post-reflective survey (similar to the pre-reflection) and presented their completed telementoring journals to the instructor for assessment and analysis (Watson, 2006).

Qualitative Analysis of Study Data

Immediately following the culmination of the project, qualitative data analysis began (Watson, 2006). It was determined that among the 29 participants (17 mentors and 12 mentees), 293 email messages were exchanged. The data were read and re-read, and minor editing took place as suggested by Marshall and Rossman (1999). A color-coded system was applied to the data to identify emerging themes, categories and patterns, and the data were ultimately reduced per Cohen, Kahn and Steeves (2000) who describe this phase of data analysis as a stage that:

...involves some decision making on the part of the researcher concerning what is relevant and what is not....The researcher can reorganize the interviews to place together discussions of the same topic, eliminate digressions that are clearly off track, and simplify the spoken language of the informants without changing the unique character of it. (p. 76)

Next, Watson (2006) coded the emergent themes, categories and patterns of the email exchanges and pre- and post- reflection responses for keywords according to Marshall and Rossman's (1999) qualitative analysis procedures.

Pre-Reflective Themes

Student participants were asked to respond to three questions prior to the start of the telementoring project:

(1) How do you feel about this project?
(2) What do you expect to learn from this interaction?
(3) What possible problems could arise? (p. 172)

Student responses to question number one (how do you feel about this project?) were mostly positive, with comments including the following (Watson, 2006): "I feel that it is a good idea. New teachers need mentors to help guide them through the beginning." "I am excited that I will get to talk to a teacher in the field and maybe pick up a few pointers." "I'm excited about having someone I can ask a lot of questions and who will give me real answers." "This seems like it will be interesting and a good way to gain educational knowledge and real life teaching skills." "I think this is a wonderful project for pre-service teachers to participate in. I have learned a lot about education through my time here, but I feel I lack any real hands-on experience in the day-to-day activities of a teacher. There are many things I would like to learn." "I am looking forward to communicating with someone who teaches what

I will teach." Nine student participants indicated that they were excited about the project, while four indicated that they were somewhat hesitant and/or nervous about the assignment stating: "I am worried that I may not be able to find someone who can actually email me back and stay with this." "I have some concerns as to how easy it will be to find a person willing or able to email twice a week." "I am nervous about finding someone in the field who will be willing to do this." "I'm a little nervous that I won't sound professional enough, that too much time will be involved, that my mentor won't respond in a timely fashion, or that my questions will not be answered sufficiently" (Watson, 2006).

Student responses to question number two (what do you expect to learn from this interaction?) fell into four major categories (Watson, 2006): teaching tips (10 students mentioned this), information about the daily life of a teacher (5), specific advice for particular teaching areas (3), and advice specific to the beginning teacher (8). Comments included the following: "I expect to get a better understanding as to what I will face as both a new teacher and an experienced teacher. Also, I hope to get some good ideas that will help me prepare for teaching." "Hopefully, some pointers about the profession that will help me become an effective teacher." "I expect to get a better feel for what life as a teacher is like. I expect to gain knowledge about how to handle situations, what a daily schedule is like, and other duties a physical education teacher might have other than teaching physical education." "I want to learn how to manage an art budget, connect units, and manage the transfer of art information to the community." "I've had some questions lingering in my head about teaching music (specifically in the elementary school). I hope to acquire some information that will enable me to have realistic expectations as I enter this profession. Also, I would like to receive some information on the practical side of teaching. Now that I've had some theory in teaching music, it would be nice to see how these ideas/strategies are put into practice." "I hope to receive some great insight from a teacher who has been in the field for some time. I'm interested in what he/she is currently doing in his/her classes, how he/she organizes coursework, and some terrific advice about what to do and not do as a first year teacher. By the end of the semester, I would like to have a friend I can contact when I start teaching." "I would like to learn some basic classroom management techniques, disciplinary techniques, teaching strategies, and socialization techniques. I want to learn how to motivate students to work together as a team since choir is more like a team than a class. I want to learn how to use constructive criticism effectively without making students self-conscious about their voices. I'd like to gather information that will help me to sharpen my personal educational philosophy" (Watson, 2006).

A variety of concerns were voiced in response to question three (what possible problems could arise?). The most frequently occurring concern among the student participants was that mentors would not respond to emails in a timely fashion, jeopardizing the completion of the project by the deadline (9 students indicated this as a possible issue). Four students were worried about the quality of responses of teacher mentors (due to the time constraints teachers face). Three students were concerned about locating teacher mentors willing to participate in the project. Two mentioned the possibility that technical issues regarding computers and emails might negatively affect the project. Other singular concerns included: teacher mentors quitting the project prior to its completion, the mentor not seeming to like the student, lack of time to adequately address the project, and possible philosophical differences between mentor and mentee (Watson, 2006).

Prioritized Concerns

Early on in the project, students were instructed to review the list of discussion topics, add any additional topics they wished to address with their mentors, and prioritize those topics/concerns so that those most important to them would be addressed early in the project. Qualitative data analysis across the collective prioritized concerns of the class revealed "eleven general categories of issues (themes) discussed within the email exchanges and forty-five subcategory issues" (Watson, 2006, p. 172). The eleven major issues included the following with subcategory issues indicated parenthetically following each major category issue: (1) socialization (overt and covert school routines; handling assemblies, fire drills, etc; extra duties; high risk students; interaction with other teachers; support for new teachers; inappropriate student male/female contact); (2) producing a positive learning environment (necessary conditions; cooperative learning strategies); (3) assessment/evaluation and paperwork issues (used to inform next steps; developing range of practices; grading policies; student and parental feedback; parent conferences; handling paperwork; report cards); (4) classroom management/ discipline (classroom rules and procedures; behavioral strategies; student violence; reward systems; student disrespect/insubordination; lockdowns/ bomb threats); (5) curriculum/resource materials (obtaining needed materials; access to literature and professional materials; attending conferences; writing grants); (6) time management (typical day; amount of work taken home; types of daily lesson plans required; length and structure of daily lesson plans); (7) teaching strategies (recognizing learner differences; repertoire of teaching strategies; student motivation); (8) certification and legal issues (maintaining current certification; summers; teacher contract issues; teacher professional insurance; professional organizations; teacher observations); (9) special needs students (inclusive classroom issues; special education meetings and documentation; accommodations/ modifications) and; (10) issues pertaining to new teachers (challenges faced; interview issues; teacher created materials). Other students mentioned many specific issues related to particular content areas (11) (Watson, 2006).

Post-Reflective Themes

Student participants were asked to respond to four questions at the culmination of the telementoring project:

(1) Did this project meet your expectations? Why or why not?
(2) What did you learn from your mentor that was particularly beneficial to you?
(3) What was problematic, if anything, about the project?
(4) What suggestions could you offer to improve this project? (pp. 172-173)

Ten out of twelve students (two did not answer this question) indicated that the experience was very beneficial. Student participants' post-reflective responses to question one (Did this project meet your expectations? Why or why not?) included the following (Watson, 2006): "Yes, I learned some very good strategies for classroom management." "My experience exceeded my expectations because the whole experience was really insightful." "Yes, it was really good to get a sense of what teaching is like…I felt like I got to ask several questions that I have had about teaching music. This was a really good forum to do so." "Yes, I learned a lot about what teaching is really like." "Yes, my mentor was helpful and informative. He worked with my crazy schedule and we are now friends. It exceeded my expectations."

Two students voiced difficulties locating mentors willing to participate in the project. One had a mentor who dropped out of the project, making completion impossible: "I had a very difficult time locating a mentor and then that person just stopped writing…with this project I felt a bit helpless" (Watson, 2006).

"All student participants indicated that they learned information pertaining to the education profession that was beneficial to them" (Watson, 2006, p. 173). Student participants' post-reflective responses to question two (What did you learn from your mentor that was particularly beneficial to you?) included the following: "I learned how to deal with insubordination and school violence. The most important information that I learned from this project is that there are many correct ways to do something. We will be given rules and regulations, but each teacher develops his or her own teaching style and method of handling problems." "I learned from my mentor that I have to be organized and love what I do. The classroom management information and real world insight she provided will be very beneficial when I start teaching. I learned about budgeting, unit development and the importance of arts advocacy." "I learned tips on classroom management and grading organization. Overall she helped me to be less apprehensive about teaching." Some mentors even provided mentees with documents (in the form of email attachments or pasted directly into the email exchange) such as class syllabi, lesson plans, entire units, graphic organizers, and assessment information (Watson, 2006).

Student participants' post-reflective responses to question three (What was problematic, if anything, about the project?) indicated that most participants did not experience any problems with the project. Those who did have difficulty mentioned the following as problematic: locating a mentor willing to participate or even responsive to the query for participation, untimely and vague responses to questions on the part of mentors, and the large amount of time the project required on the part of some student participants. Responses to question three included: "The only problem I found to be an issue was actually finding someone who wanted to participate in the project." "Finding the time to complete the project was difficult as I also work full-time." "It was hard sometimes because my mentor wouldn't write back for a week or so and I didn't want to send another email and seem rude, but I really needed her to respond."

"It was very hard to get my mentor to respond to my questions. When she would respond, she did not elaborate on anything" (Watson, 2006).

Suggestions for improvement were offered as the students responded to the final post-reflective question (number four). These suggestions were made regarding mentor selection and the time commitment of the project. Student responses to question number four included the following: "The biggest improvement I think that could be made is locating teachers who are willing to participate. One suggestion would be either to get a system down where you have a pool of teachers for students to choose from, or let the students choose teachers they already know" and "The only suggestion I would make for this project is to require only one email exchange per week" (Watson, 2006).

DISCUSSION

Tele-Conversations

Of the eleven major areas listed as concerns by participants in the pre-reflective survey, only those identified ten or more times by student participants as concerns will be discussed here, with the exception of one category: Issues Pertaining to Specific Content Areas. Because this category involved multiple varying specific issues pertaining to specific content areas, it would be difficult to address each of them here. Under the eleven major category areas were 45 subcategory issues as identified by student participants in the pre-reflective surveys. It is important to note that although these concerns were identified by student participants, many of them were never discussed in mentor/mentee conversations. What follows is a discussion of the electronic conversations pertaining to the top six concerns cited by students (ten or more times): socialization, time management/typical day, classroom management, assessment, handling records and paperwork and classroom supplies and materials procurement.

Socialization

One of the identified major causal factors of teacher stress is poor or no colleague relationships (Dussault, Deaudelin, Royer, & Loiselle, 1997). Although schools are busy places, teachers often find themselves spending large amounts of time with students, cut off from colleagues by the natural compartmentalization that is the structure of U.S. schools, and thus unable to discuss teaching problems and concerns (Ray, Waldhart & Seibert, 1985; Rosenholtz, 1985). Mentor participants provided encouraging information in this area, stating that they got along well with their colleagues and suggestions were made to consult with veteran teachers for answers to questions, classroom management strategies, lesson plan ideas and other words of advice. One teacher at a school that utilizes a particular curriculum noted that lesson plan creation to meet that curriculum's requirements was very time consuming so all of the teachers in one department divided up the lessons and shared what they had created with one another. Some teacher mentors indicated that they were personal friends with their colleagues, often socializing with them on the weekends.

Time Management/Typical Day

Meister and Melnick (2003) list "feelings of being overwhelmed by time constraints and workload" as especially problematic for beginning teachers (p. 87). The teachers in Meister and Melnick's study spoke about "time constraints in terms of the amount of time required to plan and implement a lesson, as well as deal with all the paperwork" (p. 87). In fact, Meister and Melnick (2003) found that only 55% of the beginning teachers who participated in their survey identifying new teacher concerns indicated that they were well prepared for the amount of work required of them.

Many student participants wanted to talk about what a day in the life of a teacher is really like and how teachers manage their time to be most productive. Student participants wanted to know more about how much time is devoted to lesson planning, how much work is taken home each evening, and how a typical day is structured. The teacher mentors provided lots of feedback on this particular topic. Some of the feedback was very positive and some was negative. One high school literature teacher with 21 years of teaching experience described her typical teaching day as follows (Watson, 2006):

A typical day is very busy: I hate to say it but it is also very stressful. This week I have morning duty, which means that I have to be here at 7:00 am to stand in the Student Center and greet students...I teach three classes of American Literature, then I have Journalism I, planning, and Journalism II. Yesterday we had a faculty meeting after school. Then I stayed and worked until 7:30 pm. I have more of those kinds of days than I don't. In fact, last week I got home around 5:30 and my husband said, "Gee honey, you're home early today." (p. 174)

Another similar response was provided by a high school math teacher with 20 years of experience (Watson, 2006):

I get up at 5:30 a.m., take a shower, get my son up, eat breakfast, take him to school across town and get to school at about 7:30. It takes me 30 minutes just to drive to work. I usually have a student to tutor or bus duty for a few minutes in the mornings...I teach first period, have planning second, teach third, go to lunch, then teach fifth and sixth periods. After school I often have parent conferences, special education IEP meetings, faculty meetings, or stay in my room and grade papers. I used to take work home but it was getting frequent flyer miles so I do the work before I leave school or get here early to do the grading, copying and planning...then I finally get to

Telementoring in Teacher Education

go home, but I really don't because then I make parent phone calls.

A more positive description of a typical day was provided by an elementary physical education teacher with five years of teaching experience (Watson, 2006):

I just want to start off by saying, I love my job! I get to school at 7:15 in the morning wearing gym shorts and tennis shoes. I'm the envy of every teacher wearing dress clothes and dress shoes every day. I assist in the car loop every morning from 7:40-8:00, making sure to greet the students as they are dropped off. From 8:00 to 8:40 I have my planning time. My first class starts at 8:40... lunch from 11:35-12:05. My final class ends at 2:15 and I then go back to the car loop and assist with dismissal until all the students are picked up. I then go back to my office and answer emails, make phone calls, or whatever else needs to be done. Our day ends at 3:15. I normally don't take much work home with me. It really depends on what I am working on. Sometimes I would rather take some work home and be able to visit with my family, fix dinner, or do some laundry while I am working on school "stuff." (p. 174)

Another description of her typical teaching day was provided by a high school math teacher with 26 years of teaching experience:

A typical day for me starts with arrival at school between 7:00 and 7:15 to get ready for the day. I really like the quiet time in the morning. I have time to check my email and get my supplies ready for the day. I teach five 55-minute classes and have one planning period. First period starts at 8:05 and our students are dismissed at 3:10 in the afternoon. I have six weeks of early morning bus duty this year; last year I had after school detention duty. I leave school usually by 4:00 and I do take work home with me. I use overhead transparency sheets to teach and I take them home at night to clean them. This year I am trying really hard not to take a lot of papers home to grade because I have worked myself to death the last few years. I used to work on the weekends a lot too, but I have not been doing that this year.

Every student participant was pleased with the descriptions their mentors provided about their daily teaching lives. Some were surprised at the amount of work involved in teaching and the long days many teachers experience. All mentees felt they gained a much better insight into what a typical day in the life of a teacher was like as a result of this project (Watson, 2006).

Classroom Management

Veenman (1984) conducted a comprehensive literature review concerning new teacher concerns and found classroom management/discipline to be the most serious problem they face. Meister and Melnick (2003) conducted a study in which forty-two teachers from four states were interviewed about their first year of teaching. The teachers in this study consistently identified student behavior/classroom management as their greatest concern. In Watson's study (2006) classroom management and student behavioral issues were not the greatest concerns of the participants, but were in the top three. Mentor teacher participants were particularly vocal about and willing to share ideas and plans about classroom management techniques with their pre-service teacher mentees. Themes that emerged after qualitative analysis of the email conversations included the following: how to develop a succinct and appropriate set of classroom rules; how to enforce those rules; documentation of disciplinary events and cautions about not becoming friends with students. Some mentors provided mentees with copies of their classroom rules and procedures documents as attachments, others just typed them into their email responses (Watson, 2006).

One mentor remarked that disciplinary issues are always changing with time: "Each year we are dealing with a new set of problems that we didn't see in the past." For example, this teacher mentioned that new rules had to be created to deal with student possession of cell phones and to address changes in student clothing styles (such as sagging pants). Another teacher mentioned that new rules have been enforced regarding increasingly inappropriate contact between male and female students (Watson, 2006).

One teacher participant offered the following advice about discipline:

First of all, don't try to be their friend. They have friends. Be their teacher. Establish firm, fair rules that you follow consistently. I have very few: (1) Be on time; (2) Be prepared; (3) Don't talk while someone else is talking; (4) Don't chew gum, eat, or drink in class; (5) Don't groom in class; and (6) Be courteous! Of course, you have to enforce school rules too. I haven't had an uproar in my class in quite some time but they do occur occasionally. Students don't like to be corrected. I have learned through the years to be careful of the tone of voice I use when dealing with students. A gentle tone seems to work better than an accusatory one.

Another teacher believed that troubled students either lack attention from home or are insecure. He shared this information with his mentee about discipline (Watson, 2006):

I always try to identify the troubled students early on and make a deal with them. I tell them that jokes and other behaviors have their time and place and sometimes that is in the classroom. I tell them to recognize the nature of class daily, and to prepare themselves for the "culture" of class that day. The worse thing a teacher can do is embarrass or challenge these kids during class out loud. That is attention that can fuel their fires…they deserve as much respect as we do. In other words, my attempt is to love the troubled kids, allow them some fun, yet let them gauge their attitudes and allow them to make some mistakes. Kids need direction and you must be that force.

This teacher went on to suggest that the mentee seek discipline strategies from experienced teachers and that he document all discipline infractions completely and keep a record of those infractions. Other mentors suggested some classroom procedures that were conducive to good classroom management such as: utilizing a seating chart (getting to know students' names at the start of a new school year is a first step toward identifying misbehaving students); arranging desks so that it is easy for the teacher to maneuver past each student; posting classroom rules in a prominent location in the classroom; making sure to consistently enforce classroom rules; allowing students ownership in the development of classroom rules; having a set procedure for daily tasks such as turning in and passing out homework and locating paperwork needed by an absent student; and making sure students understand the consequences for violating classroom rules (Watson, 2006).

Assessment

Several issues regarding assessment emerged as concerns from the pre-reflective data, which supports the findings in the literature that assessment is a primary concern of the beginning teacher (Meister & Melnick, 2003; Veenman, 1984). The assessment of special needs students in the regular education classroom was one such concern mentioned by several student participants. Qualitative analysis of mentor responses regarding assessing special needs students revealed the following strategies: test modification strategies: reading the test aloud to the student, allowing extra time for test completion, redirecting questions, creating a series of shorter quizzes rather than one large exam, and shortening assignments; making use of graphic organizers to help students pick out the main points of a lesson and to summarize a lesson; providing opportunities for group work; and providing individualized instruction whenever possible (Watson, 2006). One physical education teacher shared how he evaluates students with special needs in his class:

I try to include our special needs students in every activity, making as many or as few adaptations necessary to allow those students to participate in the activity. Sometimes it may be as simple as having a buddy to mirror what they should be doing, sometimes the need is greater and the special needs students may need greater support (like having a buddy roll a ball for them). There is always a way to include all the children; sometimes we just need to be creative.

A music teacher provided insight into how she teaches special needs students in her music classroom:

Sometimes I will have to change the way I teach a lesson: more hands-on types of strategies rather than lecture or even visual teaching. Also, I might have a student who is mentally impaired and in that case I adjust my lesson so that student can succeed. The most common disability is LD (learning disabled). These students might have to have a little more time to process the lesson or might even need a little more help or attention from me.

Student participants also had specific assessment concerns related to their particular content areas. Advice provided by mentors regarding assessment was analyzed to reveal the following themes: the use of rubrics for assessment whenever possible and presenting the students with the rubric when the assignment is given so that students know how to craft their work according to the criteria provided in the rubric; the use of a variety of assessment strategies to meet the different learning styles of all students; providing students multiple assessment opportunities so that students' class grades do not result from a small number of heavily weighted assessments; and the suggestion that teachers always provide prompt feedback on all assignments (Watson, 2006).

Handling Records and Paperwork

Meister and Melnick (2003) cite paperwork volume as one of the top six concerns of beginning teachers. Teachers spend extremely large amounts of time documenting on paper (events at parent conferences, discipline infractions, modifications made for special needs students, etc.), grading papers, creating lesson plans and student response sheets, creating assessments, completing evaluations, writing letters of recommendation for students, taking attendance, maintaining records (book assignments, lock and locker assignments, etc.), completing a plethora of forms (student tardy forms, hall pass forms, discipline referral forms, media center forms, etc.), ordering supplies for a new school year, inventorying equipment and materials, etc.

The teacher participants in this study had much advice to offer their mentees regarding paperwork issues in education. The following themes emerged in this category: (1) making use of routines: students can do much of a teacher's work for him or her if she teaches them routines and procedures for handing in homework, for obtaining missed handouts due to absences and for the distribution and collection of classroom materials; (2) handling all paperwork on a daily basis so that it does not pile up and become overwhelming; (3) storing lesson plans in an organized format in clearly labeled file folders or binders; and (4) adopting a filing system for all categories of documentation (special education student documentation, resources available in the media center, student information such as phone numbers and addresses, disciplinary documentation, records of parent conferences, etc.) (Watson, 2006).

Classroom Supplies and Materials Procurement

Under one of the major category issues identified by student participants (curriculum/resource materials) emerged a subcategory that appeared often enough to warrant mention here. Student participants were very concerned about how they would obtain the materials and equipment they would need to effectively teach their classes. Meister and Melnick (2003) also found funding to be in the top eight issues of concern to all teachers. Many student participants had heard stories about teachers given very little money to buy start-up supplies at the beginning of the school year and often resorting to dipping into their own personal funds to purchase necessary teaching materials. The teacher participants mostly indicated that they do spend their own money on teaching supplies because the materials fee they are allocated is woefully inadequate. No teacher participant reported receiving more than $100 to fund the purchase of materials for an entire school year (Watson, 2006). One 6-8th grade art teacher shared her frustrations with this issue:

Budget? When I first came here I was allotted $3000 for the year. Dividing that by the number of students I served, meant each child received $5. The last two years I have been asked to try to collect $5 per child from the students and was given what every teacher receives for materials: $100.

A high school literature teacher shared her funding situation:

Yes, I pay for things out of my own pocket and you will too. All teachers do, unfortunately. We get a $50 allowance at the end of the year to buy supplies for the next year. We haven't always received that much money, and it really helps. I do hunt bargains; I frequent discount stores to buy art supplies, etc.

A high school math teacher related how she handles the lack of funding for materials and supplies at her school:

We are given an allotment of $50 to purchase materials for our room, which is certainly not enough. So I end up buying supplies on my own, keeping the receipts and taking up to $250 off on our income taxes. We get markers for the white boards from the office and receive three packages of paper a month. I use cloth on my bulletin board instead of paper; it looks so much better and lasts a lot longer.

CONCLUSION

Research Problems and Limitations

Because teacher telementoring is a relatively recent phenomenon, the literature is lacking in the documentation of best practices associated with it. This study, therefore was developed and implemented based on relatively few documented successful teacher telementoring practices. Not surprisingly, problems arose. The major problems that emerged during the study included mentor recruitment and retention and mentor/mentee matching problems (Watson, 2006).

The primary problem with this project as indicated by the student participants was the difficulty of locating appropriate mentors who were willing to participate in a six-week telementoring initiative. The professor had a list of educators she personally knew who indicated their willingness to participate and some student participants already knew practicing teachers who had also agreed to serve as mentors. Student mentees who did not know any teachers personally and who could not find a subject/grade level mentor match on the professor's list turned to Education World's database of teachers. This site was initially identified as the primary resource for locating possible mentors, but ended up being woefully inadequate.

Contact information is available on that site for thousands of teachers so both the mentees and the professor thought it would be relatively easy to locate willing participants. It was not determined if the contact information was outdated or if the teachers just did not respond, but many emails were sent to teacher email addresses across the country with only one teacher responding and participating. Local teachers were finally identified who were willing to participate, but the students in those situations did get a late start on the project (Watson, 2006).

Developing a website associated with the project and linking it to the professional associations teachers belong to could possibly strengthen mentor recruitment efforts. Interested potential mentors could access the website through their association's link and peruse the list of mentees, their biographical information, teaching areas, extra-curricular interests, academic programs and career goals and perhaps identify a matching mentee.

Providing a stipend for mentors would also likely greatly increase the mentor pool. No such funds were available for this study. Therefore, writing a grant that would provide cash incentives for mentors could have quite a positive impact on a project such as this.

Another problem faced by a couple of mentees during the course of the project was mentor bail-out. A few mentors who agreed to participate, and started out doing so, ended all contact and mentees were left wondering how they could ever possibly complete the project. Additional time allowances were made for these students, new mentors were obtained and the project was eventually completed. As a result of the early mentors' abandonment, these mentees were left frustrated and upset about the entire assignment. Perhaps contact from the professor throughout the project would deter mentor bail-out. de Janasz, Ensher and Heun (2008) corroborate this idea as they suggest a third party be available throughout the process to keep tabs on the interaction and provide guidance and assistance. Mentor stipends and contractual agreements would likely also aid in ensuring that mentors fulfilled their part of the project (Watson, 2006).

Because the mentors involved in this project received no instruction or coaching in mentoring, the success of the project greatly depended on the conscientious levels of the volunteer mentors. It would be useful to compare the results of this study with another similar study whose mentors had received stipends and had attended training prior to the project's inception. Single, Jaffe, and Schwartz (1999) advocate that mentor training include instruction on methods to assess and respond to mentee needs. This training could take place electronically through email, chat forums and discussion boards or could occur in a face-to-face setting.

Because the participant sample was limited in size, the study's findings cannot be easily generalized to other telementoring contexts (Bonnet, Wildemuth & Sonnenwald, 2006). This study involved a specific group of mentees (pre-service teachers) and mentors (practicing teachers) and as mentioned by Bonnett, Wildemuth and Sonnenwald, it is unknown if the findings "are influenced by participants' discipline" (education), "organizational and institutional settings" (UTC and several public school systems in Georgia, Tennessee, Florida, and Kentucky), "socio-economic class, ethnicity and/or gender or participants" (p. 56).

Mentor/mentee matching could have also influenced the outcomes of the project (Watson, 2006). Do differences in age and gender among mentors and mentees influence dialogue? Do more experienced teachers provide higher quality responses than less experienced teachers? Do teachers nearing retirement have more negative views of teaching? Do rural and urban teachers give different types of responses to questions based on their student populations? Do elementary teachers respond differently than high school teachers? These are questions that should be further explored as these issues certainly could impact the total quality of the experience for the student mentees. Single, Jaffe, and Schwartz (1999) advocate the use of formative data collection prior to mentor/mentee matching, such as the use of short reflections and surveys to examine how mentors and mentees bond, "thus establishing predictors of good mentoring and good mentors" (p. 245).

One additional limitation of the study involves the motivation of the student participants. Because this project was an assignment in a required education course, it is difficult to assess the motivational levels of student participants. Did the students really prioritize their list of concerns or did they randomly select them to save time? Did the students ask personally meaningful questions of their mentors or did they just follow the order of the suggested discussion topics list? Did the student participants view this project as just another assignment to be completed in just another course in order to satisfy program requirements for graduation or did they seize this project as an opportunity to make connections with practicing teachers who have valuable information to share? Although student post-reflections indicated that they all seemed genuinely pleased with what transpired during the course of the mentoring project, these responses could also be crafted in a positive way in the hopes of positively influencing their grade for the project (Watson, 2006).

Research Implications

Positive implications for teacher education were identified from this study. The telementoring format provided mentees a "field experience" without venturing out into the field. College students often have hectic schedules, maintaining full course loads and often working part- or full-time. It is difficult for these students to schedule time during the weekday (when they are attending university classes) to travel out to a school site for a face-to-face mentoring session. Asking students to do this two times a week for six weeks would have been unfair and impractical. Factor in the additional cost to the students to travel to teacher locations, and the project becomes nearly impossible. The telementoring format eliminated these issues. Students were able to complete all of the requirements for this project from the comfort of their homes, dorm rooms, or university library and could read and respond to mentor emails whenever they chose as long as that happened twice each week.

Despite the aforementioned problems some students experienced, all student participants were pleased with the practical information they received from their mentors regarding the following issues: socialization, learning environments, assessment/evaluation, paperwork, classroom management/discipline, curriculum/resource materials, time management, teaching strategies, certification and legal concerns, concerns pertaining to special needs students, issues pertinent to specific content areas, and issues relevant to beginning teachers. Single, Jaffe, and Schwartz (1999) have identified many of these issues as especially problematic to new teachers and often collectively result in their exodus from the teaching field. Since these issues are pre-identified as particularly problematic to new teachers, mentoring in these areas prior to obtaining teaching positions could possibly positively influence new teacher retention rates.

Final Thoughts

The literature has indicated that electronic mentoring has been highly successful in corporate and educational contexts, so it is not surprising that it was found to also be successful for pre-service teachers. This initiative has room for expansion and further development. Possible alterations to this project that would yield more data for further analysis and possible critically valuable information could include: implementing the project during the first education course students take, assigning different mentors to student mentees at selected points throughout their educational programs of study (perhaps as components of various education courses), or assigning two mentors per mentee. Other educational contexts in which telementoring could be implemented and studied include: the telementoring of students in their first introductory education course (mentees) by students at the final phase of their programs (mentors) and the telementoring of pre-service teachers at any level by first-year retired veteran teachers. In any case, little has been documented in the literature about telementoring programs for pre-service teachers. As this study proves, telementoring in the teacher education setting is a methodology that shows promise, is cost and time-efficient, and can be managed with structure and organization. The data it yields is rich, comprehensive and critical and therefore should be further explored.

REFERENCES

Abbot, L. (2003). *Novice teachers' experiences with telementoring as learner-centered professional development.* Retrieved February 28, 2009, from http://teachnet.edb.utexas.edu/~lynda_abbott?ABBOTT-DISSERTAION.pdf

Achilles, C. M., & Gaines, P. (1991, April). *Collegial groups in school improvement: Project SIGN.* Paper presented at the meeting of the American Educational Research Association, Chicago, IL.

Alvarado, A. (2006, April). *New directions in teacher education: Emerging strategies from the Teachers for a New Era initiative.* Paper presented at the American Educational Research Association, San Francisco, CA.

Anderson, E., & Shannon, A. (1988). Toward a conceptualization of mentoring. *Journal of Teacher Education, 39*(1), 38–42. doi:10.1177/002248718803900109

Bennett, D., Harris, J., Klemmer, D., & Neils, D. (1997). *Telementoring ways of learning.* Panel presentation at the BBN National School Network Conference, Cambridge, MA. Retrieved March 9, 2009, from alpha.musenet.org/81/telementor-wrkshp/confnote/pane/1.html

Bennett, D., Tsikalas, K., Hupert, N., Meade, T., & Honey, M. (1998). *The benefits of online mentoring for high school girls: Telementoring young women in science, engineering, and computing project, Year 3 evaluation* (New York, Center for Children and Technology). Retrieved March 9, 2009 from: http://www2.edc.org/CCT/admin/publications/report/telement_bomhsg98.pdf

Billingsley, B. S., & Cross, L. H. (1992). Predictors of commitment, job satisfaction, and intent to stay in teaching: A comparison of general and special educators. *The Journal of Special Education, 25,* 453–471. doi:10.1177/002246699202500404

Bonnett, C., Wildemuth, B. M., & Sonnenwald, D. H. (2006). Interactivity between protégés and scientists in an electronic mentoring program. *Instructional Science, 34,* 21–61. doi:10.1007/s11251-005-4115-9

Bush, J. (1998). *Promoting electronic reflective practice.* Paper presented at Fifth International Technological Directions in Music Learning Conference, San Antonio, TX.

Cavarallaro, F., & Tan, K. (2006). Computer mediated peer-to-peer mentoring. *AACE Journal, 14*(2), 129–138.

Chubbuck, S. M., Clift, R. T., Allard, J., & Quinlan, J. (2001). Playing it safe as a novice teacher: Implications for programs for new teachers. *Journal of Teacher Education, 52*(5), 365–376. doi:10.1177/0022487101052005003

Clowes, G. (1997). Survey: Education teachers out of touch with the real world. *School Reform News.* Retrieved March 1, 2009 from: http://www.heartland.org/Article.cfm?artId=13665

Cohen, M., Kahn, D., & Steeves, R. (2000). *Hermeneutic phenomenological research: A practical guide for nurse practitioners*. Thousand Oaks, CA: Sage Publications.

Colky, D. L., & Young, W. H. (2006). Mentoring in the virtual organization: Keys to building successful schools and businesses. *Mentoring & Tutoring, 14*(4), 433–447. doi:10.1080/13611260500493683

Cory, R. C., & Burgstahler, S. (2007). Creating virtual community: Mentoring kids with disabilities on the Internet. *Journal of School Public Relations, 28*, 283–296.

de Janasz, S. C., Ensher, E. A., & Heun, C. (2008). Virtual relationships and real benefits: Using e-mentoring to connect business students with practicing managers. *Mentoring and Tutoring: Partnership in Learning, 16*(4), 394–411. doi:10.1080/13611260802433775

Deshler, D., Ellis, E., & Lentz, B. (1996). *Teaching Adolescents with Learning Disabilities: Strategies and Methods* (2nd ed.). Denver, CO: Love Publishing.

Dickey, C. A. (1997). Mentoring women of color at the University of Minnesota: Challenges for organizational transformation. *Journal of Vocational Special Needs Education, 36*(1), 22–27.

Dussault, M., Deaudelin, C., Royer, N., & Loiselle, J. (1997, April). *Professional isolation and stress in teacher.* Paper presented at the annual meeting of the American Educational Research Association, Chicago, IL.

Feiman-Nemser, S. (1998). *Teacher mentoring: A critical review.* ERIC Digests. Washington, D.C. (ERIC Document Reproduction Service No. ED397060).

Freedman, M. (1992). *The kindness of strangers: Reflections on the mentoring movement.* Philadelphia, PA: Public/Private Ventures.

Ganser, T. (1997). Similes for beginning teaching. *Kappa Delta Pi Record, 33*(3), 106–108.

Gareis, C. R., & Nussbaum-Beach, S. (2008). Electronically mentoring to develop accomplished professional teachers. *Journal of Personnel Evaluation in Education, 20*, 227–246. doi:10.1007/s11092-008-9060-0

Gentry, L. B., Denton, C. A., & Kurz, T. (2008). Technology-based mentoring provided to teachers: A synthesis of the literature. *Journal of Technology and Teacher Education, 16*(3), 339–373.

Gersten, R., Keating, T., Yovanoff, P., & Harniss, M. (2001). Working in special education: Factors that enhance special educators' intent to stay. *Exceptional Children, 67*, 549–567.

Harrington, A. (1999). *E-Mentoring: The advantages and disadvantages of using email to support distance mentoring.* Retrieved March 3, 2009, from European Social Fund Website: http://www.mentorsforum.co.uk/cOL1/discover.htm

Harris, J., O'Bryan, E., & Rotenberg, L. (1996). 'It's a simple idea, but it's not easy to do: Practical lessons on telementoring. *Learning and Leading with Technology, 24*(2), 53–57.

Harris, J., Rotenberg, L., & O'Bryan, E. (1997). *Results from electronic emissary project: Telementoring lessons and examples* (Denton, TX, Texas Center for Educational Technology). Retrieved March 9, 2009 from: http://www.tcet.unt.edu/pubs/em/em01.pdf

Heider, K. L. (2005). Teacher isolation: How mentoring programs can help. *Current Issues in Education, 14.* Retrieved April 22, 2009 from http://cied.ed.asu.edu/volume8/number14/June23/

Ingersoll, R. (2002). The teacher shortage: A case of wrong diagnosis and wrong prescription. *NASSP Bulletin, 86*, 16–31. doi:10.1177/019263650208663103

Ingersoll, R., & Kralik, J. M. (2004). *The impact of mentoring on teacher retention: What the research says*. Denver: Education Commission of the States. Retrieved February 2009 from, http://www.ecs.org/clearinghouse/50/36/5036.htm

Kasprisin, C. A., Single, P. B., Single, R. M., & Muller, C. B. (2003). Building a better bridge: Testing e-training to improve e-mentoring programmes in higher education. *Mentoring & Tutoring, 11*(1), 67–78. doi:10.1080/1361126032000054817

Kilgore, K. L., & Griffin, C. C. (1998). Beginning special educators: Problems of practice and the influence of school context. *Teacher Education and Special Education, 21*, 155–173. doi:10.1177/088840649802100302

Kram, K. E. (1983). Phases of the mentor relationship. *Academy of Management Journal, 26*(4), 608–625. doi:10.2307/255910

Marshall, C., & Rossman, G. (1999). *Designing Qualitative Research*. Thousand Oaks, CA: Sage Publications.

Martin, K., & McGrevin, C. (1990). Making mathematics happen. *Educational Leadership, 47*(8), 20–22.

Meister, D. G., & Melnick, S. A. (2003). National new teacher study: Beginning teachers' concerns. *Action in Teacher Education, 24*(4), 87–94.

Mihkelson, A. (1997). *A model of research mentoring for higher education – An overview.* (ERIC Document Reproduction Service No. ED418661).

Moran, S. W. (1990). Schools and the beginning teacher. *Phi Delta Kappan, 72*(3), 210–213.

Muller, C. B. (1997, November). The potential of industrial 'e-mentoring' as a retention strategy for women in science and engineering. Paper presented at the *Annual Frontiers in Education (FIE) Conference,* Pittsburgh, PA. Retrieved March 9, 2009 from http://fairway.ecn.purdue.edu/~fie/fie97/papers/1268.pdf

Muller, C. B. (1999). *The potential of industrial "e-mentoring" as a retention strategy for women in science and engineering*. Paper presented at the proceedings of the Annual Frontiers in Education Conference, New Orleans, LA.

Myerson, D., Weick, K. E., & Kramer, R. M. (1996). Swift trust and temporary groups. In Kramer, R. M., & Tyler, T. R. (Eds.), *Trust in organizations: Frontiers of theory and research* (pp. 166–195). Thousand Oaks, CA: Sage.

National Mentoring Center. (2002). *Perspectives on e-mentoring: A virtual panel holds an online dialogue*. Retrieved April 24, 2009 from www.nwrel.org/mentoring/pdf/bull9.pdf

Noe, R. A. (1988). An investigation of the determinants of successful assigned mentoring relationships. *Personnel Psychology, 41*, 457–479. doi:10.1111/j.1744-6570.1988.tb00638.x

O'Neill, D. K., Wagner, R., & Gomez, L. M. (1996). Online mentors: Experimenting in science class. *Educational Leadership, 54*(3), 39–42.

Peyton, A. L., Morton, M., Perkins, M. M., & Dougherty, L. M. (2001). Mentoring in gerontology education: New graduate student perspectives. *Educational Gerontology, 27*(5), 347–359. doi:10.1080/03601270152053384

Ray, E. B., Waldhart, E. S., & Seibert, J. H. (1985). *Communication networks and job stress among teachers*. Paper presented at the annual meeting of the Southern Speech Communication Association, Winston-Salem, N.C.

Rosenholtz, S. J. (1985). Political myths about education reform: Lessons from research on teaching. *Phi Delta Kappan, 66*(5), 349–355.

Schlichte, J., Yssel, N., & Merbler, J. (2005). Pathway to burnout: Case studies in teacher isolation and alienation. *Preventing School Failure, 50*(1), 43–40. doi:10.3200/PSFL.50.1.35-40

Seabrooks, J. J., Kenney, S., & LaMontagne, M. (2000). Collaboration and virtual mentoring: Building relationships between pre-service and in-service special education teachers. *Journal of Information Technology for Teacher Education, 9*(2), 219–236.

Single, P. B., Jaffe, A., & Schwartz, R. (1999). Evaluating programs for recruiting and retaining community faculty. *Family Medicine, 31*(2), 114–121.

Single, P. B., & Muller, C. B. (1999, April). *Electronic Mentoring: Issues to Advance Research and Practice*. Paper presented at the International Mentoring Association Conference, Atlanta, GA.

Single, P. B., & Muller, C. B. (2001). When email and mentoring unite: The implementation of a nationwide electronic mentoring program. In Stromei, L. K. (Ed.), *Creating Mentoring and Coaching Programs* (pp. 107–122). Alexandria, VA: American Society for Training and Development.

Single, P. B., & Single, R. M. (2005). E-mentoring for social equity: review of research to inform program development. *Mentoring & Tutoring, 13*(2), 301–320. doi:10.1080/13611260500107481

Smith, S. C., & Scott, J. J. (1990). *The collaborative school: A work environment for effective instruction* (Report No. ISBN-0-86552-092-5). Reston, VA: National Association of Secondary School Principals. (ERIC Document Reproduction Service No. ED316918).

Sproull, L., & Kiesler, S. (1992). *Connections: New ways of working in the networked organization*. Cambridge, MA: MIT Press.

Spuhler, L., & Zetler, A. (1994). Montana teacher support program: Research report for year two 1993-94. East Lansing, MI: National Center for Research on Teacher Learning. (ERIC Document Reproduction Service No. ED390802).

Sylwester, E. (2005, February 9). Professors honored for work with women. *Oregon Daily Emerald,* (2005). Retrieved March 1, 2009 from http://media.www.dailyemerald.com/media/storage/paper859/news/2005/02/09/News/Professor.Honored.For.Work.With.Women-1968038.shtml

Veenman, S. (1984). Perceived problems of beginning teachers. *Review of Educational Research, 54*(2), 143–178.

Watson, S. W. (2006). Virtual mentoring in higher education: Teacher education and cyber-connections. *International Journal of Teaching and Learning in Higher Education, 18*(3), 168–179.

Zelditch, M. (1990). Mentor roles. In *Proceedings of the 32nd Annual Meeting of the Western Association of Graduate Schools* (p. 11). Tempe, AZ.

KEY TERMS AND DEFINITIONS

Mentoring: A procedure in which an experienced individual provides support, advice and encouragement to an inexperienced individual in a particular format for a prescribed amount of time.

Mentor: The experienced individual in a mentoring relationship.

Mentee: The inexperienced individual in a mentoring relationship.

Virtual Mentoring, Electronic Mentoring, Online Mentoring, Computer-Mediated Conversation, e-Mentoring, Cyber-Mentoring, Telementoring: mentoring that occurs via an electronic format and is not dependent on geographic location.

Face-to-Face Mentoring: mentoring that occurs in a setting where both mentor and mentee are in close physical proximity (i.e. sitting across from each other).

Teacher Education: Program of study for students seeking licensure to teach in the K-12 setting.

Chapter 10
Virtual Mentoring:
A Response to the Challenge of Change

Thomas T. Peters
South Carolina's Coalition for Mathematics & Science, USA

Terrie R. Dew
Anderson Oconee Pickens Greenville Regional S²MART Center, USA

ABSTRACT

In this chapter mentoring is defined as a sustained relationship between reflective practitioners. The purpose of this relationship is to build capacity to manage the complex classroom environment in ways that bring about instructional improvements. Where there is a difference in experience between these practitioners, what matters for the mentor's effectiveness is expertise with applying reflective practices. Reflective practices within a virtual (distance) mentoring setting are identified and explored. Developing trust from a distance and understanding representational preferences are essential virtual mentoring practices. These practices were developed as ways to provide ongoing support to field-based instructional coaches charged with improving mathematics and science instruction in South Carolina middle schools. They are applicable in any P-12 classroom mentoring setting.

INTRODUCTION

We are a pragmatic bunch. We have to be. Our charge is to improve instruction in each and every public school in South Carolina that will have us. Increasingly, those that will have us are in dire straits. Our middle school work, funded by Mathematics & Science Partnership grants, takes us to schools with an average poverty rating, based on Free/Reduced Lunch qualifications, of over 50%. Nearly every school with which we work has not met its Annual Yearly Progress goals and thus faces negative consequences if student achievement does not quickly show gains. The lessons we have learned about virtual mentoring are learned by doing, not via a comprehensive literature review and controlled research design.

In setting out to share what we know, we take aim directly at where our credibility lies; experiences, "best practices" and pragmatic viewpoints. We also seek to inform the audience of professionals working daily in the P-12 environment.

DOI: 10.4018/978-1-61520-861-6.ch010

This is the audience we know best. Within this book there are other chapters that balance out our pragmatism with learning theories, rigorous experimental design and deep knowledge about what has been researched. That's not us. We are well informed, but by choice we are action researchers with a heavy emphasis on action. Our actions are about facilitating positive change.

Change? It's a pervasive theme in the lives of educators. "We have to change ____." "Isn't it time we changed ____?" "Why are we still doing ____? We will bet you can easily fill in the blanks with exasperated pleas for change that you have heard in your own school. So, with all the cries for change in the classroom, how do we work together to make good choices about what to do? How do we avoid being overwhelmed by an education environment that demands never-ending flexibility? How do we overcome the urge to change right back once a change has been made? Why is a chapter on virtual mentoring starting with change anyway?

According to Kegan and Lahey, the "challenge of change…is often misunderstood as the need to better 'deal with' or 'cope with' the greater complexity of the world" (2009, P. 11). Yes, the educational world is constantly growing more complex. It is not sufficient, however, just to *deal with* change. We must develop mental capabilities to view the world clearly through an increasingly more complex lens.

Mentoring is one response to the challenge of change. It is purposeful action to promote the growth in the cognitive complexity of educators seeking to manage constantly changing school environments.

Our journey in mentoring instructional coaches in South Carolina schools began in 2003 with a face-to-face training and support model developed by the South Carolina Department of Education's Mathematics and Science Unit (now known as S²MART Centers SC). Scaling up this face-to-face coaching effort proved to be a daunting task. Geography and numbers overwhelmed our best efforts to stay in constant face-to-face contact with our coaches as the initiative spread across our state. With the support of a Math Science Partnership grant from our state we began to explore virtual strategies in place of some of the face-to-face support built into our original coach-training model.

Mentoring, whether face-to-face or virtual, begins and ends with reflective practice.

METHOD

Part 1: Beginning with the End in Mind

The reflective practitioner. To manage a changing environment in ways that bring about improved instruction and increased student achievement requires an increasingly complex pattern of thinking and acting. Reflection grooms educators to extend learning beyond specific events and make generalizations to guide future decisions. Costa and Garmston (2002), identify five energy sources, called *States of Mind*, in their Cognitive Coaching[SM] model. These *States of Mind* are mental abilities that guide reflective, intentional decision-making. Like most any mental ability, these too can be enhanced with guided practice. While we employ both the practice strategies and terminology of Cognitive Coaching[SM,] our context is rather specific. The reflective practitioners of interest to us are teachers, instructional coaches, and our own selves too. Thus, our operational definitions of these mental abilities for reflection, as seen in Table 1, are more focused on instruction in schools.

To manage a changing environment in ways that bring about improved instruction and accelerated student achievement also requires dedication to making meaning from the myriad of events, actions and activities that make up a typical school day. Nieto (2003), reminds us that, "Given the dynamics of their work," teachers "need to continually rediscover who they are and what they

Table 1. Cognitive Coaching^{SM} States of Mind as we operationally define them

Craftsmanship	As would a craftsman, the school practitioner must artfully mix instructional strategies with knowledge about components of an effective school-based infrastructure. It is this blend of research and craft-knowledge that guides the practitioner in intentionally selecting strategies for instructional improvement.
Efficacy	An efficacious school practitioner has high expectations for himself and is able to navigate around barriers and possible failure. Armed with knowledge from previous learning, he knows that new experiences are challenges, not impossibilities.
Flexibility	The flexible school practitioner knows the value of creating a plan that guides efforts at instructional improvement. The flexible practitioner also knows how to read the classroom landscape to make adjustments when the best-laid plans meet unanticipated realities.
Interdependence	The interdependent school practitioner recognizes that improving instruction is a team sport. Knowing how to recognize the expertise of others and the limits of his own expertise defines the interdependent practitioner.
Consciousness	The conscious school practitioner recognizes the value of interpersonal relationship on instructional improvement. She recognizes that her actions impact herself and others and takes a systems approach to thinking about intstructional improvement.

stand for through dialogue and collaboration with peers, through ongoing and consistent study, and through deep reflection about their craft" (pp. 395-396). This ongoing need to rediscover is true for our instructional coaches and for those of us who support them as well. In essence, we are always novice in some aspects of reflective practice. So, how then might we as mentors be mindful of others and ourselves in growing the abilities of reflective practitioners?

Coaching as a pathway to growth in reflective practice. There are many people called "coach" in schools. Some are the traditional athletic team leaders. Some are persons granted the title as an outcome of being terrific classroom teachers. Generally, these latter folks are offered little in the way of mentoring or training in the work of coaches or in ways of developing the reflective capacities in others.

By coaching, we mean engaging other practitioners in purposeful ways that promote reflective practice. Coaching involves listening, observing, questioning, and offering support to help practitioners grow, reflect, and make intentional instructional decisions.

Well-prepared coaches, as Killion (2008), puts it, "coach heavy." They are able to "ask thought-provoking questions, uncover assumptions, and engage teachers in dialogue about their beliefs and goals..." (p. 3). These coaches are able to "facilitate teachers' exploration of who they are as teachers as much or more than what they do as teachers" (p. 3).

Well-prepared coaches do not simply arrive. They journey. There is no fast lane to developing the content and competencies needed to be an effective coach. Our coach preparation model draws upon the body of research on effective coaching, including Costa and Garmston (2002). It is informed by the work of others with expertise in carrying learners to new ways of thinking and resolving complex dilemmas in classroom instruction. Our goals are to prepare our coaches to promote continuous improvement in instruction and to increase student learning in their schools.

This chapter, however, is not about our coaching model. It is about lessons we've learned about mentoring, from a distance, those seeking to be more reflective in their own practice. So then, what are some ways that coaching and mentoring are alike and different?

Coaching vs. mentoring. Mentoring, according to Dennis (1993), is derived from the Greek word meaning enduring and is defined as a sustained relationship between a youth and an adult. Indeed, it is easy to find multiple examples of adult to youth mentoring programs in education and other settings. It is also easy to find multiple examples of mentoring as a relationship between new teachers and their more experienced counterparts. "In a traditional sense", writes Petersen (2007), "the mentor has a given or assumed role as a guide or advisor to someone seeking help. In the academic education environment, this is invariably a new, less experienced teacher wanting or needing assistance with aspects of their teaching practice" ("This article begins" para. 1). In a traditional sense, to be a mentor is to consult: to share one's expert knowledge with another who is a novice.

Coaching, Everd and Selman (1989), tell us, is about conveyance: carrying colleagues from where they are to where they want to be. An effective instructional coach need not be more experienced or expert as a classroom teacher. The experience that matters in conveyance is in knowing how to activate the reflective capacity of others such that they can bring their own knowledge to bear in solving problems.

We define mentoring as a sustained relationship between reflective practitioners, the purpose of which is to build capacity to manage the complex classroom environment in ways that bring about desired outcomes. Where there is a difference in experience between these practitioners, what matters for the mentor's effectiveness is expertise with reflective practices.

To be fair, many mentors coach and many coaches mentor.

While we typically describe our work as coaching instructional coaches, we will use mentoring as a verb and coach as noun from this point on.

Part 2: It's All About TRUST

Characteristics of trust. Consider for a moment, people you trust. Who are they? Where are they? How often do you see them? What are some things they have done to earn your trust? What are some reasons that you trust them even if they are far away from you?

In a face-to-face relationship, trust is established over time through multiple social interactions, based on viewing the actions of others as well as listening to their thoughts expressed through language. It is trust too that sustains relationships between mentors and mentees.

Tschannen-Moran (2004) identifies five facets of relational trust: benevolence, honesty, openness, reliability, and competence. In face-to-face relationships, we assess whether others are trustworthy based on our observations of their behaviors around each of these five facets. Observations are made regarding the ways in which we interact professionally and socially, our communication styles, our non-verbal cues, even the types of food and drink we prefer. Face-to-face relationships are built around these observations.

Technology enables us to connect with people, many of whom we've never met in a traditional sense. In reading these words, you are choosing to connect with us…or at least with our ideas. We are probably strangers to you. Blogging, electronic social networks and other more instantaneous ways of sharing ideas offer you the same choice. You may connect with strangers and their ideas or not. You can choose to develop a more sustained relationship or not. One challenge of virtual mentoring is in creating technology-supported relationships that have the same characteristics and levels of trust found in face-to-face relationships.

In a virtual relationship, trustworthiness is also based on observations of behaviors. Instead of a combination of both visually observable and non-visual behaviors, we must make our assessment of the trustworthiness of others using a series of possibly sporadic interactions via email, phone conversations, or other online technologies. The formation of trust in a virtual relationship happens somewhat differently than in a face-to-face relationship, but the need to trust at both the cognitive and affective levels remains the same (Greenberg, et al, 2007). When virtual colleagues feel they can count on one another to do what they say they will do, trust builds quickly, at least at the cognitive level. Mentoring to promote reflective practices demands more than cognitive trust. It demands a deliberate focus on connection making. When seeking to make connections virtually, it essential that we are clear about our purposes. If we are choosing mentoring behaviors specifically to build a personal connection, that purpose should be shared to avoid the perception that we are "wasting time" or "goofing off".

A confession. In our mentoring work we are not exclusively virtual in our support of those whose reflective capacity we seek to build. Though our ongoing relationship with those we mentor is largely virtual, we begin with extensive and sometimes intensive face-to-face interactions. As such we've seen each other, swapped personal and professional stories, observed each other in action and inaction and have socialized in ways that allow us to assess trustworthiness in traditional ways and promote a personal, affective connection.

We know that emotional and social bonding are essential to sustaining a trusting relationship, and we are convinced that this bonding can occur without any initial face-to-face interaction.

Personal connection in virtual settings: Terrie's perspective. Every day, millions of people from around the world come together in virtual worlds to interact and socialize. Over the past decade, Massive Multi-player Online Role-Playing Games (MMORPG) have become popular and people around the world have been forming virtual relationships around play through these games (Achterbosch, Pierce, and Simmons, 2008). Although our professional work with virtual mentoring includes face-to-face contact, my experiences in the gaming world consist of many social relationships formed over time with no face-to-face interaction. Similar to what I've seen in developing relationships through a combination of face-to-face and virtual contact, relationships with only virtual contact hold many of the same characteristics. Players in MMORPGs depend on one another to be online at appointed times, to perform their appointed duties well, and to show compassion and caring for one another. As in other relationships, the loss of trust is just as devastating in a virtual environment. What makes these online relationships different from just "playing together" is the ongoing nature of the relationship; the personal connection players have with each other and their team. As an active participant in a virtual social world, I find that my gaming team is like family—we worry for one another as we experience the trials and tribulations of life, we share our hopes and fears with one another, we shed tears when our team members experience hardships. I've sent birthday presents to people I may never meet face-to-face and trusted them with some of my most private thoughts. It is this personal connection that makes the virtual world of MMORPG's like being on a team that plays its games face-to-face. It is the realization that behind each computer generated character in the game is a human being with whom I have a relationship.

Likewise, personal compassion and caring are vital to my virtual mentoring relationships. Since we do not have the opportunity to meet over coffee or lunch, I must pay special attention to forming social bonds with coaches as we interact virtually. Virtual conversations are not always about working on the work—often coaches need emotional or social support, in addition to cognitive support. Effective virtual mentoring includes making personal connections around family or friends as well as offering professional support. Effective virtual mentoring centers on relational trust.

Positive presupposition. In addition to personal connections, the trusting mentoring relationship is built around positive presuppositions. Positive presuppositions indicate our trust in the coach's craftsmanship and efficacy. Our actions are guided by a belief that the coach is able to make quality, intentional decisions about their work. In mentoring we must choose our language carefully to promote reflective practice. We choose paraphrases and questions that hold positive assumptions rather than negative ones. For example, the statement "Even Krista could teach this lesson." holds two negative assumptions. The first is that Krista is not a very good teacher. The second is lesson is rather simplistic. Instead, we use language to convey positive presuppositions such as, "How might you support Krista as she practices the student journaling strategies she's been learning?" This question carries the assumption that the instructional coach has the knowledge and capability to enhance Krista's ability to teach the lesson.

Because our mentoring is virtual, and we are not making observations of the complex classroom environment, we must trust the accuracy of perceptions and events reported by the coach through online interactions. Having positive presuppositions about the instructional coach's perceptions of this environment keeps our mentoring focused on the issues and concerns generated by the coach. It is their issues, not ours, that they are most ready to reflect and act upon.

Having positive presuppositions does not replace asking hard questions of the coaches we mentor. Our job is to promote growth in the coach's capacity to manage an increasingly complex school environment. Avoiding difficult topics or areas of concern does not promote growth. Maintaining positive presuppositions and mentoring "heavy" are not mutually exclusive. Managing the balance is not so easy.

Table 2 contains a few examples of questions we've asked our coaches during virtual mentoring sessions. They are out of context, but they still serve as good cases to consider for their potential as trust builders or trust breakers in a virtual mentoring setting.

Reflect back on the questions in Table 2 for a few moments. As you consider the challenges of staying positive in your presuppositions about someone you are mentoring while still addressing opportunities for growth, what are some of your thoughts?

Table 2. Example coaching questions

As you walk the line between administrator and teacher, what are some things you want to stay mindful of so that you don't stray to far to either side of the line?
So, as you reflect back on the joys of being a teacher again...even briefly this week...what are some insights this experience gives you about how you'd want to be coached?
If you were a teacher who was resistant to coaching, what are some things you might be saying about the math coach at your school? How would knowing what these teachers say inform choices you make in your work as a coach?
Twice you mentioned teachers saying they wish they had begun some instruction earlier in the year. Since wishful thinking is not a particularly effective planning strategy, what are some resources these teachers might draw on to help them pace their lessons?
As you think about low expectations that teachers have for students, what might be some causes? What might be some cures?
So with all the usual beginning of school shifting and sorting, what are some things you'll want to stay aware of about yourself so that taking care of yourself does not get lost in the shuffle?
What might you be telling yourself about what needs to happen for you to feel a sense of security and satisfaction as a coach?

Part 3: Representational Systems as Cues for Making Meaning and Establishing Trust

"Representational systems", states Ellerton (2009), "are the primary ways we represent, code, store and give meaning or language...to our experiences" (para. 1). These systems are related to our senses, especially to visual, auditory and kinesthetic activity. Each of us has a preferred system for sorting out the world around us, though our preferences may be context specific. To mentor effectively, we must understand how the coaches we are mentoring are experiencing the complexities of their world. This is especially challenging if we are processing experiences differently than our coaches.

Probing for Cues. Cues, very simply are the subtle or not-so-subtle actions, gestures, intonations and word choices people use to clarify their meaning when communicating with others. In the virtual environment we can easily miss many cues we rely upon to make meaning in a face-to-face

Virtual Mentoring

Figure 1. A prompt for visual cues

environment. This increases the possibility that the intent of the communication is missed as well. In virtual mentoring, we must seek cues where they are instead of making assumptions about meaning.

To mentor, we are trained to pay attention to non-verbal cues to know when a change in thinking has happened or when we've gone too far, or not far enough in activating reflective thinking. Such cues include facial expressions, posture, gestures, voice tone, pitch, and breathing. Studies on the impact of non-verbal communication on human meaning-making vary. Argyle, et al (1970) found that non-verbal cues had about 4.3 times the effect of verbal cues on communication. Mehrabian (1972) concluded that meaning constructed from communication was 93% non-verbal and 7% verbal. He further classified non-verbal communication as body language (55%) and paralanguage (38%). Body language refers to expressions, posture, and gestures. Paralanguage includes non-verbal cues such as voice tone, pitch, and speed.

Visual cues: Tom's perspective. What are some things the image in Figure 1 tells you? Seriously, take a few moments to just think before you continue reading!

According to John Medina (2008), "Vision trumps all other senses" (p. 221). If you are like me, you can see enough in Figure 1 to imagine quite a lot. Since I am able to see the picture in color, I can tell there are quite a few people wearing jeans and white t-shirts. I'm imagining a sporting event because of the angle at which the rows of people are stacked. I see lots of arms and legs so it must be warm. Maybe it's a football game or a NASCAR race in a warm sunny place. If you are like Terrie, the picture probably does not tell you much at all...but you can imagine a few dozen conversations that are taking place among the folks in the crowd. She sees the picture as "noisy" and can imagine the sounds of cheerleaders, announcers, and car engines. If you are like some of our other colleagues, the picture might inspire you to drop this book and go toss a football or drive in circles. What this picture reminds us all to consider is that we are inherently meaning making creatures and we seek cues about our surroundings and people in them as a pathway to trust.

In a virtual setting we are disconnected from the visual cues our brain relies upon to make meaning in face-to-face interactions. That said, my learning strength is visual. I am a better at

Table 3. Visual cues in journal responses

Concern	An expression of emotional state. This could be positive or negative.
Conflict	A disconnect between the existing and desired state of some aspect(s) of instruction
Consistency	A logical connection between what the coach states as values and their reported actions
Congruence	A logical connection between what we intend for instructional coaches to do in our model and their and reported actions

mentoring when I can "see" what coaches are experiencing. None-the-less, there are still cues from which even the visually oriented can draw an impression.

One very low-tech strategy that allows me some sight into the coach's world is the electronic journal. Entries are submitted, via e-mail, weekly throughout the school year. Most of my virtual mentoring is based on asynchronous conversations related to coaches' journals.

Take a look below at an excerpt from an electronic journal submitted by one of our instructional coaches. What do you see happening in this school?

In the afternoon, I observed a third grade teacher. It was a little freaky. The last time I observed her was well over a month ago. At that time she was completing her unit on animals. The students were completing the unit by doing research and putting it together in an animal report. I had helped her when the students were doing research. Believe it or not, today they were finishing it. They had put it away for all of that time. Now the teacher had them pull out all of their information to complete the projects, amazing!

I am trying to get the fourth grade teachers motivated to start their science fair projects. Weeks ago I gave them project ideas that match their standards. Later, I discussed the options they have for completing the projects. First they were still in the middle of a social studies unit. Now it is close to Christmas. They keep making excuses. What can I do to get them started? I even offered to help them get the materials. I really don't know what else I can do. (Anonymous instructional coach, personal communication, December 5, 2007)

Please take a few moments to just think before you continue reading! The words in a coach's journal can act as a window into the coach's world, if you know what to look for. I look for four specific kinds of cues as defined in Table 3.

Take another look at the journal excerpt. The questions in Table 4 are meant to provoke reflection about visual cues in journals. They are not meant to test your knowledge of mentoring. Some of us like to ponder quietly and alone. Others need a pondering partner. If that's you, you may want to think aloud with a colleague.

Just as window-shopping gives us only a glimpse at what wares a store has to offer, journals show only that which a coach wants us to see. The journal, like the store display window, is an invitation to inquiry. What are some other things you might want to know before having a mentoring conversation with our instructional coach? If you knew those things, what might you do next to help grow our instructional coach's capacity to manage instructional improvement in her school?

Auditory cues: Terrie's perspective. I often close my eyes to listen to my coaches. In virtual mentoring, we must be highly attuned to listening for auditory cues in addition to the actual words that are spoken. I want to attend fully to the coach during the conversation to notice subtle changes in language patterns such as pauses or changes in breathing patterns that indicate changes in thinking are happening. Sighs and pauses are both forms of paralanguage, non-verbal elements of communication used to modify the meaning of what we say and convey emotion. Paralanguage offers

Table 4. Questions to consider when looking for visual cues in the sample coach's journal

What are some conflicts you are seeing between what our instructional coach would like teachers to be doing to improve instruction and what they are willing to do?
What might our instructional coach be feeling? What is your evidence?
What are some ways our instructional coach's actions are congruent with our intention that she help teachers to grow their own capacity to manage good science instruction?
What are some things this journal entry tells you about our instructional coach's consistency in enacting our intentions?

auditory processors like me with a rich source of cues that our coaches are thinking.

Paralanguage also includes the pitch and pace of the spoken language. For example, if I begin a conversation with a coach with "How are things going this week?" and the response is a fast-paced run-on response of multiple events and happenings, then I have a paralanguage cue that a focus area is helping my coach slow down and process. A fast paced conversation may be an indicator of being overwhelmed with the job of coaching or it may be an indicator that the timing is not right for this particular conversation. Again, openness is key with virtual mentoring. I ask if the conversation needs to be rescheduled. If not, then I listen, paraphrase and probe to help the coach find a calmer place to reflect, rather than react.

To encourage thinking and reflection, wait time is needed. Wait time may seem awkward at first when visual cues are missing. Several times, I've had coaches ask "are you still there?" when I was waiting for them to process. A conversation that seems painfully slow may be an indicator of multiple things. Perhaps the responses I am giving when mentoring are not promoting thinking or perhaps the coach I am mentoring is just tired. Again, I ask questions to clarify what is going on when I don't have body language cues to read. As in face-to-face coaching, I have to be flexible in my response once an understanding is reached.

I must also stay aware that processing data through auditory senses may not be a strength of those with whom I am conversing. When mentoring virtually, I must make clear the purposes of my communication whether it be making a personal connection to build a relationship or to mediate their thinking especially since those who process visually do not have the non-verbal cues—such as facial expression and gestures—they rely upon to make clear the meaning of the language I'm using.

DON'T LOOK YET at the excerpt from a journal submitted by one of our instructional coaches. Instead, ask a friend to read it to you. Hearing it over the phone is even better than having it read to you in person. This will really help you focus on just auditory cues.

Oh goodness. I really need to figure this one out. One point of contention is that by being consistent we are not going to be able to be creative and innovative as teachers, my thought is that it shows the students that their teachers are a team. Also it frees me up to take care of other things. Another teacher sees anything like this as BS, of course he doesn't abbreviate. Others want to get along with the group and so for the most part they stay silent. So instead of a discussion, a list was thrown together. I see what causes these tensions as people who have always operated as individuals and have given lip service to teamwork. What happens is that either they are in charge so people do as they say or pretend to, or they pretend to go along and do their own thing. I know that some feel threatened and I think some of that may be because they feel insecure in their ability when they compare themselves to other teachers. I've worked with these teachers trying to help them understand that everyone has some gift or skill to share, but even after 2.5 years. Some of it I believe stems to before I walked in the building when they were told I was coming to fix them. (Anonymous instructional coach, personal communication, December 12, 2008)

What are you cluing in on as you listen? What do you hear is happening in this school?

When mentoring in a virtual setting where auditory cues are all you have to go by, there's a very simple action you can take to make meaning for your self and those you mentor: paraphrasing. Paraphrasing is simply rewording the thoughts of others to identify their main point. In its simplest form, a good paraphrase tells a coach that we have been listening and seek to be sure we understand. In its more complex forms, a good paraphrase may help the coach organize their own thinking or move beyond their own assumptions to get their thinking unstuck. If your friend is willing to read it again, listen to the journal excerpt another time. How might you restate this coach's concerns in a few simple sentences?

Knowing your own representational preferences: Tom's perspective. When mentoring, in any realm, it is important to that we are conscious of our own representational preferences. Mentoring out of my preference zone is a craftsmanship challenge for me. For our coaches, being mentored out of their preference zone may raise the bar for developing comfort with the mentoring process. Regardless of one's preferences for making sense of the world, benevolence, honesty, openness, reliability, and competence still matter in building trust.

Where craftsmanship is low, like putting a strongly visual me out to mentor in an auditory setting, I recommend honesty and compensation techniques. For me, the compensation techniques came first. I learned that I could attend better in an auditory setting by drawing pictures of what I was hearing. Admitting to those I mentor that I struggle to listen attentively came a bit later. Their responses have largely been benevolent.

Knowing your own representational preferences: Terrie's perspective. Likewise, it is important for me as an auditory processor to recognize that others may process information differently than I do. I have to be careful to allow time for others to think when I may be tempted to dominate the conversation. I've learned over time to "talk" to myself in my head instead of out loud. This allows the wait time needed by others to process their thoughts. As a novice mentor and expert auditory learner, my paraphrases were often longer than the original statement from the coaches I mentored. Now, I process my paraphrase silently to pare it down. This allows the conversational spotlight to remain on the coach's thinking rather than my own. Unfortunately, I have less control over my responses when I am tired or overwhelmed. I have a tendency to talk for minutes without pausing to even breathe. Like Tom, I've found that openness and honesty are the best policy. Instead of pretending to be perfect at mentoring, I share my struggles with the coaches and give them permission to say, "You're talking too much!"

A quick note on action cues. Though most us make meaning primarily by visual or auditory cues, there are those whose first line of meaning making is action. To establish trust for another, they prefer to do things together. In face-to-face settings it is easy to accommodate this representational preference by teaching a lesson together. In the gaming world, acting together to complete a mission or set out on a quest is only a few mouse clicks away. In virtual mentoring, at least as we've experienced it, we just don't know any good, low-tech ways to do things together yet. We are trying to learn to plan professional development sessions on-line with our colleagues. Neither our craftsmanship nor our efficacy is high enough at this point to share anything that might be a "best practice."

RESULTS

Things to Expect When a Mentoring Relationship is Virtual and Face-to-Face

As we get in the habit of regularly having "heavy" mentoring conversations in a virtual setting,

Table 5. Key actions for sustaining a virtual mentoring relationship

Be True to Those You Mentor	Schedule meetings well in advance and keep them. Be on time for meetings and alert those you mentor ahead of time if you'll be absent. Reschedule! Set an expectation that a virtual meeting is just as important as one that is face-to-face. Have an agenda that is understood and agreed upon prior to the meeting and be flexible if something of greater concern to the person you mentor should come up.
Stay Focused Especially on Mentoring	It is easy when mentoring virtually to multi-task. One thing we've learned is that you can't listen and pay attention at the level needed for effective mentoring if there are distractions at the ready…like e-mail or text messages. Some of us close our eyes or stare at the ceiling to limit our distractions when we are in a virtual conversation.
End with a Reflection Leave with a Plan	Cognitive growth requires the pondering of difficult questions and enacting new strategies. When mentoring, it is up to us to model the heavy cognitive lifting needed to build capacity for managing complex teaching environments. To encourage reflection, be reflective in your own practice. To encourage action, work intentionally. Set goals for yourself in growing your mentoring skills. Encourage those you mentor to be intentional about their own growth as reflective practitioners.
Out of Sight is Not Out of Mind	Responding to communications (voicemail messages, emails) promptly to ensure that persons you mentor know their messages are received and the content is being attended to. Be sure you've agreed as to what "prompt" means. Not all of us check our e-mail 30 times a day.
Do What You Say You Will	Honestly now, if you need an explanation for this one you are probably not ready to be mentoring.

we've noticed that face-to-face interactions with our coaches sometimes become a bit awkward. Sometimes our instructional coaches request assistance from others on our support team instead us when they need face-to-face mentoring. Often, the face-to-face interactions we do have tend to take on a different purpose, like collaborating on an activity or consulting on some technical aspect of the coach's work once when we've had some success at "heavy" virtual mentoring.

We are really not sure what to make of this. It might be that virtual mentoring can sometimes take on "confessional" aspects that feel safe from a distance but lead to discomfort when face-to-face. It might also be that as our coaches develop their own capacity to reflect on and control of the changing environment in which they operate, they're more open to seeking out trusting relationships with additional colleagues. Either way, the lessons to be learned here are for us as we mentor. First, we ought not become possessive of those we mentor. We do not have to be their "favorite" source of support in all settings. Second, we need to be mindful that we can mess up the trust we have in developed in virtual settings if we are not careful in what we expect in the mentoring relationship when we are face-to-face. When mentoring in two worlds, virtual and face-to-face, it seems reasonable that we should have to build trust in both.

Making the Best of Virtual Mentoring

As we have previously stated, trust in virtual relationships depends largely upon feeling connected. As a virtual mentoring relationship develops, we can do quite a bit to build and maintain trust. Mostly, these simple actions are all about treating virtual interactions like they are face-to-face. Since we all like lists of simple things to do that can improve our effectiveness, are a few from us in Table 5.

The Results that Really Matter

When we set out to explore virtual mentoring strategies our goal was to increase capacity for growing our initiative without sacrificing the quality of mentoring support we offered our coaches. While there have been glitches as we struggle with mismatched communication systems, our external evaluators at Biological Sciences Curriculum Study (Larson, Shaw and Taylor, 2009), report that "virtual communication appears to effectively meet coaching goals, save time and money, and enhance communication skills of iCoaches and specialists without sacrificing trust and rapport" (p. 12).

DISCUSSION

Novice and expert practitioners alike grow to understand and accommodate new learning best when they have pause to reflect as individuals and with others on their own practice. There is no one right medium for reflection. Whatever yours is, be it in writing, in dialog or in silent thought, please consider these three steps toward clarification of your thinking about virtual mentoring as a response to the challenges of the changing school environment.

3. *Identify three ideas you want to remember about virtual mentoring. What are some reasons why you've selected each of these? What will you do to enact your ideas?*
2. *List two things you would like to know more about or two questions you still have. Share your questions with a colleague or two. In what ways has their response modified your thinking? What will you do to learn more?*
1. *Share one idea about virtual mentoring that you would like to discuss with a virtual colleague. You can do this by accessing our Virtual Mentoring forum at http://www.s2martsc.org/*

AUTHOR NOTE

Thomas T. Peters, South Carolina's Coalition for Mathematics & Science, Clemson University; Terrie R. Dew, Anderson Oconee Pickens Greenville S²MART Regional Center, South Carolina Department of Education.

The ongoing study of instructional coaching is made possible by funding from the South Carolina Department of Education and its Office of Standards and Support. This funding includes Mathematics & Science Partnership grants SC070701 and SC070702 awarded to South Carolina's Coalition for Mathematics & Science. We wish to acknowledge our colleagues in the South Carolina Department of Education's S²MART Regional Centers. Special thanks to our internal review team: Dr. Nan Dempsey, Dr. Steve Ulosevich, and Elizabeth Weatherley.

Correspondence concerning this chapter should be addressed to Thomas T. Peters, South Carolina's Coalition for Mathematics & Science, Sears House at Clemson University, #3 Hwy 93, Clemson, SC, 29634. E-mail: tpeters@clemson.edu

REFERENCES

Achterbosch, L., Pierce, R., & Simmons, G. (2008). Massively multiplayer online role-playing games: The past, present, and future. *ACM Computers in Entertainment*, 5(4), 1–33.. doi:10.1145/1324198.1324207

Argyle, M., Salter, V., Nicholson, H., Williams, M., & Burgess, P. (1970). The communication of inferior and superior attitudes by verbal and non-verbal signals. *The British Journal of Social and Clinical Psychology*, 9, 222–231.

Costa, A. L., & Garmston, R. J. (2002). *Cognitive Coaching – A Foundation for Renaissance Schools*. Norwood, MA: Christopher-Gordon Publishers, Inc.

Dennis, G. (1993). *Mentoring*. Office of Education Research and Improvement Consumer Guide, (OR 93-3059 ED/OERI 92-38). Retrieved from http://www2.ed.gov/pubs/OR/ConsumerGuides/mentor.html

Ellerton, R. (2009). *Modalities and representational systems*. Retrieved from http://www.renewal.ca/nlp10.htm

Everard, R. D., & Selman, J. C. (1989). Coaching and the Art of Management. *Organizational Dynamics*, *18*, 16–32..doi:10.1016/0090-2616(89)90040-5

Greenberg, P. S., Greenberg, R., & Antonucci, Y. L. (2007). Creating and Sustaining Trust in Virtual Teams. *Business Horizons*, *50*(4), 325–333. doi:10.1016/j.bushor.2007.02.005

Kegan, R., & Lahey, L. (2009). *Immunity to Change: How to Overcome It and Unlock the Potential in Yourself and Your Organization*. Boston, MA: Harvard Business Press.

Killion, J. (2008). Are You Coaching Heavy or Light? *Teachers Teaching Teachers*, *3*(8), 1–4.

Larson, J., Shaw, J., & Taylor, J. (2009), *iCoaching Instructional Coaching Year 2 Summary Report* (Report No. ER-2009-08), Colorado Springs, CO: Biological Sciences Curriculum Study, Center for Research & Evaluation.

Medina, J. J. (2008). *Brain Rules: 12 Principles for Surviving and Thriving at Work, Home and School*. Seattle, WA: Pear Press.

Mehrabian, A. (1972). *Nonverbal communication*. Chicago, IL: Aldine-Atherton.

Nieto, S. (2003). Challenging current notions of "highly qualified teachers" through work in a teachers' inquiry group. *Journal of Teacher Education*, *54*(5), 386–398..doi:10.1177/0022487103257394

Petersen, L. K. (2007) *What Distinguishes a Mentor? Self-Reflection*. Retrieved from http://www.mentors.net/03library/whatdistmentor.html

Tschannen-Moran, M. (2004). *Trust Matters. Leadership for Successful Schools*. San Francisco, CA: Jossey-Bass.

Chapter 11
Telementoring and Virtual Professional Development:
A Theoretical Perspective from Science on the Roles of Self-Efficacy, Teacher Learning, and Professional Learning Communities

Matthew J. Maurer
Robert Morris University, USA

ABSTRACT

In science, examining how teachers can effectively learn content and inquiry-based pedagogy can often be nothing short of an intellectual, cognitive, and motivational maze. Professional development (PD) programs constructed specifically to aid teacher learning may fall short of their goals due to the high background variability of the participants, especially when mixing novice and master-level teachers. Only through conscious reorganization of instructional approaches can PD programs effectively address specific content and pedagogical needs while concurrently aiding the transition from novice to master-level teachers. It is time for a shift in how PD providers think about how teachers learn. Utilizing a theoretical perspective from Science Education, this chapter will demonstrate the benefits of moving to more of a contextual-based discourse that is accomplished through a virtual telementoring-based professional learning community (PLC) in order to enhance content, pedagogy, leadership skills, and positively impact teaching self-efficacy.

INTRODUCTION

As of 2008, approximately 150 institutions of higher education, with 550 partnering K-12 school districts, had received funding from the National Science Foundation (NSF) to implement Math Science Partnership (MSP) programs which focused on improving teacher content knowledge and pedagogical skills (NSF, 2008). A common strategy for professional development (PD) in these programs was to develop professional learning communities (PLCs) between teachers and higher education faculty members to collaborate to positively impact student learning. In order to attain

DOI: 10.4018/978-1-61520-861-6.ch011

this goal, effective instruction of the participating teachers cohorts was essential (Loucks-Horsley, Love, Stiles, Mundry, & Hewson, 2003).

Many educators have likely encountered PD partnerships that have been extremely successful in training teachers, as well as programs that have struggled. Based on years of personal experiential evidence in conducting PD programs, several common challenges for teachers attending one of these programs often include:

1. A lack of background or familiarity with the content or the technology being addressed.
2. A lack of understanding of inquiry and its place in the science classroom.
3. A perceived lack of support from administrators.
4. A perceived lack of acceptance from colleagues (feeling like they are doing this alone).
5. The perception of a significant time commitment to attend the training.
6. Not enough incentive(s) to attend the training.
7. Poor understanding of the context in which the knowledge or methods can be applied in the classroom.
8. The influence of poor teaching self-efficacy.

Normally involvement in a PD program brings numerous incentives for teachers and their partnering school districts. As a result, the composition of the cohort may exhibit a large percentage of novice-level teachers (not master level teachers) who may be more extrinsically motivated to attend rather than intrinsically motivated to better themselves and their teaching. They may see the program as a means to achieve tenure, points toward re-certification, or even a source of free classroom supplies. While these reasons for participation are not inappropriate, when they become the primary reasons for participation, the long-term success of the PD program may hang in the balance.

All of these issues may impact how effectively teachers will interact with the information being communicated. Lack of personal motivation, inability to visualize context or applicability, and low self-efficacy for teaching may have negative impacts on the learner. As one examines how teachers are learning in science PD programs specifically, it is often evident how many of these issues are not addressed, and may be exacerbated by the program itself.

PD science programs involving master-level teachers have their own challenges. Master-level teachers may not participate in a PD program due to being overtaxed as a resource in the school already, serving a mentor or department chair, or may not feel they need the additional training. Here we find the crux of the issue: should the PD program focus on rudimentary levels of science content and process instruction, or should the PD be more specifically geared toward pushing the participants from a novice/technical level of understanding to a mastery level? Are teachers in current PD programs learning components of content and inquiry, or should they be learning methods, context, and techniques to plan for a more thorough implementation of pedagogy in their classroom? If effective teacher learning is the critical issue, then differing approaches must be taken to achieve the desired master-level goals. Additionally, to what extent is technology-based mentoring in a PD partnership program effective in accomplishing this? Should PD in inquiry-based science be moving more towards a virtual community model where many of the objectives of the program are achieved electronically?

This chapter will focus on addressing these questions through a literature-based discussion of current PD strategies in Science Education where effectiveness in these areas has been documented. Specifically, we will discuss:

- Novice vs. Master: Where Should PD Focus?
- How Do Master-Level Teachers Learn?

- How Can We Address Sources of Self-Efficacy as a Means to Enhance Inquiry-Based PD?
- What Are Current Examples of Science-Based Telementoring PD Programs?
- What Are Recommendations for the Future of Telementoring and Technology in Science-Based PD Programs?

Operational Definitions

In order to provide common ground to discuss these questions, the following operational definitions will be utilized for this chapter:

1. *Professional Development (PD):* PD is a process of ongoing education whereby a teacher develops skills and knowledge to benefit their teaching. In science, this includes: use of inquiry; integration of content and pedagogy; integration of theory and practice; collaboration with colleagues; long-term planning; becoming a reflective practitioner; becoming a producer of knowledge about teaching; becoming a teacher leader; becoming a member of a professional community; and becoming a facilitator and source of change (National Research Council, 1996, p. 72).
2. *Mentoring:* "Mentoring…is a teacher-to-teacher professional development strategy that sustains long-term, ongoing professional learning embedded within a school culture" (Loucks-Horseley, et al., 2003, p. 219).
3. *Professional Learning Community (PLC):* PLCs are a professional development strategy that "…are structures for continuous learning and use of knowledge in the course of conducting the work of teaching…" (Mundry and Stiles, 2009, p. 9) PLCs demonstrate characteristics of: a learning-based focus; collaborative culture; collective inquiry; action orientation; continuous improvement; and a focus on results (Mundry and Stiles, 2009).
4. *Telementoring:* "Telementoring essentially serves the same purposes as traditional mentoring but [uses] technology to facilitate mentoring relationships…Typically the interaction…occurs through e-mail…instant messaging, audio and video conferencing, and online discussion boards" (Guy, 2002, p. 28).

Summary

The overall mission of this chapter is to provide useful insights for K-12 educators, higher education faculty, and PD providers. For those who are involved in the development, teaching, or participation in a PD program in science that utilizes mentoring and technology, this chapter will offer examples of how these facets may be combined to provide an effective PD experience. Finally, a theoretical model for using the approach of telementoring for developing PD programs and PLCs will be offered.

BACKGROUND

The construction and implementation of PD programs for science teachers have recently undergone significant changes, with the inclusion of standards-based, inquiry-focused programs becoming the priority for science educators at the national, state, and local levels. As such, a large number of PD programs have come about to not only provide teachers with critical science content knowledge, but also exposure to inquiry-based methods of teaching.

The Role of Professional Learning Communities in Science PD

As stated by Loucks-Horsley, et al. (2003), science is a discipline where active engagement and inquiry must be practiced. With the constructivist educational philosophy that undergirds inquiry, approaches for students (and teachers) to learn inquiry by doing inquiry effectively flows from a collaborative effort (Llewellyn, 2007). Teachers simply cannot teach inquiry from a collaborative perspective if they are not familiar with the experience of participating in a collaborative activity.

Professional learning communities (PLCs) provide this opportunity in a way that not only enhances teachers' understanding of inquiry and science content, but also builds skills for effective leadership and collaborative participation. As discussed by Mundry and Stiles (2009), the idea of PLCs is not a new one, bordering on twenty years since the idea was first introduced. As a research-based approached to teacher learning, two of the most important facets of PLCs are ensuring that teachers are learning, and that teachers are working collaboratively with others to contextualize that learning into their own classroom practice (Mundry & Stiles, 2009). In fact, they go on to characterize PLCs in the following ways (pp. 9-11):

- an overall focus on learning;
- the creation of a collaborative culture focused on learning;
- the utilization of collective inquiry;
- an action orientation and use of experimentation;
- a continuous improvement mindset;
- an outcomes-based orientation.

Taken together, these six characteristics identify a learning environment where learning, application, assessment, and ongoing modification are done collaboratively. When put in a context of learning more about inquiry, one can see how teachers would benefit from this type of ongoing collaboration where the focus is on the successful learning by the community. Pair this with professional development, and a unique entity is created to help teachers learn about inquiry in a socially reinforcing way that benefits all members of the PD community.

Landel and Nelson (2009) and Loucks-Horsely, et al. (2003) both discussed the importance of planning and structure with a PD partnership. In order to create an effective PLC, several steps must be followed. As stated by Landel and Nelson (2009):

1. First create the partnership between higher education and K-12.
2. Focus the PLC on science content and pedagogical content knowledge (such as inquiry).
3. Be supportive of the leadership roles of teachers and administrators.
4. Find the balance between participant support and accountability.
5. Work on expanding the PLC and increasing participation.

A PLC is only as effective as its weakest partner (whether that be an individual, a department, a school, or a college/university). One of the most critical factors for individuals attempting to create effective PLCs today is recruiting participants who are dedicated to the program for more than just financial and material incentives. Recruiting PLC members who have no intention of implementing content and pedagogy learned from the PLC into their own classrooms is simply an inefficient use of time and funds. Most importantly, students in the classrooms of those teachers actually lose out on potentially significant academic opportunities because their teacher or institution chose not to fulfill their PLC obligations.

As discussed by Loucks-Horsely, et al. (2003), several critical issues need to be considered when developing PD programs since the reasons a teacher may choose not to effectively participate in a PD program or PLC are variable. These reasons can include: lack of professional knowledge, time commitments, lack of leadership skills, lack of support, or location of the training. Ultimately, one of the most critical factors affecting many teachers is their self-efficacy to teach science effectively in their classroom (Enochs & Riggs, 1990). If they are lacking the fundamental intrinsic confidence

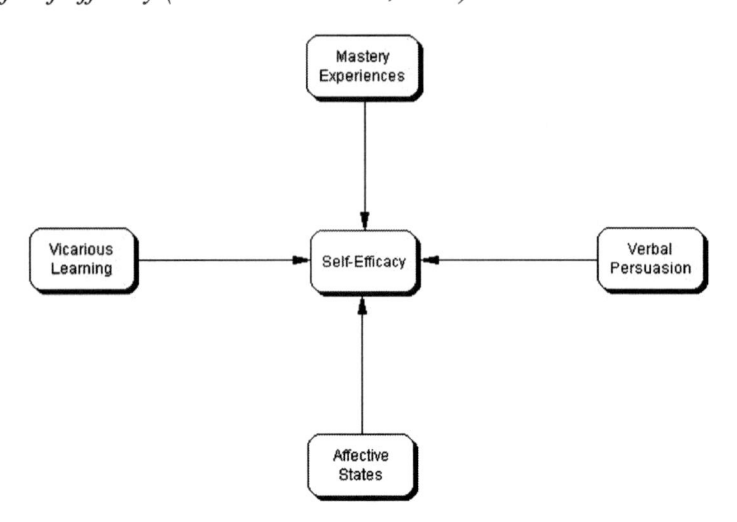

Figure 1. Sources of self-efficacy (Based on Bandura, 1997).

in their abilities to perform effectively, the training they receive as part of the PLC may be negatively impacted. For PD providers, having teachers with low self-efficacy in the PLC can be frustrating. It is difficult to see a return on investment when individuals simply do not have the background, confidence, or ability to visualize themselves being successful implementing new strategies and ideas in their classroom. Consequently, it is important that PD providers work to promote science teaching self-efficacy as a portion of their PLC planning.

Self-Efficacy and Technology as Means to Enhance Science Learning by Teachers

As stated by Bandura (1997), self-efficacy "... refers to beliefs in one's capabilities to organize and execute the courses of action required to produce given attainments" (p. 3). Self-efficacy is uniquely individual and uniquely situational. Not everyone has the same levels of self-efficacy for a given task in a given situation. When one looks at self-efficacy from an educational perspective, it is easy to see how learning and performance could be impacted (for either students or teachers). Bandura (1997) proposed four major sources of self-efficacy (see Figure 1): (a) enactive mastery experiences (being successful at a task); (b) vicarious experiences (feeling more efficacious by watching others perform); (c) verbal persuasion (verbal reinforcement by a peer or knowledgeable other); (d) physiological and affective states (influence of positive moods and attitudes).

These sources of self-efficacy are not uniquely specific to science or inquiry-based learning. They can influence self-efficacy to perform any task. However, when looking at learning science content and pedagogy specifically, a great deal of research has been done to further investigate how best to impact the low self-efficacy often observed in science teachers.

Since self-efficacy is a context-specific construct, the literature relating to self-efficacy and science teaching is diverse. Initially, one of the most recognized instruments used to measure science teacher self-efficacy was produced by Enochs and Riggs (1990): the *Science Teacher Efficacy Belief Instrument (STEBI) Form B*. This instrument has been the standard for many studies as well as the impetus for development of new instruments to measure the self-efficacy of science teachers.

A focus on new and pre-service teachers. Much of the more recent work relating to science teacher self-efficacy has focused on two specific populations: pre-service teachers learning to teach science and new/novice teachers teaching science in their own classrooms for the first time. Results have varied as to what has most impacted science teacher self-efficacy in these groups:

- Moseley, Reinke, and Bookout (2003) found that a PD program specifically designed to train environmental education teachers had little impact on their science teaching self-efficacy, which was high before and during the program, but dropped significantly several weeks after the program was completed.
- Smolleck, Zembal-Saul, and Yoder (2006) used the STEBI-B as a starting point to develop a new instrument, the *Teaching Science as Inquiry Scale* (TSI), specifically designed to measure pre-service teachers' beliefs about teaching science via inquiry.
- ·Richardson and Liang (2008) demonstrated that pre-service teacher efficacy for learning science content and process skills can be positively impacted via inquiry-based pedagogy. Similar results were obtained earlier by Britner and Finson (2005).
- Jarrett (1999) demonstrated that prior experience and number of college science courses contributed to pre-service elementary teachers' confidence in teaching science.

These representative studies of literature in this area point to a few important facts. First, self-efficacy is extremely contextual and task-specific. Each of the studies represented here examined self-efficacy from a different perspective, and obtained different results. Second, all of the research is focused on new or pre-service science teachers. While examining the science teaching self-efficacy of veteran master-level teachers is important, a significant amount of variability in self-efficacy seems to exist in the novice teacher population. This may signal an important red flag for PD providers as they construct programs to enhance pedagogical skills in their participants.

Self-efficacy, teachers, and technology. In regards to teachers' self-efficacy for the use of technology, numerous studies have been done in this area as well. With the use of technology becoming a more integral part of a teacher's daily routine, encountering an individual who is not familiar with basic types of instructional technology (interactive whiteboard, Web 2.0 tools, document cameras, etc.) is less common than even a few years ago. The following studies comprise a representative sample of recent research relating self-efficacy and the use of technology:

- Stevens, To, Harris, and Dwyer (2008) designed a continuing education program (LOGO Project) for teachers that had a goal of increasing self-efficacy for the use of technology to teach mathematics. They found that two of the critical factors affecting self-efficacy were promoting individuality and providing ongoing support from instructors.
- Watson (2006) studied the long-term self-efficacy of science and mathematics teachers who were trained, via summer workshops and online courses, to integrate the Internet into their curricula. He found that self-efficacy remained high for an extended time after the initial summer training was completed, as long as participants remained active through the online courses.
- Dawson (2008) examined Australian teachers' use of various information technology resources for communication in the classroom. It was found that new/novice teachers felt most efficacious in utilizing simple forms of technology such as word processing and presentation software, email, and the Internet. Other types of communication (webpage design, on-

line forums) were used much less often. Similarly, Wu, Chang, and Guo (2008) found that perceived computer usefulness most significantly impacted teachers' self-efficacy regarding technology integration in the classroom.

- Zeldin, Britner, and Pajares (2008) reported that gender may play a role in the predominant source of self-efficacy for individuals in careers in science, technology, engineering, and mathematics (STEM). Men were found to rely most heavily on enactive mastery experiences as the source of their career-based self-efficacy, while women favored verbal persuasion and vicarious experiences.

Three critical themes emerge from these studies: the importance of long-term support, confidence with the technology, and impacts of gender. These factors influencing technology-based self-efficacy may be keys to designing effective technology-based PLCs and other PD programs.

Given this background discussion on PLCs in science and the importance of self-efficacy, it is apparent that multiple factors may be at work in a teacher participating in a PLC. Previous experiences, expectations, and motivation may all impact how effective a PD program will be for a participant (Loucks-Horsely, et al., 2003). The other important factor to consider is experience. This leads to the next several points of discussion in this chapter. Specifically:

1. Where should PD be focused—on the novice teacher or the veteran teacher?
2. How do master-level teachers learn?
3. How can we examine self-efficacy in technology-based PD?
4. What are examples of successful current telementoring-based PLCs?

NOVICE VS. MASTER: WHERE SHOULD PD FOCUS?

How Do Master-Level Teachers Learn?

The concept of teacher learning is a relatively recent area of research (National Research Council, 2000). As described in the previous section, several studies into aspects of science teaching self-efficacy have tended to favor novice and preservice teachers, both in aspects of learning and practice. This begs a few important questions to consider prior to the design of a PD program: (1) How should participants be chosen? (2) Should participants be novice teachers or master-level teachers? (3) Should there be a mix? (4) Which group would most benefit from this type of PD? In this section, the topic of teacher learning and PD will be approached from a science-based perspective.

Novice vs. Master: Where Should PD Focus?

Vasquez and Cowan (2001) discussed the unique differences between providing PD in science for teachers who are veteran master teachers and those who are at a more novice-level of service. Several critical points were made regarding the effectiveness of many PD programs for teachers, such as: (a) While popular with many classroom teachers, the use of hands-on, kit-based training materials is not equivalent to the development of a curriculum; (b) There is a significant difference between "technical instruction of science" and "scientific discourse" (p.13); (c) PD programs must focus on the specific needs of the teachers involved; and (d) Many individuals who promote inquiry cannot effectively define inquiry.

Additionally, novice-level teachers may find themselves in PD programs where these issues are problematic. For example, a school district may be asked to participate in a PD program where several workshops are offered over time to increase in-service teacher knowledge in identified weak areas of science content and process. Novice-level teachers may jump at the chance to pick up new activities, supplies, course credit, etc. to help develop their classroom environment. Master-level teachers may be overtaxed in the school already, serving a mentor or department chair, and may not feel they need the additional training or not have the time. In a larger sense this creates two critical questions that must be addressed: (1) What is the overall goal of the PD? (2) Is it focused specifically on impacting the learning of students, or the PD of teachers? If effective teacher learning is the critical issue, then different approaches must be taken to achieve the desired master-level goals. As Britner and Finson (2005) found, more has to occur for new teachers during PD instruction than just exposure to inquiry-based activities. The real challenge is in translating the experience of inquiry into a mode of planning for inquiry. In order to progress to an effective inquiry-based educator, a continuous progression to skills exhibited by master-level teachers is required.

How do master level teachers learn? Identifying what helps one learn to become a master-level teacher is not difficult. Providing it can be a challenge. Vasquez and Cowan (2001) stated repeatedly that *time* is the key. Specifically, time to grow, time for reflection, time for self-examination, time for peer mentoring and coaching, and time for PD in science content.

One cannot learn to become a master-level science teacher in a short two-week summer PD workshop. Providing teachers with ongoing PD time, mentoring support for planning and implementation, and reflective practice are all essential (Neufeld & Roper, 2003). While learning science content is an ongoing role, application of science methodology to one's own unique classroom situation is important (Supovitz & Turner, 2000). Application of ideas and skills only comes from understanding one's own needs, limitations, and classroom context.

Vasquez and Cowan (2001) also provided common traits that master-level teachers exhibit. These are important characteristics for PD providers to include in their program development. Participants who are not given time, instruction, or mentoring support to develop these skills will likely get little out of the experience, and will not feel excited or efficacious enough to implement what they have learned in their own classrooms. Master-level science teachers view the importance of: (a) understanding that science provides success in life, (b) knowing that both science content and processes are equally important, (c) seeing mentoring as essential, (d) viewing collaborative climates as beneficial, (e) developing effective questioning skills, (f) learning to manage activities wisely, and (g) knowing what the research says and using it.

None of these characteristics are learned quickly, but come with practice and application over time. In many cases, the development of teacher leaders has led to district-wide educational reforms (Reeves, 2007). While immersion into an inquiry-based environment helps teachers experience what inquiry may be like, it is ineffective in terms of professional growth when used in isolation.

The Leadership Aspect of Teaching and PD

One of the more common aspects of PD programs today focuses on the training of teacher leaders to be effective peer mentors. Developing effective leadership skills is at the core of these programs, providing a concurrent goal of moving the novice teacher to more of a master-level. In discussing how best to provide PD programs for teachers, leadership should be a part of the conversation as it impacts these aspects of teacher training.

Donaldson (2009) likened leadership training to riding a bicycle. In essence, both activities involve a coordination of mind and body in a set of ongoing progressive steps that leads to expertise over time. It is not a quick process. It takes practice. Most importantly, it takes patience, dedication, and mentoring by someone with more experience. This provides the impetus for the creation of PLCs, as discussed earlier. Darling-Hammond and Richardson (2009) stated that the PD programs that were most effective were ones that offered 30-100 hours of training spread over 6-12 months. PD programs of 14 hours or fewer in duration showed no effects on learning. This reiterates the importance of time in PD, as discussed above by Vasquez and Cowan (2001). Becoming an effective teacher takes time. Leadership is not developed overnight. Novice-level teachers seeking PD must realize that there are no "quick fixes" for lack of content knowledge, pedagogical skills, collaborative experiences, and technological expertise. Participation in a PLC is an effective place to start, but ongoing dedication to personal growth and development are also keys. Hammerness, Darling-Hammond, Bransford, Berliner, Cochran-Smith, McDonald, and Zeichner (2005) set out a framework for teacher learning that includes the following key areas: (a) understanding (of content, pedagogy, students, and social contexts); (b) practices (constructing a repertoire of classroom activities and approaches); (c) tools (theoretical tools and practical tools); (d) dispositions (habits of mind, metacognitive strategies, reflection); and (e) vision (goals and aspirations to guide practice and future learning).

Simply put, becoming a master-level teacher leader requires a significant amount of time and commitment. It requires the teacher to develop a great deal of self-confidence in their own abilities to teach effectively and collaborate with others. In essence, it means having high self-efficacy for content, for teaching, and for one's own professional growth.

ADDRESSING SOURCES OF SELF-EFFICACY IN TECHNOLOGY-BASED PD

When one logically considers the four sources of self-efficacy discussed earlier (mastery experiences, verbal persuasion, affective states, and vicarious experiences), are not all of these predicated upon past experiences and knowledge? Similarly, is not what one has learned and how it was learned then directly related to the personal confidence in one's abilities to use those bits of knowledge and skills to perform a specific task? As is evident by the standards themselves, the Constructivist philosophy of learning underlying *National Science Education Standards* (National Research Council, 1996) should directly impact the pedagogy used by teachers. When we consider how best to structure PLCs and other PD programs to promote inquiry skills, the development of teacher leaders, and the increased use of technology within these programs, it is apparent that self-efficacy should also be a key construct that is addressed.

As discussed earlier, gender may play a role in the source(s) of self-efficacy most affecting an individual's confidence in their ability to be successful in their STEM-related career (Zeldin, Britner, & Pajares, 2008). With men relying more on mastery experiences, and women being influenced more by vicarious learning and verbal support, creating a PD model that addresses both aspects effectively would seem to be important, but also creates a more challenging PD design process. Overlay this with the use of technology as part of the PD program, and things are complicated further. The reason these create such challenges is that the participants involved are asked to perform not just one basic teaching-related task but several all at once. For example, the content focus for the day may be on developing an inquiry-based lesson to teach about cells and DNA. Content is the first hurdle. Without a solid background in basic cellular structure, organelle function, membrane structure and permeability, DNA nucleotides, and protein formation, teachers may be at a loss for where to begin. As such, self-efficacy for the science content itself may be poor.

If the PD is science-specific, now add the inquiry wrinkle. Lack of familiarity with inquiry-based instruction as a whole, how to plan for it, how to assess it, transition to it, integrate it with science content, and time required, make the overall process of creating this lesson even more difficult. Self-efficacy for inquiry now becomes a factor.

Then, include the need for technology—as part of the investigation to collect and represent data, word processing and publishing to create the lesson and handouts, use of email and/or Blackboard® types of systems to communicate with other teachers or with students—and this may simply be too much for many novice teachers to handle. While self-efficacy for the use of basic technologies for communication and daily work may be high, when it is coupled with other aspects of teaching, the context for the overall task changes dramatically, as does the self-efficacy.

So realistically, can this ever work? Let us review some current successful science PD programs and PLCs where all of these factors have come together with positive results.

The Inclusion of Telementoring in Science-Based PD Programs: Examples of Success

Science Education has maintained a technological edge to much of its PD training over the last 15 years due to multiple factors, including the *National Science Education Standards* (National Research Council, 1996), which includes a series of PD standards. With instructional forms of technology becoming prevalent in most K-12 schools today, PD has had to keep pace. All of the programs discussed below have demonstrated how a technologically-based PD mentoring program could work. Initially, we will focus on two exemplary programs where technology has been used not only for basic PD, but to form a virtual PLC to keep teachers and PD providers connected and communicating over long distances and extended periods of time.

National Science Teachers Association New Science Teacher Academy
http://www.nsta.org/academy/

Beginning its third year in 2009, NSTA[2] (as it is often referred to) was originally a collaborative effort between the National Science Teachers Association (NSTA) and the Amgen Corporation to provide PD training for novice science teachers at the secondary level. According to Ingersoll (2003), almost 50% of new teachers in science leave the profession within the first five years of teaching. For science educators, especially those in teacher preparation programs, this is an appalling trend. With a significant national shortage of teachers in science and mathematics currently, watching the best and brightest new generation of teachers fall away from their career is extremely disheartening.

NSTA[2] has a unique structure, in that it relies completely on technology for most of the PD that occurs. Each year 100-200 participants (Fellows) are chosen through a rigorous application process, done completely online. The new Fellows are then sorted into smaller cohort groups to form distinct PLCs which meet virtually online to accomplish their PD training. Each cohort is assigned a qualified science education mentor who guides the PLC and also answers questions and helps them deal with problems or concerns encountered in their classroom. Fellows are given regular assignments dealing with various aspects of science teaching, inquiry instruction, assessment, classroom management, and professionalism. Again, all discussions, deliverables, and interactions occur in a virtual world. At the end of the year, the program pays for each Fellow to attend the NSTA National Conference on Science Education, where they are able to finally meet their cohort peers and mentors face-to-face. Additional program-specific sessions and activities are offered to the Fellows at the conference.

This has been a very successful program to date. Time commitments are nominal, not overwhelming, but are long-term over the course of the year. Fellows are given the time they need to learn, plan, interact, communicate, and grow. Not only is the program content-focused, but it provides the opportunity for these novice teachers to begin the metamorphic process to master-level teachers. Creating a successful experience is key, as is verbal support from the cohort and mentors. Vicarious learning can occur as well. It is an excellent program from which to model a self-efficacy-based, technological approach to learning how to teach through inquiry. It is a unique PLC that has demonstrated very encouraging initial results.

e-Mentoring for Student Success (eMSS) http://www.newteachercenter.org/eMSS/menu.php?p=home

A precursor program to the NSTA[2], eMSS (first begun in 2002) has been offered as a collaborative effort by the National Science Foundation, The New Teacher Center at the University of California at Santa Cruz, and the Montana State University's Science/Math Resource Center. The focus of eMSS has been to provide content-based mentoring for new teachers in an online environment. Participants engage in activities and discussions that can be done literally anywhere at any time (provided they have access to the internet). Mentoring support comes on a grade-level specific and subject-specific format, while also permitting the participants access to a nationwide PLC of math and science professionals. Electronically, participants and mentors are given multiple levels of access to their mentor, including the following forums:

- *Our Place* page for private discussions.
- *Mentee Place* for larger group discussions.
- *Mentor Place* provides PD support for the mentors themselves.
- *Inquiries* are self-selected groups that focus on content and pedagogy for specific topics.
- *Community Forums and Resources* is a large scale community discussion on various topics.

eMSS has had great success since its initial inception. The fact that participants can have access to a completely virtual PD experience that permits them the opportunity to network locally and nationally with others is appealing for many new teachers. The focus on eMSS is on serving new teachers in the profession, with a goal of showing them how to begin the process of moving to a level of more effective teaching, content knowledge, pedagogical application, and self-confidence for doing their job effectively. Supplemental leadership training for veteran teachers is available as well.

Additional Technology-Based PD Programs

In addition to the two programs discussed, many other PD programs using technology-based mentoring have been created, creating an effective literature base in this area. A representative sample of these studies includes:

- Slotta (2002) discussed the development of the Web-Based Inquiry Science Environment (WISE) program to provide PD for teachers to integrate technology and inquiry.
- Signer (2008) created a model for online professional development for numerous

academic disciplines, including science and mathematics.
- Project TIES (Technology Integration Enhancing Science), a technology-focused PD partnership program, was developed by Shane and Wojnowski (2005). In addition to focusing on the development of science content and pedagogy skills in K-8 teachers, many of the participants also increased their leadership roles as a result of the program.
- Barnett (2008) documented the development of the Inquiry Learning Forum (ILF), a web-based PD program using online videos as a means to enhance pre-service and in-service pedagogy.
- National Research Council (2007) provided a unique view of an entire PD workshop on potential uses of information technology to enhance PD for teachers, especially utilizing an online format. Several guidelines for planning and implementation were discussed, as well as a number of case studies found to be effective.

The key features highlighted here include: online mentoring, focus on content and pedagogy development, and providing the skills necessary for teachers to grow as leaders in their schools. While increased leadership ability is not always a specific objective of programs, it is often an unanticipated benefit. Providing an environment that is conducive to teacher skill development, self-efficacy improvement, and pedagogical understanding is complex, but the potential benefits of doing so are enormous.

RECOMMENDATIONS FOR THE FUTURE OF TECHNOLOGY AND TELEMENTORING IN SCIENCE-BASED PD PROGRAMS AND PLCS

So where does this leave one in trying to develop more effective PLCs and PD programs? Simply stated, planning an effective PD program is not a simple task. Numerous resources exist to provide examples of how to construct PD programs and PLCs (see Loucks-Horsley & Stiles (2001); Loucks-Horsley, et al. (2003); Mundry & Stiles (2009); Petto, Patrick, & Kessel (2005)). The difficulty arises in trying to integrate numerous research-tested approaches into an effective overall plan for action. Multiple layers of PD development need to be addressed together.

Self-Efficacy

Recall from the previous discussion that self-efficacy is a context-specific construct that provides a measure of confidence in one's abilities to perform a specific task. In the context of PD, enhancing self-efficacy for teaching content and the use of pedagogies must undergird the PD plan. Recall the four main sources of self-efficacy (See Figure 1).

Additionally, gender may play a role in which source of self-efficacy is preferred. Men in STEM careers showed a preference for mastery experiences, while women relied more on verbal persuasion and vicarious learning experiences to impact their self-efficacy.

Overall, self-efficacy for any given task will vary between individuals and within individuals, depending on the context of the situation. In thinking about teacher learning, focusing on sound techniques and pedagogies for teaching provides one with the ability to solve problems and transfer ideas to new situations. What is true for the transfer of learning is also true for the transfer of teaching (National Research Council, 2000).

Novice vs. Master-Level Teachers

The professional differences between pre-service/novice teachers and veteran/master teachers are great. In developing a PLC or creating a PD program, special attention should be paid to addressing these differences yet also utilizing them for program benefit. Identifying what the needs are in each population is essential. A "one size fits all" approach to PD will not be effective. Master teachers possess numerous valuable characteristics which should be utilized to aid in the development of those less experienced. Developing leadership skills should be an integrated and ongoing theme of the program.

Several keys aspects of PD are involved in planning for PD programs with novice and master teachers. Background knowledge and experiences of everyone involved relating to content, pedagogy, leadership, and collaborative work should be considered as useful resources in planning for mentoring and other collaborative experiences. Again, the formation of leadership skills supports the rest of the model.

Virtual Mentoring, Self-Efficacy, PLCs, and PD: A Theoretical Model

Combining the multiple components of effective PLC and PD program development discussed in this chapter is a daunting task. Self-efficacy is context-specific, so creating PD situations where participants can work to enhance their task-specific confidence is ultimately a function of their prior experiences. Veteran teachers will likely have more of those experiences than novice teachers. The end result of increased participant leadership abilities and holding individuals responsible for the role in the program is an ongoing process which must develop over time. Mentoring, collaboration between individuals, and the development of successful partnerships (at the individual and institutional levels) are also time-sensitive processes which come as other programmatic factors evolve. Surrounding this entire venture is the virtual world in which it all takes place. Successful PLCs (such as eMSS, NSTA[2], and others) have utilized electronic means to structure their programs. These have been nationwide endeavors that have essentially resolved the ongoing PD issues of distance to receive training, and time expectations that were unworkable for many teachers. Figure 2 summarizes the interaction between these varying aspects to create a theoretical model for developing a virtual PLC.

It is important to note that the model proposed here is a literature-based, theoretical scaffold on which multiple pieces of a PD program that utilize a telementoring format can hang. As discussed earlier, PLCs have been shown to be very useful forms of teacher PD in science. The model described here takes the idea of a PLC and places it in a virtual world which combines overlapping aspects of leadership training, promotion of self-efficacy, collaborative partnerships and mentoring experiences, and also the incorporation of knowledge, experiences, and beliefs of the teacher participants.

While the entire model is a theoretical combination of multiple components, the individual pieces of this plan have been addressed in numerous studies, many of which have been discussed in this chapter. As the field of Education as a whole progresses further into demands for highly qualified teachers, increased teacher accountability, and requirements for ongoing PD at all grade levels, PD programs as a whole simply must adapt to keep up with these changes. Teachers' needs are changing, and a "one size, fits all" approach to PD is no longer effective. Creating virtual PLCs that utilize a telementoring approach has the potential of reaching many more teachers than traditional programs. By including aspects that relate to leadership, self-efficacy, collaboration, mentoring, and teacher knowledge, the virtual PLCs that are formed have the potential to enhance the professionalism of numerous teachers.

Implications for the K-12 Teacher and PD Provider

As a K-12 PD provider, or a teacher seeking to participate in a telementoring program, the theoretical model discussed in this chapter may seem somewhat intangible in relation to a program you are designing or considering joining. However,

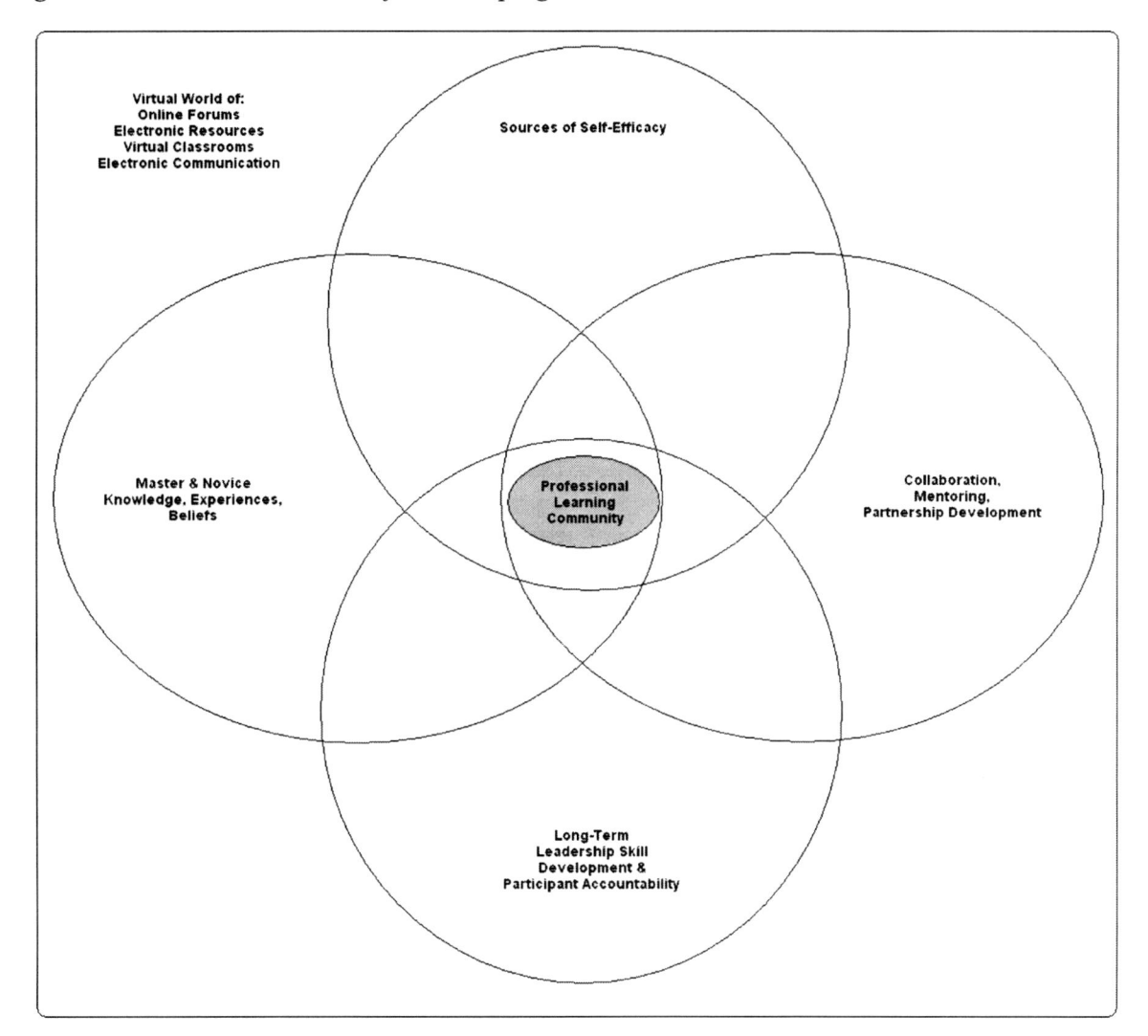

Figure 2. A theoretical PD model for developing a virtual PLC

there are several take-home messages and questions from this chapter to consider that may benefit your participation and enhance your experience.

1. Identify your goals for being involved in the PD program or PLC. What are you trying to accomplish? Be open and honest about your expectations related to tangible rewards, content, methodology, and professionalism.
2. Identify the reasons for seeking (or providing) technology-based mentoring. Is a telementoring format a useful way for you (or others) to learn and interact (as opposed to a face-to-face program)? Are you comfortable utilizing a technology-based approach? Do you have the infrastructure to support such a program?
3. What types of experiences make you (or your participants) feel most efficacious about teaching? How can those experiences be a part of your mentoring experience?
4. Is the PD program or PLC focused on mentoring novice teachers to help them become master teachers? How is leadership development a part of the community? Which category of teacher do you fall into?

5. How do you plan to implement what you learn? How will this experience better you as a teacher?
6. What long-term PD goals have you set for yourself? How will telementoring support those goals? Does the PLC you are joining have a long-term component to it?
7. Identify the needs of the participants early on, and adapt the program to address those needs. If you are a participant, be patient and flexible. Provide constructive feedback to your program planners on what you feel may be useful to include in the mentoring experience. Be involved. Be disciplined. Be ready to learn. Be ready to teach.

Translating theory into practice is not always a simple task for the PD provider or for a teacher participant. This chapter has provided numerous resources on self-efficacy, PLCs, teacher leadership, and teacher learning. Based on years of personal PD program experiences, the most useful message to gain from this discussion is not to try to euphemistically reinvent the wheel. The theoretical model outlined in this chapter provides a framework for designing virtual telementoring-based PLCs. However, your program may not have the infrastructure or the resources to include all of these components. Make changes over time. Work towards a goal of implementing more aspects of the model as it is feasible for you to do so. Based on the literature discussed here, addressing any aspects of the model individually will provide benefits to teachers participating in the mentoring experience.

CONCLUSION

Science Education has seen numerous changes in content and pedagogy over the last 20 years. Standards have been created that never existed previously, now providing guidelines for teaching, content, assessment, and PD among others (National Research Council, 1996). In response to these new inquiry-based approaches to science, numerous PD programs have been created to bring new and veteran teachers up to speed on content and pedagogy they may be lacking. In many cases, these efforts have been successful. However, in other cases programs have struggled to meet their objectives for a variety of reasons. With the widely varying backgrounds in teacher participants it is difficult to find a productive middle ground that is common to all involved and that permits collective growth. Prior experiences with content and pedagogy lead to individual differences in self-efficacy for teaching.

Teachers entering a PD program with low self-efficacy may struggle. Some individuals are more receptive to mentoring in those areas than others. Many are concerned about time, expectations, and their rewards. While it is not possible to positively impact everyone in every way, there has been a distinctive shift in PD approaches seen in the research literature.

While the concept of a PLC is not new, it has seen a resurgence of popularity among PD providers. The potential benefits are great. Even though PLCs have been shown to be successful in a number of settings (see Mundry & Stiles, 2009), expectations of time and travel for PD still remain as hurdles for many teachers. This is where the utilization of a virtual PLC has demonstrated its usefulness. PLCs in science have been an effective model for the concept of telementoring. Programs like eMSS and NSTA[2] have significantly raised the bar for virtual PLC use. The development of these online mentoring communities has reached thousands of individuals, and done so in a manner that is supportive and conducive to learning and professional growth. Creating an effective virtual PLC or PD program should address a number of key development issues, specifically: self-efficacy, leadership skill development, and identification of the unique needs of novice and master teachers. Collaboration with mutual accountability should be viewed as critical components as well. Above all, a long-term, sustained effort where time is permitted for growth, reflection, and support for implementation should be a primary goal.

All teachers are capable of professional growth and all have the potential to be leaders in some aspect. As discussed by the National Research Council (2000), teacher learning is critical to achieving an expert level of ability. They specifically state:

- Teachers need expertise in both subject matter content and in teaching.
- Teacher need to develop an understanding of theories of knowledge (epistemologies) that guide the subject matter disciplines in which they work.
- Teachers need to develop an understanding of pedagogy as an intellectual discipline that reflects theories of learning….
- Teachers are learners and the principles of learning and transfer for student learners apply to teachers.
- Teachers need opportunities…to know how teaching practices build on learners' prior knowledge.
- Teachers need to develop models of their own professional development that are based on lifelong learning….(p. 242)

As PD providers, we must provide an environment where these evolutions can occur. As demonstrated in this chapter, technology can no longer be ignored in PD programs. While face-to-face PLCs are still effective, we must realize as PD practitioners that the future of mentoring and PD lies in our current and future technologies. Only by embracing the use of online communities and other electronic forms of communication and mentoring can the field of PD continue to grow at a pace that is in-step with educational needs.

ACKNOWLEDGMENT

I would like to acknowledge the assistance of Ms. Jennifer H. Gammill for her professional development expertise, and her valuable input in the development of this chapter.

REFERENCES

Bandura, A. (1997). *Self-Efficacy: The Exercise of Control*. New York: W.H. Freeman and Company.

Barnett, M. (2006). Using a web-based professional development system to support pre-service teachers in examining authentic classroom practice. *Journal of Technology and Teacher Education, 14*(4), 701–729.

Britner, S. L., & Finson, K. D. (2005). Pre-service teachers' reflections on their growth in an inquiry-oriented science pedagogy course. *Journal of Elementary Science Education, 17*(1), 39–54. doi:10.1007/BF03174672

Darling-Hammond, L., & Richardson, N. (2009). Teacher learning: What matters? *Educational Leadership, 66*(5), 46–53.

Dawson, V. (2008). Use of information communication technology by early career science teachers in western Australia. *International Journal of Science Education, 30*(2), 203–219. doi:10.1080/09500690601175551

Donaldson, G. A. Jr. (2009). The lessons are in the leading. *Educational Leadership, 66*(5), 14–18.

Enochs, L. G., & Riggs, I. M. (1990). Further development of an elementary science teaching efficacy belief instrument: A pre-service elementary scale. *School Science and Mathematics, 90*(8), 694–706. doi:10.1111/j.1949-8594.1990.tb12048.x

Guy, T. (2002). Telementoring: Shaping Mentoring Relationships for the 21st Century. In Hansman, C. A. (Ed.), *Critical Perspectives on Mentoring: Trends and Issues. Information Series No. 388.* Columbus, OH: ERIC Clearinghouse on Adult, Career, and Vocational Education.

Hammerness, K., Darling-Hammond, L., Bransford, J., Berliner, D., Cochran-Smith, M., McDonald, M., & Zeichner, K. (2005). How teachers learn and develop. In Darling-Hammond, L., & Bransford, J. (Eds.), *Preparing Teachers for a Changing World: What Teachers Should Learn and Be Able to Do.* San Francisco, CA: Jossey-Bass.

Ingersoll, R. M. (2003). The teacher shortage: Myth or reality? *Educational Horizons, 81*(3), 146–152.

Jarrett, O. S. (1999). Science interest and confidence among pre-service elementary teachers. *Journal of Elementary Science Education, 11*(1), 49–59. doi:10.1007/BF03173790

Landel, C., & Nelson, G. (2009). Creating and sustaining science-focused professional learning communities through partnerships. In Mundry, S., & Stiles, K. E. (Eds.), *Professional Learning Communities for Science Teaching: Lessons from Research and Practice* (pp. 73–88). Arlington, VA: NSTA Press.

Llewellyn, D. (2007). *Inquire Within* (2nd ed.). Thousand Oaks, CA: Corwin Press.

Loucks-Horsley, S., Love, N., Stiles, K. E., Mundry, S., & Hewson, P. W. (2003). *Designing professional development for teachers of mathematics and science* (2nd ed.). Thousand Oaks, CA: Corwin Press.

Loucks-Horsley, S., & Stiles, K. E. (2001). Professional development designed to change science teaching and learning. In J. Rhoton & P. Bowers, P. (Eds.). *Professional development planning and design* (pp.13-24). Arlington, VA: NSTA Press.

Moseley, C., Reinke, K., & Bookout, V. (2003). The effect of teaching outdoor environmental education on elementary pre-service teachers' self-efficacy. *Journal of Elementary Science Education, 15*(1), 1–14. doi:10.1007/BF03174740

Mundry, S., & Stiles, K. E. (Eds.). (2009). *Professional Learning Communities for Science Teaching: Lessons from Research and Practice.* Arlington, VA: NSTA Press.

National Research Council. (1996). *National Science Education Standards.* Washington, DC: National Academy Press.

National Research Council. (2000). *How People Learn: Brain, Mind, Experience, and School.* Washington, DC: National Academy Press.

National Research Council. (2007). *Enhancing Professional Development for Teachers: Potential Uses of Information Technology. Report of a Workshop.* Washington, DC: National Academies Press.

National Science Foundation. (2008). *Math science partnership program: National impact report.* Retrieved August 25, 2008, from http://www.scalemsp.org/files/MSP_News/Impact_Report/final_msp_impact_report.pdf

National Science Teachers Association. (2009). *New Science Teacher Academy.* Retrieved May 1, 2009 from http://www.nsta.org/academy/

Neufeld, B., & Roper, D. (2003). *Coaching: A strategy for developing instructional capacity--Promises and practicalities.* Washington, DC: Aspen Institute Program on Education, and Providence. RI: Annenberg Institute for School Reform.

Petto, A. J., Patrick, M., & Kessel, R. (2005). Emphasizing inquiry, collaboration, and leadership in K-12 professional development. In Yager, R. E. (Ed.), *Exemplary science: Best practices in professional development* (pp. 147–160). Arlington, VA: NSTA Press.

Reeves, D. (2007). Teachers step up. *Educational Leadership, 65*(1), 87–88.

Richardson, G. M., & Liang, L. L. (2008). The use of inquiry in the development of pre-service teacher efficacy in mathematics and science. *Journal of Elementary Science Education, 20*(1), 1–16. doi:10.1007/BF03174699

Shane, P. M., & Wojnowski, B. S. (2005). Technology integration enhancing science: Things take time. *Science Educator, 14*(1), 49–55.

Signer, B. (2008). Online professional development: Combining best practices from teacher, technology, and distance education. *Journal of In-service Education, 34*(2), 205–218. doi:10.1080/13674580801951079

Slotta, J. (2002). Designing the "Web-Based Inquiry Science Environment (WISE)". *Educational Technology, 42*(5), 15–20.

Smolleck, L. D., Zembal-Saul, C., & Yoder, E. P. (2006). The development and validation of an instrument to measure pre-service teachers' self-efficacy in regard to the teaching of science as inquiry. *Journal of Science Teacher Education, 17*(2), 137–163. doi:10.1007/s10972-006-9015-6

Stevens, T., To, Y., Harris, G., & Dwyer, J. (2008). The LOGO project: Designing an effective continuing education program for teachers. *Journal of Computers in Mathematics and Science Teaching, 27*(2), 195–219.

Supovitz, J. A., & Turner, H. M. (2000). The effects of professional development on science teaching practices and classroom culture. *Journal of Research in Science Teaching, 37*(9), 963–980. doi:10.1002/1098-2736(200011)37:9<963::AID-TEA6>3.0.CO;2-0

The New Teacher Center. (2009). *e-Mentoring for student success*. Retrieved on May 1, 2009 from http://www.newteachercenter.org/eMSS/menu.php?p=home

Vasquez, J., & Cowan, M. B. (2001). Moving teachers from mechanical to mastery: The next level of science implementation. In Rhoton, J., & Bowers, P. (Eds.), *Professional development leadership and the diverse learner* (pp. 11–22). Arlington, VA: NSTA Press.

Watson, G. (2006). Technology professional development: Long-term effects on teacher self-efficacy. *Journal of Technology and Teacher Education, 14*(1), 151–166.

Wu, W., Chang, H., & Guo, C. (2008). An empirical assessment of science teachers' intentions toward technology integration. *Journal of Computers in Mathematics and Science Teaching, 27*(4), 499–520.

Zeldin, A. L., Britner, S. L., & Pajares, F. (2008). A comparative study of the self-efficacy beliefs of successful men and women in mathematics, science, and technology careers. *Journal of Research in Science Teaching, 45*(9), 1036–1058. doi:10.1002/tea.20195

ADDITIONAL READING

Association for Supervision and Curriculum Development. (2009). *PD in Focus: Online Media and Tools for Powerful Professional Development*. Retrieved on May 1, 2009 from http://www.ascd.org/pdinfocus/

Darling-Hammond, L., & Bransford, J. (Eds.). (2005). *Preparing Teachers for a Changing World: What Teachers Should Learn and Be Able to Do*. San Francisco, CA: Jossey-Bass.

Loucks-Horsley, S., Love, N., Stiles, K. E., Mundry, S., & Hewson, P. W. (2003). *Designing professional development for teachers of mathematics and science* (2nd ed.). Thousand Oaks, CA: Corwin Press.

Mundry, S., & Stiles, K. E. (Eds.). (2009). *Professional Learning Communities for Science Teaching: Lessons from Research and Practice.* Arlington, VA: NSTA Press.

National Research Council. (2000). *How People Learn: Brain, Mind, Experience, and School.* Washington, DC: National Academy Press.

Pajares, F. (2009). *Information on self-efficacy.* Retrieved on May 1, 2009 from http://www.des.emory.edu/mfp/self-efficacy.html

Rhoton, J., & Bowers, P. (Eds.). (2001). *Professional development leadership and the diverse learner* (pp. 11–22). Arlington, VA: NSTA Press.

Rhoton, J., & Bowers, P. (Eds.). (2001). *Professional development planning and design.* Arlington, VA: NSTA Press.

Yager, R. E. (Ed.). (2005). *Exemplary science: Best practices in professional development.* Arlington, VA: NSTA Press.

Section 4
Telementoring:
Web 2.0 Technologies

Chapter 12
An Orientation to Web 2.0 Tools for Telementoring

Robin Hastings
Missouri River Regional Library, USA

ABSTRACT

This chapter gives an overview of Web 2.0 technologies and how they can support telementoring partnerships. Web 2.0 tools offer opportunities for increased networking and social interactivity. Synchronous (chats) and asynchronous (email) communication are possible with these tools. Some of the Web 2.0 capabilities that are introduced in this chapter include cloud computing, Facebook, Ning, and Twitter. FriendFeed and Groupware are also discussed as methods to organize and track a number of Web 2.0 applications for ease of use. Stability, data portability, privacy, and security are issues that are indicated for future research.

INTRODUCTION WEB 2.0

Effective communication is at the heart of any mentoring process, more so with telementoring because the mentor and student are not physically close to one another and must communicate using electronic means. With the recent explosion of Web 2.0 tools, communication over distance and time has become more convenient. The concepts behind Web 2.0–communication, networking, social bonding and sharing–fit perfectly into a mentoring relationship. In this chapter, I will explain how communication using these tools can work for your mentoring relationship, what technologies and services are available in the Web 2.0 toolset for you to use and how mentors and students can use those tools today to improve communication during the mentoring process.

First, a definition of the term Web 2.0 may be in order. Darcy DiNucci first coined the phrase in 1999 (DiNucci, 1999), but it became part of the general lexicon with Tim O'Reilly's began to use it in conjunction with the first Web 2.0 conference. In an article in which he explains just what he meant by the term "Web 2.0" (O'Reilly, 2005), he explains this term with phrases such as

DOI: 10.4018/978-1-61520-861-6.ch012

"The Web As Platform", "Harnessing Collective Intelligence" and "Software Above the Level of a Single Device". The term encompasses a philosophy more than any one tool. It refers to a multitude of services, applications and web sites that encourage user-created content, sharing between contacts or friends on a site as well as providing a communication channel between users of the site or service. The driving idea behind Web 2.0 is that of the web as a platform for two-way communication and sharing - much more so than the one-way communication of websites that give the reader information, but do not encourage the reader to become a content creator or give the reader a way to easily share information with other readers of the site. Because most Web 2.0 tools encourage users to become content creators and, as such, provide many different features and applications that are there for the single purpose of assisting users in creating content, they are ideally suited to educational and telementoring uses.

One of the benefits of using one—or more—of these Web 2.0 tools in your telementoring activities is the ability to conduct both real-time (synchronous) and time-shifted (asynchronous) communications via the tool itself. Synchronous communication occurs when both parties are present and "chatting" or communicating at the same time. Instant Messaging (IM), talking on the telephone (as long as an answering machine is not involved) and face-to-face meetings are examples of synchronous communication. Asynchronous communication happens between people who may not be at the same place at the same time. Examples of asynchronous communication include leaving a message on a telephone answering machine, email and writing a letter. All of these examples of asynchronous communication include an "inbox" that holds the message until the recipient is ready to read and respond. This kind of communication is almost required for international communication: when someone in one part of the world is asleep, someone in the other part of the world can be reading the message left in his or her inbox and responding to it when it is convenient. While synchronous communication is ideal for getting a quick answer to a question or for brainstorming, asynchronous communication is useful for far-flung teams whose members may be distant from one another–even in different time zones–yet communication can still happen at a time that is convenient for each of the participants. It has the added advantage of allowing everyone breathing space to consider questions or problems and answer or suggest solutions at their own pace.

BACKGROUND

Synchronous and asynchronous communications are not new. Anyone who has used a telephone has participated in a synchronous communication channel; anyone who has written a letter (or an email message) has participated in an asynchronous communication channel. What is new are the ways in which these communications can happen. Moving from a face-to-face conversation to a telephone call to an IM conversation, the changes in communication options have been rapid and sometimes overwhelming. The one aspect that has not changed, no matter how you choose to communicate, is the reason for the communication: the sharing of knowledge between people. Synchronous communications make that possible in real-time and make getting feedback (questions, comments, etc.) on the shared information easy. Asynchronous communication is also about sharing knowledge, but it does not involve the real-time, immediate response that synchronous communication does. It does, however, make communication between time zones less of a hassle and more convenient.

With the advent of electronic communications, the line between synchronous and asynchronous communications has become thinner. Nearly everyone has experienced receiving a reply to an email message within a few seconds: that turnaround time is nearly synchronous. Nearly everyone has also experienced sending off an IM to someone who has had to leave their desk for a while and not getting a response back for an hour or more. That is much closer to an asynchronous communication method than people normally consider IM to be. I refer to the resources in this chapter as specifically synchronous and asynchronous communications, but do keep in mind that the line between the two is blurred at times.

WEB 2.0: SYNCHRONOUS AND ASYNCHRONOUS COMMUNICATION

The Web 2.0 tools that are available today provide multiple means of communication as well as many ways in which a group of people can work. Some of the more popular tools that have both synchronous and asynchronous communication channels include: MySpace, FriendFeed, Twitter (which can be synchronous in the manner of email, mentioned before), Facebook, and various forms of Web 2.0 groupware that are available today.

Issues

Groupware–software that facilitates communication and provides tools for teams to work together on projects–has traditionally been expensive and exclusive. If your group had the funding for one of these software suites and was able to standardize on one of them, then you could use groupware effectively. If you had widely dispersed teams who used different groupware suites, however, you had a problem, as the groupware each team used might not work together. You also had a problem if you had a limited budget. Because many of the traditional groupware suites are so expensive it may be difficult to justify the purchase of an entire groupware software suite for a telementoring program.

If you chose to use something besides the expensive groupware suites, you had options, but none that were both integrated and convenient. Conference calls or video conferencing require all participants to be available at the same time for the synchronous communication, as well as to have compatible hardware and software to make the conference work. Asynchronous communication such as mail, faxing or even email limited you to delayed answers and slow responses with no real recourse to a good synchronous communication channel. Any of these options were available, but no conference calling solutions offer a way to collaborate in real time on a document, and methods that would provide the ability to collaborate create too much clutter as different versions of a document are emailed–or worse yet–faxed around to the various team members.

Using a technological solution, such as a forum or discussion board, requires that everyone remember to log in regularly: something that may be difficult for busy students (and mentors) to remember on a regular basis. A software solution that is not part of a daily routine adds more work and more opportunities for information that is received too late or missed altogether.

Cloud Computing

Cloud Computing is, as Wikipedia defines it, "a style of computing in which dynamically scalable and often virtualized resources are provided as a service over the Internet" (Wikipedia). This includes just about every Web 2.0 service that is available today: Facebook, Twitter, blogs and wikis are all providing resources over the Internet for multiple people to access. When you log into any of these sites, you are moving into the "cloud". When you work in the Internet cloud, you need to keep a few things in mind: the security of your data as it is no longer resident only on your computer and access to it is now being managed by other people; the reliability of your Internet connection, since if you lose access to the Internet, you lose access to your data; and the willingness of others who are working with you to put their data "out there" in the cloud. You can

An Orientation to Web 2.0 Tools for Telementoring

gain quite a bit when using the cloud, too. You gain the economy of scale that makes many of these services completely free to end users. You gain the freedom from worrying about whether or not the server is running properly and whether someone is properly backing up all of your information. In addition, you gain the ability to access your data from any Internet-connected computer in the world. These trade-offs are things to keep in mind when you are setting up a Web 2.0-enabled telementoring program.

Stability and Data Portability

While stability is an issue with any communication method–with the possible exception of face-to-face communication–data portability is a special issue for computer-mediated communications. For documents that were emailed around in the past, team members had to choose a platform such as Microsoft Word 2007 and all had to use it in order for the data to be usable by the entire team. The same sort of issues affect Web 2.0 services, but in different ways. For some of them (Facebook, for example), the data you put into the service in the form of notes or discussion posts is in a proprietary format and may be difficult to retrieve if needed later. Others such as Ning, let you upload data in the format you choose so you would be able to download it in that format again. All Web 2.0 services have the fundamental issue of being unstable–they are not guaranteed to be around for the next decade and some have disappeared quite quickly in the past–so quickly that users lost their data before they could recover it.

Solutions

One way to get a suite of communication tools that you can use both synchronously and asynchronously is to use the Web 2.0 tools that are freely available now. While the list of tools profiled in this section are not exhaustive by any means, they are popular, have a large user base, are widely available with an Internet connection and email address and have many different uses for supporting a telementoring relationship.

Facebook

Sites such as Facebook (www.facebook.com) are familiar to students and provide multiple channels of communication. Facebook's statistics page (Facebook, n.d.) shows that over 100 million people log into the service every day and that there are over 200 million active users of the site, as of the end of April 2009. This popularity means that if you choose to use Facebook as your telementoring platform, you will likely find that many of the people in the group are already on Facebook and will be checking the site regularly for updates and new information–and that can easily include information from their mentors. Along with this strong user base, Facebook also provides several different methods of communication for your group.

For synchronous communication, Facebook includes an internal IM system that gives members a chance to "chat" with each other in real time. For asynchronous communication, Facebook includes threaded discussion forums for groups as well as internal-to-Facebook private message inboxes and a "wall" section of the site. Facebook's wall is the public area of each profile on which any of a user's friends can write. A comment left on the wall is public: any other friend of that Facebook user can see it and comment on the original wall post at any time. If you create a "page" in Facebook (either for a school or for a particular mentoring program), you can add a discussion forum to that page that permits leaving asynchronous comments for anyone else who is a fan or friend of that page to see and to which he or she can respond.

Facebook also has another asynchronous communication channel: the private message. You can leave a message for any of your Facebook friends

209

that will be stored in their inbox and that they can access and respond to it at any time. This provides for private comments that you might not want the whole world to see in an asynchronous way, unlike the Facebook IM client. The Facebook IM client offers private messaging in a synchronous way with chatting capabilities that mirror other Instant Messaging systems with which your team members may already be familiar.

Mentors and students can use the IM capabilities of Facebook to catch up quickly when both the mentor and the student are online and logged into Facebook at the same time. This does not have to be by accident–you can use the discussion board, private message system or a wall post to set up a time for both to be online to chat. Students can use the asynchronous tools–the discussion board, wall posts and private message system–to ask questions or discuss problems, and mentors can use the same tools to respond or to leave messages of their own.

Ning [$49 a month]

Another Web 2.0 site that offers all of the same benefits as Facebook, but with more controllable and granular privacy features, is Ning (www.ning.com). Ning is a social networking site builder. Ning does not release statistics on the number of registered users, but in February of 2009, they did announce on their blog (Oech, 2009) that there have been more than 850,000 different social networks created on their site. Each social network in Ning is a private, Facebook-like community with features and access controlled by the network's creator.

With Ning, you can create a site that is very much like one created in Facebook, with a comment wall, discussion forums and IM, but you can make it completely private so that only the people you invite can read and respond to the messages left on the site. With Ning, however, you may lose the familiarity that many students have with the Facebook site, as well as the fact that they will very likely be going to Facebook anyway and thus you can "catch" them as they go about their daily lives. However, you gain very strong privacy controls and the ability to minimize distractions while on the site, which have obvious advantages for a mentoring situation. Only the applications that the site manager approves are added to a Ning site–so there are no games, no outside friends and no time-wasters that are available on the site. Ning's basic service is free, though there is a paid service that eliminates advertising and gives more space for file uploads and other applications. You can use Ning's tools in the same way you would use Facebook's tools to communicate.

Twitter [free]

Less "full service" Web 2.0 sites can also be put into service for a mentoring relationship. Twitter (www.twitter.com) is a rapidly growing communication service that is useful for quick bursts of communication throughout the day. Twitter is a microblogging service: anyone who follows your account on Twitter will receive the short (140-character maximum) posts that you make to the Twitter service. You will also receive all of the posts made to the service by anyone you follow. This puts a limit on the amount of communication that can take place in a single "tweet" (a post to the Twitter service), but it also enforces concise communication styles and promotes one idea per post.

In a mentoring relationship, students can use the Twitter service to post questions for their mentor using the @username reply system. The reply system is a built-in method for Twitter users to be alerted whenever a Twitter post is directed at them. It is used simply by putting the "at" symbol (@) before the user name of the person you are speaking directly to so that they get that message in their replies inbox at Twitter. One of Twitter's strengths is its tight integration with cell phone text messaging. Because you can set up Twitter to get a person's updates through a cell phone, a mentor can subscribe to the student's Twitter account and set those "tweets" to be sent directly to the mentor's phone. This allows the mentor to follow, virtually at least, the student all day–and makes Twitter's mostly asynchronous communications far more synchronous.

FriendFeed [shut down]

Once you have a few social networking accounts set up and in use, you may find that adding a FriendFeed (www.friendfeed.com) account will help you keep everything together and assist you in keeping on top of all of the different forms of communication that you use. FriendFeed is a lifestreaming application: it takes the feeds from all of the social networking services described above (plus many more) and puts them in a single river of information about you to which other people can subscribe. If everyone you are working with has a FriendFeed account, you can subscribe to those accounts and get all of their Facebook status posts, Twitter posts and any Ning activity aggregated in the FriendFeed interface. Even if one of the people you are following does not have a FriendFeed account, you can still aggregate their information in FriendFeed by making them an imaginary friend.

You can create an imaginary friend in Friend-Feed by clicking on the "create a feed" link on the right sidebar of the FriendFeed site. You can make that friend public so that anyone can access their information or private so that only you and people you invite can see the imaginary friend's river of information. This is a one-way street: the person you are creating this imaginary friend for will not have access to your FriendFeed information unless they join the site themselves. In that case, you can then just subscribe to their account and delete the imaginary friend. This feature can be useful for mentors in that it allows them to keep track of all of the student's outputs that have a status update (Facebook Twitter, etc.) or that have an RSS feed (blogs). The process to create an imaginary friend may change in the next implementation of FriendFeed: so if you are interested in creating one and the steps have changed, go to the Help link at the bottom of the page and do a search for "imaginary friend."

Web 2.0 Groupware

Groupware has also moved into the Web 2.0 world: now you can go to a groupware site such as Grou.ps (http://grou.ps) and create an entire site that incorporates many different Web 2.0 services (Facebook, Twitter, Flickr–the photo-sharing site–and many more) into one single interface. This service, was generally expensive in the past, but is frequently provided as an advertising-supported Web 2.0 application today. Grou.ps is similar to Ning in that it gives the account owner control of what applications to add to the site so that the administrator of the site can completely customize the groupware to fit the needs of a particular group. There are many to add: chatting, wikis, blogging, calendar applications, video uploads, forums and mapping tools are just a few of the features available to any Grou.ps site.

You can also use Web 2.0 groupware to create a self-contained portal to the mentor/student relationship. Since sites like Grou.ps have many different modules that can be added as needed, all of the communication needs for a telementoring project can be included–giving mentors and students an easy way to consolidate all of the information being shared through this process in one place. Not only can groupware put everything that you are doing on other Web 2.0 sites together, but it also provides communication channels as well. The IM module, a mailing list module and a discussion board module all provide in-site communication that keeps all of the information produced and all of the ideas that are shared in one easy-to-access site.

FUTURE RESEARCH DIRECTIONS

Some of the issues that will need to be more thoroughly examined in the area of Web 2.0 and its communication channels deal with the stability of the platform you choose, the ability to move data from one service to another, the privacy controls that are available and the security issues that arise from the use of web-based tools. All of these concerns are worth further examination for any of the tools that you use in your telementoring programs.

Stability and data portability are very much related. The vast majority of the popular Web 2.0 tools are free and many of them have no revenue models beyond venture capital and advertising sales. Twitter, for example, serves no ads and collects no money from its users–others such as Facebook and Ning use advertising to help defray the cost of providing the service, but if the advertising dollars fail to materialize, the services could die very quickly. If the platform (Facebook, Ning, Twitter, etc.) that you choose for your telementoring program ends up going away, you will need to be able to pull your data off that service in a way that you can easily import into a new service so that all of your historical communications are not lost. All of your communications, any files that you have uploaded and any personal information that you have submitted to the service will need to be saved and moved into a new platform. When researching what service you will use, be sure to investigate the options for data portability in case the service becomes unstable or is discontinued. Find out how easy it is to back up the files that you have on the service as well as the communications (chat logs, forum messages, etc.) that are stored on the site.

Privacy and security are also related issues that you will need to investigate before committing to a particular Web 2.0 platform for your program. Being able to set fine-grained privacy controls and having trust in the security of the service you choose will ensure that you are comfortable using the platform to communicate without fear of someone else listening in to your conversations. It may also turn out to be a regulatory issue if you are working with children under the age of 13. There are many laws in place to protect children that may have some bearing on what services are available for you to use, so do keep that in mind while you are looking for a common platform to use during your telementoring sessions.

CONCLUSION

Taking advantage of both the synchronous and asynchronous communication channels that many of the popular Web 2.0 tools provide is easy and can help make your telementoring program easier and more successful. By incorporating both real-time communication via IM and time-shifted communication via wall posts or forum discussions, you can tailor a program that fits the needs of everyone involved.

Do your research before you embark on a new venture and make sure that the service you are using provides data portability and security that is appropriate to your needs and is as customizable as you would need it to be. Since almost all of the services that I have discussed in this chapter are completely free, at least for a basic account, you do not have to concern yourself with out-of-pocket monetary issues, but you do need to consider the amount of time that it will take to learn a new application. Most of the widely used Web 2.0 applications are popular because they are so easy to use, but what makes sense to one person may be baffling to another, so keep ease of use and the learning curve for your team members in mind.

With a bit of research, some planning and a willingness to experiment, you can take a Web 2.0 site and make it work for your purposes. The ability to communicate in many different ways and through many different time zones can be used to your advantage in a telementoring program.

REFERENCES

Facebook. (n.d.). *Statistics*. Retrieved April 2009, 2009, from Facebook: http://www.facebook.com/press/info.php?statistics

O'Reilly, T. (2005, 09 30). *What Is web 2.0*. Retrieved 04 25, 2009, from O'Reilly Media: http://www.oreillynet.com/pub/a/oreilly/tim/news/2005/09/30/what-is-web-20.html

Oech, A. V. (2009, Feb 19). *850,000 Social Networks on Ning!* Retrieved April 25, 2009, from Ning Blog: http://blog.ning.com/2009/02/850000-social-networks-on-ning.html

Wikipedia. (n.d.). *Cloud computing*. Retrieved April 25, 2009, from Wikipedia: http://en.wikipedia.org/wiki/Cloud_computing

ADDITIONAL READING

Bouwman, H., & Van Dijk, A. G. M. J., Van Den Hooff, B., &Van De Wijngaert, L. (2005). *Information and Communication Technology in Organizations: Adoption, Implementation, Use and Effects*. Thousand Oaks, CA: Sage Publications Ltd.

Branon, R. F., & Essex, C. (2001, January). Synchronous and asynchronous communication tools in distance education. *TechTrends, 45*, 36. doi:10.1007/BF02763377

Caton, M. (2006, December 18). Culture of Sharing is Possible. *eWeek*, 37.

Clark, R. C., & Kwinn, A. (2007). *The New Virtual Classroom: Evidence-based Guidelines for Synchronous e-Learning (Pfeiffer Essential Resources for Training and HR Professionals)*. Washington, D.C.: Pfeiffer.

Finkelstein, J. E. (2006). *Learning in Real Time: Synchronous Teaching and Learning Online (Online Teaching and Learning Series (OTL))*. San Francisco: Jossey-Bass.

Goldberg, M. (n.d.). *WebCT.com Library: Synchronous vs. Asynchronous: Some Thoughts*. Retrieved April 28, 2009, from http://www.webct.com/service/ViewContent?contentID=2339346

Hargadon, S. (2009). "Microblogging: It's Not Just Twitter." *School Library Journal* 55, no. 2: 15-15. *MasterFILE Premier*, EBSCO*host* (accessed April 21, 2009).

iCohere, J. A. (n.d.). *Synchronous and Asynchronous Communication Tools - Articles - Publications and Resources - ASAE & The Center for Association Leadership*. Retrieved April 28, 2009, from http://www.asaecenter.org/PublicationsResources/articledetail.cfm?ItemNumber=13572

Jin, S. H. (2005). Analyzing Student-Student And Student-Instructor Interaction Through Multiple Communication Tools In Web-Based Learning. *International Journal of Instructional Media*, 59–67.

Konijn & Barnes. (2008). *Mediated Interpersonal Communication*. New York: Routledge.

(n.a.) 1998. *Communication and Collaboration in the Online Classroom: Examples and Applications (JB - Anker Series)*. San Francisco: Jossey-Bass.

(n.a.) 2005. *Web and Communication Technologies and Internet-Related Social Issues - HSI 2005: 3rd International Conference on Human-Society@Internet, Tokyo, Japan,... (Lecture Notes in Computer Science)*. New York: Springer.

Niehues, J. (2004). *The use of (a)synchronous communication tools in e-learning*. Marburg: GRIN

Pan, C.-C., & Sullivan, M. (2005, September 1). Promoting synchronous interaction in an eLearning Environment [Technological Horizons In Education]. *T.H.E. Journal*, 27–30.

Park, J. (2007). Interpersonal and Affective Communication In Synchronous Online Discourse. *The Library Quarterly, 77,* 133–155. doi:10.1086/517841

Sapenov, K. (n.d.). *Cloud Computing Wiki.* Retrieved February 21, 2009, from sites.google.com/site/cloudcomputingwiki

Wikipedia. (n.d.). *Cloud computing.* Retrieved April 25, 2009, from Wikipedia: http://en.wikipedia.org/wiki/Cloud_computing

Chapter 13
Web 2.0 for Tele-Mentoring

Shari McCurdy Smith
University of Illinois at Springfield, USA

Najmuddin Shaik
University of Illinois Urbana-Champaign, USA

Emily Welch Boles
University of Illinois at Springfield, USA

ABSTRACT

Web 2.0 technologies are designed to be open, flexible, and collaborative offering many tools to support traditional or non-traditional tele-mentoring activities. The benefit of effortless sharing and connectivity comes with challenges in how we view such things as ownership, privacy, and duplicity. The Web 2.0 toolkit includes applications for web-based note-taking, shared documents, feedback, reflection, informal discussion, and presentation. The collaborative opportunities provided by mashable, social networking platforms allow users to flex time, geography, and projects. Professional educators continue to inform their practice and explore new ways to meet the needs of students. Web 2.0 technologies can support educational professionals by opening doors and classrooms world-wide. The chapter makes a comparison between online and mentoring instructional practice and highlights models for educational use of and aids in identification of tools for mentors and mentees.

INTRODUCTION

It is our challenge as teachers to create meaningful engaged learning experiences for students. We look for better ways to build connections in disciplines, learning outcomes, and the real world. Often the search centers on technology. When incorporating technology into an engaged learning process, educators must be willing to adjust or experiment with various applications and technology tools to determine what will best work for a given curriculum objective. (Bowen, 2000) However, the task of locating, acquiring and using technology in the classroom has, traditionally, been both time consuming and complex. If a classroom teacher were to employ technology, the room, equipment, software, operating system, and/or license were all potential barriers to success and a prudent use of time. Barriers such as browser compatibility, platform dependence, lack of home

DOI: 10.4018/978-1-61520-861-6.ch013

or school computing resources, and time often waylaid; and, over time, taught that technology adaption, whatever it was, was not worth the risk.

Fortunately, the last fifteen years has brought rapid and lasting change. The Internet helped classroom teachers overcome many barriers by making the right software and equipment easier to find. As Internet access increased, schools implemented interdisciplinary curricula and themes around Internet-based technologies. A driving force of this change was the opportunity to use authentic tasks and collaborate in learning communities in a constructivist approach to learning. Project based learning became far easier for students to accomplish using the resources of the web. Such projects "ask students to perform challenging and authentic tasks, align curriculum, instruction, and assessment into one seamless experience" (Jones, Valdez, Nowakowski, & Rasmussen, 1995).

In January 2001, the online encyclopedia Wikipedia was developed by Ward Cunningham and Richard Stillman. The encyclopedia was successfully built due to its use of several very important features; open content including open editing, no cost, and the global reach of the web (Wikipedia, History of Wikipedia, 2009). Openness in cost, geography, and contribution allowed users to easily contribute to the site leading to its rapid growth. Additional websites developed around networks and communities of users. They included MySpace in 2003 and Flickr in 2004. This community model of web site development takes advantage of the "wisdom of the crowd" or the taking into account collective opinion rather than a single expert to answer a question (Wikipedia, Wisdom of the Crowd, 2009). These principles plus the technical ability to present formerly server related functions into the user's browser combined to create what many described as Web 2.0. The origin of the term Web 2.0 is credited to Tim O'Reilly but a proper definition of what this term really entails is frequently debated (O'Reilly, 2005). In a February 2007 JISC Tech Watch, Paul Anderson points out that Tim O'Reilly was really trying to describe a set of benchmarks to tell whether or not a company was Web 1.0 or Web 2.0 when the term became a buzzword for blogs, wikis, and social connects (Anderson, 2007). Whatever its definition, open development at no or low cost, and virtually connected social communities came to define a new model for the web. Web content was still a top-down distribution model until the appearance of Web 2.0 tools and technologies. With Web 2.0, barrier free applications and user-friend technology is possible as the Web rather than a server, is the stage for applications and interactions (Asmus, Bonner, Esterhay, Lechner, & Rentfrow, 2005). Capabilities of Web 2.0 as described by O'Reilly embrace the following:

- user control of their own content
- web-based applications are services to buy not own
- applications are perfected and update, and continually changed
- applications are built from and with the help of users
- applications have classifications developed by users
- applications and services can be distributed
- access is open and uncontrolled
- shaped and assembled to new purpose
- innovation (Adobe, 2005)

These competencies have been employed in the development of a host of products designed to benefit communication and relationship building over a distance. Educational circles are now examining how to best take advantage of these competencies for learning. Certainly one of the most meaningful is the use of Web 2.0 in support of social media technologies.

The easily recognizable promise of social technologies has helped moved discussion of their use to the forefront of most educational journals, papers, and conferences. However, the recognition of benefit does not mean these tools

Web 2.0 for Tele-Mentoring

are being implemented in the classroom. Whether Web-based or desktop, issues that act as barriers to adoption still exist. Considering the many applications, software packages, and tools developed for K-12 instruction, it is difficult and time consuming to know what tools are available, how to select tools, and what works best for a given situation. Web 2.0's rapid development causes even more difficulty; the larger the pool of useful applications, the more complex the decision. We need a way to shape our understanding and, perhaps, give ourselves permission to narrow our focus.

This chapter highlights the role new learning environments and Web 2.0 tools have in supporting mentoring relationships; illustrates similarities between online course facilitation and tele-mentoring in establishing and maintaining a successful experience for both the mentor and the mentee; discusses the changing learning environment and, offers ways to select and think about the application of Web 2.0 tools for distance education and mentoring. Finally, we conclude by outlining free suites of tools that can be implemented in incremental and effective ways for distance mentoring. Professional educators continually inform their practice and explore new ways to meet the needs of students and new avenues for improvement. We present a direct course to employing Web 2.0 tools in professional mentoring.

BACKGROUND: THE PATH WELL-TRAVELED, WHERE TECHNOLOGY IS AND HAS BEEN

Some background is useful to appreciate the value of applications which reside on the web rather than on the computer. Software describes any of the applications which operate a computer. In essence, software is what you can do on a computer. Types of computer software include:

- application software used to perform tasks or operations
- system software used to support other applications
- middleware negotiates between system and application software as in converting file formats
- utility software applications used to fix or repair other software applications

The operating system (OS) of your computer manages all the application software of your computer except the boot or startup applications. The operating system performs a number of critical tasks for the user behind the scenes. Operating systems manage requests from devices such as printers, scanners, and modems, determine the order that application processes should be processed and internal memory requirements for each process, and allocate the resources of the processor in dual processor environments.

Often, users do not take full advantage of the functionality software applications. This is true for computer professionals, teachers, doctors, lawyers, and nearly everyone else. Whether for lack of time or knowledge, software applications and functions go untouched or undiscovered. The best approach to expanding your knowledge and use of application software is to try out a new function each day. If you continue to push yourself and use what you've learned, you will expand your repertoire of knowledge. The key to remembering what you learn is, of course, using it. The same is true of Web 2.0 tools. The more you use them, the more comfortable you will become.

The cost of implementing a technology often equates to more than just time spent in understanding how to use it. In 2002 the Panel on the Impact of Information Technology on the Future of the Research University observed, "individual human beings cannot modify their behavior with respect to technology as rapidly as the technology itself is changing." (Bruggeman, Hernandez, & Marcus, 2002) For web-based tools especially, the open source movement has meant even the technologies we know well change more rapidly than we can handle making it increasingly difficult to keep current. In addition, when technology moves online, new and old adoption risks and implementation problems follow. An understanding of what is needed to make online delivery of instruction effective is not intuitive. Skills that worked well face-to-face rarely transition to a distance without some modification; though assumptions, perhaps based upon a sense of engagement felt with popular media such as Television, falsely suggest otherwise.

Not long ago the Internet was an excellent resource to find, review, and download a variety of software applications. The main skill required was determining how much you would have to pay for what you found. Software was available on the Internet as freeware meaning no charge to use, to own or download the software; or as Shareware which means available for download for a trial period but if you decide to keep and use the software you are required to pay a nominal fee to the owner of the software after a set period of time. Software for sale on the Internet could be purchased through a web site as a download. For an additional fee, the manufacturer would ship a CD-Rom copy of the software to you. Much of this software was available on a try-before-you-buy basis. Sometimes the free demo version of the software would be all you'd need to create something for your class and you would not even need to buy the software. Demo versions of the software sometimes came to you as incomplete, meaning that the functionality was reduced so you might not be able to save or print, etc. Problems with this model included: OS matching, how to store the license and media, bandwidth to download and store the application, ownership, and maintenance of the software license (keeping up to date on the latest versions). Web 2.0 has changed all of this.

Web 2.0 tools have several benefits for educators. The 2008 Horizon Report noted sweeping changes in the expense and availability of web-based tools will strengthen collaborative networks for educators. The report notes recent developments in word processing suite tools such as Zoho Office (www.zoho.com) and Google Docs and Spreadsheets (www.docs.google.com) have made group work and actions surrounding collaborative tasks easier to develop, inexpensive or free, and platform independent (New Media Group, 2008).

The web-based ease of communicating ideas can have a profound effect on mentoring relationships referred to as tele-mentoring when convened over a distance. Anderson predicts, "The social aspects of the Web's topological interconnectedness are becoming increasingly important and indeed this may be the most important long-term trend" (Anderson, 2007).

Tim O'Reilly describes Web 2.0 this way, "None of the trappings of the old software industry are present. No scheduled software releases, just continuous improvement. No licensing or sale, just usage. No porting to different platforms so that customers can run the software on their own equipment, just a massively scalable collection of commodity PCs running open source operating systems plus homegrown applications and utilities that no one outside the company ever gets to see" (O'Reilly, 2005). Often when trying to define Web 2.0, a comparison is made between Web 1.0, where pages simply displayed information and Web 2.0, where data can be moved, changed, or manipulated. Many of the changes which brought about what O'Reilly described happened over the course of just five-eight years. Popular and defining Web 2.0 themes of harvesting the "wisdom of the crowd", providing easy ways to self-publishing, and opportunities to create social networks began with the Google Search Engine in 1996. Google used a unique link/request criteria based on popularity to display search results. In 1999, Blogger offered an easy and organized web-based publishing tool which meant anyone in the world could publish and share content on the web. In 2003, MySpace took the web publishing one step further by offering people an opportunity to link to others and create networks of friends within a single website.

Most of this action occurs directly on the web page, without purchasing software or even installing an application. It is accomplished much more quickly and without complicated coding through a web development programming language called AJAX. AJAX stands for Asynchronous JavaScript + XML (Garrett, 2005). Though not solely what powers Web 2.0 applications, it is the behind the scene engine that creates many of the applications defined as Web 2.0. Using a combination of web development techniques, data is retrieved in the background from a server asynchronously without interrupting the user's page display. This is a huge change from what had been possible prior to Web 2.0.

In addition to the ease with which applications can retrieve information, Web 2.0 technologies deliver on the spread of information. Really Simple Syndication (RSS) links many Web 2.0 applications and has changed the nature of web use. Instead of going to a site to check what updates have been posted, web users can use the information contained in an RSS document to have the information delivered to their desktop or cell phone. RSS uses a web programming language called XML to describe the site. This enables a variety of tools to access and manipulate the "feed" or RSS document. RSS offers web visitors a chance to subscribe to frequently updated information and have the information come or be fed to a single site. RSS has three components: sites which *provide* content descriptive RSS files; RSS aggregators that *read* RSS files; and *viewing* applications sometimes called Headline Readers because users can click on the headlines displayed by the RSS reader to view the information on the content providers site.

In addition to syndication, Web 2.0 takes advantage of open code, online services, and interoperability to create entirely new applications called Mashups. As described earlier, open code is a foundational concept of Web 2.0. Some of the first Web 2.0 applications posted their underlying code so that other developers could help improve the application. The openness of development process often led to better applications and could bridge different knowledge and abilities. New development breakthrough continue to form through open code; and, in addition, new applications are being developed by combining applications and data in new ways. This process is referred to as Mashups. Examples of mashups include: combining census data with maps, pictures with social networking sites, and applications built to help consumers locate specific items such as popular video games or electronics. Mashups are fairly easy to create allowing new mashup applications to be posted to the web every day. More often than not, the applications developed are useful but not profitable. However, for education, mashups offer the unique potential to combine disciplines and information in unusual ways. For distance mentors and online facilitators, mashups can provide engaging activities and inventive uses of data.

LITERATURE REVIEW: PARALLELS IN MENTORING ONLINE IN WEB-BASED DELIVERY

Mentoring has been described as a "planned pairing" of the skilled with the lesser-skilled to achieve purposeful outcomes, personal development and growth (Nefstead, S. & Nefstead, S., 2005). Due to the complex and resource heavy nature of the world around us, businesses and institutions are finding new motivation for establishing mentoring relationships on many levels. Knowledge needs coupled with scare resources set up ripe conditions for looking to outside assistance to answer needs for training or within an educational setting. All learners are looking for real examples and better ways to gain the specialized skills necessary for success in a completive economy. In *Passionate Voices*, a blog digest for Tech & Learning, Ryan Bretag describes what he heard students say about education in the 21st Century. Bretag reports students value "making global connections, interacting with professionals (biologists, authors, etc), and breaking down the walls of the classroom" (Bretag, 2009).

Web 2.0 technologies provide additional opportunity to mentoring relationships at a distance than have been available in the past. Mentoring is an experience of multiple conversations; mentor and mentee; teacher and mentor; teacher and mentee. These conversations happen in many ways and over a period of time. Web 2.0 tools can support the mentoring process by offering multiple channels for online interaction. Tools are currently available to support asynchronous and synchronous discussion, shared documents, feedback, reflection, informal discussion, and presentation. The collaborative opportunities provided by Organizers, Browser add-ons, Shared Start pages, Storage, and Communication applications make time, geography, and projects far easier to organize, share, and manage.

Relationships are central to successful mentoring partnerships. Illustrative of the importance of interaction and communication in mentoring, mentoring literature and research often looks for ways to evaluate and define intervals of communication structure in the relationship. A key aspect to building any successful relationship centers on providing for and even structuring appropriate communication. This is especially true for distance education and mentoring relationships. In order to establish bonds for support, people must have avenues for communication. The need for an instructional process which supports opportunities for presenting ideas, offering guidance, instruction, practice, and assessment exist in distance education communication as well as in mentor relationships. A review of literature finds similar conversational themes exist in both fields. The importance of progressively changing and timely communication, relevant inquiry, opportunities for expression and constructing knowledge reside in the literature of each field.

Progressively Changing and Timely Discourse

In their 1993 study, Maynard and Furlong outline five distinct stages of development and "focal concern" beginning educators go though as they learn to teach: early idealism, personal survival, dealing with difficulties, the plateau, and moving on. They describe new teachers as beginning their teaching practice most focused on their role and performance as teachers. With time and outside help, new teachers can 'de-centre' to view the learning needs of their students. Not surprisingly, the needs of new student teachers and what they are ready to learn changes over time (Maynard & Furlong, 1993). This view of the application of knowledge by student teachers surely transfers to what all mentees experience as they work with outside professionals in mentoring relationships. Expectations and needs are not static. They evolve and change over time depending upon the viewpoint of the participants. This means the type of communication and interaction taking place in a mentoring relationship also evolves. In distant or tele-mentoring relationships, it is import to choose technologies which will support the different stages of the relationship and foster new avenues for communication for any given point in the relationship. In a shared teaching practice which involved online class collaborations, faculty from two distinct institutions emphasized the need to find the right communication at the right time (McCurdy & Schroeder, 2005). There is no substitute for communicating thoughts and needs in a timely manner whether in an online course or a mentoring relationship. The realization that relationships evolve over time, depend upon time, and move forward must be present, acknowledged, and supported by the practices of the participants.

Relevant Inquiry

The relationship and experience of being mentored can have a residual effect for the mentee which can be used to sustain success and a positive self-image (Evans, Wilson, Hansson, & Hungerford, 1997). The shared experiences and successes can be recalled and adapted to answer additional needs down the road. In online learning, comfort and familiarity with web-based functions occur through actual use. If the mentoring relationship includes successful experiences which involve web-based technologies, as they must in tele-mentoring, mentees will also become more comfortable using Internet resources such as email, library databases, search engines, media, and other web tools to acquire knowledge, solve problems, and inform thought in future activities. Inquiry-based learning first introduced by John Dewey includes active verbs such as designing, connecting, and investigating. Web 2.0 tools provide the space and the means to support inquiry in a tele-mentoring relationship which can transfer to active use at other times in the mentee's experience.

Opportunities for Expression

A strong mentoring experience would seem to need a complicated mix of keen relationship skills, availability, and shared expectations. Hawkey describes four distinct approaches research into student teacher mentoring has taken. The four approaches included examining the level of expertise in comparison to the roles and responsibilities of the participants; studying the developmental stages and developing models to meet each stage; viewing the interpersonal stages of relationships rather than professional; and, finally, focusing on the unique aspects of the individuals involved in a mentoring relationship and the roles perspectives, assumptions, and values they bring to the task and how these help to shape what develops (Hawkey, 1997). These many approaches are testament to the complicated interplay and interactions that occur between people as they exchange knowledge, grow, and depend upon each other to fulfill the promise or purpose of the mentorship. A mentoring relationship needs a commitment of time; but,

is not an unselfish act on the part of the mentor; as with teaching itself, the ideas and discoveries of a good mentoring relationship are a two-way street with the mentor learning as much or more from the mentee (Tobin, 2004). Capturing and sharing ideas for the benefit of all and in the right way is an important aspect of the mentorship and the online classroom. In face-to-face mentoring, ideas are formed through hallway conversation, resource sharing, and in an exchange of youth and experience that is gratifying to both parties as practice is changed and ideas are tested. Tele-mentoring relationships should contain ways to enhance the collaborative presentation of ideas on both sides in formal and informal ways.

Constructing Knowledge

Hawkey suggests "Maynard and Furlong's conceptualization is useful when considering how best to structure a course of ITE (Initial Teacher Education), for understanding the possible responses and reactions of student teachers as they move through the course, and for alerting mentors to the different styles of activities that may be appropriate for their mentees at different points during their course." (Hawkey, 1997) An understanding that mentorship involves stages or points of contact and expectations is fundamental as one develops the relationship with tools and activates at a distance. When viewed as a building process, a planned selection of different tasks and tools to support the stages of learning and emotional readiness is more manageable. In any distance mentoring relationship, mentoring or teaching, it would seem important to apply a number of different activities and means of engagement in order to mimic the nature of face-to-face activities and to meet the expectations of the mentee or student at different points in the relationship. Through the application of differing Web 2.0 tools, the mentor can be present and supportive to the mentor on a number of different levels.

Online learning is as recent as the Internet itself; however, distance education has a long history with many studies covering its effectiveness. Perhaps due to the shortness of its history, studies into the effectiveness and differences between online learning and on-campus learning are sometimes conflicting. In 1999, Dr. Thomas Russell made headlines after studying more than 400 studies of distance education methods and reporting there exists generally "no significant difference" in effectiveness of distance and classroom instruction. Institutions of higher learning look to this report when asked if online learning is as good as campus-based instruction (Hirst, 2000). More recent research in the field has found a higher indication of social interaction online than on-ground (Nesler & Hanner, 2001); a much smaller level of dropouts in an electronic classroom than in a traditional classroom, and those online students are better at handing in papers on time (Stinson & Claus, 2000). Because interaction and communication is separated by space and time in an online classroom, learning relies heavily on technology and proper pedagogy. The same constraints on interaction and communication exist in a distance mentoring relationship with a similar reliance on proper tools and structure. Best practices from online learning appear relevant to the tele-mentoring experience.

Timely and Progressively Changing Communication

Similarities in delivery, roles, and expectations exist between online instruction and tele-mentoring. Best practices and research of the two disciplines can inform practitioners on both sides. O'Neill and Gomez observed tele-mentoring needs "purposeful orchestration." They also outlined three fundamental aspects of tele-mentoring; timeliness, visibility, and sensitivity to roles and limits of the roles (O'Neill & Gomez, 1998). These factors also greatly influence the success in the distant education classroom. Shearer (2003) observed the importance in timely interaction in the online classroom. Collis (1998) reports the importance of content, learning resource, communication, and technology-use flexibility among other aspects. Dallos and Comley-Ross observed five themes important to children when describing characteristic of their mentoring experience; good mentor, good relationship, attachment, building trust, and facilitating change. The last, facilitating change, consisted of listening, providing validation, offering acceptance, and above all creating change. (Dallos & Comley-Ross, 2005) An online virtual learning community requires members to be "committed to the learning process, and responsive to the contributions of other participants through 'reciprocity' based on trust between the community members" (Garber, 2004). In order to gain mutual respect and trust at a distance, communication needs to be flexible, timely and meet established expectations.

Inquiry and Validating Efforts through Feedback

Garrison, Anderson, and Archer report the distinguishing feature of online learning as opposed to earlier distance education delivery methods is the ability to create communities of inquiry. Inquiry and interaction create opportunities for engaging the participants to express and convey concerns, learning, and theories of their own (Garrison, Anderson, & Archer, 2003). Moore defined three types of interaction in distance education: learner-to-content, learner-to-learner, and learner-to-instructor (Moore, 1989). Timely attention to all three types of interaction (feedback) is vital to a creating a successful online learning experience for students and instructors. Content, when presented in a digital manner, needs to be easily manipulated and readily understood. The lack of non-verbal cues and the sometimes complex interpretations demanded of a text-heavy learning environment make interaction, in the form of feedback, particularly central to the distance classroom. Faculty would like to confirm their knowledge and facilitation matter and their instruction is understood. Students desire reassurance that their work is correct and valued. In addition, students benefit from multiple layers of targeted feedback. Tools can be developed which will collect, summarize, and display all types of data (not just assessments) to students for their own self-reflection and evaluation and to faculty for intervention and guidance. All feedback received by students influence their learning in some way (Jerome, Rinderle & Bajzek, 2008). Feedback in a mentoring relationship is not necessarily assignment specific. However, mentees are looking for signs of falsehood in the relationship and are very sensitive to how the mentor reacts or refers to the mentee. What is said and done (and not done) is critical to building trust: Especially at the start of the mentoring program, "actions speak louder. (Dallos & Comley-Ross, 2005) In distance instruction and mentoring, timely, two-way conversations; periods of inquiry-based discussion, honest representation; and sincere appreciation and validation of work and ideas are the best ways to bridge the gaps necessarily brought about by distance delivery methods.

Be Present: Opportunities for Interaction and Expression

Students have good and bad online experiences just as they do in on-campus classrooms. The quality of teaching, the learning environment and time constraints affect students in online and on campus courses. For online students, the level of teacher interaction, peer-to-peer interaction, and ease of navigation of online classes affects the success of the experience. A 2000 study by the State Universities of New York (SUNY) showed interaction to be an important factor to student satisfaction in online classes. The SUNY study found, "The greater the percentage of the course grade that was based on discussion; the more students thought they learned, the more satisfied they were, and the more interaction they thought they had with instructors and peers"(Fredericksen, Pickett & Shea, 2000). However, it is important to note research has suggested, interaction on the part of students is an individual need. The value students place on interaction in an online course can vary depending upon learning styles or individual personalities (Su, Bonk, Magjuka, Liu & Lee, 2005).

Constructing their own Knowledge

Barcena and Read (2004) describe educational cognitive technology as descriptive in nature and emphasizing thinking, remembering, understanding, and communication and list this theory as the starting point of the popular constructivist movement. Constructivism states knowledge must be "constructed rather than transferred intact" (Dwyer, Ringstaff & Sandholz, 1991). Constructivism is replacing drill and practice and teacher-centered methods of learning in many disciplines. Drill and practice often applies best in rote memory activities such as multiplication tables, spelling, or timelines of historical information. Conversely, an emphasis on the practical application of knowledge rather than on rote learning could better prepare students for complex problem-solving they will face in the future. Jacqueline and Martin Brooks describe the five key principles of constructivism as:

1. Pose problems of emerging relevance to learners
2. Structure learning around "big" ideas or concepts
3. Seek and place value on the student's point of view
4. Adapt curriculum to address student's suppositions
5. Assess student learning n the context of the teaching (Brooks & Brooks, 2004)

Constructivist learning is based on the experience of the learner; learners interpret what they are shown from their own experiences. The instructor's role is one of facilitator helping the student find circumstances or ways of piecing together knowledge. It is this emphasis on student-centered knowledge gathering that creates an opportunity for technology to play such an important role in the constructivist movement highlighted in education today. In constructivism, the instructor's role is to use various technologies and instructional activities that will deepen learner understanding of the subject matter as well as critical reflection and analysis skills." (Su, et al., 2005) The shear array of technologies available within Web 2.0 tools makes the task of gathering a variety of resources for various individual needs much more achievable. In fact, suites of tools, located within a single site, exist that compliment various needs and learning styles. In addition, Web 2.0 technologies support students in initiating their own gathering, sorting, investigating, compiling, simulating, and exploring. With control of their own learning, they can construct meaning based upon their own unique experiences and constructs. Information is coupled through their own hands in ways they assimilate making the learning outcome relevant and memorable. Web 2.0 aids in shifting the engagement of learner; moving the students from passive to active participants. Metacognition, the ability to direct and adjust one's own learning strategy, is a goal of both Instructional Technology and education. Knowledge independence supported by Web 2.0 tools can make this happen on a daily basis for online instructors or tele-mentors.

Two key web-based technologies have been the mainstays of interaction in the online learning classroom; the asynchronous discussion board and the synchronous chat. The discussion board is an integral part of online education as it allows for asynchronous communication between classmates and between students and the instructor. Threaded discussions take place in a forum or conversational theme. The staggered displayed, entry-listed threading of the conversation means you can view and post your ideas or comments to any point and any time in the thread. The conversation within the discussion board builds a community of learners in the course site that would not exist in a correspondence course. Community and engagement on the part of students and instructor is built through daily interaction. This is especially true in the first few weeks of a class. By inference, tele-mentors have a better chance of building a trusted community if the interactions, whether in email, text, or chat, are equally active. In the online classroom, facilitators are encouraged to establish the practice of conversation via the discussion boards through response modeling and frequent interaction. Tele-mentors would seem to benefit from the same approach.

The development of synchronous chat products changed the flavor of the online classroom bringing instant texted communication but sacrificing the "anywhere, anytime" nature of online learning. Though Web 2.0 technology, light weight chat products can now be run through a browser without installing an full application to the desktop. As they do in the online classroom, chat tools can provide mentors and mentees access and an instant touch-point if both parties have Internet access, via phone or computer, and are online at the same time. In the online classroom, formal chat sessions work best when they are scheduled well in advance. Informal access via chat is frequently used for office hours and by appointment. Tele-mentors who can establish set times to be online will give mentees an opportunity to gain fast answers to questions and, perhaps, an additional avenue for expression.

While discussion boards and chat rooms have been the principle means of interaction in the online classroom, at times the interactions can seem to lack the "realness" or character of true conversations. Students have reported exchanges did not seem "natural" if you cannot hear or see the other's responses (Su, et al., 2005). Web 2.0 technologies are beginning to bridge this gap and provide opportunities to see, hear, and share that are comparable to the "real" world. These changes have the potential to bring online learning to new audiences and levels of acceptance. In its 2009 report, the University Continuing Education Association suggests the popularity of Web 2.0 tools could be changing long held opinions regarding the value of online learning (UCEA, 2009).

MOVING TO WEB 2.0: USER GENERATED CONTENT AND A SINGLE LEARNING ENVIRONMENT

As illustrated by Maynard and Furlong the numerous changing dynamics of interaction in a mentoring relationship require a mix of tools and techniques. However, when finding new ways to interact online, there are challenges involved that should be identified and overcome through careful planning. The first challenge to overcome is of variety. On-ground, how we approach or set up conversations flows naturally from meetings and chance happenstance. Online interactions are forced to be more purposeful to even occur. By incorporating social networking tools that support frequent adaptation, tele-mentoring teams can make meetings and conversation happen more easily. A second challenge is that of confusion. Shifting often between different websites in order to find useful tools to track emails, set up appointments, or review collaborative products can be difficult to follow. The more often users shift from site to site to communicate the higher the likelihood of confusion, uncertainty, and perhaps missed communication. Unifying all communication tools to a single location or URL means the users never have to guess as to where the communication and interaction will take place. There is great value in addressing potential confusion on where interactions will take place but also in keeping or storing all information in a central location. To address this important concern, we focus our chapter on case studies of Web 2.0 sites which offer a variety of applications for communication, interaction, presentation, construction, and inquiry through a single portal or login. Additionally, the collaborative nature of online instruction and tele-mentoring activities must be flexible; however, it is often hard to know what tool is best for what type of activities. Models and taxonomies are available to help educators identify and focus efforts in choosing the best technologies for the desired outcome or purpose. Some helpful examples follow.

The ASSURE model (Heinich, Molenda, Russell & Smaldino, 2002) was originally used as a procedural guide when introducing technology into a lesson planning. ASSURE is an acronym for the first letter of each action word of the model; Analyze, State, Select, Utilize, Require, Evaluation. The model helps to "assure" media use is appropriate to the task and the audience. The model does not require a great deal of planning and with practice the model and stages of questions become automatic. The ASSURE steps are particularly effective in helping instructors prevent time wasting activities such as no printer hook ups, no file space, and light reflection. It can also illustrate misapplication of or incorrect preparation of technology. The guide was originally developed for classroom use; however, the criteria established can be translated to use with Web 2.0 tools and tele-mentoring activities as follows.

Analyze Learners. Who will be using the technology? What skill or experience do they have with web-based tools? Are learning styles important? Will the users have ready access to the web? When? How? Has the mentee developed a new skill or area of interest

State Objectives. Every mentoring experience needs to have clear and well-defined goals. What are the goals of the tele-mentoring experience? Considering these goals, what Web 2.0 tool best supports the learning objectives and tasks? What purpose, performance, or task is to be assigned? What type of communication? What type of information gathering? What Quality/ Quantity measures should be included? Has or will the mentoring objective(s) changed over time? How is this change reflected in the objectives?

Select Media Should the interaction be public or private? Do we need a record or archive of the events? What types of controls are necessary? Is the information subject to comment or copyright compliance? How will the selected media support interaction and/or feedback?

Utilize Media. If it was a classroom, this would be where you state what you need to do to set up the projector for all to see and hear, the preparation needed for the technology, etc. For web-based tools the questions are more value based. Do students need to create individual accounts? Do we want to register or record this material as part of our school? Do we need file storage space to store video or audio files before uploading? Do we need a microphone, web camera, or speakers?

Require Learner Participation. How do we insure tele-mentoring participants are attentive to the objectives and meet their goals?

Evaluation and Revise. How well did this work? What do the participants, both mentee and mentor say about the media and methods used? Did the media enhanced the interaction and relationship or distracted from it?

Distance or classroom technology integration takes into account considerations such as how the technology connects with curriculum and other activities, the known time frames, learning styles, and how activities including content knowledge and technology skills will be assessed. Whenever technology is involved, but especially at a distance, planning, practice, and reflection are essential components of success. The following steps can prove helpful in planning on ground or web-based educational technology activities and are outline in Lynn Rhone's 6 Step Design plan (Rhone, 1995).

1. Identify concepts or objective.
2. Plan the performance tasks linking the instruction and activity with the performance assessment
3. Choose a technology supporting the integrated curriculum theme and/or to the objectives.
4. Allow time to work with the technology using appropriate tasks, equipment, or manipulative.
5. Allow time to reflect/record or share products.
6. Allow time for explanation and sharing.

Bruce and Levin (1997) propose a catalog of educational technologies uses based on John Dewey's natural learning impulses. Existing instructional taxonomy models were based on hardware or software features, or instructional models. Levin and Bruce selected natural learning impulses. Their taxonomy areas can be used to catalog technologies and vary their use in the classroom. Whether web-based or classroom-based, learning and mentoring can strive to provide an opportunity to equally develop and use various technologies in all four classifications. "A taxonomy can be a productive step in the process of understanding and explaining what we see by organizing perceptions into categories if we are able to see the familiar in new ways or if we are able to cope with a confusing array of phenomena." (Bruce & Levin, 1997) The four areas of the Bruce/Levin taxonomy include: technology as media for inquiry, technology as media for communication, technology as media for construction, technology as media for expression. Currently available Web 2.0 technologies under each category are listed in the Appendix of this Chapter. To the extent possible, tele-mentoring activities should take advantage of the taxonomy to provide opportunities and experiences to participants that support the role and relationship needs at the time and take advantage of variety of technology tools available.

As individuals engaged in learning, students need to be given clear instructions and expectations. From the beginning of a class or an interaction, students and instructors must agree on behavior and the correct use of technology. Most important to any integration of technologies is an open mind. Technology can fail at the most inopportune time but a new answer, a new approach, or a new tool can almost always be found.

CASE STUDIES: LEARNING ENVIRONMENTS FOR WEB 2.0

The volume of and access to information acquired in the last 15 years is staggering. The impact is far-reaching and has changed our lives and culture. No longer are employees expected to stay with the same company for 30 years. "The psychological employment contract between firms and workers has altered. In the not too distant Past, workers used to be more connected to their positions and their employers working for a single firm for long periods of time. Today employees move freely between jobs" (Sullivan & Emerson, 2000). The Department of Labor reports young baby boomers, those born between 1957-64, held 10.8 jobs from age 18-42; many (almost two-thirds) were held from the ages of 18-27 (Department of Labor, 2008). This represents quite a few career changes even if you account for the temporary jobs most college age students held during that time period. Workers outside of the traditional career model, who have "boundary-less careers," are becoming the norm rather than the exception (Arthur & Rousseau, 1996).

Global economies, mobile students and workers, and single world events shape our world with immediacy unprecedented in generations past. Always available and boundless information shapes us more than we realize. For many web users today, relevance is paramount and waiting unacceptable. Because it is so easy to obtain, facts matter less than knowing how those facts will impact the world. In addition, technology is not an add-on to today's classroom any more than it is an extra in the world of commerce or government or communication. Students are using GPS to map hazards in their communities, twittering to gather real world data, and exploring the educational uses of cell phones. (Bafile, 2009) Today, information is rarely controlled by a single source. Emphasis is placed on obtaining needed information from a host of different sources rather than hearing unrequested information at a time specified by others. In the world just described, we owe students more than just an opportunity to receive and practice rote memorization of facts. Students have resources in their pockets to help them navigate the many information sources and questions they have. They should not be expected to work within a framework built for a different time.

Long and Holeton (2009) suggest classroom spaces and much of education as we know it is still designed around the industrial model of "strict rules, regimented behavior, identical curricula and expectations for all students, and an emphasis on basic skills of literacy and numeracy" (Long & Holeton, 2009). Students know this factory model of education will not prepare them for the jobs they will have. Michael Wesch, points out the injustice of designing instruction around a world we no longer have. He suggests, "Most of our classrooms were built under the assumption that information is scarce and hard to find... a physical manifestation of the all too pervasive yet narrow and naïve assumption that to learn is simply to acquire information, built for teachers to effectively carry out the relatively simple task of conveying information" (Wesch, 2008). Wesch's description of a "sage on the stage lecture hall" illustrates the failure of learning environments both physical and virtual if they do not take advantage of the collaborative and lifelong nature of learning. In constructing online learning spaces, to revert back to times where classrooms housed teachers who transferred knowledge instead of making it, is to deny students the opportunity to prepare for the world where knowledge is widely available. Instead, we should build flexible spaces where knowledge can live, move, build, change, and thrive.

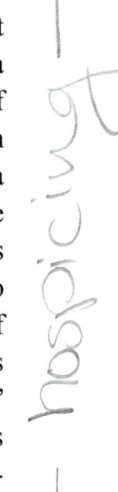

Environment matters whether we are learning about plumbing, practicing to be a trial lawyer, or taking a test. In online classroom research summary Karen Swan describes varies studies which emphasize the importance of the environment to outcomes. Shea (2003) found teaching presence including design and organization of information is linked to student learning. Mayer (2001) found learning transferred better when components of concepts were addressed first and when the pace was learner controlled. Parker and Germino (2001) and Picciano (2002) suggest online discussions might be more supportive of divergent thinking, exploration, experimentation, and reflection than face-to-face discussions (Swan, 2004). Soloway, Jackson, Klein, Quintana, Reed, Spitulnik, Stratford, Studer, Jul, Eng & Scala (1996) described the software needs of learners in three categories: provide growth, allowing the student to "learn how while doing"; address diversity in culture, gender, thought, etc.; and, provide motivation. The confluence of Web 2.0 technologies, strategic agendas, diverse learners, new course design methods, and discoveries in learning informs how we think about virtual and physical learning spaces (Jorn, Whiteside & Duin, 2009). Focusing our efforts on building an environment in which students control their tasks and can move easily from one task to another; work independently or in a group; meet new people and discover new idea, and where information is stored or easily obtained, can improve the experience of learning and, most-likely, the results. Jaffe suggests, "As new virtual learning environments are introduced, it is worth asking to what extent these environments will represent a pedagogical ecology that either reinforces or alters these institutionalized pedagogical roles and behaviors" (Jaffe, 2003). In a New York Times article reflecting on the 25th anniversary of The National Commission on Excellence in Education "A Nation At Risk", Richard Hersh advocates, in a world where everything is connected and collaborative, there is a need for more "knowledge, intellectual horsepower, rigor, and deep thinking than has been associated with education in the past" (Hersh, 2009).

As we design learning environments for tele-mentoring, we need to offer a number of channels for expression and interaction so that mentors and mentees can have the high-'touch' necessary to grow a strong bond and relationship. Web 2.0's flexible, open code, designed or inspired by a community of user for collaboration and sharing provides just the type of environment needed to maneuver through a sea of information or willow ideas down to concrete plans. Tele-mentoring participants can take advantage of this environment to explore more, with greater frequency, and perhaps for a longer period of time than they could if they were relating in a traditional face-to-face setting. Terry Andersen describes his experience with supporting student learning at a distance as this following:

Over the years, in my own distance teaching, I have been informally polling students about the relative advantage and disadvantage of various forms of mediated and face-to-face, synchronous and asynchronous, educational activities. From these polls, I conclude that there is a wide range of need and preference for different combinations of paced and un-paced, synchronous and asynchronous activity, and also a strong desire for variety and exposure to different modes and modularities of educational provision and activity. (Anderson, 2003)

By setting roles and expectations at the onset; combining useful tools into a single learning environment shaped to different relational and interactive needs; and applying technologies that support specific educational goals of expression, inquiry, construction, or communication, we can strengthen tele-mentoring partnerships, lessen the psychological distance, and provide individualized support to those who seek to learn from experience. For beginners looking to incrementally adopt a technology platform for tele-mentoring, the Ning social networking platform is a solid choice. It offers many tools integrated into a single interface and login.

CASE STUDY: NING SOCIAL NETWORKING SITE

Ning is a free, flexible platform to create both public and private online social networks. Unlike other online networks such as Facebook, MySpace, or LinkedIn, in which you create a profile and then associate yourself with groups, causes or other people, Ning lets you design the entire social network around your interest. Anyone can create a Ning about any topic, and people join Ning social networks based on similar interests rather than existing, "real world" relationships. More than four thousand Ning networks are created each month, and the company reported 4.7 million unique visitors in January 2009 (Ning, Inc., 2009).

Ning CEO Nina Binachini says that she and Marc Andreesen founded the company to help people form networks and meet new people around their interests and passions. They were inspired to create Ning "by the first wave of Internet companies truly native to the Web" that were built "around people connecting to other people" (Chen, 2009). Bianchini also notes that "Niche social networking sites are absolutely something people want to do... They […] look around and say, 'I want a social network for this particular group'" (Chen, 2009).

Many education-related groups have a presence on Ning, including Humanities, Arts, Science, and Technology Advanced Collaboratory (HASTAC), Educause Learning Initiative (ELI), and the New Century Learning Consortium (NCLC). The movement of existing human networks into social networking sites illustrates an important concept that Boyd and Ellison (2007) discuss in their review of the state of scholarship on social network sites, "What makes social network sites unique is not that they allow individuals to meet strangers, but rather that they enable users to articulate and make visible their social networks." In addition to allowing users to recreate existing relationships and networks online, Ning lets users connect with new people around their interests.

Though scholarly research on tele-mentoring and social networking sites is limited, the body of research in computer-mediated communication in education, as well as research on other social networking sites, certainly applies. Hewitt and Forte (2006) found that a third of students "did not believe that faculty should be present on Facebook at all." The notion that students or mentees may be resentful of intrusion into popular social networking sites makes the use of Ning an appealing option. The self-contained nature of Ning could help students to separate academic and social presences online.

Hawkey's observation that multiple types of activities may be appropriate during various stages of the mentoring relationship suggests that a flexible technology should be employed in tele-mentoring (1997). Choosing a broad social networking tool like Ning allows for incremental and easy adoption of new tools, as well as multiple modalities for learning and communication, as the needs of the mentoring relationship change. Ning consists of many interactive Web2.0 tools, and simplifies the process of including external technologies tools by housing them in a single location, like a virtual toolbox for tele-mentoring.

Since its release in February 2007, the Ning platform has expanded to include many tools, including photo and video sharing, chat, forums, and more. Ning joined the OpenSocial movement in October 2008. OpenSocial is an open source movement that works to allow social networking platforms to integrate (McCarthy, 2008). Ning OpenSocial application support makes it possible to build and submit your own gadget, or include other's applications on your personal profile, or "My Page." The free applications range from Twitter Tracker, a way to track your favorite tags across Twitter, to Emote, a graphical status message tool, and from RSS, a tool to mash and display RSS feeds, to Gmail Chat, which allows you to chat with Gmail friends within Ning.

Creating a Ning social network is a simple process that does not require any knowledge of programming or HTML. First, create your Ning ID at http://www.ning.com. After that, it is an easy process of selecting a Web address, choosing the tools you will use, and selecting a visual theme. Ning uses an easy drag and drop interface for selecting and arranging the tools. The tools range from synchronous (Chat) and synchronous (Forum) discussion tools to media sharing (Photo, Video, Music, Blog) to organization (Events, Notes, Pages). These tools form the framework for enabling inquiry-based learning and your tele-mentoring relationship. A large variety of themes – more than fifty – are available. Each theme may be customized further using the graphical interface, or, for more advanced users, cascading style sheets.

Once you have created your Ning, you have many opportunities to customize the network to fit your educational and mentoring goals. Ning network creators may modify the taxonomy used to describe tools. By changing the naming conventions in the Language Editor tool, labels for tools, buttons, and activity logs are changed site-wide. Customizing naming conventions to match your educational purpose can help to reinforce the purpose of mentoring activities. Additionally, Ning navigation can be customized to match the mentoring activities taking place in each area.

Explore the tools available in Ning with a critical eye. Consider the four categories of educational technologies defined by Bruce and Levin (1997) – inquiry, communication, construction, and expression. Levin and Bruce's taxonomy can help determine which technologies to use for specific stages in the learning process. Also keep the ASSURE model in mind to make sure the chosen tools are implemented successfully and are appropriate for your mentee and the tasks at hand. The tools you choose should facilitate the interpersonal relationship between mentor and mentee, and allow mentees to create content, interpret experiences, and generate knowledge.

COMMUNICATION TOOLS

Ning Forum

The Forum tool allows all users to create and reply to asynchronous discussion and upload files. You can choose to follow individual forums, and receive email notifications when any one posts a comment or reply. Network members can also choose to follow the entire Forum tool, and receive email notification any time a new forum is created.

Email/Messaging

Ning Messages is an internal email system. The Messages tool protects your email account from other members of the network. When you receive a message through Ning, it automatically sends a notification to the email account associated with your Ning account. Through the Ning applications available on your My Page area, you can integrate your Yahoo Mail and Gmail accounts.

Chat

Ning contains a basic chat tool, using plain text plus a few emoticons. The tool is accessed through the status bar of your Web browser. The chat tool can "pop out" and become a separate browser window, or it can remained anchored at the bottom of the page. Though chat is often used for administrative functions and information sharing, Reynard (2008) promotes using chat for moving critical thinking processes forward. Through the Ning Applications features, users can also integrate the more powerful Yahoo! Chat, as well as Gmail chat.

Comments

Comments can be enabled on nearly every feature within Ning. Enabling comments allows any user to post text-based replies to other users comments. The Comments tool can effectively transform Pages and Notes tools from technologies for creating content to technologies for communication and dialogue.

TOOLS TO CREATE, PUBLISH, & PRESENT CONTENT

Ning Pages

Ning Pages are places where administrators can generate and format content using HTML. The Pages feature is currently an administrator-only tool by default. Network owners can delegate administrator privileges to individual tools, such as Pages, to other members of the network.

Ning Notes

Ning Notes is an internal wiki tool Ning. Users can very easily link pages to one another. The tool does not require any HTML knowledge; it allows formatting through a basic WYSIWYG (What You See Is What Your Get) editor. Again, this is a default administrator-only tool that can be delegated to users.

Ning Blog

By default, every member of a Ning network has a blog for posting anything they like -- sharing articles, journaling, or sharing issues on which they would like feedback. Ning blogs automatically have comments enabled to support dialog between members.

Ning Photos and Flickr Integration

A photo upload and sharing tool is integrated in Ning. Every user can upload, share, display, tag, and comment on photos. Photos can be uploaded in bulk, and played in a slideshow format. Ning also allows users to add and display images from their Flickr photo sharing account and to submit photos by phone or email. Ning will display slide shows of member photos.

Ning Music

Ning's Music tool allows uploading of 100.mp3 audio files. The Music tool allows members to share songs, audio recordings, original music, and interviews, significantly expanding presentation and sharing capabilities of the site.

Ning Video

The Ning Video tools allow members to easily upload videos up to 100 MB in size in the.mov,.mpg,.avi,.wmv and.3gp file formats. Videos may also be uploaded via phone or email. Ning Video also support the embedding of YouTube, Google videos, and SlideShare/Slidecast presentations using the embed code feature. More information on ShareShare is available in the Google Applications Suite section.

TOOLS TO ORGANIZE & SHARE CONTENT

RSS Ning Application

The RSS application allows you to mash and display up to five RSS feeds on your My Page profile area. The application is an excellent to aggregate news and research. Two RSS feeds to consider including for research purposes are Google Alerts and Delicious. Google Alerts, a tool that updates an RSS feed with the newest

Google search results for the criteria you select. Delicious creates an RSS feed for every keyword, or tag, used to describe a Web site. Essentially, Delicious feeds can be considered a filtered or refined search based on articles and Web sites that other Delicious users have found relevant.

Tagging in Ning

Whenever a piece of content (photo, video, page, note, etc.) is added to Ning, the author can add tags. A tag is "a non-hierarchical keyword or term assigned to a piece of information" ("Tag," 2009). Tags help content to be located more easily through searches.

Text Boxes on My Page

The Text Box tool in the My Page area for each user will allow them to embed tag clouds from Delicious social bookmarking (http://delicious.com) and many other types of content including YouTube videos, images, Word documents, and more.

Box.net Ning Application

The Box.net application allows you to upload and share all types of files in Ning. If you do not already have a Box.net account, the Ning application prompts you to register.

Google Services Ning Application

By adding the Google Services application to your My Page profile, you can integrate the benefits of myriad Google tools into your Ning network, including Search, Maps, Blogger, Gmail, and Chat. These applications are discussed in detail in the Google Applications Suite section.

Measurement & Analysis Tools

Assessing both quantitative and qualitative use of your Ning social network is fairly simple. For easy collection and analysis of quantitative data, you can include Google Analytics, a free data collection tool. Google Analytics provides easy-to-read charts and graphs that show you when users visited, what pages they accessed, and how they navigated your Ning. The service is easily incorporated in Ning through the Analytics tool under the Manage tab.

For a more qualitative view of the communication tool choices and the nature of interactions, review the "My Page" feature of Ning. Each participant's page on the Ning contains their "Latest Activity," a running tally of their network usage as an RSS feed. Since each user is able to choose what activity is tracked through this feature, you will need to ask all your network members to enable tracking of the interactions you wish to monitor. Privacy options may be changed under user settings.

Conclusion/Synthesis

Much as Bruce and Levin (1997) suggest that technologies should not be classified by type (synchronous v. asynchronous), rather by the step in the learning process the technology enables (inquiry, communication, construction, expression); educators should focus on teaching transferable technology skills rather than specific software applications. Nielsen (2007) emphasizes that "Schools should teach deep, strategic computer insights that can't be learned from reading a manual." Through implementing Ning social networking sites to facilitate your tele-mentoring experiences, you are also giving your mentee useful technical proficiencies with increasingly common tools like wikis, blogs, and RSS, as well as professional abilities like search strategies, digital information evaluation, and presentation skills.

Though Ning can help you provide many opportunities to your mentees, it is not without its problems. The textbox editor is not robust, which can limit customization opportunities for some users. The basic Ning framework is free, but some supplemental services, such as premium support, additional storage and bandwidth, and removing context-sensitive advertisements, are fee-based services. Additionally, as with many Web 2.0 tools, you are storing your data on a remote server and sometimes give up sole copyright ownership of materials you upload. Free Web 2.0 services may be taken offline at any time, which is a risk you need to consider before adopting the technology. Are you going to keep duplicate records offline? Does it matter if you lose the materials? Often the benefits of using social web tools outweigh adverse consequences.

COMPLEMENTARY TOOLS

Elluminate vRoom

Elluminate's vRoom is free and easy-to-use web-conferencing tool for up to three people. Sign up for an account at http://www.elluminate.com/vroom/register.go, and add your vRoom link to Ning. During web conferences, you can employ tools such as voice chat, white boards, web site tours, and audience polling features.

SELECTED GUIDES FOR GETTING STARTED

- Social Networking in Plain English - http://www.commoncraft.com/video-social-networking
- Control Your Privacy on Ning - http://help.ning.com/cgi-bin/ning.cfg/php/enduser/std_adp.php?p_sid=3gisfEwj&p_faqid=3562
- Create Your Perfect Social Network on Ning - http://help.ning.com/cgi-bin/ning.cfg/php/enduser/std_adp.php?p_sid=3gisfEwj&p_faqid=3562
- Safety on Ning - http://about.ning.com/safety.php

CASE STUDY: GOOGLE APPLICATIONS SUITE AND SUPPORTING APPLICATIONS

Web 2.0 is the second generation Web that facilitates communication, collaboration, construction, and sharing of information on the Internet. It is the new business model (O'Riley, 2005). The education community, responding to the growing needs of 'Digital Natives', is embracing Web 2.0 by gradually introducing Web 2.0 tools and leveraging the power of blogs, wikis, folksonomies, and social networks in their campus environments. It is therefore appropriate that the platform and tools to support Tele-mentoring are built around the core competencies of Web 2.0 identified by O'Riley (2005), including software as services, software that is above the level of a single device, users as co-developers of content, harnessing the power of collective intelligence, leveraging the long trail, lightweight user interfaces, and promoting the creation of data sets that gets richer as more people use them. Another important factor to consider is to select services that are reliable, convenient, easy-to-learn, people-centric, scalable, and device-ready.

Web 2.0 is also leading the trend towards 'Cloud Computing' as an efficient and low cost alternative to the high-cost in-house IT services. Amazon has been aggressively expanding its marketing presence on the Internet by expanding the portfolio of its web services (Roush, 2005) and sharing revenue with many small and independent internet businesses through the Amazon Affiliate advertising program. Amazon Web Services are a collection of services and include web services such as the Amazon Elastic Compute Cloud (Amazon EC2), Amazon Simple Storage

Service (Amazon S3), Amazon SimpleDB, Amazon DevPay, Amazon Flexible Payments Service (Amazon FPS), Amazon Fulfillment Web Service (Amazon FWS), Amazon Simple Queue Service (Amazon SQS), and the Amazon Associates Web Service. Similar services are also offered by Amazon's competitors such as Google, Microsoft, and Salesforce.com.

Google is a dominant Web 2.0 Internet company and has been maintaining its market position by offering a variety of web services such as the popular Google Search Engine and numerous gadgets. Unlike Amazon, Google offers free web services to its customers and generates revenue streams from online advertisements. Google has been a pioneer in cloud computing. Google's hardware architecture, operating system components, and software programming methodologies have accelerated Google's development and deployment of cloud-based applications. Both Google and third parties have written a wide variety of gadgets that include RSS feeds, Blogs, Google Services, Google applications, News, Games etc. Even though Google offers a large collection of services and applications, it does not provide all the tools and services required for Tele-mentoring. It is therefore necessary to supplement Google Apps with services and tools from other Web 2.0 service providers.

Google Apps is a collection of web-based applications that run in a web browser and are based on the notion of software as services rather than as a product. Software as services model takes away the responsibility for software updates and maintenance from the institutional IT department, freeing IT staff from a considerable amount of software support. Instead, educational institutions will be able to focus on creative ways to use Web 2.0 technologies and services to support Tele-mentoring activities. The goal of Google Apps is to facilitate collaboration, peer review, and knowledge creation by harnessing the functionality and power of Google services from a single domain. The collection includes communication tools (Gmail, Google Talk, and Google Calendar), collaboration tools (Google Docs: text files, spreadsheets, and presentations; Google Video, and Google Sites), a customizable home page (iGoogle), develop web pages (Google Sites), work offline mode (Google Gears), administration features and APIs (for integration with existing systems), and add-on on security and compliance software (to be purchased at a discount). The central component of Google Apps is Gmail which integrates well with other Google applications such as Google Docs, Talk and voice chat, and Google Calendar.

Google Apps comes in multiple flavors in terms of enhanced functionality. The Starter Edition and the Standard Edition are both ad-supported and free to users. They are sufficient for individuals and small organizations. The Premier Edition has more storage, additional functions, and includes technical support but there is a per-user charge. The Education Edition is free to educational institutions and combines features from the Standard and Premier editions and includes communication tools, productivity tools, a customizable home page, and administration features. It is a widely deployed hosted application suite among K-12 and Higher-Ed institutions (Google Inc, 2009a). For example University of Southern California use their USC password to log into Google's applications through the USC gateway or authentication system while maintaining their@usc.edu email name (University of Southern California, 2009). An active Gmail (http://mail.google.com) account is required to use the Google applications. Having a Gmail account gives easy access to variety of Google applications and resources. Users can then create a customized home page with their choice of Google applications for easy access to Google services.

iGoogle

iGoogle is Google's customized landing page system that allows you to create your personalized home page. A customized homepage is a not a new concept. MyWay (http://www.myway.com/), MyYahoo (http://my.yahoo.com/) and others also provide a personal portal. What makes iGoogle better than the competitors? Like all browser applications, iGoogle is available to you wherever you have access to the Internet and it is supported by the market power of Google.

The process of creating a customized home page is simple. You do not have to be proficient in HTML or Internet programming language to create a customized home page. You go to http://www.google.com/ig to get started. Select topics of your interest, a theme for the home page. Google will customize the information that appears on your page based on your geographic location with the Google web search engine at the top of the home page. You are ready to launch your home page. To save your home page for access later from any web browser you need to have a Google Gmail account. With an active Gmail account, you can customize your homepage however you like and as often as you want.

The current iGoogle version features the revised design with the navigation on the left side of the page with links to the user's gadgets. The iGoogle's canvas feature allows a gadget to maximize to the size of the screen for a full-page experience when the user clicks on the navigation link. Multiple tables allow you to organize the home page based on your interests. iGoogle interface uses drag-and-drop feature for easy customization of the home page. You can pick and choose which gadgets to display by searching through thousands of gadgets and move them by dragging and dropping on the home page. Subscribing to RSS feeds works similar to gadgets. You can also add feeds and gadgets by surfing the Internet and if you find a gadget or feed that you like you can subscribe via RSS. Gadgets come with the standard option to edit, delete, and minimize the gadget. You can also group gadgets by category to minimize clutter on the web page.

Google has been a relative late comer to the Social Networking circuit. A social networking website enables people with common interests to build a 'trusted' online community with the help of online communication and collaboration tools. Critics of Google argue that iGoogle is based on Web 1.0 architecture offering nothing more than a glorified home page with a simple design customized with numerous gadgets. Even though gadgets are useful and helpful, the underlying architecture of iGoogle is not much different from Google's competitors. This is a valid and justifiable criticism against Google because social networking and the user-generated content defines Web 2.0. The suite of Google applications and gadgets consisting of Gmail, Google docs, Google base, Google Talk, Adsense, Adword, Orkut, Picassa, You tube, iGoogle, blogspot, blogger.com, API etc., constitute basic components of a social network but iGoogle needs to be more social to be treated as a social network. In response to such criticism, Google began to look at the relational links among friends to make iGoogle a customizable personal social network. With social gadgets, iGoogle can become a personalized homepage with social features and a new level of connectivity and interactions. Not all gadgets need to have social features. Only a few selected gadgets could allow sharing information with friends. To make iGoogle a launching point into social-networking applications. Google began to ask the following questions (Francisco, 2009):

- How can you connect with your friends?
- Can you play a game with a friend?
- Can you see comments that your friends are leaving on different blogs?
- Can you connect to their Picasa photo albums?

The current version of iGoogle includes the chat functionality via Gmail as a base for a social network to allow for a more social experience. Google generates social graph through Gmail user contacts. Google does not ask users to build and confirm their social graph. The social graph is generated automatically for the users. All user contacts via Gmail are added to your address book and some of those contacts with frequent emails are identified as friends to be included in each other's Google Talk. Google is also supporting OpenSocial API for writing social gadgets and OpenSocial applications with a social component to tap into iGoogle's social graph created through Gmail user contacts. Google intends to make the OpenSocial applications of iGoogle available in the near future. This will provide users with the option to opt-in to share information with their contacts, see what those contacts are doing across other Google services, share Google Reader subscriptions, gadgets, Picasa photos, Talk status messages, and iGoogle themes. For example, a books gadget could display what a user's friends are reading, allow users to request to borrow books from friends' libraries, and show users books that their friends recently rated.

COMMUNICATION TOOLS

After creating a personal home page on Google Networks using iGoogle and storing it with Google user account, the next step is to customize the home page with gadgets which support communication among friends and buddies. Popular modes of communication include the asynchronous email and the synchronous text and audio chat services supplemented with video streaming.

Gmail or Google Mail

Gmail is a free POP3 and IMAP webmail service provided by Google with a relatively larger storage capacity than its competitors. Gmail is part of Google Apps and runs on Google Servlet Engine and Google GFE/1.3 which run on Linux (Gmail, 2009). Google is not alone. Hotmail and Yahoo! also offer free email hosting services. That is the hidden cost customers pay for access to free email services in terms of intrusive advertisements and spam. Gmail puts contextual advertising next to the emails you read. Gmail serves as a passport to various Google services. Gmail has a search-oriented interface and a "conversation view" similar to an Internet forum. The interface is simple and elegant and supports keyboard shortcuts and fast operation. Gmail supports search operators such as labels and attachments. Search operations are efficient except when searching for single email. Gmail is also handy with organizing, tracking and recording users' contact lists. For instance, typing the letter D into the "To" field in Gmail will bring up a list of email address and contact name starting with the letter D. A useful feature when you can't quite remember a contact's name. Gmail saves all your email exchanges as one link in your inbox, and automatically adds and updates email addresses and names to the contact list from your emails. When you click the link, you get all the correspondence with that person in a list, similar to the threads in a message board. Google's offline mode is another useful feature because it enables users to do the majority of their Gmail triage in Offline mode and then sync up later when it is more convenient.

GTalk or Google Talk [Instant Messaging] *(discontinued)*

Google Talk is Google's approach to instant communications using Google Talk network and is available to users with Gmail account. Google Talk is a full-fledged IM client based on the Open Extensible Messaging and Presence Protocol (XMPP) also know as Jabber, with added VoIP functionality, and a complete integration with Gmail. It is Google's late entry into IM and VoIP and a direct competition to MSN Messenger, Yahoo Messenger and Skype. Since Google Talk network is based on open protocol, users can communicate with their buddies on other XMPP-compliant programs, such as GAIM, iChat, Earthlink, etc. Though it lacks video, Google Talk offers text and voice messaging services, a user-friendly interface with standard features including the ability to add contacts from Gmail, notification of new messages to Gmail inbox, real-time availability and status of online buddies when you are signed into Google Talk. Google would like to see IM and VOIP partners to support inter-service communications similar to the phone company model, because the choice of service provider should not affect who you can communicate with. According to Google (Google Inc, 2009b),

"Google's mission is to make the world's information universally accessible and useful. Google Talk, which enables users to instantly communicate with friends, family, and colleagues via voice calls and instant messaging, reflects our belief that communications should be accessible and useful as well. We're committed to open communications standards, and want to offer Google Talk users and users of other service providers alike the flexibility to choose which clients, service providers, and platforms they use for their communication needs."

Google Wave [Apache Wave] → discontinued

Google Wave (http://wave.google.com/) developed by brothers Lars and Jens Rasmussen with Stephanie Hannon is a new communication platform (Siegler, 2009). It is an online communication and collaboration service that combines Gmail and Google Docs into a free-form workspace to create documents collaboratively, communicate and work together with richly formatted text, photos, videos, and maps. According to Lars Rasmussen (Google Inc, 2009d),

"In Google Wave you create a wave and add people to it. Everyone on your wave can use richly formatted text, photos, gadgets, and even feeds from other sources on the web. They can insert a reply or edit the wave directly. It's concurrent rich-text editing, where you see on your screen nearly instantly what your fellow collaborators are typing in your wave. That means Google Wave is just as well suited for quick messages as for persistent content -- it allows for both collaboration and communication. You can also use "playback" to rewind the wave to see how it evolved."

A Wave is a balanced mix of conversation and document. A Wave inbox looks like email inbox but the replies are embedded to the original message interleaved at the paragraph level (O'Reilly, 2009). According to O'Reilly (2009), "A key point here is that Google's relentless focus on reducing the latency of online actions is bringing the online experience closer and closer to our real world experience of face-to-face communication."

COMPLEMENTARY TOOLS TO COMMUNICATE

Twitter and BeTwittered

Twitter (http://twitter.com/) is a free social networking and micro-blogging service described as the IM or SMS for grown-ups to communicate with family and friends known as followers and also includes the option to broadcast to all users. You need to sign up for Twitter to use the service. There are similar micro-blogging services within corporations as closed networks with access restricted to members only to maintain privacy and security of communications. Twitter enables users of this service to send and receive text-based posts of up to 140 characters in length, known as tweets. Users can send and receive tweets via the Twitter website, IM, as a Short Message Service (SMS) alert to a mobile, or via third-party applications. The service is free for Internet users but phone service provider may charge fees for SMS users. Tweets are delivered to the followers and also displayed on user profile pages. BeTwittered and the mobile version gadgets are Twitter clients for users to keep in touch or just follow what others are doing. BeTwittered has all of the expected Twitter features, including the option to view replies, direct messages, public timeline, detail about the sender, the application it was sent from, and send a reply (reTweet), or a direct message. The characteristic short text format of the tweet is useful for informal collaboration and quick information sharing among team members. It can also be used for formative evaluation or initial feedback between the mentor and team.

Meebo Chat *discontinued*

Meebo (http://www.meebo.com/) is a free Ajax-based in-browser instant messaging (IM) program based on the free and open source library, lib-purple. Compared to other IM platforms, Meebo has a number of unique features. A unique feature of Meebo is that it synchronizes multiple social and instant messaging platforms such as AOL Instant Messenger, MSN Messenger, Yahoo! Messenger,.NET Messenger Service, Google Talk, AIM, ICQ, MySpaceIM, Facebook Chat, and Jabber in a single Web browser interface, enabling seamless chat between multiple circles of friends in Meebo Rooms granting a degree of control to the user with invite and ban authority, all with a single sign-on. Another unique feature of Meebo is that it allows instant messaging from any web-browser anywhere without any software downloads or installs. It is an elegant solution to the problem of having multiple interoperable IM accounts requiring different software downloads. What is also unique about Meebo chat service is that it does not require participants to have an account with any IM service to chat in the in the Meebo room, even though it highly recommends participants to have a Meebo account to benefit from services provided to its members such as saving chat logs and conversations. To access the chat service, you login with your screen name and password. Once connected your buddy list appears in the right-side window. Users with IM account across multiple IM service providers will have their buddy list merged into a single list that includes your buddy name and their service provider IM icon. The Meebo chat widget can be embedded into any home page or blog and the Meebo Platform gives developers' access to Meebo's open APIs to create widgets centered on audio and video sharing, and gaming applications to support collaboration and real-time interactions among its users. Up till now, the IM space was defined by the leading IM services providers such as AIM, MSN Messenger and Yahoo! Messenger. Meebo has taken the lead by synchronizing IM services among multiple social web communities and offering users the flexibility to choose clients, service providers, and platforms for their communication needs. According to Meebo CEO Seth Sternberg,

"If Google is search, YouTube is video and Facebook is a social utility, then Meebo aims to be live interaction. These multiplayer games will make the Meebo experience more fun and give our users new ways to connect live with their buddies." (Alexander, 2007)

Tools to Create, Publish, & Present content

A personal homepage with communication gadgets such as Gmail, GoogleTalk, Twitter, and Meebo support basic interactions and communications. The level of communication and interactions is enriched if users have access to tools to create content and share with family, friends and community members such as Google Docs, Blog, and SlideShare.

Google Scholar Beta

For those who are unable or reluctant to use the library's research databases or consult the research librarian, preferring the simplicity of online searches, Google Scholar is the best alternative.

It is freely accessible to academic institutions providing useful resource for the general public, and all those who may not have access to, or are affiliated with, an academic institution. Google Scholar searches across multiple databases that contain scholarly content and is offered as a search tool for academic professionals. Google Scholar is a subset of the larger Google search index and uses the familiar uncluttered Google interface. According to Google (2009c) Google Scholar enables you to search for scholarly literature across multiple disciplines and sources including: "peer-reviewed papers, theses, books, abstracts and articles, from academic publishers, professional societies, preprint repositories, universities and other scholarly organizations." It is fast and easy to use. Although Google Scholar covers a great range of topical areas, it appears to be strongest in the sciences, particularly medicine, and secondarily in the social sciences. The articles are sorted by weighing the full text of each article, the author, the publication in which the article appears, and how often the piece has been cited in other scholarly literature. It is based on the famous PageRank criteria used in Google searches. The most relevant results appear on the top. Next to each publication is a link to other publications that cite it to enable users to determine whether a paper is influential and who it has influenced. Google's Advanced Scholar feature allows users to search specific journals, authors, and date ranges to customize and narrow the search parameters. Searches can lead to a number of freely accessible online versions of many scholarly publications which is very useful to many academic researchers with limited or no access to expensive journal articles databases.

Google Docs

Google Docs is a free, web-based suite of productivity tools offered by Google as an Internet hosted service to create, store, share, and collaboratively work in real-time on word processing documents, spreadsheets, presentations and online forms. It consists of Google Documents, Google Spreadsheets, and Google Presentations. The proprietary Microsoft Office suite applications support a large set of office functions but are limited to the desktop experience and do not support real-time online collaboration. Compared to Microsoft Office, Google Docs offers a limited set of functions but support real-time online collaborations. Google Docs was originally based on Writely and Spreadsheets services which were merged into a single product. It is similar to Microsoft proprietary SharePoint application (Google Docs, 2009). Google added basic drawing functionality to Google Docs, to allow users to add graphical elements such as org charts or diagrams to their online word-processing documents, spreadsheets, and presentations. This feature does offer several useful illustration tools that can be used within Google Docs' multi-author collaborative framework. Google Docs is integration with Google Gears to enable users to edit their documents offline. From the "Share" tab option, you enter the email addresses of users you would like to view or collaborate on the document. An email with the link is sent to the collaborator(s) which means you do not have to email the document as an attached file to the users who then have to download the document and make changes to the document and email it back to you. Manually keeping track of the changes to the document is not a trivial task. Document changes are automatically tracked. Publishing it on the web for the team to view is just a click away.

Google Translate

Google Translate is an automated machine translation application that can be used to translate words, phrases, entire Web pages from one language to another, and perform cross-language searches by using the Google online translation services. Google Translate supports up to 40 plus languages and new languages are added on a regular basis. The goal is to make making information universally accessible. It is a free online language translation service offered to all users with access to Internet and a standard browser. Users are not required to have a Google account. Google Translate service works very well and provides reliable service most of the time. Since it is a machine translation system, it does not deliver 100% accurate translations all the time. Other translation services such as Babel Fish, AOL, and Yahoo! use SYSTRAN, a rule-based translation system that applies grammatical rules to generate the translation. The algorithms of Google's proprietary translation software are based on statistical analysis and are not rule-based. Sometimes the translation might lack the correct grammar and punctuation, but the readers can still get the general context of the foreign language text (Google Translate, 2009). Google is aware of the challenge:

"Even today's most sophisticated software, however, doesn't approach the fluency of a native speaker or possess the skill of a professional translator. Automatic translation is very difficult, as the meaning of words depends on the context in which they're used. While we are working on the problem, it may be some time before anyone can offer human quality translations. In the interim, we hope you find the service we provide useful for most purposes." (Google Inc, 2009)

Google Reader & Google Reader Mobile *discontinued*

Google Reader is a browser-based online news aggregator developed by Google and supports both the RSS and ATOM feed types. It has a user-friendly conversation-like interface, a powerful search engine, and allows for feeds and links to be shared. Google Translate's auto-detect function automatically translates feed's in over 40 different languages to your preferred language. Users with interest in multi-cultural and international issues will find the Google Translate function very useful because it allows them to subscribe and read from blogs in other languages without worrying about copying and pasting the text into a separate translation tool. In conjunction with the Google Gears, Google Reader supports both online and offline modes while maintaining the state of user feed reading experience across PC and mobile devices. With a server based application like this, users are not required to manage their OPML files across platforms.

To get started with Google Reader, go to http://google.com/reader and login with your Gmail account. If you already have a collection of RSS feeds, Google Reader will import OMPL files with their links into their pre-determined folders very efficiently. There are a number of ways to add feeds. You can find RSS feeds manually searching web sites, by entering the URL and have Google Reader find the RSS feed for you, use the keyword search function to find feeds from its built in directory, or subscribe from a pre-selected bundles of feeds organized by themes. To help manage the large selection of RSS feeds, the folder function comes in handy to organize the feeds into groups by themes. Similar to Gmail, the title of the feeds are presented as a list for a quick and easy review of the title and headline, with the option to click the title for an expanded view to read the entire story. Google Reader uses the "River of News" paradigm in its listing of the titles of recent feeds in the order received (Winer, 2005). You can share feeds and links publicly or with family and friends by tagging feed with the "share" flag. You can also use Gmail to email the feed with your comments. Another feature that most users find useful is the compilation of trends of Google Reader usage. Users get an idea of what feed they are reading the most, the percentage of articles they have read from a feed, and an analytical graph detailing the frequency of usage. The trend feature is useful to analyze your reading pattern and decide which feeds you want to continue to subscribe to.

Google Videos [discontinued]

Google Video (http://video.google.com/) is a free video sharing website and also a video search engine from Google similar to YouTube. It offers a large archive of freely searchable videos. Google Video searches include results from YouTube. YouTube provides a large selection of videos and a superior video sharing community than Google Videos.

PicasaWeb [discontinued]

There are a number of photo sharing services such as Flickr (http://www.flickr.com), SmugMug (http://www.SmugMug.com), and Shutterfly (http://www.shutterfly.com). Picasaweb (http://picasaweb.google.com/) is Google's foray into online photo storage. It is designed around a simple interface to organize and share photos Picasaweb does not have a large active social community.. If you only want to store photos online then Picasaweb service will serve your needs, but if you are looking for an active social community and a group experience to share photos then Flickr is the preferred destination because according to Scheinberg (2006), "Picasaweb is a personal experience and flickr is a group one"

COMPLEMENTARY TOOLS TO CREATE, PUBLISH, & PRESENT CONTENT

Blog & BlogTalkRadio

A blog is an online journal comprised of links and content. Blogger is the person who keeps the blog. The process of authoring and updating entries is referred as blogging. The journal entries are displayed in reverse chronological order with the most recent posting displayed at the top. A blog can be on virtually any topic ranging from news and commentary to a personal diary. The content of the blog is syndicated via RSS feeds. A blog generally represents the personal views and opinion of the blogger. The goal is to communicate and interact with the audience and contribute to a healthy debate on issues by inviting reader's participation. Unlike the print medium where someone with editorial privileges edits or filters the content, blog postings and participant comments are all un-filtered. This gives blogs a personal and an informal characteristic as such it is often called "Citizen Journalism." Due to the asynchronous nature of the blog format, bloggers cannot interact with their readers in real-time. BlogTalkRadio is a response to extend the blog to the synchronous radio medium to allow for real-time interaction between the blogger and the audience. It is a social radio network merging the phone technology with Web 2.0 to promote social interactions and user generate content. Using a phone and a computer with an internet connection, hosts can create free, live, call-in talk shows with unlimited participants. The service does not require any software downloads and installs. It is a live broadcast and allows up to five callers at a time. The radio show is automatically archived and made available as podcasts. According to the founder and CEO of BlogTalkRadio, Alan Levy: "BlogTalkRadio is a platform that extends the blog, allowing any individual to host a live blogshow online. Our service is free to all users, whether you host a blogshow or listen in." (Levy, 2007)

SlideShare

So far, preparing and sharing presentations has been limited to the PC desktop environment. Users needed the presentation software and projector screen to share presentation with the audience. There was a need to host the presentation online (in the cloud) and embed presentations within weblog posts. SlideShare (http://www.slideshare.net/) offers the solution, as an online community-based presentation and free hosting service that enables people to exchange ideas and communicate information. There is also a mobile version (m.slideshare.com) for mobile browsers. SlideShare supports various copyright claims including creative commons. Users do not have to email the presentations or carry a copy on a USB drive. Users can search for presentations, view the slides, and if you have a user account you can save or download the presentation. SlideShare is similar to YouTube except instead of sharing videos online, users share presentations online. Microsoft PowerPoint, OpenOffice, and PDF formats are supported by SlideShare. After the presentation is uploaded, it is converted into shockwave/flash format and stored on the web with a permanent URL as a shareable resource. The benefit of the Flash conversion is that users do not need to have the presentation software to view the presentation. One of the drawbacks is that any embedded animations, visual effects, and sound effect are lost in the conversion to Flash which could have an adverse effect on audience attention. Like other social network sharing services, users are able to add tagging, rate, comment, and embed content. The transcripts of your presentation are indexed by internet search engines and listed in search results.

YouTube

YouTube (http://www.youtube.com/) is the most popular Internet video sharing website not only in USA but also throughout the world. Online video existed before YouTube came into vogue, but the creators of YouTube with engineering ingenuity and lots of creativity solved the issues relating to video storage and user experience (Thomas & Buch, 2007). Users with an Internet connection can easily upload and share video clips and view them in MPEG-4 format. The video clips can be shared with family, friends, and the world. Users "tag" their videos with keywords which lets others search videos by keywords. Users are invited to leave comments, pick favorites, send messages, and watch the videos. Users create "playlists" of favorite videos and join communities of users with similar interests. The real strength of YouTube is the members that interact, comment, and post videos creating a social community based on video sharing. YouTube is applauded for supporting individual creativity but it is also accused of promoting plagiarism (Williams, 2009).

Flickr

Flickr (http://www.flickr.com) owned by Yahoo is the largest an online photo sharing site. Flickr provides users to upload and share their photography. Users have a number of options such as organizing photos into categories, tagging with multiple keywords, link photo to a location on the map, create a discussion around a photo pool and share comments. Flickr has a large active social community and it is easy to find someone that share common interests. Flickr has two account options. The Free account includes advertisements and limited options. Users with Pro Account are provided with unlimited storage and bandwidth and ads-free browsing and photo sharing. Like YouTube, Flickr supports individual creativity. The downside of flickr is that unless users protect their photos with a watermark, or Creative Commons license, or restrict viewing to family and friends, anyone can download the photo and use it without proper credits.

Tools to Organize & Share Content

A personal homepage with communication gadgets such as Gmail, GoogleTalk, Meebo, and Twitter support basic communication. The level of communication and interactions are enriched if users have the tools to generate content to share with family, friends and community members.

Google Notebook *discontinued*

Google Notebook is a free online application with sharing and collaboration features for collecting bits and pieces of information as you browse the web, organize and store the information online. It serves like an interactive scratch pad and allows you to write notes, clip text, images, and links from pages during browsing. You organize the information by creating notebooks, which are user created categories, and storing notes and clips within the notebooks. The sharing function enables users publish your notes on the web to share with your collaborators. Besides being easy to use, Google Notebooks also integrated seamlessly with other Google applications such as Google Docs, and Google Bookmarks. You need to have Google account to use the service. It is similar to Furl, Yahoo! MyWeb, and Microsoft OneNote. Since late January 2009 Google stopped active development of Google Notebooks and will not be adding any new features or offer Google Notebook to new users but existing users can continue to add or delete clips in their notebooks as before. But there are many other competing products such as Zoho (http://www.zoho.com/) and EverNote (http://www.evernote.com/) offering similar functionality and the option to import your content from Google Notebook

COMPLEMENTARY TOOLS TO ORGANIZE & SHARE CONTENT

Delicious

The number of Internet web sites runs into zillions and it is growing by leaps and bounds. Users tend to bookmark their favorite web sites because it is difficult if not impossible to memorize the web address. But, bookmarking with your web browser has limitations because the bookmarks are saved on your desktop and are not available from your home computer. For those who have a large number of their favorite web sites bookmarked on multiple computers, it is difficult not only to organize all the bookmarks across browsers, but it is equally difficult to synchronize these bookmarks between multiple computers. Delicious (http://delicious.com/) offers a simple and elegant solution to this problem. Delicious, formerly del.icio.us, pronounced "delicious", is a social bookmarking web service for storing, sharing, and discovering web bookmarks. Bookmarks are organized into categories by tags which are subject keywords. Tagging is one of the important benefits of Delicious. You are not required to follow any official taxonomy to categorize the web site. You tag the web site with keyword(s) of your choose that are meaningful to you and to your peers, which is known as folksonomy. Del.icio.us replaces the inefficient folder system of organization with a system of tags. Each time you save a Del.icio.us page, you can add new tags. If the tag already exists, Del.icio.us will fill in the word as you start to type. Delicious has an add-on for Firefox and Internet Explorer browsers to make it easy to save your bookmarks. To use this service you need to create an account. Delicious allows users to not only create online bookmarks to access them from any browser, but also makes it social by sharing your bookmarks with others unless you choose to make them private. You can see links that others have collected, as well as see who else has bookmarked a specific site, and subscribe to the links of others whose lists you find interesting.

MEASUREMENT & ANALYSIS TOOLS

Google Analytics

Google Analytics is a free web analysis service offered by Google and also comes with Google's customer support. It is a bargain for that price — it is free. Google Analytics is similar to commercial OneStat and SiteTracker applications. The interface is simple, user-friendly, and easy to use. Google Analytics generates performance data on a number of metrics such as Visits, Bounce Rate, Page Views, Most Visited pages, Traffic origins, New Visitors, Returning Visitors, and User Geographic locations. Google Analytics allows administrators to determine what keywords attract the most visitors to their site and which type of promotions generates more traffic and interest in your web site. The performance data can be used to improve the usability of web site by gaining a better understanding of what visitors to the web site want, and also identify poor performing web pages for modification, and help gaining insights into what can improve their conversions. It also includes "Benchmarking" service, which shows how your website compares against similar sites. The comparison generally is based on standard web performance metrics that include Visits, Bounce Rate, Page Views, Most Visited pages, Traffic origins, New Visitors, Returning Visitors, and User Geographic locations against benchmark data from similar participating websites.

COMPLEMENTARY TOOLS FOR MEASUREMENT & ANALYSIS

Publinion Gadget

The Publinion gadget (http://www.googleminiapps.com/3925/tools/publinion-gadget/) is developed by xorstudio.com to help you create surveys online. This gadget can be used to create market research campaigns, gather feedback, and gauge public opinion on topics of general interest.

Selected Guides for Getting Started with Google

- Gmail Help http://mail.google.com/support/?hl=en
- Gmail Tutorial http://services.google.com/apps/resources/overviews/welcome/topic-Mail/index.html
- Google Talk Help http://www.google.com/support/talk/?hl=en
- Gmail User Guide http://mail.google.com/support/bin/answer.py?answer=908771
- Google Talk Tutorial http://services.google.com/apps/resources/overviews/welcome/topicTalk/index.html
- iGoogle Help http://www.google.com/support/websearch/?ctx=web&hl=en
- iGoogle Guide http://services.google.com/apps/resources/overviews/welcome/topic-Welcome/page09.html
- Google Docs Help http://docs.google.com/support/?hl=en
- Google Docs Guide http://services.google.com/apps/resources/overviews/welcome/topicDocs/index.html
- Documents http://docs.google.com/support/bin/static.py?hl=en&page=guide.cs&guide=21008
- Spreadsheet http://docs.google.com/support/bin/static.py?hl=en&page=guide.cs&guide=20322
- Presentations http://docs.google.com/support/bin/static.py?hl=en&page=guide.cs&guide=19431
- Google Reader Help http://www.google.com/support/reader/?hl=en
- How to use Google reader http://www.andywibbels.com/flash/google_reader.htm

ISSUES AND CONCLUSION

Web 2.0 has created new challenges and also opened new opportunities to educational institutions to create teaching and learning environments that also meet the needs of digital natives. Web 2.0 offers a unique platform along with a number of technologies and services to support Tele-mentoring. Ning and the Google Application suite are examples of server-based technologies and services that are free to educational institutions. Google Apps are free but the issue relating to privacy and security of data, reliability of services, nature of the web applications learning curve, and

Web 2.0 for Tele-Mentoring

intrusive advertisements need to be addressed to protect the interests of students, faculty, and staff. Google Apps in general is a powerful collaborative application in many ways than the pricy Microsoft applications but it has a relatively steep learning curve unless you purchase the paid Premier version of the service which comes with additional functionality and Google's customer support (Blum, 2008). Cloud computing is gaining support but like any emerging technology there are unresolved issues such as the reliability of services that need to be addressed by the management. For example, the sudden drop in North American Internet traffic due to Google service blackout left 14% of Google users without a wide variety of practical online services such as Gmail, Google Docs, Maps, Calendar, and Google Search for a few hours (Paul, 2009). Fortunately the Internet did not die due to the Google blackout even though for many users online activities came to a standstill causing lots of confusion during the blackout (Paul, 2009). The outage was resolved and fixed in a few hours but it made us pause and reflect on the wisdom of cloud computing while at the same time restored our trust in the ability of Internet companies such as Google to efficiently resolve the crisis. Google applications and services with the exception of Google Search are free of advertisements, pop-ups, and other clutter. But there is no guarantee that it will remain so in the future. We are aware that hackers have the ability to snoop on email with packet sniffers when email passes through routers on the Internet. We are also at the mercy of spammers and malicious hackers who disrupt our email services on a regular basis. IM services are also an easy target for delivering malware such as spyware, viruses, worms, and trojans to computer users by common methods such as file transfer with an inflected file, or an email with a URL containing active malicious code. This is the risk we all take with email and chat services. Fortunately the connections to service provider's network are secure and all hosted mail services such as AOL, Hotmail, MSN, and Yahoo! routinely scan email for viruses and spam. We applaud the efforts by email services acting on our behalf to protect our email and chat from spam and malware. Email and chat communications are captured and stored on email servers in un-encrypted format. This results in a potential for abuse by hosting services to employ automated text scanning BOTs or human readers to mine personal email and chat for confidential information. Given the potential for backlash from customers and the media, service providers will not tread this path (O'Reilly, 2004). So employing Web 2.0 technologies and services for Tele-mentoring does not involve any additional risk. We will need to be vigilant but not overly concerned about these issues

Web 2.0 tools are built around openness and access. With that openness, still follows a basic understanding of the very long life of anything digital. We have to learn to be open and wise at the time. It is a good rule of thumb to recall no amount of information is secure if it is digitally represented. Just as a private conversation can be overheard, digital information can be sent to the wrong location, copied and changed without your knowledge or saved forever on someone's hard drive. The same is true for information supplied via forms on various web sites. As the old saying goes, never put into digital form something you would not want put on the front page of the local newspaper. As accounts are created, content is published, and information is shared on Web 2.0 web sites, there are a few things for potential mentors and mentees to keep in mind.

You have a right to privacy. Most web sites will publish a means to remove personal information that web sites collect as you visit. This policy removal is normally buried deep in a site and is found by following the sites privacy policy link or FAQ. You should be aware that information is being gathered (The information is usually collected through cookies which monitor where you go on web sites or though information gathered in forms.) with every visit you make. You have a right to remove this information from business

245

databases. Where possible most application providers will help you remove unwanted content. However, there are exceptions and instances where information could be stored in someone's individual machine (cache) even if you have removed access. Again, best to consider anything digital as existing forever and act accordingly.

Any web site protected by encryption is indicated by the extra "s" after the normal http in a web address. (HTTPS) In most popular browsers, the secure web site address and information can be obtained by clicking on the locket icon at the bottom of the screen or alongside the lock icon. DO NOT purchase or give out any personal information such as social security numbers, credit card numbers, or any other private information without using a secure site.

Copyright laws are as applicable in the digital world as they are in the traditional classroom. When deciding whether the information should be used ask basic questions such as: Who owns this? How do I wish to use this material? What is the age of the material? Would I be withholding profit or compensation from the original owner of the material by my use? This is true for electronic as well as paper materials. In fact, it is even more important when dealing with digital documents due to the ease with which digital materials can be copied, multiplied, and presented to millions on the Internet. All materials have copyright protection as soon as they are created with or without the copyright phrase posted on the material. This means that almost everything, except federal government information, on the Internet is copyrighted whether it says so or not. This applies to every type of content; images, text, video, and audio.

Finally, asking permission to link to another's material is the courteous thing to do on the web. That being said, the nature of the web is to link information together. Therefore, it is generally considered acceptable to link to other information without requesting permission. As web sites are created, it is important to consider the nature of the site to determine whether permission should be obtained to link to material. Considerations and acceptable practices change if the site is commercial or large enough to generating a lot of traffic. If this is the case, it is wise to obtain written approval of any hotlinks included in the site. In creating private or small web sites for classroom or tele-mentoring use, this would not be necessary.

Web 2.0 tools can provide the flexible framework needed to support quality communication at a distance. Research seems to point to similar needs in online learning and mentoring for the development of distance communication and advancing interaction. For mentors and mentees, Web 2.0 tools represent a variety of offerings not represented previously to connect, share, and build meaningful relationships to solve problems or gain needed experience. When mentoring relationships are formed in free suites of Web 2.0 tools such as Ning or Google Apps a single portal can host synchronous and asynchronous discussions, information gathering, presentations, and reporting acting as a repository for and possibly continuing testament to the relationship.

REFERENCES

Adobe Inc. (2005, November 17) Upgrading the Internet-Web 2.0. *InterAKTOnline.com*. Retrieved May 18, 2009, from http://www.interaktonline.com/support/articles/Details/Upgrading+the+Internet+%96+Web+2.0.html?id_art=39

Alexander, L. (2007). *Q&A: Meebo's Sternberg on integrating games and chat*. Retrieved April 25, 2009, from http://www.gamasutra.com/news/casual/?story=16316

Anderson, P. (2007, February). What is Web 2.0? Ideas, technologies, and implications for education. *JISC Technology and Standards Watch*, 47.

Anderson, T. (2003).Getting the mix right again: An updated and theoretical rationale for interaction. *The International Review of Research in Open and Distance Learning*. Retrieved April 19, 2009, from http://www.irrodl.org/index.php/irrodl/article/view/149/230.

Arthur, M. B., & Rousseau, D. M. (1996). *The boundaryless career: A new employment principle for a new organizational era*. New York: Oxford University Press.

Asmus, J., Bonner, C., Esterhay, D., Lechner, A., & Rentfrow, C. (2005). *Instructional design technology trend analysis*. Retrieved April 30, 2009, from http://eduspaces.net/collinb/files/1136/2967/trendanalysisweb.pdf

Bafile, C. (2009). *Mobile technology goes to school*. Retrieved April 29, 2009, from http://www.education-world.com/a_tech/tech/tech248.shtml

Barcena, E., & Read, T. (2004, July 15). The role of scaffolding in a learner-centered tutoring system for business English at a distance. *European Journal of Open, Distance and E-Learning*. Retrieved May 29, 2009 from http://www.eurodl.org/?p=archives&year=2004&halfyear=2&article=122

Blum, J. (2008, November 19). *The hidden cost of Google Apps*. Retrieved April 25, 2009, from http://money.cnn.com/2008/11/13/smallbusiness/google_apps.smb/index.htm

Bowen, E. M. (2000, May). Research, analysis, communication: Meeting standards with technology. *Learning and Leading with Technology, 27*(8). Retrieved November 1, 2005, from http://www.iste.org/L&L/archive/vol27/no8/body.html

Boyd, D. M., & Ellison, N. B. (2007). Social network sites: Definition, history, and scholarship. *Journal of Computer-Mediated Communication, 13*(1). Retrieved April 30, 2009, from http://jcmc.indiana.edu/vol13/issue1/boyd.ellison.html

Brabham, D. (2008, April 4). Moving the crowd at Istockphoto: The composition of the crowd and motivations for participation in a crowdsourcing application. *First Monday 13*(6). Retrieved April 20, 2009, from http://ssrn.com/abstract=1122462

Bretag, R. (2009, February 6). Passionate voices. *Tech & Learning*. Retrieved April 30, 2009, from http://www.techlearning.com/blogs.aspx?id=15776.

Brooks, J. G., & Brooks, M. G. (2004, April). Concept to classroom. *Thirteen Ed Online*. Retrieved April 20, 2009, from http://www.thirteen.org/edonline/concept2class/constructivism/implementation.html

Bruce, B., & Levin, J. (1997). Educational technology: Media for inquiry, communication, construction, and expression. *Journal of Educational Computing Research 17*(1), 79-102. Retrieved June 3, 2009 from http://www.isrl.illinois.edu/~chip/pubs/taxonomy/taxonomy.pdf

Bruggeman, D., Hernandez, E., & Marcus, S. J. (2002). Preparing for the revolution: Information technology and the future of the research university. *The National Academies Press*. Retrieved April 29, 2009, from http://www.nap.edu/openbook.php?isbn=030908640X

Chen, S. (2009, May 25). *Ning: the future of online social networking?* Retrieved May 30, 2009, from http://www.cnn.com/2009/TECH/05/25/ning.social.networking.interest/index.html?iref=t2test_techmon/

Collis, B. (1998). New didactics for university instruction: Why and how? *Computers & Education, 41*(4), 373–393. doi:10.1016/S0360-1315(98)00040-2

Commons, C. (2009). Retrieved April 28, 2009, from http://creativecommons.org

Dallos, R., & Comley-Ross, P. (2005). Young people's experience of mentoring: Building trust and attachments, *Clinical Child Psychology and Psychiatry*, 10, 369. Retrieved April 25, 2009, from http://ccp.sagepub.com/cgi/content/abstract/10/3/369

Department of Labor. (2008, June 27). *Number of jobs held, labor market activity, and earnings growth among the youngest baby boomers: Results from a longitudinal survey* (USDL Publication No. 08-0860). Retrieved April 22, 2009 from http://www.bls.gov/news.release/pdf/nlsoy.pdf

Docs, G. (2009). *Wikipedia*. Retrieved April 25, 2009, from http://en.wikipedia.org/wiki/Google_docs

Dwyer, D. C., Ringstaff, C., & Sandholtz, J. H. (1991, May). Changes in teachers' beliefs and practices in technology-rich classrooms. *Educational Leadership*, 48(8), 45–52.

Evans, I. M., Wilson, N. J., Hansson, G., & Hungerford, R. (1997). Positive and negative behaviours of independent adolescent youth participation in a community support programme. *New Zealand Journal of Psychology*, 26, 29–35.

Francisco, B. (2009). iGoogle to add chat and become more social. Retrieved April 25, 2009, from http://vator.tv/news/show/2009-01-08-igoogle-to-add-chat-and-become-more-social

Fredericksen, E., Pickett, A., & Shea, P. (2000, September). Student satisfaction and perceived learning with on-line courses: Principles and examples from the SUNY Learning Network, *Journal of Asynchronous Learning Networks, 4*(2). Retrieved April 10, 2009, from http://www.aln.org/alnweb/journal/jaln-vol4issue2.htm

Garber, D. (2004). Growing virtual communities, *International Review of Research in Open and Distance Learning, 5*(2). Retrieved April 28, 2009, from http://www.irrodl.org/content/v5.2/technote4.html

Garrett, J. (2005 February). *Ajax: A new approach to web applications*. Retrieved on April, 23, 2009 from http://www.adaptivepath.com/ideas/essays/archives/000385.php.

Garrison, D. R., Anderson, T., & Archer, W. (2000). Critical inquiry in a text-based environment: Computer conferencing in higher education. *The Internet and Higher Education*, 2(2-3), 87–105. doi:10.1016/S1096-7516(00)00016-6

Garrison, D. R., Anderson, T., & Archer, W. (2003). A theory of critical inquiry in online distance education. In Moore, M. G., & Anderson, W. G. (Eds.), *Handbook of distance education* (pp. 113–128). Mahwah, N.J.: L. Erlbaum Associates.

Gmail. (2009). *Wikipedia*. Retrieved April 25, 2009, from http://en.wikipedia.org/wiki/Gmail

Google Inc. (2009). Google Translate FAQs. Retrieved April 25, 2009, from http://www.google.com/intl/en/help/faq_translation.html#statmt

Google Inc. (2009a). Google Apps Education Edition. Retrieved April 25, 2009, from http://www.google.com/a/help/intl/en/edu/customers.html

Google Inc. (2009b). Google Talk for Developers. Retrieved April 25, 2009, from http://code.google.com/apis/talk/open_communications.html

Google Inc. (2009c). Google Scholar Beta. Retrieved April 25, 2009, from http://scholar.google.com/intl/en/scholar/about.html

Google Inc. (2009d). Google Wave. Retrieved May 30, 2009, from http://googlesystem.blogspot.com/2009/05/google-wave.html

Hawkey, K. (1997). Roles, responsibilities, and relationships in mentoring: A literature review and agenda for research. *Journal of Teacher Education*, 48(5), 325. doi:10.1177/0022487197048005002

Heinich, R., Molenda, M., Russell, J. D., & Smaldino, S. E. (2002). *Instructional media and technologies for learning* (7th ed.). Upper Saddle River, New Jersey: Merrill Prentice Hall.

Hersch, R. (2009, April 20). Our 21st-century 'risk': Teaching for content and skills. *New York Times Web Education Week*. Retrieved from http://www.edweek.org/login.html?source=http://www.edweek.org/ew/articles/2009/04/22/29hersh_ep.h28.html&destination=http://www.edweek.org/ew/articles/2009/04/22/29hersh_ep.h28.html&levelId=1000

Hewitt, A., & Forte, A. (2006, November). *Crossing boundaries: Identity management and student/faculty relationships on Facebook*. Poster session presented at the Computer Supported Cooperative Work Conference. Retrieved April 30, 2009, from http://www.cc.gatech.edu/~aforte/HewittForteCSCWPoster2006.pdf

Hirst, K. (2000). Distance education: No significant difference. Retrieved June 20, 2001, from http://distancelearn.miningco.com/education/distancelearn/library/blpages/blnsd.htm

History of Wikipedia. (2009). *Wikipedia*. Retrieved April 29, 2009, from http://en.wikipedia.org/wiki/History_of_Wikipedia

History of Wikipedia. (2009). *Wikipedia*. Retrieved April 25, 2009, from http://en.wikipedia.org/wiki/History_of_Wikipedia

Jaffe, D. (2003, April). Virtual transformation: Web-based technology and pedagogical change. *Teaching Sociology, 31*(2), 227–236. doi:10.2307/3211312

Jerome, W., Rinderle, J., & Bajzek, D. (2008). Tools for constructing targeted feedback in online instruction. In G. Richards (Ed.), *Proceedings of World Conference on E-Learning in Corporate, Government, Healthcare, and Higher Education 2008* (pp. 3753-3759). Chesapeake, VA: AACE.

Jones, B. F., Valdez, G., Nowakowski, J., & Rasmussen, C. (1995). Plugging in: Choosing and using educational technology. *North Central Regional Educational Laboratory*. Retrieved April 1, 2001, from http://www.ncrel.org/sdrs/edtalk/toc.htm

Jorn, L., Whiteside, A., & Duin, A. H. (2009) Pair-up. *Educause Review, 44*(2). Retrieved April 20, 2009, from http://www.educause.edu/EDUCAUSE+Review/EDUCAUSEReviewMagazineVolume44/PAIRUp/163795

Levy, A. (2007). *What is Blogtalkradio?* Retrieved April 25, 2009, from http://blog.blogtalkradio.com/2007/04/15/what-is-blogtalkradio%22/

Maynard, T., & Furlong, J. (1995). *Mentoring student teachers the growth of professional knowledge*. New York: Routledge.

McCarthy, C. (2008, October). *Ning's OpenSocial support goes live*. Retrieved April 30, 2009, from http://news.cnet.com/8301-13577_3-10063030-36.html

McCurdy, S., & Schroeder, R. (2005). *Interinstitutional collaborations in the delivery of online learning*. Paper presented at the 21st Annual Conference on Distance Teaching and Learning. Retrieved April 30, 2009, from http://www.uwex.edu/disted/conference/Resource_library/proceedings/05_1829.pdf

Moore, M. G. (1989).Editorial: Three types of interaction. *The American Journal of Distance Education, 3*(2). Retrieved May 29, 2009, from http://www.ajde.com/Contents/vol3_2.htm

Nefstead, S., & Nefstead, S. (2005). *Mentoring in the 90's and beyond*. Retrieved April 29, 2009, from http://www.extension.umn.edu/distribution/citizenship/DH6447.html

Nesler, M. S., & Hanner, M. B. (2001). Professional socialization of baccalaureate nursing students: Can students in distance nursing programs become socialized? *The Journal of Nursing Education, 40*(7), 293–302.

New Media Consortium. (2008). *The 2008 Horizon Report*. Retrieved May 20, 2009, from http://www.nmc.org/pdf/2008-Horizon-Report.pdf

Nielsen, J. (2007, February). Life-long computer skils. *Alertbox*. Retrieved April 30, 2009, from http://www.useit.com/alertbox/computer-skills.html

Ning, Inc. (2009). *Ning Fact Sheet*. Retrieved April 30, 2009, from http://about.ning.com/press.php

O'Neilly, D. K., & Gomez, L. M. (1998). Sustaining mentoring relationships on-line. Paper presented at the Computer Supported Cooperative Work, Seattle, Washington. Retrieved April 30, 2009, from http://delivery.acm.org/10.1145/290000/289507/p325-o_neill.pdf?key1=289507&key2=5151514421&coll=GUIDE&dl=GUIDE&CFID=37944349&CFTOKEN=13733950

O'Reilly, T. (2004). The fuss about gmail and privacy: Nine reasons why it's bogus. Retrieved April 25, 2009, from, http://www.oreillynet.com/pub/wlg/4707

O'Reilly, T. (2005). What is Web 2.0? Design patterns and business models for the next generation of software. Retrieved April 25, 2009, from http://www.oreilly.de/artikel/web20.html

O'Reilly, T. (2009). Google wave: What might email look like if it were invented today? Retrieved May 29, 2009, from http://radar.oreilly.com/2009/05/google-wave-what-might-email-l.html.

Paul, I. (2009, May 15). Google outage lesson: Don't get stuck in a cloud. Retrieved May 25, 2009, from http://www.pcworld.com/printable/article/id,164946/printable.html

Reynard, R. (2008, December). Using chat to move the thinking process forward. *Technological Horizons In Education Journal, 35*(12), 4. Retrieved April 30, 2009, from Expanded Academic ASAP via Gale: http://find.galegroup.com/itx/start.do?prodId=EAIM

Rhone, L. (1995). *Measurement in a primary-grade integrated curriculum. Connecting mathematics across the curriculum*. Reston, VA: National Council of Teachers of Mathematics.

Roush, W. (2005, January). Amazon: Giving away the store. *Technology Review*. Retrieved May 25, 2009, from http://www.technologyreview.com/business/14089/

Scheinberg, A. (2006, August 8). *Review: Picasaweb vs. Flickr*. Retrieved May 25, 2009, from http://firsttube.com/read/review-picasaweb-vs-flickr/

Shearer, R. L. (2003). *Interaction in distance education. Special report 2*(1). Madison, WI: Atwood Publishing.

Siegler, M. G. (2009, May 28). Google wave drips with ambition. A new communication platform for a new web. Retrieved May 30, 2009, from http://www.techcrunch.com/2009/05/28/google-wave-drips-with-ambition-can-it-fulfill-googles-grand-web-vision/

Soloway, E., Jackson, S. L., Klein, J., Quintana, C., Reed, J., Spitulnik, J., et al. (1996). *Learning theory in practice: Case studies of learner-centered design*. Paper presented at CHI96 conference, Vancouver, British Columbia, Canada. Retrieved May 2, 2009, from http://www.sigchi.org/chi96/proceedings/papers/Soloway/es_txt.htm

Stinson, B., & Claus, K. (2000). The effects of electronic classrooms on learning English composition: A middle ground. *T.H.E. Journal*. Retrieved April 30, 2009, from http://www.thejournal.com/articles/14610

Su, B., Bonk, C. J., Magjuka, R., Liu, X., & Lee, S. (2005). The Importance of interaction in web-based education: A program-level case study of online MBA courses. *Journal of Interactive Online Learning, 4*(1).

Sullivan, S., & Emerson, R. (2000). Recommendations for successfully navigating the boundaryless career: From theory to practice. Retrieved April 30, 2009, from http://www.sba.muohio.edu/management/mwAcademy/2000/27c.pdf

Swan, K. (2004). Relationships between interactions and learning in online environments, The Sloan Consortium. Retrieved June 3, 2009, from http://www.sloan-c.org/publications/books/interactions.pdf

Tag (metadata). (2009). *Wikipedia*. Retrieved April 30, 2009, from http://en.wikipedia.org/wiki/Tag_(metadata)

Thomas, D., & Buch, V. (2007, March 18). YouTube case study: Widget marketing comes of age. *Startup Review*. Retrieved April 22, 2009, from http://www.startup-review.com/blog/youtube-case-study-widget-marketing-comes-of-age.php

Tobin, M. (2004). Mentoring: Seven roles and some specifics, *American Journal of Respiratory and Critical Care Medicine*, 170, 114-117. Retrieved April 22, 2009, from http://ajrccm.atsjournals.org/cgi/content/full/170/2/114

Translate, G. (2009). *Wikipedia*. Retrieved April 25, 2009, from http://en.wikipedia.org/wiki/Google_Translate

University Continuing Education Association (UCEA). (2009, March). *The new face of higher education lifelong learning trends*. Washington, D.C.: UCEA Publications Office.

University of Southern California. (2009). *Examples in education*. Retrieved April 25, 2009, from http://getgoogle.usc.edu/

Wesch, M. (2008, October 21). *A vision of students today (& what teachers must do)*. Retrieved April 28, 2009, from http://www.britannica.com/blogs/2008/10/a-vision-of-students-today-what-teachers-must-do/

Williams, E. (2009, May 11). The YouTube dilemma. *Creative Review*. Retrieved May 25, 2009, from http://www.creativereview.co.uk/cr-blog/2009/may/the-youtube-dilemma

Winer, D. (2005). *What is a 'River of News' style aggregator?* Retrieved April 25, 2009, from http://www.reallysimplesyndication.com/riverOfNews

Wisdom of the Crowd. (2009). *Wikipedia*. Retrieved April 25, 2009, from http://en.wikipedia.org/wiki/Wisdom_of_the_crowd

APPENDIX A

Technology as Media for Inquiry: Subsets of this use area include theory building, data access, and data collection. Software included in this area would include digital libraries, virtual reality and simulation products, and recording technologies in video and sound recording. Examples of Web 2.0 products available in this category would include:

- **Second Brain:** (http://secondbrain.com/) Organizes all online content, share and interact with friends.
- **SurveyGizmo:** (http://www.surveygizmo.com) Survey tool with reporting and usage feature. Free option available
- **Ask 500:** (http://www.ask500people.com) Free, Web-based, anonymous opinion poll
- **Audacity:** (http://www.audacity.com) Free, audio recording and editing tool which can be used to add audio to PowerPoint.
- **Second Life:** (http://www.secondlife.com) A free virtual world with its own money where avatars talk, walk and fly. Must be 18.
- **Fix8:** (http://www.fix8.com) Cool avatar chat tool that gives the avatar's expression based upon webcam input

Technology as media for Communication: This use area contains document preparation, communication technologies such as email and conferencing, collaborative media, and teaching media. Examples of Web 2.0 products available in this category would include:

- **Zoho:** (http://zoho.com) Web-based Email, Word Processing, Spreadsheet, presentation, wiki applications in one site
- **Elluminate:** (http://www.elluminate.com) Two-way, VoIP conferencing tool. Includes chat, whiteboard, web tour, polling features. Free Vroom available
- **Gliffy:** (http://www.gliffy.com) A free web-based graphical organizer
- **Gmail:** (http://mail.google.com) Free web-based email with huge, 1 gigabit of storage per user, unique conversation message display, and spam filter
- **Jing:** (http://www.jing.com) Free web capturing tool; captures anything on your computer screen

Technology as media for Construction: Subsets of this area include software used for construction design, graphing, robotics, control of equipment, or systems control.

- **NetLogo Models:** (http://ccl.northwestern.edu/netlogo/models/) Computer modeling that runs in a browser. Sample models are listed for earth science, biology, computers.
- **FloorPlanner:** (http://www.floorplanner.com/) Create and share interactive floor plans.
- **Modelling4All:** (http://modelling4all.nsms.ox.ac.uk/) A tool to create computer models online without programming skills
- **Vector Magic:** (http://vectormagic.com/home) Converts bitmap images to vectors for smoother lines and better results.
- **WriteMaps:** (http://writemaps.com) A visualization tool for creating, editing, and sharing websites

Web 2.0 for Tele-Mentoring

- **MultieyeVision Solutions:** (http://www.multieyevision.com/index.html) The site turns a camera phone into a number of different applications via the web including a document processing system which lets you use a cell phone as a scanner. Also has Observer Remote Monitoring System which turns a cell phone into a web camera and uses the web to remotely operate.
- **Evernote:** (http://www.evernote.com) Captures information in any form. Tag images of anything including documents for easy organizing and archiving. Even allows you to clip web content directly into Evernote.
- **Kartoo:** (http://www.kartoo.com) A graphic visual search engine that can be used to make connections between ideas
- **Gliffy:** (http://www.glify.com) A web-based tool for connecting and graphing concepts

Technology as media for Expression: Subsets of this area include software or technologies which create opportunities of self-expression. Examples of software programs available for classroom use would include:

- **Aviary:** (http://aviary.com/home) An entire suite of graphic editing and drawing tools in a single site. All of the tools are named after birds; Peacock, Visual Laboratory; Raven, vector editor; Phoenix, image editor; Toucan, color swatch tool.
- **Animoto:** (http://animoto.com/education) Very simple to use site that lets users combine images and sound to create a video in seconds.
- **Glog:** (http://www.glogster.com) Website that lets you create posters of yourself using tons of graphics, video, sounds, and text elements.
- **SplashUp:** (http://www.slashup.com) Full featured editing tool and photo manager where you can create and then share your creations.
- **PXN8:** (http://pixenate.com) A photo editor for the web that easily cross posts to Flickr

Compilation of References

Abbot, L. (2003). *Novice teachers' experiences with telementoring as learner-centered professional development*. Retrieved February 28, 2009, from http://teachnet.edb.utexas.edu/~lynda_abbott?ABBOTT-DISSERTAION.pdf

Abbott, L. (2005). The nature of authentic professional development during curriculum-based telecomputing. *Journal of Research on Technology in Education, 37*(4), 379–398.

Abbott, S., & Mcconkey, R. (2006). The barriers to social inclusion as perceived by people with intellectual disabilities. *Journal of Intellectual Disabilities, 10*, 275–287. doi:10.1177/1744629506067618

AbilityNet. (2008, January 18). *State of the eNation Reports: Social networking sites lock out disabled users.* Retrieved May 13, 2009, from http://www.abilitynet.org.uk/enation85

Achilles, C. M., & Gaines, P. (1991, April). *Collegial groups in school improvement: Project SIGN.* Paper presented at the meeting of the American Educational Research Association, Chicago, IL.

Achterbosch, L., Pierce, R., & Simmons, G. (2008). Massively multiplayer online role-playing games: The past, present, and future. *ACM Computers in Entertainment, 5*(4), 1–33..doi:10.1145/1324198.1324207

Adelman, M. B., Parks, M. R., & Albrecht, T. L. (1987). Beyond close relationships: Support in weak ties. In Albrecht, T. L., & Adelman, M. B. (Eds.), *Communicating Social Support* (pp. 127–147). Newbury Park, CA: Sage.

Adobe Inc. (2005, November 17) Upgrading the Internet-Web 2.0. *InterAKTOnline.com*. Retrieved May 18, 2009, from http://www.interaktonline.com/support/articles/Details/Upgrading+the+Internet+%96+Web+2.0.html?id_art=39

Albert, B. (Ed.). (2006). *In or out of the mainstream? Lesson from research on disability and development cooperation*. Leeds: The Disability Press.

Albert, M., Becker, T., Mccrone, P., & Thornicroft, G. (1998). Social networks and mental health service utilisation – A literature review. *The International Journal of Social Psychiatry, 44*, 248–266. doi:10.1177/002076409804400402

Alexander, L. (2007). *Q&A: Meebo's Sternberg on integrating games and chat.* Retrieved April 25, 2009, from http://www.gamasutra.com/news/casual/?story=16316

Allen, T. D., & Eby, L. T. (2004). Factors related to mentor reports of mentoring functions provided: Gender and relational characteristics. *Sex Roles, 50*(1-2).

Allen, L. J., & Sigafoos, J. (2000). Friendship and loneliness among Australian children with special education needs. *The Journal of International Special Needs Education, 3*, 12–20.

Alvarado, A. (2006, April). *New directions in teacher education: Emerging strategies from the Teachers for a New Era initiative.* Paper presented at the American Educational Research Association, San Francisco, CA.

American Association for the Advancement of Science (AAAS). 2009. *Science NetLinks*. Retrieved April 2, 2009, from http://www.sciencenetlinks.com/index.cfm.

American Association for the Advancement of Science. (2001). *In pursuit of a diverse science, technology, engineering, and mathematics workforce*. Washington, DC: Author.

American Association of School Librarians (AASL). (2007). *Standards for the 21st-century learner*. Chicago: American Library Association. Retrieved August 20, 2009, from http://www.ala.org/ala/mgrps/divs/aasl/guidelinesandstandards/learningstandards/standards.cfm.

American Association of School Librarians (AASL). [n.d.]. *Best web sites for teaching and learning*. Retrieved August 20, 2009, from http://www.ala.org/ala/mgrps/divs/aasl/guidelinesandstandards/bestlist/bestwebsites-top25.cfm.

American Youth Policy Forum. (1997). SOME things DO make a difference for youth. Washing ton, DC: Author. Retrieved December 4, 2009 from http://www.aypf.org/publications/compendium/comp01.pdf

Americans With Disabilities Act of 1990. 42 U.S.C.A. § 12101 et seq.

Amichai-Hamburrger, Y., MaKenna, K.Y.A., & Tal, S.A. (2008). E-empowerment: Empowerment by the Internet. *Computers in Human Behavior*, *24*(5), 1776–1789. doi:10.1016/j.chb.2008.02.002

Amill, L. (2002). *Telementoring: A view from the facilitator's screen*. Retrieved November 20, 2006, from http://www.serviceleader.org/old/w/direct/laura.html

Anderson, E., & Shannon, A. (1988). Toward a conceptualization of mentoring. *Journal of Teacher Education*, *39*(1), 38–42. doi:10.1177/002248718803900109

Anderson, P. (2007, February). What is Web 2.0? Ideas, technologies, and implications for education. *JISC Technology and Standards Watch*, 47.

Anderson, T. (2003).Getting the mix right again: An updated and theoretical rationale for interaction. *The International Review of Research in Open and Distance Learning*. Retrieved April 19, 2009, from http://www.irrodl.org/index.php/irrodl/article/view/149/230.

Andersson, G., Bergström, J., Holländare, F., Carlbring, P., Kaldo, V., & Ekselius, L. (2005). Internet-based self-help for depression: randomized controlled trial. *The British Journal of Psychiatry*, *187*, 456–461. doi:10.1192/bjp.187.5.456

Aphids Communications. (n.d.). Quotations about politics/government. *The Quotations Archive*. Retrieved August 11, 2010, from http://www.aphids.com/cgi-bin/quotes.pl?act=ShowListingsForSub&Subject=S30

Argyle, M., Salter, V., Nicholson, H., Williams, M., & Burgess, P. (1970). The communication of inferior and superior attitudes by verbal and non-verbal signals. *The British Journal of Social and Clinical Psychology*, *9*, 222–231.

Arthur, M. B., & Rousseau, D. M. (1996). *The boundaryless career: A new employment principle for a new organizational era*. New York: Oxford University Press.

Asgari, M., & O'Neill, D. K. (2005). What do they mean by "success"? Examining mentees' perceptions of success in a curriculum-based telementoring program. In Pascarelli, J., & Kochan, F. (Eds.), *Creating successful telementoring programs* (pp. 225–249). Greenwich, CT: Information Age Publishing.

Asmus, J., Bonner, C., Esterhay, D., Lechner, A., & Rentfrow, C. (2005). *Instructional design technology trend analysis*. Retrieved April 30, 2009, from http://eduspaces.net/collinb/files/1136/2967/trendanalysisweb.pdf

Augusto, C. (2009, April 6). *Making Facebook accessible for everyone*. Retrieved February 1, 2010, from http://blog.facebook.com/blog.php?post=71852922130

Bafile, C. (2009). *Mobile technology goes to school*. Retrieved April 29, 2009, from http://www.education-world.com/a_tech/tech/tech248.shtml

Bandura, A. (1982). Self-efficacy mechanism in human agency. *The American Psychologist*, *37*, 122–147. doi:10.1037/0003-066X.37.2.122

Bandura, A. (1997). *Self-efficacy: The exercise of control*. New York: Freeman.

Bandura, A. (2004). Social cognitive theory for personal and social change by enabling media. In Singhal, A., Cody, M. J., Rogers, E. M., & Sabido, M. (Eds.), *Entertainment-education and Social Change: History, Research, and Practice* (pp. 75–96). Mahwah, NJ: Lawrence Erlbaum.

Bandura, A. (1992). Albert Bandura's social-cognitive theory. In M. E. Gredler, *Learning and instruction: Theory into practice* (pp. 302-345). New York: MacMillan Publishing Co.

Banks, J. A. (2008). Diversity, group identity and citizenship education in a global age. *Educational Researcher*, *37*(3), 129–139. doi:10.3102/0013189X08317501

Barab, S. A., & Squire, K. (2004). Design-based research: Putting a stake in the ground. *Journal of the Learning Sciences*, *13*(1), 1–14. doi:10.1207/s15327809jls1301_1

Barak, A., & Dolev-Cohen, M. (2006). Does activity level in online support groups for distressed adolescents determine emotional relief? *Counselling & Psychotherapy Research*, *6*(3), 186–190. doi:10.1080/14733140600848203

Barak, A., & Sadovsky, Y. (2008). Internet use and personal empowerment of hearing-impaired adolescents. *Computers in Human Behavior*, *24*, 1802–1815. doi:10.1016/j.chb.2008.02.007

Barak, A. (2007). Phantom emotions: Psychological determinants of emotional experiences on the Internet. In Joinson, A., McKenna, K. Y. A., Postmes, T., & Reips, U. D. (Eds.), *Oxford handbook of Internet psychology* (pp. 303–329). Oxford, UK: Oxford University Press.

Barak, A. (2003, December). *Psychological determinates of emotional experiences on the Internet*. Paper presented at the workshop of Rationality and Emotion, Haifa, Israel.

Barcena, E., & Read, T. (2004, July 15). The role of scaffolding in a learner-centered tutoring system for business English at a distance. *European Journal of Open, Distance and E-Learning*. Retrieved May 29, 2009 from http://www.eurodl.org/?p=archives&year=2004&halfyear=2&article=122

Barker, R. G. (1963). On the nature of the environment. *The Journal of Social Issues*, *19*, 17–38. doi:10.1111/j.1540-4560.1963.tb00456.x

Barnes, S. B. (2003). *Computer-mediated communication: Human-to-human communication across the Internet*. Boston, USA: Allyn and Bacon.

Barnett, M. (2006). Using a web-based professional development system to support pre-service teachers in examining authentic classroom practice. *Journal of Technology and Teacher Education*, *14*(4), 701–729.

Beehr, T. A., Farmer, S. J., Glazer, S., Gudanowski, D. M., & Nair, V. (2003). The enigma of social support and occupational stress: Source congruence and gender role effects. *Journal of Occupational Health Psychology*, *8*(3), 220–231. doi:10.1037/1076-8998.8.3.220

Beier, S. R., Rosenfeld, W. D., Spitalny, K. C., Zansky, S. M., & Bontempo, A. N. (2000). The potential role of an adult mentor in influencing high-risk behaviors in adolescents. *Archives of Pediatrics & Adolescent Medicine*, *154*, 327–331.

Bell, P. (2004). On the theoretical breadth of design-based research in Education. *Educational Psychologist*, *39*(4), 243–253. doi:10.1207/s15326985ep3904_6

Bennett, D., Heinze, C., Hupert, N., & Meade, T. (n.d.). *IBM MentorPlace: Starter kit*. New York. *EDC Center for Children and Technology*.

Bennett, D., Harris, J., Klemmer, D., & Neils, D. (1997). *Telementoring ways of learning*. Panel presentation at the BBN National School Network Conference, Cambridge, MA. Retrieved March 9, 2009, from alpha.musenet.org/81/telementor-wrkshp/confnote/pane/1.html

Bennett, D., Hupert, N., Tsikalas, K., Meade, T., & Honey, M. (1998). *Critical issues in the design and implementation of telementoring environments* (CCT Technical Report No. 09-1998b). New York: Center for Children and Technology.

Bennett, D., Tsikalas, K., Hupert, N., Meade, T., & Honey, M. (1998). *The benefits of online mentoring for high school girls: Telementoring young women in science, engineering, and computing project, Year 3 evaluation* (New York, Center for Children and Technology). Retrieved March 9, 2009 from: http://www2.edc.org/CCT/admin/publications/report/telement_bomhsg98.pdf

Benson, P. L., & Pittman, K. J. (2001). *Trends in youth development: Visions, realities, and challenges*. Boston: Kluwer Academic Publishers.

Benson, P. L., Scales, P. C., Hawkins, J. D., Oesterle, S., & Hill, K. G. (2004). *Successful young adult development. A report submitted to The Bill & Melinda Gates Foundation*. Retrieved December 4, 2009 from http://depts.washington.edu/sdrg/SuccessfulDevelopment.pdf

Benz, M., Doren, B., & Yovanoff, P. (1998). Crossing the great divide: Predicting productive engagement for young women with disabilities. *Career Development for Exceptional Individuals, 21*(1), 3–16. doi:10.1177/088572889802100102

Berners-Lee, T. (1993, June). Hypertext Markup Language (HTML). Retrieved February 1, 2010, from http://www.w3.org/MarkUp/draft-ietf-iiir-html-01.txt

Bierema, L. L., & Meriam, S. B. (2002). E-mentoring: Using computer mediated communication to enhance the mentoring process. *Innovative Higher Education, 26*(3), 211–227. doi:10.1023/A:1017921023103

Billingsley, B. S., & Cross, L. H. (1992). Predictors of commitment, job satisfaction, and intent to stay in teaching: A comparison of general and special educators. *The Journal of Special Education, 25*, 453–471. doi:10.1177/002246699202500404

Blum, J. (2008, November 19). *The hidden cost of Google Apps*. Retrieved April 25, 2009, from http://money.cnn.com/2008/11/13/smallbusiness/google_apps.smb/index.htm

Bonnett, C., Wildemuth, B. M., & Sonnenwald, D. H. (2006). Interactivity between protégés and scientists in an electronic mentoring program. *Instructional Science, 34*, 21–61. doi:10.1007/s11251-005-4115-9

Boss, S., Krauss, J., & Conery, L. (2008). *Reinventing project-based learning: Your field guide to real-world projects in the digital age*. Eugene, OR: International Society for Technology in Education.

Boud, D., & Prosser, M. (2002). Appraising new technologies for learning: A framework for development. *Educational Media International, 39*(2/4), 237–245. doi:10.1080/09523980210166026

Bowe, F. G. (2002). Deaf and hard of hearing Americans' instant messaging and e-mail use: A national survey. *American Annals of the Deaf, 147*(4), 6–10.

Bowen, D. D. (1985). Were men meant to mentor women? *Training and Development Journal*, 30–34.

Bowen, E. M. (2000, May). Research, analysis, communication: Meeting standards with technology. *Learning and Leading with Technology, 27*(8). Retrieved November 1, 2005, from http://www.iste.org/L&L/ar chive/vol27/no8/body.html

Bowker, N. I., & Tuffin, K. (2007). Understanding positive subjectives made possible online for disabled people. *New Zealand Journal of Psychology, 36*(2), 63–71.

Boyd, D. M., & Ellison, N. B. (2007). Social network sites: Definition, history, and scholarship. *Journal of Computer-Mediated Communication, 13*(1). Retrieved April 30, 2009, from http://jcmc.indiana.edu/vol13/issue1/boyd.ellison.html

Brabham, D. (2008, April 4). Moving the crowd at Istockphoto: The composition of the crowd and motivations for participation in a crowdsourcing application. *First Monday 13*(6). Retrieved April 20, 2009, from http://ssrn.com/abstract=1122462

Braithwaite, D. O., Waldron, V. R., & Finn, J. (1999). Communication of social support in computer-mediated groups for people with disabilities. *Health Communication, 11*(2), 123–151. doi:10.1207/s15327027hc1102_2

Brescia, W. (2005). Developing a telementoring taxonomy to improve online discussions. In Kochan, F., & Pascarelli, J. (Eds.), *Creating successful telementoring programs* (pp. 75–103). Greenwich, CT: Information Age Publishing.

Bretag, R. (2009, February 6). Passionate voices. *Tech & Learning*. Retrieved April 30, 2009, from http://www.techlearning.com/blogs.aspx?id=15776.

Britner, S. L., & Finson, K. D. (2005). Pre-service teachers' reflections on their growth in an inquiry-oriented science pedagogy course. *Journal of Elementary Science Education, 17*(1), 39–54. doi:10.1007/BF03174672

Brooks, J. G., & Brooks, M. G. (2004, April). Concept to classroom. *Thirteen Ed Online*. Retrieved April 20, 2009, from http://www.thirteen.org/edonline/concept2class/constructivism/implementation.html

Bruce, B., & Levin, J. (1997). Educational technology: Media for inquiry, communication, construction, and expression. *Journal of Educational Computing Research 17*(1), 79-102. Retrieved June 3, 2009 from http://www.isrl.illinois.edu/~chip/pubs/taxonomy/taxonomy.pdf

Bruggeman, D., Hernandez, E., & Marcus, S. J. (2002). Preparing for the revolution: Information technology and the future of the research university. *The National Academies Press*. Retrieved April 29, 2009, from http://www.nap.edu/openbook.php?isbn=030908640X

Buck Institute for Education (BIE). (n.d.). *Project based learning handbook*. Novato, CA. Buck Institute for Education.

Buck Institute for Education (BIE), & Boise State University, Department of Educational Technology. (2005). *PBL Online: Designing your project*. Retrieved April 8, 2009, from http://www.pbl-online.org/pathway2.html.

Bureau of Labor Statistics. (2009). New monthly data series on the employment status of people with a disability. Retrieved December 4, 2009 from http://www.bls.gov/cps/cpsdisability.htm

Burger, L. (2007). Transforming reference. *American Libraries, 38*(3), 5–6.

Burgstahler, S., & Chang, C. (2007). Gender differences in perceived value of components of a program to promote academic and career success for students with disabilities. *Journal of Science Education for Students with Disabilities, 12*(1).

Burgstahler, S., Comden, D., & Fraser, B. (1997). Universal access: Designing and evaluating Websites for accessibility. *CHOICE: Current Reviews for Academic Libraries, 34*(Suppl.), 19–22.

Burgstahler, S., & Cronheim, D. (2001). Supporting peer-peer and mentor-protégé relationships on the internet. *Journal of Research on Technology in Education, 34*(1), 59–74.

Burgstahler, S., & Doyle, A. (2005). Gender differences in computer-mediated communication among adolescents with disabilities: A case study. *Disability Studies Quarterly, 25*(2).

Burgstahler, S. (2008). Universal design of technological environments: From principles to practice. In Burgstahler, S. E., & Cory, R. C. (Eds.), *Universal design in higher education: From principles to practice* (pp. 213–224). Cambridge, MA: Harvard Education Press.

Burgstahler, S. (2007). Accessibility training for distance learning personnel. *Access Technologists Higher Education Network (ATHEN) E-Journal, 2*. Retrieved February 1, 2010, from http://athenpro.org/node/56

Burke, R. J., & McKeen, C. A. (1996). Gender effects in mentoring relationships. *Journal of Social Behavior and Personality, 11*(5), 91–104.

Bush, J. (1998). *Promoting electronic reflective practice*. Paper presented at Fifth International Technological Directions in Music Learning Conference, San Antonio, TX.

Campbell-Whatley, G. (2001). Mentoring students with mild disabilities: The "nuts and bolts" of program development. *Intervention in School and Clinic, 36*, 211–216. doi:10.1177/105345120103600403

Casey, M., & Savastinuk, L. C. (2006, September). Library 2.0. *Library Journal, 131*(14), 40–42.

CAST. (n.d.b). *R & D projects*. Retrieved May 13, 2009, from http://www.cast.org/research/projects/index.html

CAST. (n.d.c). *What is universal design for learning?* Retrieved February 1, 2010, from http://www.cast.org/research/udl/

Cavarallaro, F., & Tan, K. (2006). Computer mediated peer-to-peer mentoring. *AACE Journal, 14*(2), 129–138.

Center for Applied Special Technology [CAST]. (n.d.a). *CAST Transforming education through universal design for learning*. Retrieved February 1, 2010, from http://www.cast.org

Center for Children & Technology. (1998, September). *Critical issues in the design & implementation of telementoring environments*. Retrieved March 1, 2010, from http://cct.edc.org/admin/publications/report/09_1998.pdf

Center for Universal Design [CUD] (n.d.a) *About the Center: Ronald L. Mace*. Retrieved February 1, 2010, from http://www.design.ncsu.edu/cud/about_us/usronmace.htm

Chadsey, J., & Beyer, S. (2001). Social relationships in the workplace. *Mental Retardation and Developmental Disabilities Research Reviews, 7*, 128–133. doi:10.1002/mrdd.1018

Chen, S. (2009, May 25). *Ning: the future of online social networking?* Retrieved May 30, 2009, from http://www.cnn.com/2009/TECH/05/25/ning.social.networking.interest/index.html?iref=t2test_techmon/

Childress, C. A. (2000). Ethical issues in providing online psychotherapeutic interventions [online]. *Journal of Medical Internet Research, 2*(1). http://www.jmir.org/2000/1/e5/ Retrieved July, 2007. doi:10.2196/jmir.2.1.e5

Chubbuck, S. M., Clift, R. T., Allard, J., & Quinlan, J. (2001). Playing it safe as a novice teacher: Implications for programs for new teachers. *Journal of Teacher Education, 52*(5), 365–376. doi:10.1177/0022487101052005003

Closing the Gap. (n.d.). *Closing the Gap solutions: Producers*. Retrieved February 1, 2010, from http://www.closingthegap.com/solutions/producers/

Clowes, G. (1997). Survey: Education teachers out of touch with the real world. *School Reform News*. Retrieved March 1, 2009 from: http://www.heartland.org/Article.cfm?artId=13665

Cobb, B. (1997). *HP e-mail mentor program evaluation. September 1996 – May 1997*. Retrieved September 12, 1998 from http://mentor.external.hp.com/eval/eval9697.html

Cohen, K. J., & Light, J. C. (2000). Use of electronic communication to develop mentor-protégé relationships between adolescent and adult AAC users: Pilot study. *Augmentative and Alternative Communication, 16*, 227–238. doi:10.1080/07434610012331279084

Cohen, M., Kahn, D., & Steeves, R. (2000). *Hermeneutic phenomenological research: A practical guide for nurse practitioners*. Thousand Oaks, CA: Sage Publications.

Colky, D. L., & Young, W. H. (2006). Mentoring in the virtual organization: Keys to building successful schools and businesses. *Mentoring & Tutoring, 14*(4), 433–447. doi:10.1080/13611260500493683

Colley, A., & Comber, C. (2003). Age and gender differences in computer use and attitudes among secondary school students: What has changed? *Educational Research, 45*(2), 155–165. http://www.informaworld.com/smpp/content~content=a713766213~db=all~order=page Retrieved February 1, 2010. doi:10.1080/0013188032000103235

Collins, A., Joseph, D., & Bielaczyc, K. (2004). Design research: Theoretical and methodological issues. *Journal of the Learning Sciences, 13*(1), 15–42. doi:10.1207/s15327809jls1301_2

Collins, A. (1996). Design issues for learning environments. In Vosniadou, S., De Corte, E., Glaser, R., & Mandl, H. (Eds.), *International perspectives on the psychological foundations of technology-supported learning environments*. Mahwah, NJ: Erlbaum.

Collis, B. (1998). New didactics for university instruction: Why and how? *Computers & Education, 41*(4), 373–393. doi:10.1016/S0360-1315(98)00040-2

Conklin, M. (2007, February 25). *101 uses for Second Life in the college classroom*. Retrieved March 3, 2010, from http://citeseerx.ist.psu.edu/viewdoc/download?doi=10.1.1.133.9588&rep=rep1&type=pdf

Cory, R. C., & Burgstahler, S. (2007). Creating virtual community: Mentoring kids with disabilities on the Internet. *Journal of School Public Relations, 28*, 283–296.

Costa, A. L., & Garmston, R. J. (2002). *Cognitive Coaching – A Foundation for Renaissance Schools*. Norwood, MA: Christopher-Gordon Publishers, Inc.

Coulson, N. S. (2005). Receiving Social Support Online: An Analysis of a Computer-Mediated Support Group for Individuals Living with Irritable Bowel Syndrome. *Cyberpsychology & Behavior, 8*(6), 580–584. doi:10.1089/cpb.2005.8.580

Cuban, L. (1986). *Teachers and machines: The classroom use of technology since 1920*. New York: Teachers College.

CUD. (n.d.b). *About UD*. Raleigh: CUD. Retrieved May 13, 2009, from http://www.design.ncsu.edu/cud/about_ud/about_ud.htm

Cutrona, C. A., & Shur, J. A. (1992). Controllability of stressful events and satisfaction with spouse support behaviors. *Communication Research, 19*(2), 154–174. doi:10.1177/009365092019002002

Dallos, R., & Comley-Ross, P. (2005). Young people's experience of mentoring: Building trust and attachments, *Clinical Child Psychology and Psychiatry, 10*, 369. Retrieved April 25, 2009, from http://ccp.sagepub.com/cgi/content/abstract/10/3/369

D'Amico, L. (1999). *The implications of project-based pedagogy for the classroom assessment infrastructres of science teachers*. Paper presented at the Annual meeting of the American Educational Research Association, Montreal, Quebec, Canada.

Darling-Hammond, L., & Richardson, N. (2009). Teacher learning: What matters? *Educational Leadership, 66*(5), 46–53.

Dawson, V. (2008). Use of information communication technology by early career science teachers in western Australia. *International Journal of Science Education, 30*(2), 203–219. doi:10.1080/09500690601175551

Day, A. L., & Livingstone, H. A. (2003). Gender differences in perceptions of stressors and utilization of social support among university students. *Canadian Journal of Behavioural Science, 35*, 73–83. doi:10.1037/h0087190

de Janasz, S. C., Ensher, E. A., & Heun, C. (2008). Virtual relationships and real benefits: Using e-mentoring to connect business students with practicing managers. *Mentoring and Tutoring: Partnership in Learning, 16*(4), 394–411. doi:10.1080/13611260802433775

Dede, C. (Ed.). (2006). *Online professional development for teachers: Emerging models and methods*. Cambridge, MA: Harvard Education Press.

Dede, C. (2007). Reinventing the role of information and communications technologies in Education. *Yearbook of the National Society for the Study of Education, 106*(2), 11–38. doi:10.1111/j.1744-7984.2007.00113.x

Dennis, G. (1993). *Mentoring*. Office of Education Research and Improvement Consumer Guide, (OR 93-3059 ED/OERI 92-38). Retrieved from http://www2.ed.gov/pubs/OR/ConsumerGuides/mentor.html

Department of Labor. (2008, June 27). *Number of jobs held, labor market activity, and earnings growth among the youngest baby boomers: Results from a longitudinal survey* (USDL Publication No. 08-0860). Retrieved April 22, 2009 from http://www.bls.gov/news.release/pdf/nlsoy.pdf

Deshler, D., Ellis, E., & Lentz, B. (1996). *Teaching Adolescents with Learning Disabilities: Strategies and Methods* (2nd ed.). Denver, CO: Love Publishing.

Design-Based Research Collective. (2003). Design-based research: An emerging paradigm for educational inquiry. *Educational Researcher, 32*(1), 5–8. doi:10.3102/0013189X032001005

Deubel, P. (2009, September 16). Social networking in schools: Incentives for participation. *Collaboration 2.0 Newsletter.* Retrieved August 10, 2010, from http://thejournal.com/articles/2009/09/16/social-networking-in-schools-incentives-for-participation.aspx

Dickey, C. A. (1997). Mentoring women of color at the University of Minnesota: Challenges for organizational transformation. *Journal of Vocational Special Needs Education, 36*(1), 22–27.

Dimock, K. V. (1996). *Building relationships, engaging students: A naturalistic study of classrooms participating in the electronic emissary project.* Retrieved September 20, 1998, from http://www.tapr.org/emissary/

Dinerstein, R. D. (2004, January). *Disability and the Law.* Paper presented at the inaugural conference of MISHAL – The Israeli University Center on Disabilities – Education, Empowerment & Research. Haifa, Israel: University of Haifa.

diSessa, A. (2002). A history of conceptual change research. In Sawyer, R. (Ed.), *Cambridge handbook of the learning sciences* (pp. 265–281). West Nyack, NY: Cambridge University Press.

Docs, G. (2009). *Wikipedia.* Retrieved April 25, 2009, from http://en.wikipedia.org/wiki/Google_docs

DO-IT. (n.d.). *DO-IT video search.* Retrieved February 1, 2010, from http://www.washington.edu/doit/Video/Search/

Donaldson, G. A. Jr. (2009). The lessons are in the leading. *Educational Leadership, 66*(5), 14–18.

Donker, H. (1993, November). *Experiences in telementoring during a computer-mediated communication (CMC) process.* Paper presented at the Conference of the New Educational Technologies and the TEMUS Programme – A Contribution to their Dissemination in Bulgaria, Sofia, Bulgaria. Retrieved September 12, 1998 from http://nsn.bbn.com/telementor_wrkshp/tmlink.htm

Doren, B., & Benz, M. R. (1998). Employment inequity revisited: Predictors of better employment outcomes of young women with disabilities in transition. *The Journal of Special Education, 31*(4), 425–442. doi:10.1177/002246699803100402

Doyle, C. S. (1995). Telementoring takes off in California: The telemation project develops integrated curriculum. *Internet Research: Electronic Networking Applications and Policy, 5,* 40–45. doi:10.1108/10662249510084453

Drayton, B., & Falk, J. (2003). Discourse analysis of web texts: Initial results from a telementoring project for middle school girls. *Education Communication and Information, 3*(1), 71–104. doi:10.1080/14636310303149

DuBois, D. L., Holloway, B. E., Valentine, J. C., & Cooper, H. (2002). Effectiveness of mentoring programs for youth: A meta-analytic review. *American Journal of Community Psychology, 30*(2), 157–197. doi:10.1023/A:1014628810714

DuBois, D. L., & Karcher, M. J. (2005). Youth mentoring. In DuBois, D. L., & Karcher, M. J. (Eds.), *Handbook of youth mentoring* (pp. 2–11). Thousand Oaks, CA: Sage.

Dussault, M., Deaudelin, C., Royer, N., & Loiselle, J. (1997, April). *Professional isolation and stress in teacher.* Paper presented at the annual meeting of the American Educational Research Association, Chicago, IL.

Dwyer, D. C., Ringstaff, C., & Sandholtz, J. H. (1991, May). Changes in teachers' beliefs and practices in technology-rich classrooms. *Educational Leadership, 48*(8), 45–52.

Edelson, D. C. (2002). Design Research: What We Learn When We Engage in Design. *Journal of the Learning Sciences, 11*(1), 105–121. doi:10.1207/S15327809JLS1101_4

Electronic Emissary. (n.d.a). *What is the Electronic Emissary?* Retrieved February 1, 2010, from http://emissary.wm.edu/index.php?content=what.html

Electronic Emissary. (n.d.b). *Project overview.* Retrieved February 1, 2010, from http://emissary.wm.edu/index.php?content=project_overview.html

Elgort, I., Smith, A. G., & Toland, J. (2008). Is wiki an effective platform for group course work? *Australasian Journal of Educational Technology, 24*(2), 195–210.

Ellerton, R. (2009). *Modalities and representational systems*. Retrieved from http://www.renewal.ca/nlp10.htm

Enochs, L. G., & Riggs, I. M. (1990). Further development of an elementary science teaching efficacy belief instrument: A pre-service elementary scale. *School Science and Mathematics, 90*(8), 694–706. doi:10.1111/j.1949-8594.1990.tb12048.x

Ensher, E. A., & Murphy, S. E. (1997). Effects of race, gender, perceived similarity, and contact on mentor relationships. *Journal of Vocational Behavior, 50*, 460–481. doi:10.1006/jvbe.1996.1547

Ensher, E. A., Heun, C., & Blanchard, A. (2003). Online mentoring and computer-mediated communication: New directions in research. *Journal of Vocational Behavior, 63*, 264–288. doi:10.1016/S0001-8791(03)00044-7

Evans, I. M., Wilson, N. J., Hansson, G., & Hungerford, R. (1997). Positive and negative behaviours of independent adolescent youth participation in a community support programme. *New Zealand Journal of Psychology, 26*, 29–35.

Everard, R. D., & Selman, J. C. (1989). Coaching and the Art of Management. *Organizational Dynamics, 18*, 16–32..doi:10.1016/0090-2616(89)90040-5

Fabian, E. S., Edelman, A., & Leedy, M. (1993). Linking workers with severe disabilities to social supports in the workplace: Strategies for addressing barriers. *Journal of Rehabilitation, 57*, 118–124.

Facebook (n.d.a). *Accessibility and assistive technology*. Retrieved February 1, 2010, from http://www.facebook.com/help.php?page=440

Facebook (n.d.b). *The official petition for a more accessible Facebook*. Retrieved February 1, 2010, from http://www.facebook.com/home.php#/group.php?gid=2384051749

Facebook. (n.d.). *Statistics*. Retrieved April 2009, 2009, from Facebook: http://www.facebook.com/press/info.php?statistics

Federal Communications Commission. (n.d.). *What you need to know about TRS*. Retrieved February 1, 2010, from http://www.fcc.gov/cgb/dro/trs.html

Feiman-Nemser, S. (1998). *Teacher mentoring: A critical review*. ERIC Digests. Washington, D.C. (ERIC Document Reproduction Service No. ED397060).

Fish, T. R., Rabidoux, P., Ober, J., & Graff, V. L. W. (2006). Community literacy and friendship model for people with intellectual disabilities. *Mental Retardation, 44*, 443–446. doi:10.1352/0047-6765(2006)44[443:CLAFMF]2.0.CO;2

Francisco, B. (2009). iGoogle to add chat and become more social. Retrieved April 25, 2009, from http://vator.tv/news/show/2009-01-08-igoogle-to-add-chat-and-become-more-social

Fredericksen, E., Pickett, A., & Shea, P. (2000, September). Student satisfaction and perceived learning with on-line courses: Principles and examples from the SUNY Learning Network, *Journal of Asynchronous Learning Networks, 4*(2). Retrieved April 10, 2009, from http://www.aln.org/alnweb/journal/jaln-vol4issue2.htm

FrEdWriter and FrEdMail. (n.d.). In Global SchoolNet's Global Schoolhouse. Retrieved August 11, 2010, from http://www.globalschoolnet.org/gsnabout/history/fred-history.cfm

Freedman, M. (1992). *The kindness of strangers: Reflections on the mentoring movement*. Philadelphia, PA: Public/Private Ventures.

Friedman, A. A., Zibit, M., & Coote, M. (2004). Tele-mentoring as a collaborative agent for change. *Journal of Technology, Learning, and Assessment, 3*(1). Retrieved January 29, 2010 from http://www.jtla.org

Ganser, T. (1997). Similes for beginning teaching. *Kappa Delta Pi Record, 33*(3), 106–108.

Garber, D. (2004). Growing virtual communities, *International Review of Research in Open and Distance Learning, 5*(2). Retrieved April 28, 2009, from http://www.irrodl.org/content/v5.2/technote4.html

Garcia, P., & Rose, S. (2007). The influence of technocentric collaboration on preservice teachers' attitudes about technology's role in powerful learning and teaching. *Journal of Technology and Teacher Education, 15*(2), 247–266.

Gareis, C. R., & Nussbaum-Beach, C. (2007). Electronically mentoring to develop accomplished professional teachers. *Journal of Personnel Evaluation in Education, 27*, 227–246. doi:10.1007/s11092-008-9060-0

Garrett, J. (2005 February). *Ajax: A new approach to web applications*. Retrieved on April, 23, 2009 from http://www.adaptivepath.com/ideas/essays/archives/000385.php.

Garringer, M., Fulop, M., & Rennick, V. (2003). *Foundations of successful youth mentoring: A guidebook for program development*. Portland, OR: National Mentoring Center. Retrieved February 1, 2010, from http://gwired.gwu.edu/hamfish/merlin-cgi/p/downloadFile/d/20699/n/off/other/1/name/foundationspdf/

Garrison, D. R., Anderson, T., & Archer, W. (2000). Critical inquiry in a text-based environment: Computer conferencing in higher education. *The Internet and Higher Education, 2*(2-3), 87–105. doi:10.1016/S1096-7516(00)00016-6

Garrison, D. R., Anderson, T., & Archer, W. (2003). A theory of critical inquiry in online distance education. In Moore, M. G., & Anderson, W. G. (Eds.), *Handbook of distance education* (pp. 113–128). Mahwah, N.J.: L. Erlbaum Associates.

Gentry, L. B., Denton, C. A., & Kurz, T. (2008). Technology-based mentoring provided to teachers: A synthesis of the literature. *Journal of Technology and Teacher Education, 16*(3), 339–373.

Gersten, R., Keating, T., Yovanoff, P., & Harniss, M. (2001). Working in special education: Factors that enhance special educators' intent to stay. *Exceptional Children, 67*, 549–567.

Gilligan, C. (1982). *In a different voice: Psychological theory and women's development*. Cambridge, MA: Harvard University Press.

Gmail. (2009). *Wikipedia*. Retrieved April 25, 2009, from http://en.wikipedia.org/wiki/Gmail

Golden, D. C. (2002). Instructional software accessibility: A status report. *Journal of Special Education Technology, 17*(1), 57–60.

Goleman, D. (2006). *Social intelligence: The revolutionary new science of human relationships*. New York: Bantam Dell.

Goodnough, K. C., & Hung, W. (2008) Engaging teachers' pedagogical content knowledge: Adopting a nine-step problem-based learning model. *Interdisciplinary Journal of Problem-based Learning, 2*(2), 61-90. Retrieved April 2, 2009, from http://docs.lib.purdue.edu/ijpbl/vol2/iss2/6.

Google Inc. (2009). Google Translate FAQs. Retrieved April 25, 2009, from http://www.google.com/intl/en/help/faq_translation.html#statmt

Greenberg, P. S., Greenberg, R., & Antonucci, Y. L. (2007). Creating and Sustaining Trust in Virtual Teams. *Business Horizons, 50*(4), 325–333. doi:10.1016/j.bushor.2007.02.005

Greenglass, E. R. (1993). Structural and social-psychological factors associated with job functioning by women managers. *Psychological Reports, 73*(3), 979–987.

Gresham, F. M., Evans, S., & Elliott, S. N. (1988). Self-efficacy differences among mildly handicapped, gifted, and nonhandicapped students. *The Journal of Special Education, 22*, 231–241. doi:10.1177/002246698802200208

Gross, E. F. (2004). Adolescent Internet use: What we expect, what teens report. *Applied Developmental Psychology, 25*, 633–649. doi:10.1016/j.appdev.2004.09.005

Gross, E. F., Juvonen, J., & Gable, S. L. (2002). Internet use and well being in adolescence. *The Journal of Social Issues*, *58*, 75–90. doi:10.1111/1540-4560.00249

Grossman, J. B. (1999). The practice, quality and cost of mentoring. In J. B. Grossman (Ed.), *Contemporary issues in mentoring* (pp. 5-9). Philadelphia: Public/Private Ventures. Retrieved December 4, 2009 from http://www.ppv.org/ppv/publications/assets/37_publication.pdf

Guy, T. (2002). Telementoring: Shaping Mentoring Relationships for the 21st Century. In Hansman, C. A. (Ed.), *Critical Perspectives on Mentoring: Trends and Issues. Information Series No. 388*. Columbus, OH: ERIC Clearinghouse on Adult, Career, and Vocational Education.

Hackett, G., & Betz, N. E. (1981). A self-efficacy approach to the career development of women. *Journal of Vocational Behavior*, *18*, 326–339. doi:10.1016/0001-8791(81)90019-1

Hamilton, B. A., & Scandura, T. A. (2003). E-mentoring: Implications for organizational learning and development in a wired world. *Organizational Dynamics*, *31*, 388–402. doi:10.1016/S0090-2616(02)00128-6

Hammerness, K., Darling-Hammond, L., Bransford, J., Berliner, D., Cochran-Smith, M., McDonald, M., & Zeichner, K. (2005). How teachers learn and develop. In Darling-Hammond, L., & Bransford, J. (Eds.), *Preparing Teachers for a Changing World: What Teachers Should Learn and Be Able to Do*. San Francisco, CA: Jossey-Bass.

Hansman, C. A. (2002). Facing forward: Implications for practice and suggestions for future research. In C. A. Hansman (Ed.), *Critical Perspectives on Mentoring: Trends and Issues* (pp.49-52). Columbus, OH: Center on Education and Training for Employment. Retrieved May 13, 2009, from http://www.calpro-online.org/eric/docs/mott/mentoring7.pdf

Harada, V. H., Kirio, C. H., & Yamamoto, S. H. (2008b). Project-based learning: Rigor and relevance in high schools. *Library Media Connection*, *26*(6), 14–16, 18, 20.

Harada, V. H., & Yoshina, J. M. (2004. *Inquiry learning through librarian-teacher partnerships*. Worthington, OH: Linworth. Harada, V. H., Kirio, C. H., & Yamamoto, S. H. (2008a). *Collaborating for project-based learning in grades 9-12*. Columbus, OH: Linworth.

Hargadon, S. (2009). *Educational networking: The important role Web 2.0 will play in education*. Calgary, Alberta: Elluminate Canada. Retrieved August 10, 2010, from http://www.scribd.com/doc/22279609/Hargadon-Educational-Social-Networking

Harrington, A. (1999). *E-Mentoring: The advantages and disadvantages of using email to support distance mentoring*. Retrieved March 3, 2009, from European Social Fund Website: http://www.mentorsforum.co.uk/cOL1/discover.htm

Harris, J. (1998). *Virtual architecture: Designing and directing curriculum-based telecomputing*. Eugene, OR: International Society for Technology in Education, University of Oregon.

Harris, J., & Hofer, M. (2009). "Grounded" technology integration: Planning with curriculum-based learning activity types. *Learning and Leading with Technology*, *37*(2), 22–25.

Harris, J. B., & Figg, C. (2000). Participating from the sidelines, online: Facilitating telementoring projects. *Journal of Computer Documentation*, *24*, 227–236. doi:10.1145/353927.353934

Harris, J., & Jones, G. (1999). A descriptive study of telementoring among students, subject matter experts, and teachers: Message flow and function patterns. *Journal of Research on Computing in Education*, *42*(1), 36–53.

Harris, J., O'Bryan, E., & Rotenberg, L. (1996). It's a simple idea, but it's not easy to do! Practical lessons in telementoring. Learning and leading with technology. *The ISTE Journal of Educational Technology Practice and Policy*, *24*, 53–57.

Harris, J. (2010). Facilitated telementoring for K-12 students and teachers. In Berg, G. A. (Ed.), *Cases on online tutoring, mentoring, and educational services* (pp. 1–11). Hershey, PA: IGI Global. doi:10.4018/978-1-60566-876-5.ch001

Harris, J. (2005). Curriculum-based telecomputing: What was old could be new again. In Kearsley, G. (Ed.), *Online learning: Personal reflections on the transformation of education* (pp. 128–143). Englewood Cliffs, NJ: Educational Technology Publications.

Harris, J. B. (2003). Electronic Emissary. In Kovalkchick, A., & Dawson, K. (Eds.), *Education and Technology: An encyclopedia* (*Vol. 1*). Santa Barbara, CA: ABC-CLIO.

Harris, J. (1999). *About the Electronic Emissary Project*. Retrieved February 1, 2010 from http://emissary.wm.edu/index.php?content=about.html

Harris, J. B. & Jones, G. (1999). A descriptive study of telementoring among students, subject matter experts, and teachers: Message flow and function patterns. *Journal of Research on Computing in Education, 32*.

Harris, J. B. (2008). TPACK in inservice education: Assisting experienced teachers' planned improvisations. In AACTE Committee on Innovation & Technology (Eds.). *Handbook of technological pedagogical content knowledge for educators* (pp. 251-271). New York: Routledge.

Harris, J. B., & Figg, C. (2000). Participating from the sidelines, online: Facilitating telementoring projects. *ACM Journal of Computer Documentation, 24*(4), 227-236. Retrieved August 9, 2010, from http://portal.acm.org/citation.cfm?id=353927.353934

Harris, J. B., & Hofer, M. J. (in press). Technological pedagogical content knowledge (TPACK) in action: A descriptive study of secondary teachers' curriculum-based, technology-related instructional planning. *Journal of Research on Technology in Education, 43*(3).

Harris, J., Rotenberg, L., & O'Bryan, E. (1997). *Results from electronic emissary project: Telementoring lessons and examples* (Denton, TX, Texas Center for Educational Technology). Retrieved March 9, 2009 from: http://www.tcet.unt.edu/pubs/em/em01.pdf

Hasselbring, T.S., & Williams Glaser, C.H. (2000). Use of computer technology to help students with special needs. *The future of children – Children and computer technology, 10*(2), 102-122.

Hawkey, K. (1997). Roles, responsibilities, and relationships in mentoring: A literature review and agenda for research. *Journal of Teacher Education, 48*(5), 325. doi:10.1177/0022487197048005002

Hazari, S., North, A., & Moreland, D. (2009). Investigating pedagogical value of wiki technology. *Journal of Information Systems Education, 20*(2), 187–198.

Headlam-Wells, J., Gosland, J., & Craig, J. (2006). Beyond the organization: The design and management of e-mentoring systems. *International Journal of Information Management, 26*, 372–385. doi:10.1016/j.ijinfomgt.2006.04.001

Heider, K. L. (2005). Teacher isolation: How mentoring programs can help. *Current Issues in Education, 14*. Retrieved April 22, 2009 from http://cied.ed.asu.edu/volume8/number14/June23/

Heinich, R., Molenda, M., Russell, J. D., & Smaldino, S. E. (2002). *Instructional media and technologies for learning* (7th ed.). Upper Saddle River, New Jersey: Merrill Prentice Hall.

Hernandez, B., Keys, C., & Balcazar, F. (2000). Employer attitudes toward workers with disabilities and their ADA employment rights: A literature review. *Journal of Rehabilitation, 66*, 4–16.

Herrera, C., Sipe, C., & McClanahan, W. S. (2000). *Mentoring school-age children: Relationship development in community-based and school-based programs*. Philadelphia, PA: Private/Public Ventures.

Herrera, C., Sipe, C. L., & McClanahan, W. S. (2000). *Mentoring school-age children: Relationship development in community-based and school-based programs*. Philadelphia: Public/Private Ventures. (Published in collaboration with MENTOR/National Mentoring Partnership, Alexandria, VA.

Hersch, R. (2009, April 20). Our 21st-century 'risk': Teaching for content and skills. *New York Times Web Education Week*. Retrieved from http://www.edweek.org/login.html?source=http://www.edweek.org/ew/articles/2009/04/22/29hersh_ep.h28.html&destination=http://www.edweek.org/ew/articles/2009/04/22/29hersh_ep.h28.html&levelId=1000

Hewitt, A., & Forte, A. (2006, November). *Crossing boundaries: Identity management and student/faculty relationships on Facebook*. Poster session presented at the Computer Supported Cooperative Work Conference. Retrieved April 30, 2009, from http://www.cc.gatech.edu/~aforte/HewittForteCSCWPoster2006.pdf

Hirst, K. (2000). Distance education: No significant difference. Retrieved June 20, 2001, from http://distancelearn.miningco.com/education/distancelearn/library/blpages/blnsd.htm

History of Wikipedia. (2009). *Wikipedia*. Retrieved April 25, 2009, from http://en.wikipedia.org/wiki/History_of_Wikipedia

History of Wikipedia. (2009). *Wikipedia*. Retrieved April 29, 2009, from http://en.wikipedia.org/wiki/History_of_Wikipedia

Hitchcock, M. A., & Mylona, Z. E. (2000). Teaching faculty to conduct problem-based learning. *Teaching and Learning in Medicine*, *12*(1), 52–57. doi:10.1207/S15328015TLM1201_8

Hitchcock, C., Meyer, A., Rose, D., & Jackson, R. (2002). Providing new access to the general curriculum: Universal design for learning. *Teaching Exceptional Children*, *35*(2), 8–17.

Hitchcock, C., & Stahl, S. (2002). Assistive technology, universal design, universal design for learning: Improved learning opportunities. *Journal of Special Education Technology*, *18*(4).

Hmelo-Silver, C. E., & Barrows, H. S. (2006). Goals and strategies of a problem-based learning facilitator. *The Interdisciplinary Journal of Problem-based Learning*, *1*(1), 21–39.

Hoffman, M., & Blake, J. (2003). Computer literacy: Today and tomorrow. *Journal of Computing Sciences in Colleges*, *18*(5), 221–233.

Houston, T. K., Cooper, L. A., & Ford, D. E. (2002). Internet support groups for depression: A 1-year prospective cohort study. *The American Journal of Psychiatry*, *159*(12), 2062–2068. doi:10.1176/appi.ajp.159.12.2062

Huett, J., Moller, L., Foshay, W., & Coleman, C. (2008). The evolution of distance education: Implications for instructional design on the potential of the web. *TechTrends*, *52*(5), 63–67. doi:10.1007/s11528-008-0199-9

IBM. (2008). *What is Virtual Worlds User Interface for the Blind?* Retrieved February 1, 2010, from http://services.alphaworks.ibm.com/virtualworlds/

Illinois Mathematics and Science Academy (IMSA). (2009). *Introduction to problem based learning*. Retrieved April 9, 2009, from http://pbln.imsa.edu/model/intro/index.html.

Individuals with Disabilities Education Improvement Act of 2004. (P.L. 108-446). Retrieved December 4, 2009 from http://idea.ed.gov/download/statute.html

Ingersoll, R. (2002). The teacher shortage: A case of wrong diagnosis and wrong prescription. *NASSP Bulletin*, *86*, 16–31. doi:10.1177/019263650208663103

Ingersoll, R. M. (2003). The teacher shortage: Myth or reality? *Educational Horizons*, *81*(3), 146–152.

Ingersoll, R., & Kralik, J. M. (2004). *The impact of mentoring on teacher retention: What the research says*. Denver: Education Commission of the States. Retrieved February 2009 from, http://www.ecs.org/clearinghouse/50/36/5036.htm

Jaffe, D. (2003, April). Virtual transformation: Web-based technology and pedagogical change. *Teaching Sociology*, *31*(2), 227–236. doi:10.2307/3211312

Jarrett, O. S. (1999). Science interest and confidence among pre-service elementary teachers. *Journal of Elementary Science Education*, *11*(1), 49–59. doi:10.1007/BF03173790

Jerome, W., Rinderle, J., & Bajzek, D. (2008). Tools for constructing targeted feedback in online instruction. In G. Richards (Ed.), *Proceedings of World Conference on E-Learning in Corporate, Government, Healthcare, and Higher Education 2008* (pp. 3753-3759). Chesapeake, VA: AACE.

John, P. D. (2006). Lesson planning and the student teacher: Re-thinking the dominant model. *Journal of Curriculum Studies*, 38(4), 483–498. doi:10.1080/00220270500363620

Johnson, D. W., & Johnson, R. T. (2009). Energizing learning: The instructional power of conflict. *Educational Researcher*, 38(1), 37–51. doi:10.3102/0013189X08330540

Johnson, D., Stodden, R., Emmanuel, E., Luecking, R., & Mack, M. (2002). Current challenges facing secondary education and transition services: what research tells us. *Exceptional Children*, 68(4), 519–531.

Johnson, L., Levine, A., Smith, R., & Smythe, T. (2009). *The 2009 horizon report: K-12 edition*. Austin, Texas: The New Media Consortium. Retrieved April 8, 2009, from http://www.nmc.org/pdf/2009-Horizon-Report-K12.pdf.

Joinson, A. N. (2001). Self-disclosure in computer-mediated communication: The role of self-awareness and visual anonymity. *European Journal of Social Psychology*, 31, 177–192. doi:10.1002/ejsp.36

Jonassen, D. H. (2000). Toward a design theory of problem solving. *Educational Technology Research and Development*, 48(4), 63–85. doi:10.1007/BF02300500

Jonassen, D. H., Carr, C., & Yueh, H. P. (1998). Computers as MindTools for engaging learners in critical thinking. *TechTrends*, 43(2), 24–32. doi:10.1007/BF02818172

Jonassen, D. H., & Hung, W. (2008). All problems are not equal: Implications for problem-based learning. *The Interdisciplinary Journal of Problem-based Learning*, 2(2), Article 4. Retrieved August 20, 2009, from http://docs.lib.purdue.edu/ijpbl/vol2/iss2/4.

Jones, B. F., Valdez, G., Nowakowski, J., & Rasmussen, C. (1995). Plugging in: Choosing and using educational technology. *North Central Regional Educational Laboratory*. Retrieved April 1, 2001, from http://www.ncrel.org/sdrs/edtalk/toc.htm

Jorn, L., Whiteside, A., & Duin, A. H. (2009) Pair-up. *Educause Review*, 44(2). Retrieved April 20, 2009, from http://www.educause.edu/EDUCAUSE+Review/EDUCAUSEReviewMagazineVolume44/PAIRUp/163795

Jucovy, L. (2001). *Training new mentors*. Philadelphia, PA: Public/Private Ventures.

Kasprisin, C. A., Single, P. B., Single, R. M., Ferrier, J. L., & Muller, C. B. (2008). Improved mentor satisfaction: emphasizing protégé training for adult-age mentoring dyads. *Mentoring & Tutoring*, 16(2), 163–174. doi:10.1080/13611260801916424

Kasprisin, C. A., Single, P. B., Single, R. M., & Muller, C. B. (2003). Building a better bridge: Testing e-training to improve e-mentoring programmes in higher education. *Mentoring & Tutoring*, 11(1), 67–78. doi:10.1080/1361126032000054817

Kaye, S. (2000). Disability and the digital divide. *Disability Statistics Abstract*, 22. Retrieved December 4, 2009 from http://dsc.ucsf.edu/publication.php?pub_id=6

Kegan, R., & Lahey, L. (2009). *Immunity to Change: How to Overcome It and Unlock the Potential in Yourself and Your Organization*. Boston, MA: Harvard Business Press.

Keller, T. E. (2005). The stage and development of mentoring relationships. In DuBois, D. L., & Karcher, M. J. (Eds.), *Handbook for youth mentoring* (pp. 82–99). Thousand Oaks, CA: Sage.

Kelton, A. J. (2007). *Second Life: Reaching into the virtual world for real-world learning*. EDUCAUSE Center for Applied Research (ECAR) Research Bulletin, 2007 (17). Retrieved February 1, 2010, from http://www.educause.edu/ECAR/SecondLifeReachingintotheVirtu/161863

Kerka, S. (1998). *New perspectives on mentoring.* Retrieved October 5, 1998, from http://www.peer.ca/Perspectives.html

Kessler, M. (2004). *The transition years: Serving current and former foster youth ages eighteen to twenty-one.* Tulsa: University of Oklahoma, National Resource Center for Youth Services.

Kilgore, K. L., & Griffin, C. C. (1998). Beginning special educators: Problems of practice and the influence of school context. *Teacher Education and Special Education, 21,* 155–173. doi:10.1177/088840649802100302

Killion, J. (2008). Are You Coaching Heavy or Light? *Teachers Teaching Teachers, 3*(8), 1–4.

Kimball, L., & Eunice, A. (1999, November). *Zen and the art of facilitating virtual learning communities.* Paper presented at the ThinkQuest Teachers' Summit, Los Angeles, CA.

Kim-Rupnow, W. S., & Burgstahler, S. (2004). Perceptions of students with disabilities regarding the value of technology-based support activities on postsecondary education and employment. *Journal of Special Education Technology, 19*(2), 43–56.

King, R., Bambling, M., Lloyd, C., Gomurra, R., Smith, S., Reid, W., & Wegner, K. (2006). Online counseling: The motives and experiences of young people who choose the Internet instead of face to face or telephone counseling. *Counselling & Psychotherapy Research, 6,* 169–174. doi:10.1080/14733140600848179

Kram, K. E. (1985). *Mentoring at work: Developmental relationships in organizational life.* New York: University Press of America.

Kram, K. E. (1983). Phases of the mentor relationship. *Academy of Management Journal, 26*(4), 608–625. doi:10.2307/255910

Lab, F. W. For Educational Research and Development. (1995). *Telemation project evaluation, Final report* (ERIC Document Reproduction Service No. ED 396 705). Sacramento, CA: California State Department of Education.

Labaree, D. F. (1997). Public goods, private goods: The American struggle over educational goals. *American Educational Research Journal, 34*(1), 39–81.

Landel, C., & Nelson, G. (2009). Creating and sustaining science-focused professional learning communities through partnerships. In Mundry, S., & Stiles, K. E. (Eds.), *Professional Learning Communities for Science Teaching: Lessons from Research and Practice* (pp. 73–88). Arlington, VA: NSTA Press.

Larson, J., Shaw, J., & Taylor, J. (2009), *iCoaching Instructional Coaching Year 2 Summary Report* (Report No. ER-2009-08), Colorado Springs, CO: Biological Sciences Curriculum Study, Center for Research & Evaluation.

Laux, L. F., McNally, P. R., Paciello, M. G., & Vanderheiden, G. C. (1996). Designing the World Wide Web for people with disabilities: A user centered design approach. In *Proceedings of the Second Annual ACM Conference on Assistive Technologies.* Association for Computing Machinery, Special Interest Group on Accessible Computing, Vancouver, B. C., 94-101.

Lave, J., & Wenger, E. (1991). *Situated learning: Legitimate peripheral participation.* Cambridge: Cambridge University Press.

Lee, P. (2004). Understanding history. In Seixas, P. (Ed.), *Theorizing Historical Consciousness.* Toronto: University of Toronto Press.

Leh, A. S. C. (2001). Computer-Mediated Communication and Social Presence in a Distance Learning Environment. *International Journal of Educational Telecommunications, 7*(2), 109–128.

Lehman, J. D., George, M., Buchanan, P., & Rush, M. (2006). Preparing teachers to use problem-centered, inquiry-based science: Lessons from a four-year professional development project. *The Interdisciplinary Journal of Problem-based Learning, 1*(1), 9–19.

Lembree, D. (2009). *Accessible Twitter.* Retrieved February 1, 2010, from http://www.accessibletwitter.com

Lemon, G. (2009). *Twitter focus*. Retrieved February 1, 2010, from http://juicystudio.com/article/twitter-focus.php

Lenert, K. F., & Harris, J. B. (1994). *Redefining expertise and reallocating roles in text-based asynchronous teaching/learning environments*. Retrieved October 8, 1998 from http://www.tapr.org/emissary/

Lenhart, A., Ling, R., Campbell, S., & Purcell, K. (2010). *Teens and mobile phones* (Research report, April 20, 2010). Washington, DC: Pew Research Center, Pew Internet & American Life Project. Retrieved August 10, 2010, from http://pewinternet.org/Reports/2010/Teens-and-Mobile-Phones.aspx

Levy, A. (2007). *What is Blogtalkradio?* Retrieved April 25, 2009, from http://blog.blogtalkradio.com/2007/04/15/what-is-blogtalkradio%22/

Lewis, J., Coursol, D., & Herting, W. (2004). Researching the cybercounseling process: A study of the client and counselor experience. In Bloom, J. W., & Walz, G. R. (Eds.), *Cybercounseling & cyberlearning: An encore* (pp. 307–325). Alexandria, VA: American Counseling Association.

Limon, M. (2001). On the cognitive conflict as an instructional strategy for conceptual change: A critical appraisal. *Learning and Instruction*, *11*, 357–380. doi:10.1016/S0959-4752(00)00037-2

LinkedIn. (n.d.). *Professional and Amateur Mentoring Group*. Retrieved February 1, 2010, from http://www.linkedin.com/groups?gid=36602

Linn, M., Lewis, C., Tsuchida, I., & Songer, N. (2000). Beyond fourth-grade science: Why do U.S. and Japanese students diverge? *Educational Researcher*, *29*(3), 4–14.

Llewellyn, D. (2007). *Inquire Within* (2nd ed.). Thousand Oaks, CA: Corwin Press.

Lombard, M., & Ditton, T. (1997). At the heart of it all: The concept of presence. *Journal of Computer Mediated Communication, 3*(2). Retrieved November, 2007, from http://jcmc.indiana.edu/vol3/issue2/lombard.html

Longmore, P. (2003). *Why I burned my book and other essays on disability*. Philadelphia, PA: Temple University Press.

Loucks-Horsley, S., Love, N., Stiles, K. E., Mundry, S., & Hewson, P. W. (2003). *Designing professional development for teachers of mathematics and science* (2nd ed.). Thousand Oaks, CA: Corwin Press.

Loucks-Horsley, S., & Stiles, K. E. (2001). Professional development designed to change science teaching and learning. In J. Rhoton & P. Bowers, P. (Eds.). *Professional development planning and design* (pp.13-24). Arlington, VA: NSTA Press.

Mallen, M. J., Vogel, D. L., Rochlen, A. B., & Day, S. X. (2005). Online Counseling: Reviewing the Literature from a Counseling Psychology Framework. *The Counseling Psychologist*, *33*(6), 819–871. doi:10.1177/0011000005278624

Marshall, C., & Rossman, G. (1999). *Designing Qualitative Research*. Thousand Oaks, CA: Sage Publications.

Martin, K., & McGrevin, C. (1990). Making mathematics happen. *Educational Leadership*, *47*(8), 20–22.

Martin, A. (2005). *Shared responsibilities of teachers and mentors in a curriculum-based telementoring project in the humanities*. Unpublished Master's thesis, Simon Fraser University, Burnaby, British Columbia.

Maynard, T., & Furlong, J. (1995). *Mentoring student teachers the growth of professional knowledge*. New York: Routledge.

McCarthy, C. (2008, October). *Ning's OpenSocial support goes live*. Retrieved April 30, 2009, from http://news.cnet.com/8301-13577_3-10063030-36.html

McConkey, R. (2005*). Inclusion in society: Delivering on the promise*. Paper presented at the International Special Education Conference on Inclusion: Celebrating diversity? 1st – 4th August, Galsgow, Scotland.

McCurdy, S., & Schroeder, R. (2005). *Inter-institutional collaborations in the delivery of online learning*. Paper presented at the 21st Annual Conference on Distance Teaching and Learning. Retrieved April 30, 2009, from http://www.uwex.edu/disted/conference/Resource_library/proceedings/05_1829.pdf

McDonald, K. E., Balcazar, F. E., & Keys, C. B. (2005). Youth with disabilities. In DuBois, D. L., & Karcher, M. J. (Eds.), *Handbook of youth mentoring* (pp. 493–507). Thousand Oaks, CA: Sage.

McGee. P. (1997). *Collaboration and unintentional teacher learning in telementoring contexts*. Retrieved October 7, 1998 from http://www.tapr.org/emissary/

McLoughlin, C., Brady, J., Lee, M. J. W., & Russell, R. (2007, November). Peer-to-peer: An e-mentoring approach to developing community, mutual engagement and professional identity for pre-service teachers. Paper presented at the Australian Association for Research in Education (AARE) Conference Fremantle, Western Australia. Retrieved April 4, 2009, from http://www.aare.edu.au/07pap/mcl07393.pdf.

Medina, J. J. (2008). *Brain Rules: 12 Principles for Surviving and Thriving at Work, Home and School*. Seattle, WA: Pear Press.

Mehrabian, A. (1972). *Nonverbal communication*. Chicago, IL: Aldine-Atherton.

Meister, D. G., & Melnick, S. A. (2003). National new teacher study: Beginning teachers' concerns. *Action in Teacher Education*, 24(4), 87–94.

MentorNet. (n.d.a). *About MentorNet*. Retrieved February 1, 2010, from http://www.mentornet.net/documents/about/

MentorNet. (n.d.b). *MentorNet E-Forum*. Retrieved May 13, 2009, from http://www.mentornet.net/community/eforum/

Mesch, G. S., & Talmud, I. (2006). Online friendship formation, communication channels, and social closeness. *International Journal of Internet Science*, 1(1), 29–44.

Michalko, R. (2002). *The difference that disability makes*. Philadelphia, PA: Temple University Press.

Mid-continent Research for Education and Learning (McREL). (2009). *Content knowledge* (4th ed.) Retrieved April 8, 2009, from http://www.mcrel.org/standards-benchmarks/.

Mihkelson, A. (1997). *A model of research mentoring for higher education – An overview*. (ERIC Document Reproduction Service No. ED418661).

Miller, H., & Griffiths, M. (2005). E-Mentoring. In DuBois, D. L., & Karcher, M. J. (Eds.), *Handbook of youth mentoring* (pp. 300–313). Thousand Oaks, London, New Delhi: Sage.

Mishra, P., & Koehler, M. J. (2006). Technological pedagogical content knowledge: A framework for integrating technology in teacher knowledge. *Teachers College Record*, 108(6), 1017–1054. doi:10.1111/j.1467-9620.2006.00684.x

Moen, D. (2000). *Cargill/Olson e-mentoring program evaluation report 1999-2000: Linking youth with employees through the use of computer technology*. Unpublished manuscript.

Moller, L., Huett, J. B., & Harvey, D. M. (2008). *Learning and instructional technologies for the 21st century: Visions of the future*. New York: Springer.

Monnier, J., Stone, B. K., Hobfoll, S. E., & Johnson, R. J. (1998). How antisocial and prosocial coping influence the support process among men and women in the U.S. Postal Service. *Sex Roles*, 39(1-2), 1–20. doi:10.1023/A:1018821631246

Moore, M. G. (1989).Editorial: Three types of interaction. *The American Journal of Distance Education*, 3(2). Retrieved May 29, 2009, from http://www.ajde.com/Contents/vol3_2.htm

Moran, S. W. (1990). Schools and the beginning teacher. *Phi Delta Kappan*, 72(3), 210–213.

Moseley, C., Reinke, K., & Bookout, V. (2003). The effect of teaching outdoor environmental education on elementary pre-service teachers' self-efficacy. *Journal of Elementary Science Education, 15*(1), 1–14. doi:10.1007/BF03174740

Muller, C. B. (1997, November). The potential of industrial 'e-mentoring' as a retention strategy for women in science and engineering. Paper presented at the *Annual Frontiers in Education (FIE) Conference,* Pittsburgh, PA. Retrieved March 9, 2009 from http://fairway.ecn.purdue.edu/~fie/fie97/papers/1268.pdf

Mundry, S., & Stiles, K. E. (Eds.). (2009). *Professional Learning Communities for Science Teaching: Lessons from Research and Practice.* Arlington, VA: NSTA Press.

Myerson, D., Weick, K. E., & Kramer, R. M. (1996). Swift trust and temporary groups. In Kramer, R. M., & Tyler, T. R. (Eds.), *Trust in organizations: Frontiers of theory and research* (pp. 166–195). Thousand Oaks, CA: Sage.

National Alliance for Secondary Education and Transition. (2004). *NASET overview.* Retrieved December 4, 2009 from http://www.nasetalliance.org/about/index.htm

National Collaborative on Workforce and Disability for Youth. (2003). *The guideposts for success.* Washington, DC: Author. Retrieved December 4, 2009 from http://www.ncwd-youth.info/resources_&_Publications/guideposts/

National Council on Disability. (2004). *Design for inclusion: Creating a new marketplace.* Washington, DC: Author. Retrieved February 1, 2010, from http://www.ncd.gov/newsroom/publications/2004/online_newmarketplace.htm#afbad

National Mentoring Center. (2002). *Perspectives on e-mentoring: A virtual panel holds an online dialogue.* Retrieved April 24, 2009 from www.nwrel.org/mentoring/pdf/bull9.pdf

National Organization on Disability and Harris Survey. (2004). *Landmark disability survey finds pervasive disadvantages.* Retrieved December 4, 2009 from http://www.nod.org/index.cfm?fuseaction=feature.showFeature&FeatureID=1422&C:\CFusion8\verity\Data\dummy.txt

National Research Council. (1996). *National Science Education Standards.* Washington, DC: National Academy Press.

National Research Council. (2000). *How People Learn: Brain, Mind, Experience, and School.* Washington, DC: National Academy Press.

National Research Council. (2007). *Enhancing Professional Development for Teachers: Potential Uses of Information Technology. Report of a Workshop.* Washington, DC: National Academies Press.

National Science Foundation. (2001). *Programs for persons with disabilities: Regional Alliances for Persons with Disabilities in Science, Mathematics, Engineering and Technology Education* (NSF 01-67). Retrieved February 1, 2010, from http://www.nsf.gov/pubs/2001/nsf0167/nsf0167.htm

National Science Foundation. (2008). *Math science partnership program: National impact report.* Retrieved August 25, 2008, from http://www.scalemsp.org/files/MSP_News/Impact_Report/final_msp_impact_report.pdf

National Science Teachers Association. (2009). *New Science Teacher Academy.* Retrieved May 1, 2009 from http://www.nsta.org/academy/

Nefstead, S., & Nefstead, S. (2005). *Mentoring in the 90's and beyond.* Retrieved April 29, 2009, from http://www.extension.umn.edu/distribution/citizenship/DH6447.html

Nesler, M. S., & Hanner, M. B. (2001). Professional socialization of baccalaureate nursing students: Can students in distance nursing programs become socialized? *The Journal of Nursing Education, 40*(7), 293–302.

Neufeld, B., & Roper, D. (2003). *Coaching: A strategy for developing instructional capacity--Promises and practicalities.* Washington, DC: Aspen Institute Program on Education, and Providence. RI: Annenberg Institute for School Reform.

New Media Consortium (NMC). (2005). *A global imperative: The report of the 21st Century Literacy Summit.* Austin, TX: The New Media Consortium. Retrieved April 8, 2009, from http://archive.nmc.org/pdf/Global_Imperative.pdf.

New Media Consortium. (2008). *The 2008 Horizon Report*. Retrieved May 20, 2009, from http://www.nmc.org/pdf/2008-Horizon-Report.pdf

Nielsen, J. (1996, October). Accessible design for users with disabilities. *Albertox: Current Issues in Web Usability*. Retrieved February 1, 2010, from http://www.useit.com/alertbox/9610.html

Nielsen, J. (2007, February). Life-long computer skils. *Alertbox*. Retrieved April 30, 2009, from http://www.useit.com/alertbox/computer-skills.html

Nieto, S. (2003). Challenging current notions of "highly qualified teachers" through work in a teachers' inquiry group. *Journal of Teacher Education, 54*(5), 386–398.. doi:10.1177/0022487103257394

Ning, Inc. (2009). *Ning Fact Sheet*. Retrieved April 30, 2009, from http://about.ning.com/press.php

Noe, R. A. (1988). An investigation of the determinants of successful assigned mentoring relationships. *Personnel Psychology, 41*, 457–479. doi:10.1111/j.1744-6570.1988.tb00638.x

O'Neill, D. K., & Harris, J. B. (2004). Bridging the perspectives and developmental needs of all participants in curriculum-based telementoring programs. *Journal of Research on Technology in Education, 37*(2), 111–128.

O'Neill, D. K., Sensoy, Ö., & Guloy, S. (2009). *Final research paper, fostering metahistorical knowledge in Canadian history learning project*. Burnaby, BC: Simon Fraser University.

O'Neill, D. K. (2000). *The telementor's guidebook*. Toronto: Ontario Institute for Studies in Education, University of Toronto.

O'Neill, D. K. (2004). Building social capital in a knowledge-building community: Telementoring as a catalyst. *Interactive Learning Environments, 12*(3), 179–208. doi:10.1080/10494820512331383419

O'Neill, D. K., Weiler, M., & Sha, L. (2005). Software support for online mentoring programs: a research-inspired design. *Mentoring & Tutoring, 13*(1), 109–131. doi:10.1080/13611260500040617

O'Neill, D. K. (2001). Knowing when you've brought them in: Scientific genre knowledge and communities of practice. *Journal of the Learning Sciences, 10*(3), 223–264. doi:10.1207/S15327809JLS1003_1

O'Neill, D. K., Wagner, R., & Gomez, L. M. (1996). Online mentors: Experimenting in science class. *Educational Leadership, 54*(37), 39–42.

O'Neill, K. (1996). Telementoring: One researcher's perspective. *National School Network Testbed Newsletter, 12*, 223–264.

O'Neill, D. K., & Guloy, S. (2010, April, 2010). *The Historical Account Differences survey: Enriching methods for assessing metahistorical understanding in complex school environments*. Paper presented at the Annual Meeting of the American Educational Research Association, Denver, CO.

O'Neill, D. K., & Harris, J. B. (2005). Bridging the perspectives and developmental needs of all participants in curriculum-based telementoring programs. *Journal of Research on Technology in Education, 37*(2), 111-128. Retrieved May 13, 2009, from http://www.eric.ed.gov:80/ERICDocs/data/ericdocs2sql/content_storage_01/0000019b/80/2a/0d/16.pdf

O'Neilly, D. K., & Gomez, L. M. (1998). Sustaining mentoring relationships on-line. Paper presented at the Computer Supported Cooperative Work, Seattle, Washington. Retrieved April 30, 2009, from http://delivery.acm.org/10.1145/290000/289507/p325-o_neill.pdf?key1=289507&key2=5151514421&coll=GUIDE&dl=GUIDE&CFID=37944349&CFTOKEN=13733950

O'Donnell, A. M. (2004). A commentary on design research. *Educational Psychologist, 39*(4), 255–260. doi:10.1207/s15326985ep3904_7

Oech, A. V. (2009, Feb 19). *850,000 Social Networks on Ning!* Retrieved April 25, 2009, from Ning Blog: http://blog.ning.com/2009/02/850000-social-networks-on-ning.html

Office of the Federal Register, National Archives and Records Service, General Services Administration. (2000, December 21). Electronic and information technology accessibility standards. *Federal Register*, *65*(246), 80499–80528.

O'Neill, D. K. (2004). Building social capital in a knowledge-building community: Telementoring as a catalyst. *Interactive Learning Environments*, *12*(3), 179–208. doi:10.1080/10494820512331383419

O'Neill, D. K. (2001). Knowing when you've brought them in: Scientific genre knowledge and communities of practice. *Journal of the Learning Sciences*, *10*(3), 223–264. doi:10.1207/S15327809JLS1003_1

O'Neill, D. K., & Weiler, M. J. (2006). Cognitive tools for understanding history: What more do we need? *Journal of Educational Computing Research*, *35*(2), 179–195. doi:10.2190/H22P-7718-81G5-0723

O'Neill, D. K. (2007). *Designing a telementoring program to improve secondary students' understanding of history.* Paper presented at the Annual Meeting of the American Educational Research Association, Chicago, IL.

O'Neill, D. K., & Guloy, S. (2010, April, 2010). *The Historical Account Differences survey: Enriching methods for assessing metahistorical understanding in complex school environments.* Paper presented at the Annual Meeting of the American Educational Research Association, Denver, CO.

O'Neill, D. K., Weiler, M., & Sha, L. (2003). *The telementoring orchestrator: Research, design and implementation.* Paper presented at the annual meeting of the American Educational Research Association, Chicago, IL.

O'Reilly, T. (2004). The fuss about gmail and privacy: Nine reasons why it's bogus. Retrieved April 25, 2009, from, http://www.oreillynet.com/pub/wlg/4707

O'Reilly, T. (2005). What is Web 2.0? Design patterns and business models for the next generation of software. Retrieved April 25, 2009, from http://www.oreilly.de/artikel/web20.html

O'Reilly, T. (2009). Google wave: What might email look like if it were invented today? Retrieved May 29, 2009, from http://radar.oreilly.com/2009/05/google-wave-what-might-email-l.html.

Osgood, D., Foster, E., Flanagan, C., & Ruth, G. (2004). *Why focus on transition to adulthood for vulnerable populations?* (Research Network Working Paper No. 2). Network on Transitions to Adulthood. Retrieved December 4, 2009 from http://www.transad.pop.upenn.edu/downloads/vulnerable.pdf

Paine, C., Joinson, A. N., Buchanan, T., & Reips, U. D. (2006, April 22-27). Privacy and self-disclosure online. *Conference on Human Factors in Computing Systems* (pp. 1187-1192). Montréal, Québec, Canada.

Pajares, F. (1997). Current directions in self-efficacy research. In Maehr, M., & Pintrich, P. R. (Eds.), *Advances in motivation and achievement* (Vol. 10, pp. 1–49). Greenwich, CT: JAI Press.

Pajares, F. (1993). *Self-efficacy defined.* Retrieved September 1, 1998 from http://userwww.service.emory.edu/~mpajare/eff.html

Pajares, F. (1996, April). Assessing self-efficacy beliefs and academic outcomes: The case for specificity and correspondence. In B. J. Zimmerman (Chair), *Measuring and mismeasuring self-efficacy: Dimensions, problems, and misconceptions.* Symposium conducted at the annual meeting of the American Educational Research Association, New York, NY.

Parker, K. R., & Chao, J. T. (2007). Wikis as a teaching tool. *Interdisciplinary Journal of Knowledge and Learning Objects*, *3*, 57–72.

Parra, G. R., DuBois, D. L., Neville, H. A., & Pugh-Lilly, A. O. (2002). Mentoring relationships for youth: Investigation of a process-oriented model. *Journal of Community Psychology*, *30*(4), 367–388. doi:10.1002/jcop.10016

Partnership for 21st Century Skills. (2008). *21st century skills, education & competitiveness: A resource and policy guide.* Retrieved April 8, 2009, from http://www.21stcenturyskills.org/documents/21st_century_skills_education_and_competitiveness_guide.pdf.

Pascale, M., Mulatto, S., & Prattichizzo, D. (2008). Bringing haptics to Second Life. In *Proceedings of the 2008 Ambi-Sys workshop on Haptic user interfaces in ambient media systems* (pp.1-6). Quebec City, Canada: Haptic in Ambient Systems.

Patrick, D. L. (correspondence to Senator Tom Harkin, September 9, 1996). Retrieved February 1, 2010, from http://www.usdoj.gov/crt/foia/cltr204.txt

Paul, I. (2009, May 15). Google outage lesson: Don't get stuck in a cloud. Retrieved May 25, 2009, from http://www.pcworld.com/printable/article/id,164946/printable.html

Pennebaker, J. W. (1997). Writing about emotional experiences as a therapeutic process. *American Psychological Society*, *8*, 162–166.

Perez, S., & Dorman, S. M. (2001). Enhancing youth achievement through telementoring. *The Journal of School Health*, *71*(3), 122–123. doi:10.1111/j.1746-1561.2001.tb07307.x

Perreault LaCoursiere, S. (2001). A theory of online social support. *ANS (Nijmegen)*, *24*(1), 60–77.

Petersen, L. K. (2007) *What Distinguishes a Mentor? Self-Reflection*. Retrieved from http://www.mentors.net/03library/whatdistmentor.html

Petto, A. J., Patrick, M., & Kessel, R. (2005). Emphasizing inquiry, collaboration, and leadership in K-12 professional development. In Yager, R. E. (Ed.), *Exemplary science: Best practices in professional development* (pp. 147–160). Arlington, VA: NSTA Press.

Peyton, A. L., Morton, M., Perkins, M. M., & Dougherty, L. M. (2001). Mentoring in gerontology education: New graduate student perspectives. *Educational Gerontology*, *27*(5), 347–359. doi:10.1080/03601270152053384

Pink, D. H. (2005). *A whole new mind: Why right-brainers will rule the future*. New York: Riverhead.

Pintrich, P. R., & Schunk, D. H. (2002). *Motivation in Education*. Upper Saddle River, NJ: Pearson Education, Inc.

Pitler, H., Hubbell, E. R., Kuhn, M., & Malenoski, K. (2007). *Using technology with classroom instruction that works*. Alexandria, VA: Association for Supervision and Curriculum Development.

Pitts, V. (2004). Illness and Internet empowerment: Writing and reading breast cancer in cyberspace. *Health*, *8*(1), 33–59.

Poetz, C. L. (2003). Reflections on 30 years of involvement in self-advocacy. *Journal of Intellectual & Developmental Disability*, *28*, 84–87. doi:10.1080/1366825031000086920

Preiser, W. F. E., & Ostroff, E. (Eds.). (2001). *Universal Design Handbook* (pp. 3.3–3.14). New York: McGraw-Hill.

Presidential Task Force on Employment of Adults with Disabilities. (1999). *Report from the subcommittee on expanding employment opportunities for young people with disabilities to the Presidential Task Force on Employment of Adults with disabilities*. Washington, DC: Author.

Price, M. A., & Chen, H. H. (2003). Promises and challenges: Exploring a collaborative telementoring programme in a preservice teacher education programme. *Mentoring & Tutoring*, *11*(1), 105–117. doi:10.1080/1361126032000054844

Putman, M. (2009). Running the race to improve self-efficacy. *Kappa Delta Pi Record*, *45*(2), 53–57.

Quinn, M., Rutherford, R., & Leone, P. (2001). *Students with disabilities in correctional facilities*. Arlington, VA: ERIC Clearinghouse on Disabilities and Gifted Education, Council for Exceptional Children. (ERIC Document Reproduction Service No. ED461958). Retrieved December 4, 2009 from http://www.ericdigests.org/2002-4/correctional.html

Ragins, B. R., & Cotton, J. L. (1999). Mentor functions and outcomes: A comparison of men and women in formal and informal mentoring relationships. *The Journal of Applied Psychology*, *84*(4), 529–550. doi:10.1037/0021-9010.84.4.529

Ragins, B. R. (1989). Barriers to mentoring: The female manager's dilemma. *Human Relations*, *42*, 1–22. doi:10.1177/001872678904200101

Randall, S. (2009). Jawter: Twitter from Jaws with no software in the middle. *Randy Laptop.* Retrieved May 13, 2009, from http://randylaptop.com/software/jawter-2/

Ravitz, J. (2009). Introduction: Summarizing findings and looking ahead to a new generation of PBL research. *Interdisciplinary Journal of Problem-based Learning, 3*(1). Retrieved April 8, 2009, from http://docs.lib.purdue.edu/ijpbl/vol3/iss1/2.

Ray, E. B., Waldhart, E. S., & Seibert, J. H. (1985). *Communication networks and job stress among teachers.* Paper presented at the annual meeting of the Southern Speech Communication Association, Winston-Salem, N.C.

Reeves, D. (2007). Teachers step up. *Educational Leadership, 65*(1), 87–88.

Rehabilitation Act of 1973. 29 U.S.C. § 79 et seq.

Reiter, S. (2008). *Disability from a humanistic perspective: Towards a better quality of life.* New York: Nova Science Publishers.

Reynard, R. (2008, December). Using chat to move the thinking process forward. *Technological Horizons In Education Journal, 35*(12), 4. Retrieved April 30, 2009, from Expanded Academic ASAP via Gale: http://find.galegroup.com/itx/start.do?prodId=EAIM

Rhodes, J. E. (2002). *Stand by me: The risks and rewards of mentoring today's youth.* Cambridge, MA: Harvard University Press.

Rhodes, J. E., & DuBois, D. L. (2008). Mentoring relationships and programs for youth. *Current Directions in Psychological Science, 17*(4), 254–258. doi:10.1111/j.1467-8721.2008.00585.x

Rhodes, J. E., Grossman, J. B., & Resch, N. L. (2000). Agents of change: Pathways through which mentoring relationships influence adolescents' academic adjustment. *Child Development, 71,* 1662–1671. doi:10.1111/1467-8624.00256

Rhodes, J. E. (2005). A model of youth mentoring. In DuBois, D. L., & Karcher, M. J. (Eds.), *Handbook of youth mentoring* (pp. 30–43). Thousand Oaks, London, New Delhi: Sage.

Rhodes, J. E. (2003). Online mentoring: The promise and pitfalls of an emerging approach. *National Mentoring Partnership.* Retrieved August, 2004, from http://www.mentoring.org/research_corner/11_03_online.adp

Rhone, L. (1995). *Measurement in a primary-grade integrated curriculum. Connecting mathematics across the curriculum.* Reston, VA: National Council of Teachers of Mathematics.

Rice, R. E., & Katz, J. E. (Eds.). (2001). *The Internet and health communication: Experiences and expectations.* Thousand Oaks, CA: Sage.

Richardson, W. (2008). *Blogs, wikis, podcasts, and other powerful web tools for classrooms* (2nd ed.). Thousand Oaks, CA: Corwin.

Richardson, G. M., & Liang, L. L. (2008). The use of inquiry in the development of pre-service teacher efficacy in mathematics and science. *Journal of Elementary Science Education, 20*(1), 1–16. doi:10.1007/BF03174699

Richardson, K. W. (2009). *Looking at/looking through: Teachers planning for curriculum-based learning with technology* (Doctoral dissertation). Available from ProQuest Dissertations and Theses database. (AAT 3371354)

Robinson, K. (2006, February). Do schools kill creativity? Presentation at TED2006 conference, Monterey, CA. Video retrieved from http://www.ted.com/talks/ken_robinson_says_schools_kill_creativity.html.

Rochlen, A. B., Zack, J. S., & Speyer, C. (2004). Online therapy: review of relevant definitions, debates, and current empirical support. *Journal of Clinical Psychology, 60*(3), 269–283. doi:10.1002/jclp.10263

Rose, D. H., & Meyer, A. (2002). *Teaching every student in the digital age: Universal design for learning.* Alexandria, VA: Association for Supervision and Curriculum Development.

Rose, D. H., Meyer, A., & Hitchcock, C. (Eds.). (2005). *The universally designed classroom: Accessible curriculum and digital technologies.* Cambridge, MA: Harvard Education Press.

Rosenholtz, S. J. (1985). Political myths about education reform: Lessons from research on teaching. *Phi Delta Kappan, 66*(5), 349–355.

Roush, W. (2005, January). Amazon: Giving away the store. *Technology Review*. Retrieved May 25, 2009, from http://www.technologyreview.com/business/14089/

Rousso, H. (2001). What do Frida Kahlo, Wilma Mankiller, and Harriet Tubman have in common? Providing role models for girls with (and without) disabilities. In Rousso, H., & Wehmeyer, M. (Eds.), *Double jeopardy: Addressing gender equity in special education* (pp. 337–360). Albany: State University of New York Press.

Rowland, C., & Smith, T. (1999). Web site accessibility. *The Power of Independence* (Summer Edition), 1–2. Logan: Center for Persons with Disabilities, Utah State University.

Russell, A., & Perris, K. (2003). Telementoring in community nursing: A shift from dyadic to communal models of learning and professional development. *Mentoring & Tutoring, 11*(2), 227–237. doi:10.1080/13611260306856

Russell, M. (2007). The difference between a chef and a cook. Retrieved December 17, 2007, from http://chefguide.com/a/321859/The+Difference+Between+A+Chef+And+A+Cook.html

Saito, R. N., & Blyth, D. A. (1992). *Understanding mentoring relationships*. Minneapolis, MN: Search Institute.

Sanchez, B., & Harris, J. (1996). Online mentoring: A success story. Learning and leading with technology. *The ISTE Journal of Educational Technology Practice and Policy, 23*, 57–60.

Savery, J. R. (2006). Overview of problem-based learning: Definitions and distinctions. *Interdisciplinary Journal of Problem-based Learning, 1*(1). Retrieved April 2, 2009, from http://docs.lib.purdue.edu/ijpbl/vol1/iss1/3.

Savin-Baden, M. (2007). *A practical guide to problem-based learning online*. London: Routledge.

Scheinberg, A. (2006, August 8). *Review: Picasaweb vs. Flickr*. Retrieved May 25, 2009, from http://firsttube.com/read/review-picasaweb-vs-flickr/

Schlichte, J., Yssel, N., & Merbler, J. (2005). Pathway to burnout: Case studies in teacher isolation and alienation. *Preventing School Failure, 50*(1), 43–40. doi:10.3200/PSFL.50.1.35-40

Schunk, D. H. (1996, April). *Self-efficacy for learning and performance*. Paper presented at the Annual Conference of the American Education Research Association, New York, NY.

Scigliano, D. (1999). *The effects of a drama telementoring model upon students' self-efficacy beliefs*. Published doctoral dissertation, Duquesne University, Pittsburgh, PA.

SciLands. (n.d.). SciLands Virtual Continent. Retrieved February 1, 2010, from http://www.scilands.org/

Seabrooks, J. J., Kenney, S., & LaMontagne, M. (2000). Collaboration and virtual mentoring: Building relationships between pre-service and in-service special education teachers. *Journal of Information Technology for Teacher Education, 9*(2), 219–236.

Second Life (n.d.a). *Accessibility—Second Life Wiki*. Retrieved February 1, 2010, from http://wiki.secondlife.com/wiki/Accessibility

Second Life (n.d.b) *Volunteer Portal*. Retrieved March 02, 2010, from http://wiki.secondlife.com/wiki/Volunteer_Portal

Second Life (n.d.c). *Second Life*. Retrieved May 13, 2009, from http://secondlife.com

Section 504 of the Rehabilitation Act of 1973. 29 U.S.C. § 794.

Section 508 of the Rehabilitation Act of 1973. (1998, amended). 29 U.S.C. 794(d). Retrieved February 1, 2010, from http://www.access-board.gov/sec508/guide/act.htm

Seeger, K. L. (2007). *Mentoring youth with disabilities: The mentor's lived experiences*. Unpublished master's thesis, The School of Human Resource Education and Workforce Development, Louisiana State University, U.S.A.

Seixas, P. (Ed.). (2004). *Theorizing Historical Consciousness*. Toronto: University of Toronto Press.

Shamp, S. (1991). Mechanomorphism in perception of computer communication partners. *Computers in Human Behavior*, *7*, 147–161. doi:10.1016/0747-5632(91)90004-K

Shane, P. M., & Wojnowski, B. S. (2005). Technology integration enhancing science: Things take time. *Science Educator*, *14*(1), 49–55.

Shaw, B. R., Hawkins, R., McTavish, F., Pingree, S., & Gustafson, D. H. (2006). Effects of insightful disclosure within computer mediated support groups on women with breast cancer. *Health Communication*, *19*(2), 133–142. doi:10.1207/s15327027hc1902_5

Shearer, R. L. (2003). *Interaction in distance education. Special report 2*(1). Madison, WI: Atwood Publishing.

Shemilt, D. (1987). Adolescent ideas about evidence and methodology in History. In Portal, C. (Ed.), *The History curriculum for teachers*. London, England: The Falmer Press.

Shemilt, D. (2000). The caliph's coin: The currency of narrative frameworks in History teaching. In Stearns, P. N., Seixas, P., & Wineburg, S. (Eds.), *Knowing, teaching and learning History: National and international perspectives* (pp. 83–101). New York: New York University Press.

Shpigelman, C. N., Reiter, S., & Weiss, P. L. (2008). E-mentoring for youth with special needs: Preliminary results. *Cyberpsychology & Behavior*, *11*(2), 196–200. doi:10.1089/cpb.2007.0052

Shrestha, C. H., May, S., Edirisingha, P., Burke, L., & Linsey, T. (2009). From face-to-face to e-mentoring: Does the "e" add any value for mentors? *International Journal of Teaching and Learning in Higher Education*, *20*(2), 116–124.

Shulman, L. S. (2002). Making differences: A table of learning. *Change*, *34*(6), 36–44. doi:10.1080/00091380209605567

Shulman, L. S. (2004). Knowledge and teaching: Foundations of the new reform. In Wilson, S. M. (Ed.), *The wisdom of practice: Essays on teaching, learning, and learning to teach* (pp. 217–248). San Francisco: Jossey-Bass.

Siegle, D. (2003). Mentors on the net: Extending learning through telementoring. *Gifted Child Today*, 26.

Siegler, M. G. (2009, May 28). Google wave drips with ambition. A new communication platform for a new web. Retrieved May 30, 2009, from http://www.techcrunch.com/2009/05/28/google-wave-drips-with-ambition-can-it-fulfill-googles-grand-web-vision/

Signer, B. (2008). Online professional development: Combining best practices from teacher, technology, and distance education. *Journal of In-service Education*, *34*(2), 205–218. doi:10.1080/13674580801951079

Simon, H. (1969). *The sciences of the artificial*. Cambridge, MA: MIT Press.

Single, P. B., & Single, R. M. (2005). E-mentoring for social equity: Review of research to inform program development. *Mentoring & Tutoring*, *13*(2), 301–320. doi:10.1080/13611260500107481

Single, P. B., Jaffe, A., & Schwartz, R. (1999). Evaluating programs for recruiting and retaining community faculty. *Family Medicine*, *31*(2), 114–121.

Single, P. B., & Single, R. M. (2005). E-mentoring for social equity: review of research to inform program development. *Mentoring & Tutoring*, *13*(2), 301–320. doi:10.1080/13611260500107481

Single, P. B., & Muller, C. B. (2001). When email and mentoring unite: The implementation of a nationwide electronic mentoring program. In Stromei, L. K. (Ed.), *Creating Mentoring and Coaching Programs* (pp. 107–122). Alexandria, VA: American Society for Training and Development.

Single, P. B., & Muller, C. B. (1999, April). *Electronic Mentoring: Issues to Advance Research and Practice*. Paper presented at the International Mentoring Association Conference, Atlanta, GA.

Sipe, C. L. (1996). *Mentoring: A synthesis of P/PV's research: 1988-1995*. Philadelphia, PA: Public/Private Ventures.

Slotta, J. (2002). Designing the "Web-Based Inquiry Science Environment (WISE)". *Educational Technology, 42*(5), 15–20.

Smith, R. M., & Erevelles, N. (2004). Towards and enabling education: The difference that disability makes. Book Reviews. *Educational Researcher*, (November): 31–36. doi:10.3102/0013189X033008031

Smith, S. C., & Scott, J. J. (1990). *The collaborative school: A work environment for effective instruction* (Report No. ISBN-0-86552-092-5). Reston, VA: National Association of Secondary School Principals. (ERIC Document Reproduction Service No. ED316918).

Smolleck, L. D., Zembal-Saul, C., & Yoder, E. P. (2006). The development and validation of an instrument to measure pre-service teachers' self-efficacy in regard to the teaching of science as inquiry. *Journal of Science Teacher Education, 17*(2), 137–163. doi:10.1007/s10972-006-9015-6

Solomon, G., & Schrum, L. (2007). *Web 2.0: New tools, new schools*. Eugene, OR: International Society for Technology in Education.

Soloway, E., Jackson, S. L., Klein, J., Quintana, C., Reed, J., Spitulnik, J., et al. (1996). *Learning theory in practice: Case studies of learner-centered design*. Paper presented at CHI96 conference, Vancouver, British Columbia, Canada. Retrieved May 2, 2009, from http://www.sigchi.org/chi96/proceedings/papers/Soloway/es_txt.htm

Sproull, L., & Kiesler, S. (1992). *Connections: New ways of working in the networked organization*. Cambridge, MA: MIT Press.

Spuhler, L., & Zetler, A. (1994). Montana teacher support program: Research report for year two 1993-94. East Lansing, MI: National Center for Research on Teacher Learning. (ERIC Document Reproduction Service No. ED390802).

Sternberg, R. J. (1996). *Successful intelligence*. New York: Simon & Schuster.

Stevens, T., To, Y., Harris, G., & Dwyer, J. (2008). The LOGO project: Designing an effective continuing education program for teachers. *Journal of Computers in Mathematics and Science Teaching, 27*(2), 195–219.

Stiggins, R. J. C. Nancy Faires. (1992). *In teachers' hands: Investigating the practices of classroom assessment*. Albany, NY: State University of New York Press.

Stinson, B., & Claus, K. (2000). The effects of electronic classrooms on learning English composition: A middle ground. *T.H.E. Journal*. Retrieved April 30, 2009, from http://www.thejournal.com/articles/14610

Su, B., Bonk, C. J., Magjuka, R., Liu, X., & Lee, S. (2005). The Importance of interaction in web-based education: A program-level case study of online MBA courses. *Journal of Interactive Online Learning, 4*(1).

Suler, J. (2001). Assessing a person's suitability for online therapy: The ISMHO clinical case study group. *Cyberpsychology & Behavior, 4*(6), 675–679. doi:10.1089/109493101753376614

Suler, J. (2004). The online disinhibition effect. *Cyberpsychology & Behavior, 7*(3), 321–326. doi:10.1089/1094931041291295

Suler, J. (1996-2005). *The psychology of cyberspace* [online]. Retrieved 13 July 2008 from http://www-usr.rider.edu/~suler/psycyber/psycyber.html

Sullivan, S., & Emerson, R. (2000). Recommendations for successfully navigating the boundaryless career: From theory to practice. Retrieved April 30, 2009, from http://www.sba.muohio.edu/management/mwAcademy/2000/27c.pdf

Supovitz, J. A., & Turner, H. M. (2000). The effects of professional development on science teaching practices and classroom culture. *Journal of Research in Science Teaching, 37*(9), 963–980. doi:10.1002/1098-2736(200011)37:9<963::AID-TEA6>3.0.CO;2-0

Swan, K. (2004). Relationships between interactions and learning in online environments, The Sloan Consortium. Retrieved June 3, 2009, from http://www.sloan-c.org/publications/books/interactions.pdf

Sword, C., & Hill, K. (2003). Creating mentoring opportunities for youth with disabilities: Issues and suggested strategies. *American Rehabilitation, 27*(1), 14–17.

Sword, C., & Hill, K. (2002). Creating mentoring opportunities for youth with disabilities: Issues and suggested strategies. *Issue Brief: Examining Current Challenges in Secondary Education and Transition, 1*(4). Retrieved February 1, 2010, from http://www.ncset.org/publications/viewdesc.asp?id=704

Sylwester, E. (2005, February 9). Professors honored for work with women. *Oregon Daily Emerald,* (2005). Retrieved March 1, 2009 from http://media.www.dailyemerald.com/media/storage/paper859/news/2005/02/09/News/Professor.Honored.For.Work.With.Women-1968038.shtml

Tag (metadata). (2009). *Wikipedia.* Retrieved April 30, 2009, from http://en.wikipedia.org/wiki/Tag_(metadata)

Telecommunications and Electronic and Information Technology Advisory Committee [TEITAC]. (2008). *Report to the Access Board: Refreshed accessibility standards and guidelines in telecommunications and electronic and information technology.* Retrieved February 1, 2010, from http://www.access-board.gov/sec508/refresh/report/

Tellez, K. (1992). Mentors by choice, not design: Help-seeking by beginning teachers. *Journal of Teacher Education, 43*(3), 214–221. doi:10.1177/0022487192043003008

Text, S. L. (n.d.). *TextSL a Second Life client for visually impaired and blind users.* Retrieved February 1, 2010, from http://textsl.org/

The New Teacher Center. (2009). *e-Mentoring for student success.* Retrieved on May 1, 2009 from http://www.newteachercenter.org/eMSS/menu.php?p=home

Thomas, D., & Buch, V. (2007, March 18). YouTube case study: Widget marketing comes of age. *Startup Review.* Retrieved April 22, 2009, from http://www.startup-review.com/blog/youtube-case-study-widget-marketing-comes-of-age.php

Thompson, T. (2008). Universal design of computing labs. In Burgstahler, S. E., & Cory, R. C. (Eds.), *Universal design in higher education: From principles to practice* (pp. 235–244). Cambridge, MA: Harvard Education Press.

Tidwell, L. C., & Walther, L. B. (2002). Computer-mediated communication effects on disclosure, impression and interpersonal evaluations: Getting to know one another a bit at a time. *Human Communication Research, 28,* 317–348. doi:10.1111/j.1468-2958.2002.tb00811.x

Timmons, J., Mack, M., Sims, A., Hare, R., & Wills, J. (2006). *Paving the way to work: A guide to career-focused mentoring for youth with disabilities.* Washington, DC: Institute for Educational Leadership, National Collaborative on Workforce and Disability for Youth. Retrieved December 4, 2009 from http://www.ncwd-youth.info/paving-the-way-to-work

Tobin, M. (2004). Mentoring: Seven roles and some specifics, *American Journal of Respiratory and Critical Care Medicine, 170,* 114-117. Retrieved April 22, 2009, from http://ajrccm.atsjournals.org/cgi/content/full/170/2/114

Todis, B., Powers, L., Irvin, L., & Singer, G. (1996). A qualtitive study of a mentor intervention with children who have multiple disabilities. In Powers, L., Singer, G., & Sowers, J. (Eds.), *On the road to autonomy: Promoting self-competence for children and youth with disabilities* (pp. 237–254). Baltimore: Paul H. Brookes.

Translate, G. (2009). *Wikipedia.* Retrieved April 25, 2009, from http://en.wikipedia.org/wiki/Google_Translate

Tschannen-Moran, M. (2004). *Trust Matters. Leadership for Successful Schools.* San Francisco, CA: Jossey-Bass.

Tsikalas, K. (1997). *Telementoring now.* Retrieved September 15, 1998 from http://www.uwnyc.org/7mentor.htm

Tsikalas, K., & McMillan-Culp, K. (2000). Silent negotiations: A case study of roles and functions utilized by students, teachers, and mentors in project-based, telementoring relationships. In B. Fishman & S. O'Connor-Divelbiss (Eds.), *Fourth International Conference of the Learning Sciences* (pp. 350-357). Mahwah, NJ: Erlbaum. Retrieved April 2, 2009, from http://www.umich.edu/~icls/proceedings/pdf/Tsikalas.pdf.

Tsikalas, K., McMillan-Culp, K., Friedman, W., & Honey, M. (2000, April). *Portals: A window into telementoring relationships in project-based computational science classes.* Paper presented at the Annual Meeting of the American Educational Research Association, New Orleans, LA.

Turban, D. B., & Dougherty, T. W. (1994). Role of protege personality in receipt of mentoring and career success. *Academy of Management Journal, 37*(3), 688–702. doi:10.2307/256706

U.S. Access Board. (2007). *Update of the 508 Standards and the Telecommunications Act Guidelines.* Retrieved February 1, 2010, from http://www.access-board.gov/sec508/update-index.htm

U.S. Census Bureau. (2005). *Americans with disabilities: 2005.* Retrieved December 4, 2009 from http://www.census.gov/hhes/www/disability/sipp/disable05.html

U.S. Department of Education. (n.d.). *Building the legacy: IDEA 2004.* Retrieved February 1, 2010, from http://idea.ed.gov/explore/home

U.S. Department of Justice Civil Rights Division. (2005, September). *A guide to disability rights laws.* Retrieved February 1, 2010, from http://www.ada.gov/cguide.htm

United States Access Board. (n.d.). *Section 508 home page: Electronic and information technology.* Retrieved February 1, 2010, from http://www.access-board.gov/508.htm

University Continuing Education Association (UCEA). (2009, March). *The new face of higher education lifelong learning trends.* Washington, D.C.: UCEA Publications Office.

University of California Museum of Paleontology. (2009). A blueprint for scientific investigations. *Understanding science.* Retrieved April 2, 2009, from http://undsci.berkeley.edu/article/0_0_0/howscienceworks_03

University of California Museum of Paleontology. (2009). The real process of science. *Understanding science.* Retrieved April 2, 2009, from http://undsci.berkeley.edu/article/0_0_0/howscienceworks_02.

University of California Museum of Paleontology. *Understanding science.* (2009). Retrieved April 2, 2009, from http://www.understandingscience.org.

University of Southern California. (2009). *Examples in education.* Retrieved April 25, 2009, from http://getgoogle.usc.edu/

Usher, E. L. (2009). Sources of middle school students' self-efficacy in mathematics: A qualitative investigation. *American Educational Research Journal, 46*(1), 275–314.. doi:10.3102/0002831208324517

Usher, E. L., & Pajares, F. (2008). Sources of self-efficacy in school: Critical review of the literature and future directions. *Review of Educational Research, 78*(4), 751–797. doi:10.3102/0034654308321456

Van Uden-Kraan, C. F., Drossaret, C. H. C., Taal, E., Lebrun, C. E. I., Drossares-Bakker, K. W., & Smit, W. M. (2008). Coping with somatic illnesses in online support groups: Do the feared disadvantages actually occur? *Computers in Human Behavior, 24,* 309–324. doi:10.1016/j.chb.2007.01.014

Vanderheiden, G. C., & Vanderheiden, K. R. (1992). Guidelines for the design of consumer products to increase their accessibility to people with disabilities or who are aging (Working Draft 1.7). Madison, WI: Trace Research and Development Center. Retrieved February 1, 2010, from http://trace.wisc.edu/docs/consumer_product_guidelnies/toc.htm

Vasquez, J., & Cowan, M. B. (2001). Moving teachers from mechanical to mastery: The next level of science implementation. In Rhoton, J., & Bowers, P. (Eds.), *Professional development leadership and the diverse learner* (pp. 11–22). Arlington, VA: NSTA Press.

Veenman, S. (1984). Perceived problems of beginning teachers. *Review of Educational Research, 54*(2), 143–178.

Vincenti, W. G. (1990). *What engineers know and how they know it: Analytical studies from aeronautical history.* Baltimore, MD: The Johns Hopkins University Press.

Vosniadou, S. (2007). Conceptual change and education. *Human Development, 50*(1), 47–54. doi:10.1159/000097684

W3C. (1999). *Web content accessibility guidelines 1.0: W3C recommendation 5-May-1999*. Retrieved February 1, 2010, from http://www.w3.org/TR/WAI-WEBCONTENT/

W3C. (2007). *W3C Mission*. Retrieved May 13, 2009, from http://www.w3.org/Consortium/mission

Wagner, M., Newman, L., Cameto, R., Garza, N., & Levine, P. (2005). *After high school: A first look at the postschool experiences of youth with disabilities. A report from the National Longitudinal Transition Study-2 (NLTS2). (Executive Study)*. Menlo Park, CA: SRI International. Retrieved December 4, 2009 from http://www.nlts2.org/reports/2005_04/index.html

WAI. (2005). *Introduction to Web accessibility*. Cambridge, MA: World Wide Web Consortium. Retrieved February 1, 2010, from http://www.w3.org/WAI/intro/accessibility.php

Wallis, C. (2006). The multitasking generation. *Time, 167*(13).

Walsh, T. R., & Hollister, C. V. (2009). Creating a digital archive for students' research in a credit library course. *Reference and User Services Quarterly, 48*(4), 391–400.

Walther, J. B., & Boyd, S. (2002). Attraction to computer-mediated social support. In Lin, C. A., & Atkin, D. (Eds.), *Communication technology and society: Audience adoption and uses* (pp. 153–188). Cresskill, NJ: Hampton Press.

Wang, S., & Wu, P. (2008). The role of feedback and self-efficacy on web-based learning: The social cognitive perspective. *Computers & Education, 51*(4), 1589–1598.. doi:10.1016/j.compedu.2008.03.004

Waters, C. (1997). *Universal Web design*. Indianapolis, IN: New Riders.

Watson, S. W. (2006). Virtual mentoring in higher education: Teacher education and cyber-connections. *International Journal of Teaching and Learning in Higher Education, 18*(3), 168–179.

Watson, G. (2006). Technology professional development: Long-term effects on teacher self-efficacy. *Journal of Technology and Teacher Education, 14*(1), 151–166.

WebAIM. (n.d.). TEITAC Archives. Retrieved February 1, 2010 from http://www.webaim.org/teitac/

Wehmeyer, M. L., Smith, S. J., Palmer, S. B., & Davis, D. K. (2004). Technology use by students with intellectual disabilities: An overview. *Journal of Special Education Technology, 19*(4), 1–33.

Weir, S. (1992). *Electronic communities of learners: Fact or fiction*. Cambridge, MA/Washington, D. C.: TERC Communications/Department of Education and National Science Foundation.

Weiss, P. L., Bialik, P., & Kizony, K. (2003). Virtual reality provides leisure time opportunities for young adults with physical and intellectual disabilities. *Cyberpsychology & Behavior, 6*, 335–342. doi:10.1089/109493103322011650

Weiss, P. L., Whiteley, C. P., Treviranus, J., & Fels, D. I. (2001). PEBBLES: A personal technology for meeting educational, social and emotional needs of hospitalized children. *Personal and Ubiquitous Computing, 5*, 157–168. doi:10.1007/s007790170006

Weizman, A., Covitt, B. A., Koehler, M. J., Lundenberg, M. A., Oslund, J. A., & Low, M. R. (2008). Measuring teachers' learning from a problem-based learning approach to professional development in science education. *The Interdisciplinary Journal of Problem-based Learning, 2*(2), 29–60.

Wesch, M. (2008, October 21). *A vision of students today (& what teachers must do)*. Retrieved April 28, 2009, from http://www.britannica.com/blogs/2008/10/a-vision-of-students-today-what-teachers-must-do/

Wheeldon, R. S., & Lehmann. (1999). Establishing a telementoring program that can be used in vocational classes. *Journal for Vocational and Special Needs Education, 21*, 32–37.

White, M., & Dorman, S. M. (2001). Receiving social support online: Implications for health education. *Health Education Research*, *16*(6), 693–707. doi:10.1093/her/16.6.693

Wiggins, G., & McTighe, J. (1998). *Understanding by design*. Alexandria, VA: Association for Supervision and Curriculum Development.

Wighton, D. J. (1993). *Telementoring: An examination of the potential for an educational network*. Education Technology Centre of British Columbia.

Williams, E. (2009, May 11). The YouTube dilemma. *Creative Review*. Retrieved May 25, 2009, from http://www.creativereview.co.uk/cr-blog/2009/may/the-youtube-dilemma

Wineburg, S. (2001). *Historical thinking and other unnatural acts: Charting the future of teaching the past*. Philadelphia: Temple University Press.

Winer, D. (2005). *What is a 'River of News' style aggregator?* Retrieved April 25, 2009, from http://www.reallysimplesyndication.com/riverOfNews

Wisdom of the Crowd. (2009). *Wikipedia*. Retrieved April 25, 2009, from http://en.wikipedia.org/wiki/Wisdom_of_the_crowd

Wolf, S. E., & Witte, M. M. (2005). Technology and mentoring practices within academic settings. In F. K. Kochan & J. T. Pascarelli (Eds.), *Creating Successful Telementoring Programs* (pp. 105-121). Greenwich, CT: Information Age Publishing.

Wolin, S., & Wolin, S. (1993). *The resilient self: How survivors of troubled families rise above adversity*. New York: Villard Books.

Woolfolk Hoy, A. (2003/2004). Self-efficacy in college teaching. *Essays on Teaching Excellence: Toward the Best in the Academy, 15*(7). Retrieved on July 7, 2008 from http://gozips.uakron.edu/~mcgurk/number7.htm

World Wide Web Consortium [W3C]. (n.d.a.). *Web Accessibility Initiative (WAI)*. Retrieved February 1, 2010, from http://www.w3.org/WAI/

Wright, K. B. (2000). Perceptions of on-line support providers: An examination of perceived homophily, source credibility, communication and social support within on-line support groups. *Communication Quarterly*, *48*, 44–59.

Wright, K. B., & Bell, S. B. (2003). Health-related support groups on the Internet: Linking empirical findings to social support and computer-mediated communication theory. *Journal of Health Psychology*, *8*(1), 39–57. doi:10.1177/1359105303008001429

Wu, W., Chang, H., & Guo, C. (2008). An empirical assessment of science teachers' intentions toward technology integration. *Journal of Computers in Mathematics and Science Teaching*, *27*(4), 499–520.

Yinger, R. (1979). Routines in teacher planning. *Theory into Practice*, *18*(3), 163–169. doi:10.1080/00405847909542827

Youth Connections. (n.d.). Improving transition outcomes: An innovative state alignment grant for improving transition outcomes for youth with disabilities through the use of intermediaries. Youth Connections: E-Mentoring and Vocational Exploration for Students with Disabilities. Retrieved December 4, 2009 from http://publications.iowa.gov/5618/2/ementoring_RepTemp.txt

Yukawa, J., Harada, V. H., & Suthers, D. D. (2007). Professional development in communities of practice. In Hughes-Hassell, S., & Harada, V. H. (Eds.), *The School Library Media Specialist and Education Reform* (pp. 179–192). Westport, CT: Libraries Unlimited.

Yukawa, J. (2005). *Hearts and minds through hands online: A narrative analysis of learning through co-reflection in an online action research course*. Unpublished doctoral dissertation, University of Hawaii at Manoa, 2005.

Yukawa, J., & Harada, V. H. (2009). Librarian-teacher partnerships for inquiry learning: Measures of effectiveness for a practice-based model of professional development. *Evidence Based Library and Information Practice*, *4*(2). Retrieved August 20, 2009, from http://ejournals.library.ualberta.ca/index.php/EBLIP/article/view/4633.

Zeldin, A. L., Britner, S. L., & Pajares, F. (2008). A comparative study of the self-efficacy beliefs of successful men and women in mathematics, science, and technology careers. *Journal of Research in Science Teaching*, *45*(9), 1036–1058. doi:10.1002/tea.20195

Zelditch, M. (1990). Mentor roles. In *Proceedings of the 32nd Annual Meeting of the Western Association of Graduate Schools* (p. 11). Tempe, AZ.

Zinn, H. (2003). *A people's history of the United States, 1492-present*. New York: HarperCollins.

Zmuda, A., & Harada, V. H. (2008). *Librarians as learning specialists: Meeting the learning imperative for the 21st century*. Westport, CT: Libraries Unlimited.

About the Contributors

Deborah A. Scigliano is a visiting Assistant Professor at Duquesne University in Pittsburgh, PA in the Department of Foundations and Leadership. Dr. Scigliano was an elementary educator for 30 years and has been an educational consultant on a national level. Her research interests include telementoring, self-efficacy, and peer coaching. She is passionate about professional learning for educators. Dr. Scigliano is the recipient of the Duquesne University Creative Teaching Award and the Henderson Prize for Educational Leadership.

* * *

Emily A. Boles is an instructional developer in the Center for Online Learning, Research and Service at the University of Illinois at Springfield. She offers faculty development workshops on technology and pedagogy for online learning and works with faculty to develop online courses. Her experience in online education includes work at community colleges and four-year institutions. Emily has presented nationally on online learning and Web 2.0 technologies. Her areas of research are Web 2.0 technologies, cloud computing, and the impact of online learning in rural areas.

Sheryl Burgstahler is the director of Accessible Technology within University Technology Services at the University of Washington. Within her role at the University, in 1992 she founded and continues to direct the DO-IT (Disabilities, Opportunities, Internetworking, and Technology) Center. This Center—supported with federal, state, and private funds—has hosted an award-winning telementoring community that helps high school and college students with disabilities pursue college studies and challenging careers. She has edited a book on applications of universal design in higher education and has authored and co-authored several books on the use of the Internet in K-12 education. She has published dozens of articles in peer-reviewed journals and chapters in books; her work focuses on Internet use with K-12 students, mentoring, assistive technology, universal design, and transition issues for people with disabilities.

Terrie R. Dew has fifteen years experience working with mathematics education in South Carolina. As a high school teacher, her work focused on integration of technology into algebra, calculus and statistics teaching. In 2001, Terri received certification from the National Board for Professional Teaching Standards in Adolescent and Young Adulthood Mathematics. She was also named one of Greenville County's top ten teachers of the year for the same year. Terrie joined the S. C. Statewide Systemic Initiative in 2001 as Mathematics Specialist for the Greenville Hub. Her work with the Greenville Hub

About the Contributors

focused on designing and providing professional development for teachers of mathematics, specifically focused on implementation of the S. C. Mathematics Standards and NCTM's Principles and Standards for Mathematics. As the SCSSI transitioned to the SC Mathematics and Science Unit, Terrie's work also transitioned to focus on professional development for coaching. Terrie is currently serving dual roles as an Agency Trainer for the Center of Cognitive Coaching and Mathematics Coaching Specialist for the S2MART Centers SC.

Sheryl Guloy is a doctoral student in the Educational Technology and Learning Design program at Simon Fraser University in British Columbia, Canada. Sheryl obtained her B.Comm. in International Business at Concordia University in Montreal, Canada. She also earned an M.A. in Educational Technology at Concordia University. Sheryl has carried out research and program development in both the private and nonprofit sectors. For her Ph.D. thesis, she is developing a telementoring program to aid in leadership development for a nonprofit. Sheryl's broader interests include instructional design and the application of technological innovations to improve human performance.

Judi Harris is a professor and the Pavey Family Chair in Educational Technology in the School of Education at the College of William & Mary in Virginia, where she coordinates the Curriculum and Educational Technology doctoral program. Dr. Harris' research and service focus upon K-12 curriculum-based technology integration and teacher professional development. During her 30 years of work in educational computing, she has authored more than 210 research and pedagogical publications. While a faculty member at the University of Texas from 1992-2002, Dr. Harris founded and directed WINGS ("Welcoming Interns and Novices with Guidance and Support") Online, a suite of online services that support new teachers in multiple ways. That work became the foundation of William & Mary's ENDAPT ("Electronic Networking to Develop Accomplished Professional Teachers;" http://endapt.wm.edu/). Her nonprofit Electronic Emissary (http://emissary.wm.edu/) telementoring service, begun in 1992, is the longest-running K-12 effort of its kind, serving students and teachers worldwide.

Robin Hastings is the Information Technology Coordinator for the Missouri River Regional Library in Jefferson City, Missouri. She manages the library's network, websites, training classes, and social sites. She presents all over the world on topics from the use of RSS in websites to the use of the cloud in libraries. She has written the following books, Microblogging and Lifestreaming in Libraries and Collaboration 2.0. Her personal blog is http://www.rhastings.net/, but she spends far more time on FriendFeed and Twitter (and can be found as "webgoddess" in both places) these days.

Katharine Hill, MSW, MPP, is an Assistant Professor at the School of Social Work at St. Catherine's University and the University of St. Thomas in St. Paul, MN. She teaches social policy, community practice, and research. Her research interests include youth and family policy, disa-bility policy and services, and community practice. Katharine is a doctoral candidate at the University of Minnesota, a 2001 graduate of the University of Minnesota's Humphrey Institute of Public Affairs and School of Social Work and a 1994 graduate of Macalester College.

Matthew Maurer is currently an Assistant Professor of Science Education at Robert Morris University, located in Moon Township, PA. He also serves as Program Coordinator for their Biology Teacher Certification Program. Dr. Maurer received his Bachelors degree in Biology from Heidelberg University in Tiffin, OH, and both his Master's and Ph.D. in Science Education from The Ohio State University in Columbus, OH. Dr. Maurer has been involved in designing and implementing a number of science teacher professional development programs at the K-12 level. His research interests include self-efficacy, self-regulation, and also best practices in professional development. Additionally, Dr. Maurer is actively involved in a number of professional organizations, including the National Science Teachers Association, the Pennsylvania Science Teachers Association, the National Association for Research in Science Teaching, and the National Association of Biology Teachers.

Shari McCurdy Smith is Associate Director of The Center for Online Learning Research and Service (COLRS) formerly The Office of Technology-Enhanced Learning (OTEL) at the University of Illinois Springfield (UIS) where she began teaching online graduate courses in educational technology in Spring 2001. She has supported faculty in the development of online course delivery since 1999 and technology integration since 1995. She currently teaches an undergraduate blended course in Business Communication. She has a Masters in Communications from UIS and background in web design, technology consulting, grant writing and development, and state-wide program development. Research interests include online faculty development, online instructional workload, leadership, marketing of online programs on a local and national level, learning outcomes using Web 2.0 tools, and inter-institutional collaborations. An online workshop and faculty development facilitator for Sloan Consortium, she recently completed an administrative fellowship with the University of Illinois. As Associate Director of COLRS, McCurdy Smith has directed grant projects that examine the assessment of learning outcomes and the use of synchronous technologies in online learning and presented at numerous technology conferences on multiple topics. She has recently been named Director of the New Century Learning Consortium (NCLC) a collaboration of online institutions who are committed to developing vigorous online and blended learning initiatives to expand the student base and stabilize enrollments.

Kevin O'Neill is an Associate Professor of Education and Technology at Simon Fraser University in British Columbia, Canada, where he helped to found the Master's and Ph.D. programs in Educational Technology and Learning Design. Kevin earned his B.Sc. in Great Books and Computing Science at Brock University in St. Catharines, Ontario, and his Ph.D. in Learning Sciences at Northwestern University in Evanston, IL. He began his design-based research on telementoring in Chicago-area science classrooms in 1995, and has continued this work in a variety of forms ever since. Kevin's research has been published in the Journal of the Learning Sciences, the Journal of Research on Technology in Education, Mentoring & Tutoring, and Interactive Learning Environments. He lives with his wife and two energetic children on Burnaby Mountain.

Chris Opsal is a researcher at the Institute on Community Integration, University of Minnesota, currently working on projects related to community college retention, college access for students with intellectual disabilities, and successful transition for youth with disabilities. She is also the University of Minnesota coordinator for the SUMIT e-mentoring program.

Thomas T. Peters - As the Executive Director of South Carolina's Coalition for Mathematics and Science (SCCMS), Tom continues a tradition of improving science and mathematics instruction begun in 1994 through the National Science Foundation funded, South Carolina Statewide Systemic Initiative. SCCMS is an action and advocacy group that partners with business, government and informal education organizations to accelerate student achievement in science, technology, engineering and mathematics. Tom's professional career began in Illinois where he was a high school science and mathematics teacher. He has also served as a science specialist for the Wichita Falls Independent School District in Texas. Tom has been actively involved in the leadership of the Association of Science Materials Centers for over a dozen years, and has helped to establish science materials centers in several states. Tom is proud to be recognized as the National Science Education Leadership Association's 2010 Outstanding Leader in Science Education.

Najmuddin Shaik (Naj) is a research programmer with the University of Illinois Urbana-Champaign. He has a PhD in Human Resource Education from University of Illinois Urbana-Champaign and a MS in Computer Science from Northern Illinois University. He has been an active researcher in the field of student retention, marketing distance learning programs, and in the design of Student Relationship Management system. He has published papers, book chapters, and presented research based on collaborations with various institutions. URL: http://www.ao.uiuc.edu/ao/najshaik/

Shunit Reiter - For more than 30 years I have been involved in developing a theoretical framework for understanding people with disabilities first and foremost as human beings who are not different than other people except for the need to overcome difficulties arising out of their disabilities. My research and related academic activities in recent years focus on the following: the evaluation of special education program; research on the variables that re-late to the successful inclusion of children in schools and adults in the community; continuing education in institutions of higher education for persons with disabilities. I also founded "MISHAL" the Israeli University Center on Disabilities at the University of Haifa. MISHAL is an affiliate member of the American University Centers on Disabilities (AUCD). The center runs research programs, demonstration projects, organizes conferences and disseminates information. Its vision is the enhancement of quality of life for persons with disabilities.

Carmit-Noa Shpigelman- I am an Israeli researcher that promotes the empowerment of people with disabilities through rehabilitation, educational and computer-mediated programs. In my Ph.D. dissertation (2009) at the University of Haifa, I conducted and explored an electronic mentoring (e-mentoring) intervention program designed to provide social and emotional support for youth with physical, sensory, cognitive and/or emotional disabilities. Young adult students with disabilities tutored via email adolescents who had also disabilities. The findings highlighted both the considerable potential and the challenges of e-mentoring for this population. My research interests are related to special education, rehabilitation, mentoring and e-mentoring, assistive technologies and cyberpsychology. In my future researches I would like to promote the participation of people with disabilities in their communities through self-determination practices and computer-mediated environments.

Terrill Thompson is technology accessibility specialist with DO-IT (Disabilities, Opportunities, Internetworking, & Technology) at the University of Washington. Since 1993, DO-IT has worked to increase the participation of individuals with disabilities in challenging academic programs and careers. Terrill's role in this effort is to promote information technology (IT) accessibility by developing resources, delivering lectures and workshops, providing consultation, and conducting research. Terrill has over 15 years experience in the IT accessibility field, and has presented internationally at numerous conferences and consulted widely with local and state government, private industry, and K-12 and postsecondary education entities on IT accessibility issues.

Joe Timmons has been a Researcher with the Institute on Community Integration at the University of Minnesota for seven years and has worked with adolescents and adults with disabilities in rehabilitation and education settings for twenty-five years. Since 2003, he has been a coordinator with the National Collaborative on Workforce and Disability for Youth, focusing on the transition needs of youth with disabilities and providing technical assistance to individuals and organizations, including state agencies, school districts, and federal partners. Mr. Timmons is currently directing the first High School/High Tech initiative in Minnesota, a project that strengthens connections between schools, workforce centers, vocational rehabilitation agencies, and area businesses.

Patrice L. (Tamar) Weiss is an occupational therapist with a M.Sc degree in kinesiology (Waterloo) and a Ph.D degree in physiology and biomedical engineering (McGill). In 2001, she founded the Laboratory for Innovations in Rehabilitation Technology (LIRT) at the University of Haifa where she and her team develop and evaluate novel virtual environments and co-located technologies to explore their effects on individual and collaborative rehabilitation. Rehabilitation populations of interest include spinal cord injury, stroke, cerebral palsy, developmental coordination disorder, autism and head trauma. Research funding has been received from numerous national and international agencies such as the Israeli Science Foundation, Israel Ministries of Health, Defense and Education, the US-Israel Science and Technology Foundation, the Koniver Foundation, Keren Shalem, Autism Speaks Foundation, the Rich Foundation, the Zeit Foundation and the European Union Framework 7 ICT Program.

Sandy White Watson is an Associate Professor of Science Education at the University of Tennessee at Chattanooga. Dr. Watson has ten years of high school teaching experience in the areas of physical science and biology. She has presented at state, regional, national and international conferences on a wider variety of science education topics and has numerous publications in refereed journals in science education, educational technology, multicultural education, and teacher education. Dr. Watson is the recipient of many awards at the University of TN at Chattanooga, including the Elizabeth Dalton Award, given to a faculty member who is exceptional in service, research and teaching.

Joyce Yukawa is assistant professor in the Master of Library and Information Science Program of St. Catherine University. She teaches introduction to LIS, reference and online services, internet fundamentals and design, library user education, Library 2.0 and social networking technologies, information seeking behavior, and qualitative research methods. Her teaching, research, presentations, and service draw upon interests in the blending of face-to-face and online interaction in education, librarianship, and professional development, with a particular focus on social learning within communities of practice. She has had experience as a librarian in academic, public, and special libraries in the U.S. and Asia. She received her Ph.D. in Communication and Information Sciences from the University of Hawai`i.

Index

Symbols

4-H program 135

A

academic performance 137, 138, 139
academic success 137
academic telementoring 31, 32, 43, 44
accountability 64
adaptive social behaviors 116
administrators with disabilities 89, 90, 91, 104, 106, 107
affective states 190, 194
AJAX (Asynchronous JavaScript + XML) programming language 219
AmeriCorps 135
apprenticeships 31
ask-an-expert services 31, 32, 39, 43, 44, 91, 98
assistive technology 91, 92, 103, 110
asynchronous communication 118
at-risk youth 135, 137, 142
attention deficits 91, 93
auditory cues 180, 181, 182
augmentative and alternative communication (AAC) 119, 130

B

backgrounders 59, 64, 66
backward mapping 35
barriers to participation 89
barriers to participation: engagement strategies 89
barriers to participation: physical locations 89
barriers to participation: technological tools 89

Braille output devices 92, 102

C

career awareness 137, 138, 139, 140, 142
career telementoring 31, 32, 43, 44
Carolina Department of Education's Mathematics and Science Unit (S2MART Centers SC) 174
cerebral palsy 119
civic engagement 137
classroom observation 57, 58, 65, 67, 68
classroom teachers 31, 33
cloud computing 206, 208, 209
coaches 173, 174, 175, 176, 177, 178, 180, 181, 182, 183
coaching 173, 174, 175, 176, 178, 181, 184, 185
Cognitive CoachingSM 174, 175
communication, asynchronous 206, 207, 208, 209, 210, 211, 212, 213
communication, synchronous 206, 207, 213, 214
communities of practice (CoPs) 31
Compassionate Canada? program 57, 58, 59, 60, 63, 68, 69
competitor mentors 150
computer-mediated communication (CMC) 118, 119, 120, 124, 125, 126, 127, 128
computer-mediated environments 119, 124, 128
Connecting to Success (CTS) program 135, 138, 139, 140, 141, 142, 143
constructive engagement 137
constructivist educational philosophy 188
craft knowledge 25

critical thinking skills 79
curricular goals 20

D

data portability issues 206, 209, 212
depressed mood 74
design 16
design space 15, 17, 18
digital media literacy 31, 33, 42, 43, 44, 46, 50
Disabilities, Opportunities, Internetworking & Technology (DO-IT) program 118, 119, 154
disability 136, 138, 139, 140, 141, 143, 144, 145
disability awareness training 118
disabled people 116, 117, 118, 119, 120, 121, 123, 124, 125, 126
disabled youth 135, 136, 138, 139, 140, 141, 142, 143, 145, 146
division of labour 64
drama telementoring model 72, 77, 86
drama telementoring project 75, 77
duplicity issues 215

E

educational attainment 137
educational design 16
educational networking 1, 2, 4, 10, 11, 12
Electronic Emissary project 1, 5, 6, 10, 11, 13, 23, 26, 28, 34, 45, 56, 90, 110, 111, 154
e-mentoring 135, 136, 138, 139, 142, 143, 144. *See* telementoring
emotional well-being 137
ethical behavior 137

F

Facebook 206, 208, 209, 210, 211, 212, 213
face-to-face educational contexts 1
Federal Youth Coordination Act 135
feedback 215, 220, 222, 223, 226, 231, 238, 244, 249
Flickr 216, 231, 241, 242, 250, 253
forum lurking 61
Free Educational Mail (FrEdMail) network 2, 13

FriendFeed 206, 208, 211

G

grandparent mentors 150
group mentoring 91, 98
Groupware 206, 208, 211
group work 64, 66, 67, 69

H

healthy relationships 137
horseshoe debate 60, 61, 62, 63, 64, 70

I

Illinois Mathematics and Science Academy's PBLNetwork 34
in-class essay 60, 63, 65
individualized education programs 136, 138
individual reflection 76
Individuals with Disabilities Education Improvement Act (2004) 91, 136, 144
informal discussion 215, 220
information literacy 31, 33, 37, 38, 43, 44, 46, 49, 50
information mentors 150
initial teacher education (ITE) 221
inquiry-based activities 193
inquiry-based learning 190
inquiry learning 31, 32, 33, 37, 38, 39, 42, 43, 44, 49, 55
instructional coaches 173, 174, 175, 176, 180, 181, 183
instructional planning 2, 3, 4, 5, 6, 13, 14
instructional technology specialists 31, 33, 44
International Telementor Program 6
interpersonal development 116
interpersonal relationships 116, 118, 119, 121, 123, 124, 126, 127, 128, 130, 131, 132, 133

K

K-12 education 15, 16, 18, 19, 20, 21, 22, 24, 25, 27, 89, 148, 152, 154, 155, 156, 172, 186, 217, 234
K-12 students 1, 2, 10, 13
K-12 teachers 5, 10, 148, 156

K-12 telementoring 15, 18, 19, 22, 25, 27
Komagata Maru incident 61, 62, 66, 71

L

leadership training 186, 189, 193, 194, 196, 197, 198, 199, 200, 202, 203, 204
learning activities 4, 5
learning activity types 1, 4, 5, 6, 7, 13
learning assessments 4
learning, curriculum-based 2, 5, 9, 10, 13, 14
life skills 137
LOGO Project 191

M

Massive Multi-player Online Role-Playing Games (MMORPG) 177
master-level teachers 186, 187, 191, 192, 193, 194, 196
mastery experiences 72, 73, 74, 75, 76, 77, 78, 79, 84, 87, 190, 192, 194, 197
mathematics education 191, 192, 195, 197, 202, 203
Math Science Partnership (MSP) programs 186, 202
mentees 20-24, 27, 31, 79-83, 87, 90, 99, 102, 105-109, 149-153, 157, 159, 161, 164, 166-169, 172, 215, 220-224, 228, 229, 230, 233, 245, 246
mentor functions 6
mentor functions: advise/coach 6, 7
mentor functions: assistance 6, 7
mentor functions: chat 7
mentor functions: co-creation 7, 8
mentor functions: discussion/debate 8
mentor functions: feedback provision 7, 8
mentor functions: impersonation 7, 8
mentor functions: information sharing 7, 9
mentor functions: problem-solving 7, 8
mentor functions: question-and-answer 7, 9
mentor functions: supervision 7, 9
mentor functions: tutoring 7, 9
mentoring 149-156, 167-184, 188, 196, 198, 202, 203, 215-234, 244, 245, 246, 248, 250
mentoring, active facilitation of 21, 23
mentoring: cultivation 149, 153
mentoring, duration of 21, 22, 25
mentoring, face-to-face 17, 18, 22, 32, 116, 118, 119, 121-125, 128, 149, 152, 153, 155, 168, 174, 176-183
mentoring, grading of 23, 24, 25, 26
mentoring, immediacy of 23, 26
mentoring: initiation 149, 153
mentoring, masterminding of 23, 26
mentoring, openness of 22
mentoring ratio 22
mentoring: redefinition 149, 150, 153
mentoring relationships 57, 58
mentoring: separation 149, 150, 153
mentor matching 21
mentor/mentee relationships 90
MentorNet program 154
MENTOR program 118, 131
mentor recruitment 20
mentors 1, 2, 6, 7, 9, 10, 11, 20-26, 29, 31, 32, 36, 41, 42, 43, 46, 47, 49, 56, 89, 90, 91, 99, 102, 104-110, 149, 175, 176, 185, 215, 219, 221, 224, 228, 245, 246
mentors, training of 24, 26, 27, 28
MySpace 208, 216, 218, 229

N

National Alliance for Secondary Education and Transition (NASET) 137, 144
National Collaborative on Workforce and Disability for Youth (NCWD/Y) 137
National Science Foundation (NSF) 186
networking 206, 210, 211
New Media Consortium (NMC) 33, 40, 53
Ning 206, 209, 210, 211, 212, 213

O

observational data 57, 67
occupational goals 137
online course facilitation 217
online learning environments 217, 227, 228, 244
online mentoring. *See* telementoring
online support interventions 118, 119, 120, 123
outreach programs 118
ownership issues 215, 218, 233

P

P-12 education 57, 173
paralanguage 179, 180, 181
Partners for Youth Disabilities (PYD) 118
pedagogy 186, 187, 188, 189, 190, 191, 194, 196, 197, 198, 200, 201
peer mentors 150
performance accomplishment. *See* mastery experiences
personal presence 76
physical accessibility 91, 93, 96
physical health 137
physiological states 72, 73, 75, 78, 83, 84, 87
pilot implementation 60, 63
positive development 117, 124
positive mood 74
positive presuppositions 177, 178
presentation 215, 220, 221, 225, 231, 232, 241, 242, 252
pre-service education students 148
pre-service teachers 148, 149, 152, 155, 156, 157, 158, 167, 168, 169, 190, 191, 192, 201, 202, 203
pre-service teachers, telementoring of 148, 149, 156, 169
pre-survey 63, 65
privacy issues 206, 210, 212, 215, 237, 244, 245, 250
professional development (PD) 186, 187, 188, 189, 190, 191, 192, 193, 194, 195, 196, 197, 198, 199, 200, 201, 203, 204
professional development school (PDS) 148, 151, 152
professional learning communities (PLC) 186, 188, 189, 190, 192, 194, 195, 196, 197, 198, 199, 200, 201
project-based learning (PBL) 31, 32, 33, 34, 35, 36, 37, 39, 40, 42, 44, 45, 46, 47, 48, 49, 50, 51, 52, 53, 54, 55
project-based telementoring 33
protégés. *See* mentees
proximal goals 82
psychological well-being 137

R

really simple syndication (RSS) 219, 230, 231, 232, 234, 235, 240, 241
reflection 174, 183, 185, 215, 220, 223, 224, 225, 226, 228
reflective practices 173, 174, 175, 176, 177
reflective practitioners 173, 174, 175, 176, 183
reflective thinking 179
representational preferences 173, 182
resilience 135, 137
retiree mentors 150
robust efficacy 79

S

school librarians 31, 33, 37, 38, 39, 44
science education 186, 187, 188, 189, 190, 191, 192, 193, 195, 196, 197, 198, 200, 201, 202, 203, 204
Science Teacher Efficacy Belief Instrument (STEBI) 190, 191
science, technology, engineering, and mathematics (STEM) 192, 194, 197
scientific inquiry 31, 32, 33, 34, 35, 36, 37, 38, 39, 40, 42, 43, 44, 45, 49, 53, 55
screen readers 92, 93, 94, 106, 107
security issues 206, 208, 212
self-appraisal 80
self-disclosure 119, 120, 123, 126, 128, 132
self-efficaacy interventions 75, 78
self-efficacy 72, 73, 74, 75, 76, 77, 78, 79, 80, 81, 82, 83, 84, 85, 86, 87
self-reflection 119
self-reliance 153
shared documents 215, 220
social context cues 118, 119
social inaccessibility 117
social interactivity 206
social mobility 18, 21
social networking 1, 2, 10, 11, 12, 90, 93, 95, 215, 219, 225, 229, 232, 235, 237, 247
social presence 119
social skills 135, 137, 139, 143
social stigmas 119

South Carolina 173, 174, 184
specific goals 82
stability issues 206, 209, 212
states of mind 174, 175
students with disabilities 89, 90, 91, 92, 93, 94, 95, 97, 98, 99, 103, 104, 105, 106, 107, 109, 110, 111
subject matter experts 31, 33, 34, 37, 44, 52, 90
support networks 135, 137
synchronous communication 118, 121, 123

T

teachers with disabilities 89, 90, 91, 92, 93, 99, 104, 106, 107
Teaching Science as Inquiry Scale (TSI) 191
teaching self-efficacy 186, 187, 189, 190, 191, 192, 194, 195, 196, 197, 198, 200, 201, 203, 204
technological pedagogical content knowledge (TPACK) 1, 5, 13
telementoring 1, 2, 4, 5, 6, 7, 9, 10, 11, 12, 13, 17, 18, 72, 75, 78, 79, 81, 83, 84, 85, 86, 87, 89, 90, 91, 92, 93, 99, 104, 105, 111, 118, 129, 186, 188, 195, 197, 202
telementoring activity types 6
telementoring, curriculum-based 1, 2, 4, 5, 6, 9, 10, 11, 12
telementoring, extracurricular 1, 2
telementoring, observation of 57, 58, 63, 65, 67, 68
telementoring partnerships 206
telementoring program design 19
telementoring program designers 16, 18, 19, 20, 21, 22, 23, 24, 25, 26, 27, 57, 58
telementoring programs 15, 16, 17, 18, 19, 20, 22, 23, 25, 26, 27, 29, 30, 116
telementoring program technology 89
telementoring project design 72, 74, 78, 84
telementoring, transformative capacity of 72, 75

telementors 76, 77, 78, 79, 80, 81, 82, 83, 84, 85, 87
Telementor's Guidebook 34
transition goals 137, 140, 141
transition planning 136
trust 173, 176, 177, 178, 179, 182, 183, 184
tutoring 31, 32, 43, 56
Twitter 206, 208, 210, 211, 212, 213

U

universal design 89, 99, 103, 104, 107, 108, 110, 111
University of Tennessee at Chattanooga (UTC) 148, 156, 157, 167

V

verbal persuasion 72, 73, 75, 76, 77, 78, 81, 82, 83, 84, 87, 190, 192, 194, 197
vicarious experiences 72, 73, 74, 75, 77, 78, 80, 81, 83, 84, 87, 190, 192, 194
virtual communities 216
virtual mentoring 173, 174, 176, 177, 178, 179, 180, 181, 182, 183, 184
virtual mentoring practices 173
virtual relationships 176
visual cues 179, 180, 181
visual impairments 91, 92, 99, 101
volunteer subject matter experts 90

W

Web 2.0 technologies 206, 207, 208, 209, 210, 211, 212, 215, 216, 217, 218, 219, 220, 221, 224, 225, 226, 228, 233, 234, 245, 246
Web 2.0 toolkit 215
Web-based note-taking 215
Wikipedia 216, 248, 249, 251

Y

youth development 135, 137, 142, 143, 145, 146